M000247859

Praise for *Applying Domain-Driven Design and Patterns*

"I don't know what it was I professed to doing before I had added Domain-Driven Design and Test-Driven Development to my toolkit, but from my present perspective, I'm reticent to call it anything but chaotic hacking. Domain-Driven Design and Test-Driven Development are two approaches that have consistently guided me toward a practical application of software design principles, and brought my projects to fruition with healthy, sustainable software. This is a book that puts its money where its mouth is in terms of concretely communicating Agile software development practice. It's potentially one of the most impactful guides to software development success practices yet offered to the .NET software development community."
—Scott Bellware, Microsoft MVP for C#, DDD and TDD Blogger

"Jimmy Nilsson does his readers a great service by showing them how to apply the foundational principles of enterprise application design and development taught by Evans, Fowler, and other thought leaders. The book uses a worked example not only to explain, but also to demonstrate Domain-Driven Design, Patterns of Enterprise Application Architecture, and Test-Driven Development. Jimmy's insight and experience make reading it a pleasure, and leave the reader with the certainty that they have learned from a master practitioner. Enterprise developers looking to master these principles will find the book a valuable guide."
—Jack Greenfield, Enterprise Tools architect, Visual Studio Team System, Microsoft

"Good software architects reserve the right to get smarter. Beyond the goal of shipping their current system, they're on a quest to discover better ways to design and build software. This book is travelogue of sorts in which Jimmy documents his journey through a wide range of patterns, practices, and technologies, explaining how his thinking about enterprise systems has evolved along the way. If you're traveling the same road, this book is a good companion."
—Tim Ewald, principal architect at Foliage Software Systems and author of *Transactional COM+: Building Scalable Applications*

"This book does an excellent job at making tangible the large but very important ideas of Domain-Driven Design."
—Floyd Marinescu, author of *EJB Design Patterns* and creator of InfoQ.com and TheServerSide.com

"Understanding the concepts and driving forces in the problem domain is paramount to the success of software development. Jimmy Nilsson has drawn inspiration from the past ten years of studies into patterns and Domain-Driven Design as well as recorded his own experiences from concrete development projects. This book contains compelling examples of how theory can be translated into practice. It demonstrates the author's profound understanding of design choices and trade-offs involved in object-oriented development."
—Anders Hessellund, IT University of Copenhagen, Denmark

"This book tackles an area that is a challenge for most developers on the .NET platform. As the patterns and practices architect who initiated and drove the efforts around enterprise guidance for .NET, I know how important this area is for our customers, and am painfully aware of the gaps that still exist in our guidance.

"I was thrilled to see Jimmy would be sharing his insights based on his experience doing DDD and TDD. I believe this topic can be best tackled at this point in time through a focus on simplicity, patterns, and awareness of the social aspects of building applications.

"I trust Jimmy's experience and knowledge of .NET, and have enjoyed his style of sharing concepts and stories. I can hardly imagine someone better suited to explain this topic on the platform I work on every day.

"I will definitively recommend Jimmy's book to my customers, my team, and other Microsoft engineers.

"Ultimately, I hope that our industry can get better at expressing rich concepts in code, and that it gets better at the social process of articulating and evolving shared knowledge. TDD and DDD lie together at the heart of this path."
—Edward Jezierski, architect of Microsoft patterns and practices

"Jimmy has woven together best-of-bread techniques—Domain-Driven Design, Test-Driven Development, refactoring, and design patterns—into a convincing alternative to the Data-Driven Development style that has been the mainstay of Microsoft applications. The core of the book breathes life into the techniques advocated in Domain-Driven Design; it is relentlessly practical, gives the reader insight into the thought process that underlies applying proven techniques and technologies, and, like all of Jimmy's work, is an easy read— well done Jimmy!"
—Christian Crowhurst, analyst developer

"I've been working on a joint project with Jimmy for 18 months now. Jimmy really lives as he preaches. In this book he tells you how he is working in practice. He uses O/R Mapping and NHibernate daily and he also really uses TDD to help understand and distill the customer's business logic and to make sure that he only delivers tested, high-quality code. Just as he delivers a high-quality book containing tested concepts to you. Enjoy."
—Dan Byström, software developer, www.visual-design.se/blog

"By showing how to apply Domain-Driven Design and enterprise application patterns, Jimmy makes a difficult topic approachable for a larger audience. This book has something for the experienced architect and aspiring pattern implementer alike. In fact, any developer or architect who wants to improve the way he/she designs and implements software solutions should read this book."
—Per-Ola Nilsson, head of development and software architect for Luvit

"Constantly abreast with the latest trends in software development but never swept away by the hype, Jimmy expertly extracts the value and leaves the fluff behind. Always humble and with both his ears wide open, he is uniquely well suited to guide and enlighten the reader using the practical applicability as the standard, shunning the ivory tower. Jimmy doesn't offer his help from above— he actually manages to convince us that we have just learned about the cutting edge from a peer."
—Mats Helander, software developer, www.matshelander.com

"As with Jimmy's previous book, this book is a true masterpiece: a well-laid out balance between pragmatic software engineering and deep theory."
—Frans Bouma, creator of LLBLGen Pro, weblogs.asp.net/fbouma

"With this book being based on solid ground, Jimmy tackles the real issues in applying Domain-Driven Design practices. Finally we have a manual to keep us from hitting the wall in coping with ever-increasing complexity in tomorrow's domain model-based enterprise applications."
—Paul Gielens, senior consultant for Capgemini, weblogs.asp.net/pgielens

"Speaking from experience, combining the substance behind acronyms such as DDD, DP, and TDD in .NET can lead to very efficient and adaptive enterprise software architectures. This book outlines how, and why, these concepts together make such a powerful whole. Hence, the reader is given an invaluable shortcut to successful enterprise software architectures, making it a must read for any developer of such."
—Martin Rosén-Lidholm, software architect for Exense Healthcare

"Do you want to build a high-quality enterprise system with object orientation and a relational database? Don't miss this one. Jimmy shows you how Test-Driven Development can be the driving force throughout the whole project. He shows how to map the OO design to the database, a step often treated very briefly in literature, which alone makes the book worth the money. There are also plenty of design tips and discussions so you can follow his reasoning."
—Ingemar Lundberg, passionate software developer, www.ingolundberg.com

"This important and timely book is a must read for anyone wanting to get into Domain-Driven Design in C#."
—Gregory Young, Microsoft MVP for C#, independent consultant

"This book deals with several important concepts used in modern software development, such as Test-Driven Development, refactoring, patterns, and of course, Domain-Driven Design. Jimmy Nilsson writes about these things in a very conversational tone, and you almost get the feeling that he is actually sitting next to you, showing you his examples and having a conversation about the pros and cons of different solutions with you personally."
—Niclas Nilsson, software developer and educator for Activa; not a brother to Jimmy, not even related

"This book does an excellent job of bringing Domain-Driven Design (DDD) into practical context by bridging the gaps between different abstraction levels starting from the business perspective down to the system level. The book is ideal for software architects and developers because it is written in a way that allows it to be used as a primer or reference. The author excels in presenting all aspects of DDD in a way that is not only educational but also fun to read."
—Gunther Lenz, program manager and author

"Not so very long ago, I blogged about my overall feeling that as architects we may be failing to provide enough guidance for developers to sort through the hundreds of different ways to build software. There are many ideas out there that are excellent by themselves and come with perfectly well-reasoned justifications, working examples, and an impassioned community of believers. Very few of them can be used by themselves to build applications, much less systems of applications and services. This leaves it up to developers to find ways to put the individual ideas together into applications. This is always much harder in reality than the proponents of any particular approach, like to think about. Developers, on the other hand, need to get some work done and often don't care to wade through all this every time they start a new application. This is true even when they are truly interested in the potential gains of new approaches or ideas. Jimmy's book is pointed directly at this problem. How do you apply some of the great ideas that have come forward in the last few years to real, live development? I think this book does a great job of both explaining the underlying ideas with enough detail to make them practical and putting the group of ideas together in a way that will help developers see a path from start to end. Domain-Driven Design, Test-Driven Development, Dependency Injection, persistence, and many other practical issues are covered. After reading this book, I think a reader will really be able to take these important ideas and use them together effectively. Considering the great value of the individual ideas presented, but the limited numbers of examples of people really using them, this work represents a great win for us all. I highly recommend it."
—Philip Nelson, chief scientist for PAi, xcskiwinn.org/community/blogs/panmanphil/default.aspx

"Taking the leap from a data-centric mindset to the deeper realization of OOP found in Domain-Driven Design, Test-Driven Development, object/relational persistence, and other Agile methods and patterns can be an arduous and disorienting undertaking for the uninitiated.

"With a patient, pragmatic, and mentoring style, Jimmy takes the reader along for the leap, exploring the issues and the options, giving sound advice along the way. This book shows you how to integrate the various methods and patterns into a fully coherent approach to designing and creating superbly maintainable .Net software."
—George Hicks, senior developer for Property Works

"If you have ever read his blog, you already know that Jimmy Nilsson likes to challenge established 'truths' in the .NET community, looking for better ways to design software. He acknowledges that software design is hard, and that one-size-fits-all solutions do not work; pros and cons have to be balanced in context of the problem at hand before ruling a winner. For building testable and maintainable software with complex business requirements, Jimmy chooses to use Domain-Driven Design, and he brings along a toolbox of proven and established principles, patterns, and practices to carry it out. Jimmy's informal writing style and use of examples and Test-Driven Development make this book very approachable, especially considering all the ground that is covered. Because he is on top of the DDD stuff, Jimmy (and friends) brings you distilled knowledge on, and references to, many of the most valuable techniques and resources within software development today. I believe this book to be a valuable guide to applying DDD, and for developers who want to improve their general design skills."
—Andreas Brink, software developer

"In Applying Domain-Driven Design and Patterns, Jimmy Nilsson strengthens his position as an authority on applied software architecture. With a nice blend of his personal thoughts on the subjects, Jimmy takes the reader on a tour through most of the modern must-know design techniques, leaving nothing untouched. Jimmy shows how to implement the thoughts of other, more theoretical thought leaders in an appealing and easy to follow structure. I am certain that Applying Domain-Driven Design and Patterns will become a mandatory title in the enterprise bookshelf."
—Mikael Freidlitz, vice president of Content and Knowledge Programs at IASA

"Domain-Driven Design is an important technique that can help produce quality business applications that evolve with the needs of the business. In an ideal world, practicing DDD would be about OO design—but in reality, the technologies we work with impose numerous constraints.

"This book tackles that challenge head on, bridging the gap between DDD concepts and the action of translating them into practice on the .NET platform. Jimmy not only has a deep understanding of DDD and enterprise technologies, but has learned many lessons from his extensive industry experience, and takes a refreshingly pragmatic approach. This is a valuable book."
—Rod Johnson, founder of Spring Framework, CEO of Interface21

"This is a great book. It takes you on a hands-on informative travel in the world of Domain-Driven Design. A great number of important issues are discussed, explained, and shown in relevant contexts. These will give you a great foundation when you are working with your own Domain Model-based system. Both the actual development techniques as well as practical work methods (as incorporation of Test-Driven Development) are discussed."
—Trond-Eirik Kolloen, software architect and developer

"Can we focus on the house projects now?"
—Lotta, wife

"Aaa, dee, dee, dee, pee..." (Swedish pronunciation of the book abbreviation)
—Leo, son, four years old

"Dad, do you really think someone will read it?"
—Tim, son, eight years old

Applying Domain-Driven
Design and Patterns

Applying Domain-Driven Design and Patterns

With Examples in C# and .NET

Jimmy Nilsson

✦✦ Addison-Wesley

Upper Saddle River, NJ • Boston • Indianapolis • San Francisco
New York • Toronto • Montreal • London • Munich • Paris • Madrid
Cape Town • Sydney • Tokyo • Singapore • Mexico City

Many of the designations used by manufacturers and sellers to distinguish their products are claimed as trade-marks. Where those designations appear in this book, and the publisher was aware of a trademark claim, the designations have been printed with initial capital letters or in all capitals.

The author and publisher have taken care in the preparation of this book, but make no expressed or implied warranty of any kind and assume no responsibility for errors or omissions. No liability is assumed for incidental or consequential damages in connection with or arising out of the use of the information or programs contained herein.

The publisher offers excellent discounts on this book when ordered in quantity for bulk purchases or special sales, which may include electronic versions and/or custom covers and content particular to your business, training goals, marketing focus, and branding interests. For more information, please contact:

U.S. Corporate and Government Sales
(800) 382-3419
corpsales@pearsontechgroup.com

For sales outside the United States please contact:

International Sales
international@pearsoned.com

 This Book Is Safari Enabled

The Safari® Enabled icon on the cover of your favorite technology book means the book is available through Safari Bookshelf. When you buy this book, you get free access to the online edition for 45 days. Safari Bookshelf is an electronic reference library that lets you easily search thousands of technical books, find code samples, download chapters, and access technical information whenever and wherever you need it.

To gain 45-day Safari Enabled access to this book:

- Go to http://www.awprofessional.com/safarienabled
- Complete the brief registration form
- Enter the coupon code HGIJ-MT3G-PF6P-1EG8-5TZI

If you have difficulty registering on Safari Bookshelf or accessing the online edition, please e-mail customer-service@safaribooksonline.com.

Visit us on the Web: informit.com\aw

Library of Congress Cataloging-in-Publication Data

Nilsson, Jimmy.
  Applying domain-driven design and patterns with examples in C# and .NET / Jimmy Nilsson.
    p. cm.
  Includes bibliographical references.
  ISBN 0-321-26820-2
  1. Computer software--Development. 2. C# (Computer program language) 3. Microsoft .NET. I. Title.
  QA76.76.D47N645 2006
  005.1--dc22
                                        2006004371

Copyright © 2006 Pearson Education, Inc.

All rights reserved. Printed in the United States of America. This publication is protected by copyright, and per-mission must be obtained from the publisher prior to any prohibited reproduction, storage in a retrieval system, or transmission in any form or by any means, electronic, mechanical, photocopying, recording, or likewise. For information regarding permissions, write to:

Pearson Education, Inc.
Rights and Contracts Department
501 Boylston Street, Suite 900
Boston, MA 02116
Fax: (617) 671-3447

ISBN-10: 0-321-26820-2
ISBN-13: 978-0-321-26820-4

Text printed in the United States on recycled paper at R. R. Donnelley in Crawfordsville, Indiana.

Fifth Printing, October 2008

To Lotta, Tim, and Leo: the centers of my universe.

Contents

About the Author

Jimmy Nilsson owns and runs the Swedish consulting company JNSK AB. He has written numerous technical articles and two books. He has also been training and speaking at conferences, but above everything else, he is a developer with almost 20 years of experience (www.jnsk.se/weblog/).

Forewords

Building enterprise software is rarely easy. Although we have a plethora of tools and frameworks to make it easier, we still have to figure out how to use these tools well. There are lots of approaches you can take, but the trick is knowing which one to use in specific situations—hardly ever does one approach work in all cases. Over the last few years there's grown up a community of people looking to capture approaches to design enterprise applications and document them in the form of patterns (I keep an overview with links at http://martinfowler.com/articles/enterprisePatterns.html). People involved in this effort, such as me, try to find common approaches and describe how to do them well and when they are applicable. The resulting work is pretty wide ranging, and that can lead to too much choice for the reader.

When I started writing *Patterns of Enterprise Application Architecture* (Addison-Wesley, 2002), I looked for this kind of design advice in the Microsoft world. I struggled to find much of anything, but one rare book that tackled the territory was Jimmy's earlier book. I liked his informal writing style and eagerness to dig into concepts that many others skimmed over. So it's fitting that Jimmy decided to take many of the ideas from me and the others in the enterprise patterns community and show how you can apply them in writing .NET applications.

The focus of this enterprise patterns community is documenting good designs, but another thread runs through us. We are also big fans of agile methods, embracing techniques such as Test-Driven Development (TDD) and refactoring. So Jimmy also brought these ideas into this book. Many people think that pattern-people's focus on design and TDD's focus on evolution are at odds. The huge overlap between pattern-people and TDDers shows this isn't true, and Jimmy has weaved both of these threads into this book.

The result is a book about design in the .NET world, driven in an agile manner and infused with the products of the enterprise patterns community. It's a book that shows you how to begin applying such things as TDD, object-relational mapping, and domain-driven design to .NET projects. If you haven't yet come across these concepts, you'll find that this book is an introduction to techniques that many developers think are the key for future software development. If you are familiar with these ideas, the book will help you pass those ideas on to your colleagues.

Many people feel the Microsoft community has not been as good as others in propagating good design advice for enterprise applications. As the technology becomes more capable and sophisticated, it becomes more important to understand how to use it well. This book is a valuable step in advancing that understanding.
—Martin Fowler
   http://martinfowler.com

The best way to learn how to do Domain-Driven Design (DDD) is to sit down next to a friendly, patient, experienced practitioner and work through problems together, step-by-step. That is what reading this book is like.

This book does not push a new grand scheme. It unaffectedly reports on one expert practitioner's use of and combination of the current practices he has been drawn to.

Jimmy Nilsson reiterates what many of us have been saying: that several currently trendy topics—specifically, DDD, Patterns of Enterprise Application Architecture (PoEAA), and Test-Driven Development (TDD)—are not alternatives to each other, but are mutually reinforcing elements of successful development.

Furthermore, all three of these are harder than they look at first. They require extensive knowledge over a wide range. This book does spend some time advocating these approaches, but mostly it focuses on the details of how to make them work.

Effective design is not just a bunch of techniques to be learned by rote; it is a way of thinking. As Jimmy dives into an example he gives us a little window into his mind. He not only shows his solution and explains it, he lets us see how he got there.

When I am designing something, dozens of considerations flit through my mind. If they are factors I've dealt with often, they pass so quickly I am barely conscious of them. If they are in areas where I have less confidence, I dwell on them more. I presume this is typical of designers, but it is difficult to communicate to another person. As Jimmy walks through his examples, it is as if he were slowing this process down to an observable pace. At every little juncture, three or four alternatives present themselves and get weighed and rejected in favor of the one he eventually chooses.

For example, we want model objects that are implemented free of entanglement with the persistence technology. So what are eight ways (eight!) that a persistence framework can force you to contaminate the implementation of a domain object? What considerations would lead you to compromise on some of these points? What do the currently popular frameworks, including the .NET platform, impose?

Jimmy thinks pragmatically. He draws on his experience to make a design choice that will likely take him toward the goal, adhering to the deeper design principle, rather than the choice that looks the most like a textbook example. And all of his decisions are provisional.

The first design principle Jimmy holds in front of himself is the fundamental goal of DDD: a design that reflects deep understanding of the business problem at hand in a form that allows adaptation to new wrinkles. So why so much discussion of technical framework and architecture?

It is a common misperception, perhaps a natural one, that such a priority on the domain demands less technical talent and skill. Would that this were true. It would not be quite so difficult to become a competent domain designer. Ironically, to render clear and useful domain concepts in software, to keep them from being suffocated under technical clutter, requires particularly deft use of technology. My observation is that those with the greatest mastery of technology and architectural principles often know how to keep technology in its place and are among the most effective domain modelers.

I do not refer to the knowledge of every quirk of complex tools, but to the mastery of the sort of knowledge laid out in Martin Fowler's PoEAA, because naïve application of technology paradoxically makes that technology more intrusive into the application.

For many people this book will fill in gaps of how to implement expressive object models in practice. I picked up a number of useful ways of thinking through the application of technical frameworks, and I especially firmed up my understanding of some particulars of doing DDD in a .NET setting.

In addition to technical architecture, Jimmy spends a great deal of time on how to write tests. TDD complements DDD in a different way. In the absence of a focus on refining an ever more useful model, TDD is prone to fragmented applications, where a single-minded attack on one feature at a time leads to an unextendable system. A comprehensive test suite actually allows such a team to continue making progress longer than would be possible without it, but this is just the basest value of TDD.

At its best, the test suite is the laboratory for the domain model and a technical expression of the ubiquitous language. Tests of a particular style drive the modeling process forward and keep it focused. This book steps us through examples of developing such tests.

Jimmy Nilsson has a rare combination of self-confidence and humility, which I have observed to be characteristic of the best designers. We get a glimpse of how he got to his current understanding as he tells us what he used to believe and why that opinion changed, which helps to take the reader past the specifics of the techniques to the underlying principles. This humility makes him open to a wide range of influences, which gives us this fusion of ideas from different sources. He has tried a lot of things and has let his results and experience be his guide. His conclusions are not presented as revealed truth, but as his best understanding so far with an implicit recognition that we never have complete knowledge. All this makes the advice more useful to the reader. And this attitude, in itself, illustrates an important element of successful software development leadership.

—Eric Evans

Preface: Bridging Gaps

On the cover of this book is a picture of the Øresund Bridge that connects Sweden and Denmark. It seems that all software architecture books must have a bridge on the cover, but there are some additional reasons the bridge is appropriate for this book.

This bridge replaced a ferry that I took many times as a child. I enjoy very much driving over it even after dozens of times.

On a personal note, my father was on the team that built the highest parts of the bridge.

But beyond these, the main reason is that this book is very much about bridging gaps; bridging gaps between users and developers; bridging gaps between business and software; bridging gaps between logic and storage. Bridging gaps between "DB-guys" and "OO-guys"…

I will refrain from making a joke about the Bridge pattern [GoF Design Patterns]. Hey, how geeky can a preface be?

Focus of This Book

The main focus of the book is how a Domain Model could be constructed to be clean, yet still be persistence-friendly. It shows what the persistence solution could look like for such a Domain Model and especially how to bridge that gap between the Domain Model and the database.

Put another way, my vision has been to provide a book that will put Eric Evans' *Domain-Driven Design* [Evans DDD] and Martin Fowler's *Patterns of Enterprise Application Architecture* [Fowler PoEAA] in context.

DDD might be perceived as a bit abstract. Therefore, more concrete examples are helpful regarding persistence, for example. Mine may be fairly basic, but it is a platform to start from. This book not only explains how to use the patterns, but also how the patterns are used in O/R Mappers, for example.

It has become very clear to me that "one size does not fit all" when it comes to architecture. Having said that, patterns have proven to be general enough to use and reuse in context after context.

The focus isn't on the patterns themselves, but this book uses patterns in every chapter as a tool and language for discussing different design aspects. A nice side effect is that patterns-ignorant readers will also gain some insight and interest into patterns along the way.

That also goes for TDD. Not all developers have become interested in this yet. I think it's especially common in the .NET community that TDD (just as patterns) is considered a niche technique at best, or it might even be totally unknown. Readers will learn how to apply TDD.

Why This Book?

Writing my first book [Nilsson NED] was a really tough project on top of all my other ordinary projects and obligations. I was pretty sure I wouldn't write another, but the time came when I thought I had something to say that I couldn't leave unsaid.

My change of heart started when I read two recent books that inspired me and changed my thinking. First, there was Martin Fowler's *Patterns of Enterprise Application Architecture* [Fowler PoEAA]. This book inspired me to give the Domain Model pattern another try after having failed with several earlier attempts.

Then I read Eric Evans' book *Domain-Driven Design* [Evans DDD]. This book provided me with insights about how to think and act regarding development with a strong domain focus and with a certain style of how to apply the Domain Model pattern.

Another important influence was all that I learned from teaching my patterns course over a couple of years. As I interacted with students and the material evolved, I had insights myself.

My views of DDD transformed as I worked on an ambitious (though unfortunately unfinished) open source project called Valhalla, which I developed in collaboration with Christoffer Skjoldborg. (Christoffer did by far the most work.)

To summarize all this, I felt that a book that dealt more with application than theory was needed, but one that was based on solid ground, such as the DDD and PoEAA books. "Applying" feels close to my heart because I consider myself a developer above anything else.

Target Audience

This book is aimed at a wide target audience. It will help if you have *some* knowledge of

- Object-orientation

- .NET or a similar platform

- C# or a similar language

- Relational databases; for example, SQL Server

However, interest and enthusiasm will compensate for any lack of prior experience.

I'd like to elaborate on my statement that the target audience is wide. First, we can think about the way we put people into platform boxes. The book should serve .NET people who want a more core-based approach than drag-till-you-drop (if I may use some weak generalizations). Java people should get something out of the discussions and examples of how to combine DDD and O/R Mapping.

I think the chosen language/platform is less and less important, so it feels a little strange to talk about .NET people and Java people. Let's try to describe the target audience by using another dimension. Then I think that the book is for developers, team leaders, and architects.

Choosing yet another dimension, I think there might be something in this book both for intermediate and advanced readers. There's probably also something for beginners.

Organization of This Book

The book is arranged in four parts: "Background," "Applying DDD," "Applying PoEAA," and "What's Next?"

Part I: Background

In this part, we discuss architecture and processes in general terms. There is a lot of emphasis on Domain Models and DDD [Evans DDD]. We also introduce patterns and TDD. The chapters include the following:

- Chapter 1, "Values to Value"

This chapter discusses properties of architecture and process to value for creating quality results when it comes to system development. The discussion is influenced by Extreme Programming.

- Chapter 2, "A Head Start on Patterns"

This chapter focuses on providing examples and discussions about patterns from different families, such as design patterns, architectural patterns and domain patterns.

- Chapter 3, "TDD and Refactoring"

Chapter 1 talks quite a lot about TDD and refactoring, but in this chapter there is more in-depth coverage with pretty long examples and also different flavors of TDD.

Part II: Applying DDD

In this part, it's time to apply DDD. We also prepare the Domain Model for the infrastructure, and focus quite a lot on rules aspects.

- Chapter 4, "A New Default Architecture"

This chapter lists a set of requirements of an example application, and a first-try model is created as a start for the coming chapters. A Domain Model-based architecture is used.

- Chapter 5, "Moving Further with Domain-Driven Design"

The requirements set up in the prior chapter are used in this chapter as the basis for slowly, with TDD, starting to build the Domain Model in a DDD-ish style.

- Chapter 6, "Preparing for Infrastructure"

Even though we try to push the infrastructure aspects as far off in the future as possible, it's good to think a little bit ahead and prepare the Domain Model for the infrastructure needs. In this chapter, there is a lot of discussion about pros and cons of Persistence Ignorant Domain Models.

- Chapter 7, "Let the Rules Rule"

This chapter talks about business rules in the form of validation and how a Domain Model-based solution can deal with the need for such rules, connecting back to the requirements set up in Chapter 4.

Part III: Applying PoEAA

In this part, we put several of the patterns in Fowler's *Patterns of Enterprise Application Architecture* [Fowler PoEAA] into context by discussing what we need from the infrastructure for providing persistence support to our Domain Model. We will take a look at how those requirements are fulfilled by an example tool.

- Chapter 8, "Infrastructure for Persistence"

  When we have a fairly good Domain Model, it's time to think about infrastructure, and the main type of infrastructure in this book is infrastructure for persistence. This chapter discusses different properties of persistence solutions and how to categorize a certain solution.

- Chapter 9, "Putting NHibernate into Action"

  This chapter uses the categorizations of the prior chapter with an example of a persistence solution, namely NHibernate [NHibernate].

Part IV: What's Next?

In this part, there is a focus on other design techniques to keep an eye on and start using. The other focus is on how you can deal with the presentation layer when it comes to bridging that gap to the Domain Model, but also how to deal with developer testing of the UI. This part is almost exclusively written by guest authors.

- Chapter 10, "Design Techniques to Embrace"

  After a short discussion about Bounded Context, this chapter discusses design techniques to keep an eye on now and for the future, such as Service Orientation, Dependency Injection/Inversion of Control, and Aspect Orientation.

- Chapter 11, "Focus on the UI"

  This chapter focuses on how the UI can be connected to the Domain Model and how to increase testability for the user interface when using a Domain Model, both for rich client applications and Web applications.

Appendices

There are two appendices providing further examples of Domain Model styles and an overview-type patterns catalog.

Why C# for the Examples?

In no way is this a book for teaching C#. But I still need a language (or possibly several, but I have chosen one) for the examples, and that's where C# comes in.

The reasons for the choice are mainly that C# is my current main language and that most VB.NET and Java developers can read C# code pretty easily.

Regarding the version, most of the code examples work in both C# 1.1 and 2.0, but there are some rare sections that are focused on 2.0.

Topics That Aren't Covered

There are loads of topics that aren't covered in the book, but I think there are two missing topics that spring to mind. They are distribution and advanced modeling.

Distribution

It was in my early plans of the book to include thorough coverage of the distribution aspects, but later on I came to the conclusion that the book would become too unfocused. Still, there is some coverage here and there.

Advanced Modeling

The title of the book might suggest that you find advanced and interesting examples of modeling of certain problem areas. That's not exactly the case. Instead, the application focus is more about applying TDD and adding infrastructure to DDD.

finally{}

As you can appreciate, a book project like this is hardly ever the work of only one person. On the contrary, it's a joint effort. See the list of people in the Acknowledgments section, and also remember that even more people have been involved, especially during production. That said, any errors we didn't catch before the book went to print are mine and mine alone.

I will post information of interest to readers of the book at www.jnsk.se/adddp.

Getting back to bridging gaps, the photo of the Øresund Bridge was taken by my friend Magnus von Schenck on one of his sailing trips.

Even though this book has not been as tough to write as the first one, there has been a fair amount of blood, sweat, and tears. I hope the book might save you some of that. Have fun and good luck!

Jimmy Nilsson
www.jnsk.se/weblog/
Listerby, Sweden
September 2005

Acknowledgments

With the risk of forgetting some people that should get a mention here (if so, you know who you are and a big thanks to you, too), I say a huge thanks to the following:

My foreword authors: Martin Fowler and Eric Evans.

My guest authors: Frans Bouma, Dan Byström, Udi Dahan, Erik Dörnenburg, Mats Helander, Ingemar Lundberg, Philip Nelson, Claudio Perrone, Aleksandar Seović, and Christoffer Skjoldborg.

My reviewers who provided lots of valuable feedback: William Bulley, Mark Burhop, Dan Byström, Russ Condick, Andy Conrad, Christian Crowhurst, Mike Dörfler, Steve Eichert, Eric Evans, Martin Fowler, Paul Gielens, Chris Haddad, Kim Harding Christensen, Mats Helander, Neeraj Gupta, Anders Hessellund, Roger Johansson, Roger Kratz, Trond-Eirik Kolloen, Ingemar Lundberg, Patrik Löwendahl, Marcus Mac Innes, Philip Nelson, Per-Ola Nilsson, Fredrik Normén, Johan Normén, Michael O'Brien, Michael Platt, Sébastien Ros, Martin Rosén-Lidholm, Enrico Sabbadin, Aleksandar Seović, Christoffer Skjoldborg, George Vish II, Gregory Young, and Christer Åkesson.

My artist of the figures for the parts introductions: Kjell Warnquist

My language editor: Lydia West

My development editor: Chris Zahn

My project editor: Michael Thurston

My copy editor: Elise Walter

My marketing manager: Curt Johnson

My acquisitions editor: Karen Gettman (and Sondra Scott who talked me into the project in the first place)

Without you there would be no book, or at least a book of inferior quality. Thanks guys, I owe you!

PART I

Background

In the "Background" part, we discuss architecture and processes in general terms. There is a lot of emphasis on Domain Models and *Domain-Driven Design* (DDD) [Evans DDD]. We also introduce patterns and *Test-Driven Development* (TDD).

The first part is about setting the scene. Romeo and Juliet must have a scene.

Chapter 1

Values to Value

Or Embarrassing Ramblings When Self-Reflecting on the Last Few Years

This chapter's intention is to set the scene. I will do that by looking back in time over the last few years regarding how I have thought about different concepts and how my ideas have changed over time.

We will jump around quite a lot and cover a lot of ground, but the overall idea is to discuss *values to value* regarding architecture and processes for development.

On this journey, we will introduce and talk about many concepts that we will discuss in depth later on in the book.

Start the camera...Action!

Overall Values

In the past, I was very good at planning ahead. I often added functionality, structures, and mechanisms to my projects proactively. That part usually turned out pretty well, but I often forgot about the artifacts added on that never came to any good use. Of course, I added loads of them, too. The cost was pretty large, both in development time and in increased complexity.

Over the last few years, we've been encouraged to use another approach: "Do the simplest thing that could possibly work." To a large extent, the idea comes from the *Extreme Programming* (XP) movement [Beck XP]. Another fairly similar way to put it is "You Aren't Going to Need It" (YAGNI), which is a good way of helping you stay in line. I guess "Keep It Simple Stupid" (KISS) could go here, too.

3

Both approaches are kind of the two extremes (add all you can think of up front versus do the simplest thing), but I think they both miss something in that they don't address the tradeoffs they make. Just about every question regarding "is this or that best" can be answered with "it depends." It's about tradeoffs. I tend to prefer an approach that is somewhere in the middle, moving in one or the other direction depending upon the situation. The word "lagom" is a Swedish word meaning something like "just right" or "not too much, not too little." Lagom or "to balance" together with being context sensitive are the overall values I'd like to value, as well as continuous learning.

Let's have a closer look at a couple of more specific areas of values (architecture and process ingredients), starting with some aimed at architecture to get us into the right mood.

Architecture Styles to Value

Architects and developers must make design decisions based on the requirements of the project. I haven't collected an exhaustive list of values regarding architecture styles here, but I have decided on a few main things I'd like to comment on to some extent, such as model focus, domain models, databases, distribution, and messaging. First, I think it's wise to keep a model focus.

Focus on the Model

For a long time, I have liked the object-oriented paradigm a lot, but it wasn't until pretty recently that I made the full move to that paradigm myself. There have been platform problems with using the paradigm before, but now the platforms are mature.

> ### Note
>
> As a reviewer pointed out, maturity depends on the platform we are talking about. If you come from a VB background, what was just said is reasonable, but if you come from Java, SmallTalk, C#, and so on, the platform has been mature for quite some time.

Around 13 years ago, I tried to use a visual model to communicate my understanding of the requirements of a system I was about to build, and I used some OMT [Rumbaugh OMT] sketches. (OMT stands for *Object Modeling*

Technique and was a method with a process and a notation. The notation was very similar to the one in *Unified Modeling Language*, UML, which isn't just a coincidence because OMT was the main inspiration for the notation in UML.) We were discussing multiplicity between classes, where behavior should belong, and so on. I realized after a few sessions that using my technique for discussion with expert users, instead of their technique, was a complete failure. They answered my questions randomly and didn't see or add much value at all in the discussion. (The system at large wasn't a failure, it's still being used and it's the core system there, but the development process didn't go as smoothly as it could have. I had to change method.)

Use Case Focus

I have thought about that experience several times and have actually joked about how naïve I was. In the years following, I always tried to play by the methodologies of the target groups; I mean the methodologies of the users with the users, and the methodologies of software development with developers. One technique that worked pretty well in both camps was the use case technique [Jacobson OOSE]. (At least it worked out well in the informal manner of XP [Beck XP] stories, short text descriptions, which was what I used. Such a description is a short description of a piece of functionality in a system. An example is "Register Order for Company Customer.")

It was very natural to users and could be made natural to developers, too, so it became the bridging tool of mine for years. The way I did the bridging was to have one class per use case in the software.

It did come to my attention that thanks to my way of applying use cases, I became pretty procedural in my thinking. I was designing a little bit like Transaction Script [Fowler PoEAA], but I tried to balance it by generalizing as much behavior as possible (or at least suitable).

A few years ago I heard Ivar Jacobson talking about use cases, and I was pretty surprised when I realized that he didn't encapsulate the use cases in classes of their own as I had expected and had done for a long time.

Another thing that got me kind of worried about this method was the constant struggle I was having with my friend and Valhalla-developer Christoffer Skjoldborg when we worked with the Domain Model pattern [Fowler PoEAA]. He saw little value in the use case classes, maintaining that they could even get in the way because they might become a hindrance when mixing and matching use case parts.

Different Patterns for Dealing with the Main Logic

Before we continue, I must say a few words about Transaction Script and Domain Model, which we have already touched upon.

Martin Fowler discusses three ways of structuring the main logic in application architecture in his book *Patterns of Enterprise Application Architecture* [Fowler PoEAA]. Those are Transaction Script, Table Module, and Domain Model.

Transaction Script is similar to batch programs in that all functionality is described from start till end in a method. Transaction Script is very simple and useful for simple problems, but breaks down when used for dealing with high complexity. Duplication will be hard to avoid. Still, very many very large systems are built this way. Been there, done that, and I've seen the evidence of duplication even though we tried hard to reduce it. It crops up.

Table Module encapsulates a Recordset [Fowler PoEAA], and then you call methods on the Table Module for getting information about that customer with id 42. To get the name, you call a method and send id 42 as a parameter. The Table Module uses a Recordset internally for answering the request. This certainly has its strengths, especially in environments when you have decent implementations for the Recordset pattern. One problem, though, is that it also has a tendency to introduce duplication between different Table Modules. Another drawback is that you typically can't use polymorphistic solutions to problems because the consumer won't see the object identities at all, only value-based identities. It's a bit like using the relational model instead of the object-oriented model.

Domain Model instead uses object orientation for describing the model as close to the chosen abstractions of the domain as possible. It shines when dealing with complexity, both because it makes usage of the full power of object orientation possible and because it is easier to be true to the domain. Usage of the Domain Model pattern isn't without problems, of course. A typical one is the steep learning curve for being able to use it effectively.

Domain-Driven Design Focus

The real eye-opener for me regarding the usage of use cases was *Domain-Driven Design* (DDD) [Evans DDD]. (We will talk a lot about DDD soon, but for now, let's just say it's about focusing on the domain and letting it affect the software very much.) I still think that the use case technique is a great way of communicating with users, but DDD has made me think it can help a lot if we can manage to actively involve the users in discussions about the core model. It can head off mistakes very early and help the developers understand the domain better.

Note

"Model" is one of those extremely overloaded terms in software. I think we all have an intuitive idea about what it is, but I'd like to describe how I think about it. Instead of trying to come up with *the* definition, here in all simplicity (this could fill a book of its own by the right author) are a few properties of a model that you can compare to your own understanding of the term. A model is

Partial

For a certain purpose

A system of abstractions

A cognitive tool

Also,

A model has several presentations (for example: language, code, and diagrams).

There are several models in play in a system.

If you would like to read more, very much has been written about what a model is. A good place to start is the first pages in Eric Evans' book [Evans DDD]. (A special thanks to Anders Hessellund and Eric Evans for inspiration.)

The model is a great tool for communication between developers and users, and the better the communication is between those groups, the better the software will become, both in the short and the long run.

We (including me) have been using models forever, of course, but the difference between one of my old models and those that have been built with the ideas of DDD is that my old models had much more infrastructure focus and technical concept focus. My new models are much cleaner from such distractions and instead focus totally on the core domain, its main concepts, and the domain problems at hand. This is a big mind shift.

Another way of expressing it is that technicalities (such as user interface fashion) come and go. Core business lasts. And when the core business changes, we *want* to change the model and the software.

It's not rocket science so far, and I'm probably just kicking in open doors. I think, however, this lies at the very core of how to achieve efficient software development, and in my experience it is rarely used. By this I mean focusing on the model, having a model (with different presentations) that is used by both users and developers, and not getting distracted by unimportant details.

Why Model Focus?

I'd like to exaggerate this a bit. Let's play a game: What kind of developer would be the best one for building a vertical system in a special field, let's say in finance? It goes without saying that developer should be technically savvy, very skilled and experienced, have a huge social network, and so on. It would also be very nice if he was extremely skilled in the business domain itself and it wouldn't hurt if he had worked as, say, a trader for ten years, if that's the kind of system to be built.

Finding developers like that does happen, but in my experience it's more the exception than the rule. In the case of the developer being able to move on to another domain for a new system when the financial system is up and running, that exception becomes even more rare. This is because developers just can't have ten years of experience in logistics, health care, insurance, and the rest.

Another solution can be to let the domain expert users develop the software themselves. This has been an old dream for decades, and to a degree it's slowly becoming more and more viable all the time. At the same time, it takes away time from them, time they often can use better for their core work. There's also too many technical problems still involved.

So what's the next best thing? The answer is obvious (at least from today's standpoint): make the developer learn as much as possible about the domain he or she is working on and add users to the picture to bring the domain expertise to the project team and to actively and constructively work within the project. The users would not just set the requirements—although that is also very important—but would actually help out with designing the core of the system. If we can manage to create this atmosphere, nobody is more skilled than the domain expert user at deciding on what the core is, what the key abstractions are, and so on.

Of course, as developers we are also necessary. The whole thing is done in cooperation. For example, what might be seen as a tiny detail to businesspeople can be a huge thing to us in the domain model. They might say: "Oh, sometimes it's like this instead," and everything is totally different, but because it's not the most common variant, they think it's unimportant.

Time to Try Discussing the Model with Customers Again

Why would I now succeed in discussing the model with the customers when I failed before? Many things have changed. First, it's important to have a sense of the context and the project group. Second, use cases can help a lot when getting started, and then you can switch the focus later to the core model itself. Third, building systems is something many more people have experience in and have been taught about now. Fourth, to be picky, the model represented as graphical, UML-like sketch for example is not the most important thing to have users work on; it's still typically a representation that developers like better than users. What we are looking for is the *ubiquitous language* [Evans DDD].

The ubiquitous language is not something like UML, XML Schema, or C#; it's a natural, but very distilled, language for the domain. It's a language that we share with the users for describing the problem at hand and the domain model. Instead of us listening to the users and trying to translate it to our own words, a ubiquitous language would create fewer reasons for misunderstandings, and it will become easier for the users to understand our sketches and actually to help correct mistakes, helping us gain new knowledge about the domain. If it's suitable, you can discuss ubiquitous language in the context of the graphical/code models with the users. If not, you still have the most important thing done if you catch the ubiquitous language.

Note

Eric Evans commented on the previous with the following: "Something to make clear is that the ubiquitous language isn't just the domain expert's current lingo. That has too many ambiguities and assumptions and also probably too large a scope. The ubiquitous language evolves as a collaboration between the domain experts and the software experts. (Of course, it will resemble a subset of the domain jargon.)"

The ubiquitous language is something that you should work hard to keep well-defined and in synch with the software. For example, a change in the ubiquitous should lead to a change in the software and vice versa. Both artifacts should influence each others.

If You Have a Model Focus, Use the Domain Model Pattern

If we have agreed on having a deep model focus and using object-orientation, I believe the natural result is to use the Domain Model pattern [Fowler PoEAA] for structuring the core logic of the applications and services. You find an example of a small Domain Model in Figure 1-1.

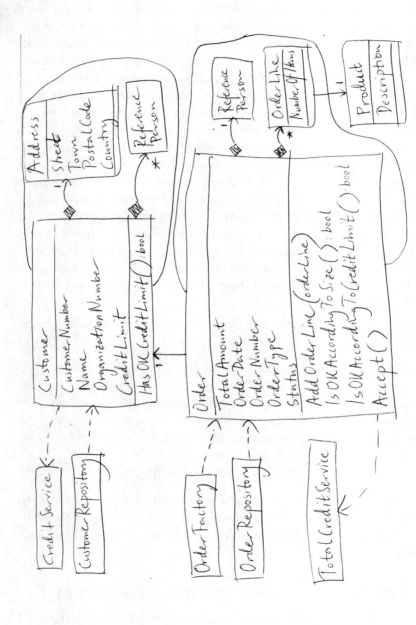

Figure 1-1   An example of a Domain Model, an early sketch for the example application, further discussed in Chapter 4, "A New Default Architecture"

> **Note**
>
> If you aren't up to speed on UML, I think a good book to read is *UML Distilled* [Fowler UML Distilled]. It's not essential that you understand UML, but I think it will be helpful to know the bones because I will be using UML as a sketch tool here and there (of course, you will benefit from it at other times as well, not just with this book).

Even though Figure 1-1 shows just an early sketch of a small domain model, I think we can see that the model expresses domain concepts and not technical distractions. We can also see that it contains several cooperating small pieces, which together form a whole.

> **Note**
>
> If you wonder why Figure 1-1 is handwritten, it is to stress the point that it is a sketch. We will explore and develop the details in code—for example, with the help of Test-Driven Development (TDD). (We will discuss TDD later in this chapter, as well as in Chapter 3, "TDD and Refactoring.")

Before we talk more about the specific style I used for the Domain Model, I think it's time to look back again.

Domain Model History from My Rear View Mirror

I still remember the first time I tried to use the Domain Model, even though I didn't call it that at the time. It was around 1991, and I couldn't understand how it should match up in the UI. I don't remember what the application was, but I remember that I tried to decide on what the menus should look like in order to be object-oriented. I didn't come over that first hurdle that time. I think I was looking for a very close mapping between the UI and the Domain Model and couldn't find out how to achieve it.

A few years prior to that, I worked on an application that was said to use object-oriented ideas, for example, for the UI. There were no big breakthroughs, perhaps, but it managed to achieve small things. For example, instead of first choosing a function and then deciding to what object (such as a portfolio) to apply it, the user first chose the object and then decided between the different functions that were possible for the chosen object. At the time this was pretty different from how most business applications were navigated in the UI.

A Few Words About Naked Objects

Perhaps I wasn't totally off with my intentions. Perhaps what I was trying to achieve was something like *Naked Objects* [Pawson/Matthews Naked Objects], but I really didn't get very far with it.

Without going into details about Naked Objects, I think a short explanation is in order. The basic idea is that not only developers but users also like object-orientation. They like it even more than we normally think, and they would quite often be happy with a UI that is very close to the Domain Model itself, so close that the UI can be created automatically by a framework directly based on the Domain Model.

A system based on naked objects automatically presents a form to a user that contains widgets exposing the properties in the Domain Model class.

For more complex tasks, there is some need for customization (as always), but the idea is to cut down on that as well, again thanks to the framework that understands what UI to create from the Domain Model fragments. So when the Domain Model is "done," the UI is more or less done as well.

For the moment I don't have first-hand experience with the concept and technique, but an appealing twist to me of the idea is that the users will really get a chance to see and feel the model, which should be very helpful in bridging the gap between developers and users.

After that, I tried Domain Model approaches many times over the years. I found problems with using it, especially related to performance overhead (especially in distributed scenarios). That said, some of my real world applications were built in that style, especially the simpler ones. What is also important to say is that however much I wanted to build very powerful, well-designed Domain Models, they didn't turn out as I had anticipated.

That wasn't the only problem I had, though....

Old Truths Might Be Wrong

I've believed in Domain Models and tried to use them several times in the past, but most attempts to implement it in object-oriented fashion led me to the conclusion that it doesn't work. That was, for example, the case with my COM+ applications in Visual Basic 6 (VB6). The main problem was that performance overhead was too high.

When I wrote my previous book [Nilsson NED], which described a default-architecture for .NET applications, I reused my old VB6/COM+ knowledge and didn't make the discussed architecture Domain Model-based at all.

Later on I started up new experiments again, trying to see if I could get down to something like 10% in response-time overhead on common scenarios (such as fetching a single order, fetching a list of orders for a customer, or saving an order) when using Domain Model in .NET compared with Transaction Scripts and Recordset. To my surprise, I could get *lower* overhead. The old truths had become wrong. The Domain Model-based architecture is very much more possible now in .NET than in VB6. One reason for this is that the instantiation time is reduced by orders of magnitude. Therefore, the overhead is just much lower when you have very many instances. Another reason is that it's trivial to write Marshal By Value (so that not only is the reference to the instance moved, but the whole instance, at least conceptually, is moved) components in .NET. It was *not* simple in the COM world. (It wasn't even possible to do it in the ordinary sense in VB6.)

Note

The importance of Marshal By Value is of less importance because we now most often prefer to not send the Domain Model as-is over the wire, but my early tests were using that.

Yet another reason is that .NET better supports object-orientation; it's just a much better toolbox.

Note

Also worth mentioning is that there hasn't been much emphasis on the Domain Model in the Microsoft community in the past. The Java community, on the other hand, is almost the opposite. I remember when I went to a workshop with mostly Java people. I asked them about what their favorite structure for the logic was, perhaps if they used Recordset (added in JDBC version 3) a lot. They looked at me funnily as if they hadn't understood the question. I quickly realized that Domain Model was more or less the de facto standard in their case.

Architecture
Styles to
Value

To set all this straight, I'd like to clarify two things. First, I do *not* say that you should choose the Domain Model pattern because of performance reasons. Rather that you often *can* choose the Domain Model pattern without getting performance problems.

Second, I do *not* say that to be able to use a model focus, you need a certain technology. Different technologies are more or less appropriate for expressing the model in software in close resemblance with the domain. Of course, there is not a single technology that is always best. Different domains and different problems set different factors for what is an appropriate technology. So I see technology as an enabler. Different technologies can be better enablers than others.

To summarize this, it's very much a matter of design if the Domain Model pattern can be used efficiently enough or not.

Some good news regarding this is that there is lots of good information to gain. Domain-Driven Design and its style for structuring Domain Models provides lots of valuable help, and that is something we will spend a lot of time trying out in the book.

One Root Structure

So if we choose to focus on a Domain Model, it means that we will get all the people on the project to buy into the model. This goes for the developers, of course.

It might even be that the DBAs can agree on seeing the Domain Model as the root, even though the database design will be slightly different. If so, we have probably accomplished getting the DBA to speak the ubiquitous language, too! (As a matter of fact, the more you can get your DBA to like the Domain Model and adhere to it, the easier it will be to implement it. This is because you will need to create less mapping code if the database design isn't radically different from the Domain Model, but more like a different view of the same model.) Oh, and even the users could buy into the Domain Model. Sure, different stakeholders will have different needs from the Domain Model, different views regarding the detail level, for example, but it's still one root structure—a structure to live with, grow with, change....

As you will find, I'm going to put a lot of energy into discussing Domain Model-based solutions in this book from now on, but before doing that, I'd like to talk a bit about other architecture values. Let's leave the domain focus for a while and discuss some more technically focused areas. First is how to deal with the database.

Handle the Database with Care

In the past, I've thought a lot about performance when building systems. For example, I used to write all database access as handwritten, stored procedures.

Doing this is usually highly effective performance-wise during runtime, especially if you don't just have CRUD (Create Read Update Delete) behavior for one instance—such as a single customer—at a time, but have "smarter" stored procedures; for example, doing several operations and affecting many rows in each call.

The Right Efficiency

Even though hardware capability is probably still growing in accordance with something like Moore's law, the problem of performance is an everyday one. At the same time as the hardware capabilities increase, the size of the problems we try to solve with software also increases.

In my experience, performance problems are more often than not the result of bad database access code, bad database structure, or other such things. One common reason for all this is that no effort at all has been spent on tuning the database, only on object-orientation purity. This in its turn has led to an extreme number of roundtrips, inefficient and even incorrect transaction code, bad indexing schemes, and so on.

To make it a bit more concrete, let's look at an example where object orientation has been thought of as important while database handling has not. Let's assume you have a Customer class with a list of Orders. Each Order instance has a list of OrderLine instances. It looks something like Figure 1-2.

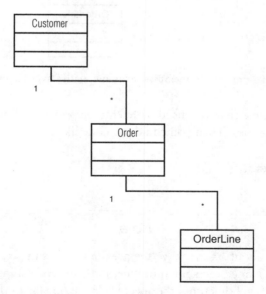

Figure 1-2 UML diagram for Customer/Order example

Moreover, let's assume that the model is very important to you and you don't care very much about how the data is fetched from and stored to the relational database that is being used. Here, a possible (yet naïve) schema would be to let each class (Customer, Order and OrderLine) be responsible for persisting/depersisting itself. That could be done by adding a Layer Supertype [Fowler PoEAA] class (called PersistentObject in the example shown in Figure 1-3) which implements, for example, GetById() and from which the Domain Model classes inherit (see Figure 1-3).

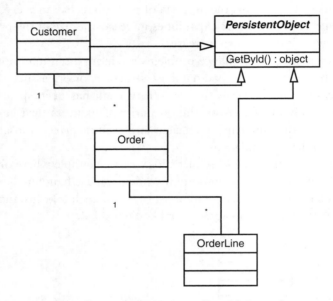

Figure 1-3   UML diagram for Customer/Order example, with Layer Supertype

Now, let's assume that you need to fetch a Customer and all its Orders, and for each order, all OrderLines. Then you could use code like this:

```
//A consumer
Customer c = new Customer();
c.GetById(id);
```

Note

If you wonder about //A consumer in the previous code snippet, the idea is to show the class name (and sometimes methods) for code snippets like that to increase clarity. Sometimes the specific class name (as in this case) isn't important, and then I use a more generic name instead.

C++ kind of has this concept built in because method names are written like `ClassName::MethodName`, but I think some small comments should provide the same effect.

What happens now is that the following SQL statements will execute:

```
SELECT CustomerName, PhoneNumber, ...
FROM Customers
WHERE Id = 42
```

Next the `customer`'s `GetById()` method will fetch a list of `orders`, but only the keys will be fetched by calling `GetIdsOfChildren()`, which will execute something like this:

```
SELECT Id FROM Orders
WHERE CustomerId = 42
```

After that, the `Customer` will instantiate `Order` after `Order` by iterating over the `DataReader` for `Order` identifiers, delegating the real work to the `GetById()` method of the `Order` like this:

```
//Customer.GetById()
...
Order o;

while theReader.Read()
{
    o = new Order();
    o.GetById(theReader.GetInt32(0));
    c.AddOrder(o);
}
```

Then for each `Order` it's time to fetch the identifiers of all the `OrderLines`...well, you get the picture. What happened here was that the object perspective was used to a certain extent (at least that was the intention of the designer) instead of thinking in sets, as is what relational databases are based on. Because of that, the number of roundtrips to the database was extremely high (one for every row to fetch plus a few more). The efficiency plummeted through the floor.

Note

Worth mentioning is that the behavior just described might be exactly what you need to avoid massive loading of data in a specific scenario. It's hard to point out something that is *always* bad. Remember the context.

On the other hand, if we think about the other extreme, handwritten and hand optimized stored procedures, it could look like this:

```
CREATE PROCEDURE GetCustomerAndOrders(@customerId INT) AS
    SELECT Name, PhoneNumber, ...
    FROM Customers
    WHERE Id = @customerId

    SELECT Id, ...
    FROM Orders
    WHERE CustomerId = @customerId

    SELECT Id, ...
    FROM OrderLines
    WHERE OrderId IN
        (SELECT Id
        FROM Orders
        WHERE CustomerId = @customerId)
```

They are often efficient (as I said) during runtime. They are very inefficient during maintenance. They will give you lots of code to maintain by hand. What's more, stored procedures in Transact SQL (T-SQL, the SQL dialect used for Sybase SQL Server and Microsoft SQL Server), for example, don't lend themselves well to ordinary techniques for avoiding code duplication, so there will be quite a lot of duplicate code.

> ### Note
>
> I know, some of my readers will now say that the previous example could be solved very efficiently without stored procedures or that that stored procedure wasn't the most efficient one in all circumstances. I'm just trying to point out two extreme examples from an efficiency point of view. I mean badly designed code—at least from an efficiency point of view—that uses dynamic SQL compared to better design and well-written stored procedures.

So the question is if runtime efficiency is the most important factor for choosing how to design?

Maintainability Focus

If I only have to choose one "ability" as the most important one, these days I would choose maintainability. Not that it's the only one you need, it absolutely is not, but I think it's often more important than scalability, for example.

With good maintainability, you can achieve the other abilities easily and cost-effectively. Sure, this is a huge simplification, but it makes an important point.

Another way to see it is to compare the total cost of producing a new system with the total cost of the maintenance of the system during its entire life cycle. In my experience, the maintenance cost will be much greater for most successful systems.

To conclude this, my current belief is that it is worth giving some attention to the database. You should see it as your friend and not your enemy. At the same time, however, hand writing all the code that deals with the database is most often not the "right" approach. It has little or nothing to do with the model that I want to focus on. To use a common quote by Donald Knuth, "Premature optimization is the root of all evil." It's better to avoid optimizations until you have metrics saying that you have to do them.

To make a quick and long jump here, I think that decent design, together with Object Relational Mapping (O/R Mapping), is often good enough, and when it isn't, you should hand tune. O/R Mapping is a bit like the optimizer of database servers—most of the time it is smart enough, but there are situations when you might need to give it a hand.

Note

Decent design and O/R Mapping will be discussed a lot throughout the book. For now, let's define O/R Mapping as a technique for bridging between object orientation and relational databases. You describe the relationship between your object-oriented model and your relational database and the O/R Mapper does the rest for you.

So one approach is to use tools such as O/R Mappers for most of the database access code and then hand write the code that needs to be handwritten for the sake of execution efficiency.

Let's take a closer look at the problem something like an O/R Mapper will have to deal with, namely mapping between two different worlds, the object-oriented and the relational.

The Impedance Mismatch Between Domain Model and Relational Database

I mentioned previously that mapping to the UI is one problem when using Domain Models. Another well-known problem is mapping to relational databases. That problem is commonly referred to as *impedance mismatch* between the two worlds of relational and object-orientation.

I'd like to give my thoughts on what that impedance mismatch is, although it is something of a pop version. For further and more formal information see Cattel [Cattell ODM].

First of all, there are two type systems if you use both a relational database and an object-oriented model. One part of the problem is caused by the fact that the type systems are in different address spaces (even if not on different machines), so you have to move data between them.

Secondly, not even primitive types are exactly the same. For example a string in .NET is of variable length, but in Microsoft SQL Server a string is typically a varchar or a char or text. If you use varchar/char, you have to decide on a maximum width. If you use text, the program model is totally different than for the other string types in SQL Server.

Another example is DateTime. DateTime in .NET is pretty similar to SQL Server, but there are differences. For instance, the precision is down to 100 nanoseconds for .NET, but "only" down to 3/1000 of a second in SQL Server. Another "fun" difference is if you set a DateTime in .NET to DateTime.MinValue it will lead to an exception if you try to store it in a SQL Server DateTime.

Yet another difference is that of nullability. You can't store null in an ordinary int in .NET, but that's perfectly valid in SQL Server.

> **Note**
>
> The problems mentioned so far exist whether you use a Domain Model or not.

A big difference is how relationships are dealt with. In a relational database, relationships are formed by duplicated values. The primary key of the parent (for example, Customers.Id) is duplicated as a foreign key in the children (for example, Orders.CustomerId), effectively letting the child rows "point" to their parents. So everything in a relational model is data, even the relationships. In an object-oriented model, relationships can be set up in many different ways (for example, via values similar to those in the relational, but that is not typical). The most typical solution is to use the built-in object identifiers letting the parent have references to object identifiers of its children. This is, as you can see, a completely different model.

Navigation in a relational model can be done in two ways. First, one can use a parent primary key and then use a query to find all children that have foreign keys with the same value as the primary key of the parent. Then, for each child, the child primary key can be used with a new query to ask for all the children of the child, and so on. The other and probably more typical way of navigating in the relational model is to use relational joins between the parent set and the children set. In an object-oriented model, the typical way of navigating is to simply traverse the relationships between instances.

Next you find two code snippets where I *have* an order with ordernumber 42. Now I want to see what the name of the customer for that order is.

C#:

```
anOrder.Customer.Name
```

SQL:

```
SELECT Name
FROM Customers
WHERE Id IN
    (SELECT CustomerId
    FROM Orders
    WHERE OrderNumber = 42)
```

Note

I could just as well have used a JOIN for the SQL case, of course, but I think a subquery was clearer here.

Another navigation-related difference is that for objects, the navigation is one-way. If you need bidirectional navigation it is actually done with two separate mechanisms. In the relational model, the navigation is always bidirectional.

Note

The question about directionality can be seen as the opposite also to what I just explained, because in the relational database, there is just a "pointer" in one direction. I still think that "pointer" is bidirectional because you can use it for traversal in both directions, and that's what I think is important.

As we have already touched upon, the relational model is set-based. Every operation deals with sets. (A set can be just one row, of course, but it is still a set.) However, in the object-oriented model, we deal with one object at a time instead.

Moreover, the data in the relational model is "global," while we strive hard to maintain privacy of the data in an object-oriented model.

When it comes to design, the granularity is quite different. Let's take an example to make this clear. Assume that we are interested in keeping track of one home phone number and one work phone number for certain people. In a relational model it is normally alright to have one table called `People` (plural is the de facto name standard—at least among database people—to make it obvious we are dealing with a set).

Note

If I'm picky, I should use the word "relation" instead of "table" when I'm talking about the relational *model*.

The table has three columns (probably more, but so far we have only talked about the phone numbers) representing one primary key and two phone numbers. Perhaps there could be five columns, because we might want to break down the phone numbers into two columns each for area code and local number, or seven if we add country code as well. See Figure 1-4 for a comparison.

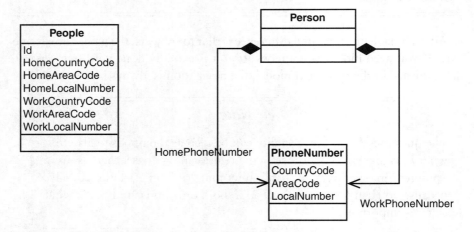

Figure 1-4   The same model expressed as relational and object-oriented

What's important here is that even for 1:1, all columns are normally defined in one table. In an object-oriented model, it would be usual to create two classes, one called Person and one called PhoneNumber. Then a Person instance would be a composition of two PhoneNumber instances. We *could* do a similar thing in the relational model, but it would not usually make any sense. We try not to reuse *definitions* a lot in the relational model, especially because we don't have behavior tied to the table definitions. It's just the opposite in the object-oriented model. Another way to say this is that in the relational model, we don't increase the satisfied normal form if we move PhoneNumbers out into a separate table. We have probably just increased the overhead. What it comes down to is that the relational model is for dealing with tabular, primitive data, and this is both good and bad. The object-oriented model deals neatly with complex data as well.

Note

The relational model has a pretty strong concept when it comes to definition reuse, which is called *domain*. Unfortunately, the support for that concept still isn't very strong in today's products.

It's also the case that many of the products have support for complex datatypes, but it's still in its infancy.

We just discussed one example of granularity where a relational model is more coarse-grained than an object-oriented model. We could also look at it the other way around. For example, in a relational model an order might have many orderLines, but the orderLines are on their own, so to speak. Each orderLine is just a row; each order is other such rows. There is a relationship between them, but the rows are the units. In an object-oriented model, it might be a good solution to see the order as the unit and let it be a composition of orderLines. This time the relational model was finer-grained than the object-oriented model.

Note

I'm not implying that there won't be an OrderLine class in the Domain Model. There should be. What I'm saying is that what I ask for and work with as the unit is an order, and orderLines is part of the order.

Last but not least, the relational model doesn't support inheritance (again, at least it's not mainstream in the most popular products). Inheritance is at the core of the object-oriented model. Sure, you can simulate inheritance in the relational model, but that is all it is, a simulation. The different simulation solutions to choose among are all compromises and carry overhead in storage, speed, and/or relational ugliness.

> ### Note
>
> Deep and native XML integration in the database seems to be the newest way of trying to lessen the problem of impedance mismatch. But XML is actually also a third model, a hierarchical one, which has impedance mismatch with the object-oriented world and the relational world.

Because it has been typical for my applications to use relational databases, the impedance mismatch has created a big problem.

The Data Mapper pattern [Fowler PoEAA] can be used for dealing with the problem. The Data Mapper pattern is about describing the relationship between the Domain Model and the Database, and then the shuffling work is taken care of automatically. Unfortunately the Data Mapper pattern itself is a tough one, especially in the .NET platform where Object-Relational Mapper (O/R-mapper) products are a couple of years behind. In Java-land there are several mature products and even a standardized spec called JDO [Jordan/Russell JDO], which makes the two platforms, as similar as they are, totally different from each other in this respect.

So it's time to leave the area of Domain Models and databases and end the architecture section by talking about distribution.

Handle Distribution with Care

Do you recognize the "I have a new tool, let's really use it" syndrome? I do. I've been known to suffer from it from time to time. It can be problematic, but I like to think about it not just negatively, but actually a bit positively, too. After all, it could be a sign of productive curiosity, healthy progressive thinking, and a never-ending appetite for improvements.

OK, now I have set up some excuses before telling you some horror stories from my past. About ten years ago, out came *Microsoft Transaction Server* (MTS) and suddenly it became pretty easy for all COM developers to build distributed systems. What happened? Loads of distributed systems have been built. I was there with the rest of them.

> ### Note
>
> I'm going to use MTS as the name here, but you could just as well use COM+ or COM+ Component Services or Enterprise Services.

Fine, for some systems it was very suitable to be distributed. Moving some processing out from the client and from the database to an application server had its benefits, like resource sharing (for example, connection pooling at the server-side so that hundreds of clients could be served by just a handful of database connections). These benefits were very much needed for some systems, and it became easier and more productive to get those benefits.

Overuse Is Never Good

Unfortunately, the benefits were so appealing that things went a bit overboard from time to time. For example, the server-side work might be split at several different application servers. Not that the application servers were cloned so that all clients could use any of them and get all services needed, but rather the client called one of the application servers. That server called another application server, which called another application server. There were small benefits, but huge drawbacks because of increased latency and lower availability.

Another mistake was that simple applications with just two simultaneous users were written for and executed in MTS. It's a very good example of making a mountain out of a molehill because of a belief that the application will probably be very popular in some distant future and be used by thousands of users simultaneously. The problem wasn't just a more complex operational environment, but that the design of the application had lots of implications if you wanted to be a good MTS citizen. A typical example of this was to avoid chatty communication between certain (or even worse, between all) layers. Those implications did increase the complexity of the design to quite an extent. Well, overuse is never good.

Did you notice that I avoided talking about the normal pitfalls that beginners of distributed systems encounter when making their first attempts with distributed systems, such at chatty communication? Well, even if, against all odds, for some reason those mistakes were avoided, there are other, slightly more subtle problems.

All these problems led Martin Fowler to come up with his First Law of Distributed Object Design, which is "Don't distribute" [Fowler PoEAA]. If you absolutely don't have to, don't do it. The cost and complexity will just go sky high. It's a law of nature.

Distribution Might Be Useful

Still, there are good things about distribution too, both now and in the future, for example:

- **Fault tolerance**

  If there is just one single machine that runs everything, you have a problem if that machine starts burning. For some applications that risk is OK; for others it's unthinkably bad.

- **Security**

  There is a heated debate over whether or not it increases security to split the application across several machines. Anyway, security concern is a common reason for why it is done.

- **Scalability**

  For some applications, the load is just too high for a single machine to cope with it. It might also be that, financially, you don't want to buy the most expensive machine around on day one. You may instead want to add more machines to the problem when the problem increases, without throwing away the old machines.

If you do need a distributed system, it's extremely important to think long and hard about the design, because then you have one big design challenge that can easily create big throughput problems, for example. When talking about distribution, messaging is an important concept.

Messaging Focus

The focus of this book is design of *one* application or *one* service, not so much about how to orchestrate several services. Even so, I think it's good to at least start thinking about messaging (if you haven't already). I guess this will just become more and more important for us in the future.

Messages as a Core Programming Model Thingy

I used to think it was good to abstract away or hide the network in distributed systems. In this way, the client programmer didn't know if a method call was going to translate to a network jump or if it was just a local function call. I liked that approach because I wanted to simplify the life of the client programmer so he or she could focus on stuff that's important to create great user interfaces and not get distracted with things such as network communication.

Let's take a look at a simple example. Assume you have a Customer class, as shown in Figure 1-5.

Figure 1-5 A Customer class

Instances of that Customer class would typically (and hopefully) live their life in the same address space as the consumer code, so that when the consumer asks for the name of the Customer, it's just a local call.

There is nothing, however, to physically stop you from letting Customer just be a Proxy [GoF Design Patterns], which in its turn will relay the calls to a Customer instance living at an application server. (OK, it's a bit simplified, but that's more or less what is going on behind the scenes if you configure the Customer class in MTS at an application server, for example.)

Szyperski points out [Szyperski Component Software] that location transparency is both an advantage and a burden. The advantage is that all types of communication (in process, interprocess, and intermachine) are mapped to one abstraction, the procedure call. The burden is that it hides the significant cost difference between the different types of calls. The difference is normally orders of magnitude in execution time.

I think the current trend is the opposite of location transparency and to make the costly messages obvious by making messages a core thing in the programming model. Trend-conscious as I am, I do like that evolution. I like it just because it's obvious to the client programmer that there is going to be a network call—it doesn't really mean that it must be hard to make. For example, message factories could be provided, yet it still makes it much clearer what will probably take time and what will not.

You might wonder how will messaging affect a domain model? The need for a domain model won't go away, but there will probably be slight changes. The first example that comes to mind is that inserts, as in a journal, are favored over updates (even for modifications). That makes asynchronous communication much more usable.

If Possible, Put It Off Until It's Done Better

One very important advantage of messaging is that it increases the execution flexibility so much. In the past, I think I've been pretty good at using batch jobs for long executions that didn't have to execute in real time. It's an old, and in my opinion underused, method for vastly increasing response time for the real time part of the work, because then the long executions would execute in windows of low load, typically at night, for example.

Currently I have written too many of my applications to be synchronous. When a piece of functionality takes too long to execute and doesn't have to execute in real time, I then have to change the functionality into a batch process instead. What is executing in real time is changed from being the complete piece of functionality into the request itself only.

A more efficient solution to the problem would be to think asynchronous messages from the start as often as possible. Then the functionality could run in real time if it's appropriate or be put on a message queue to be executed as soon as possible or at given intervals. (The batch solution would be kind of built in from the beginning.)

A solution based on asynchronous messages might require quite a different mindset when you build your user interface, but if you really challenge the different design problems, I think you will find that asynchronicity is possible and a suitable way to go more often than you may have thought in the past.

A few words to end this discussion: In my opinion it's a good idea to focus on the core model itself, no matter what the execution environment is. Then you can probably use it in several different situations, as the need arises.

Those were a few words about architecture values to value. Let's move over to the process side.

Process Ingredients to Value

I'm not much of a process guy, but I still would like to add a couple of thoughts. Before I get started, what do I mean by "process"? It's the methodology for moving forward in projects: What should be done, when, and how?

The classic process was the so-called waterfall. Each phase followed after the other in a strictly linear fashion with no going back whatsoever. A condensed description could be that first a specification was written, and then the system was built from that specification, then tested, then deployed.

Since then, numerous different processes have been introduced over the years, all with merits and pitfalls of their own. A recent one, Extreme Programming (XP) [Beck XP], gathered as one process under the umbrella of Agile [Cockburn Agile] processes, could probably be described as the opposite of waterfall. One of the basic ideas of XP is that it's impossible to know enough to write a really good, detailed specification on day one. Knowledge evolves during the project, not just because time passes, but because parts of the system are built, which is a very efficient way of gaining insight.

Note

There's much more to XP than what I just said. See, for example, [Beck XP] for more information. I will discuss TDD and Refactoring, which have their roots in XP.

Also note that XP doesn't always start from scratch. In the XP forums there is also a lot of interest for XP and legacy systems. See, for example, *Object-Oriented Reengineering Patterns* [Demeyer/Ducasse/Nierstrasz OORP].

I try to find a good combination of smaller ingredients for the situation. I have a couple of different current favorite ingredients. I'd like to discuss Domain-Driven Design, Test-Driven Development, and Refactoring, but let's start with Up-Front Architecture Design.

XP and a Focus on the User

Another thing that was considered new with XP was its focus on user-centric development. Users should be involved in the projects throughout the complete development.

For a Swedish guy, that wasn't very revolutionary. I don't know why, but we have a fairly long history of user-centric development in Sweden, long before XP.

Without meaning to sound as if Sweden is better than any other country, we have a long history of also using the waterfall processes.

Up-Front Architecture Design

Even though I like many of the Agile ideas about not making up front and premature decisions about things that couldn't possibly be known at that stage, I don't think that we should start the construction of new projects with only a blank sheet of paper, either. Most often, we have a fair amount of information from the very beginning (the more the better) about production environment, expected load, expected complexity, and so on. At least keep that in the back of your mind and use the information for doing some initial/early proof of concept of your up-front architecture.

Reuse Ideas from Your Successful Architectures

We can't afford to start from scratch with every new application, and this is especially true when it comes to the architecture. I usually think about my current favorite default architecture and see how it fits with the situation and requirements of the new application that is to be built. I also evaluate the last few applications to think of how they could have been improved from an architecture perspective, again with the context of the new application in mind. Always evaluating and trying to improve is definitely something to value.

If I assume for the moment that you like the idea of the Domain Model pattern [Fowler PoEAA], the architecture decisions could actually be a bit less hard to make initially because a great deal of the focus will go just there, on the Domain Model. Deciding whether or not to use the Domain Model pattern is actually an up-front architecture design decision, and a very important one because it will affect a lot of your upcoming work.

It is also important to point out that even though you do make an up front decision, it's not written in stone, not even your decision about whether or not to utilize the Domain Model pattern.

Note

I recently heard that the recommendation from some gurus was to implement the Transaction Script pattern [Fowler PoEAA] with the Recordset pattern [Fowler PoEAA] for as long as possible and move to another solution when it proved to be a necessity. I disagree. Sure, there are worse things that could happen, but that transition is not something I'd like to do late in the project because it will affect so much.

Consistency

An important reason for why it's good to make early architecture decisions is so that your team of several developers will work in the same direction. Some guidelines are needed for the sake of consistency.

The same is also true for IS departments that build many applications for the company. It's very beneficial if the architectures of the applications are somewhat similar as it makes it much easier and more efficient to move people between projects.

Software Factories

This brings us nicely to talking a little bit about Software Factories [Green-field/Short SF] (with inspiration from Product Line Architecture [Bosch Product Line]). The idea of Software Factories is to have two lines in the software company. One line creates architectures, frameworks, and such to be used for families of applications. The other line creates the applications by using what the first line has produced, and thereby amortizing the cost of the frameworks on several projects.

> **Note**
>
> A problem is that it's troublesome to just invent a framework. It's probably a better idea to harvest instead [Fowler HarvestedFramework].

Another thing that is somewhat problematic with Software Factories, though, is that they probably require pretty large organizations before being efficient to use. A friend that has used Product Line Architectures said that the organization needs to have a head count of thousands rather than fifty or a hundred because of the large investments and overhead costs. He also said (and I've heard the same from others) that even in organizations that have started to use Product Line Architectures, it's not necessarily and automatically used all the time. The overhead and bureaucracy it brings with it should not be underestimated. Think about a tiny framework that you use in several applications and then think much bigger and you get a feeling for it.

That said, I definitely think the Software Factories initiative is interesting.

At the heart of Software Factories is that of *Domain Specific Languages* (DSL) [Fowler LW]. A pop-description could be that DSL is about dealing with sub-problems with languages specialized for the task at hand. The languages themselves can be graphical or textual. They can also be generic, as with XML, UML and C#, or specific, like the WinForms editor in VS.NET or a little language you define on your own for a certain task.

Another approach, but with many similarities to DSL, is Model-Driven Architecture.

Model-Driven Architecture

Model-Driven Architecture (MDA) [OMG MDA] is something like "programming by drawing diagrams in UML." One common idea from the MDA arena is to create a *Platform Independent Model* (PIM) that can then be transformed into a *Platform Specific Model* (PSM), and from there transformed into executable form.

Thinking about it, it feels like writing 100% of a new program with a 3GL, such as C#, is overkill. It should be time to increase the abstraction level.

I think one problem many are seeing with MDA is its tight coupling to UML. One part of the problem is the loss of precision when going between code and UML; another part of the problem is that UML is a generic language with the pros and cons that comes with that.

For the moment, let's summarize those approaches (both DSL and MDA) with the term Model-Driven Development. I feel confident to say that we are moving in that direction, so Model-Driven Development will probably be a big thing. Even today, you can go a pretty long way with the current tools for Model-Driven Development.

Further on, I also think both approaches of DSL and MDA fit very well with Domain-Driven Design, especially the mindset of focusing on the model.

Domain-Driven Design

We have already discussed model focus and *Domain-Driven Design* (DDD) in the architecture section, but I'd like to add a few words about DDD in the process perspective also. Using DDD [Evans DDD] as the process will focus most of the energy on building a good model and implementing it as closely as possible in software.

What it's all about is creating as simple a model as possible, one that still captures what's important for the domain of the application. During development, the process could really be described as knowledge-crunching by the developers and domain experts together. The knowledge that is gained is put into the model.

Find Old Knowledge as a Shortcut

Of course, not all knowledge has to be gained from scratch. Depending upon the domain, there could well be loads of knowledge available in books, and not just in specific books for the domain in question. There is actually information in a couple of software books, too. Until recently, I would only consider the books called *Data Model Patterns* [Hay Data Model Patterns] and *Analysis Patterns* [Fowler Analysis Patterns], but I would strongly suggest that you get your hands on a book about Archetype Patterns as well. The book is called *Enterprise Patterns and MDA* [Arlow/Neustadt Archetype Patterns].

Refactor for Deeper Knowledge

A value I definitely think should be valued is continuous evaluation, and that goes for DDD, as well. Is the current model the best one? Every now and then, question the current model constructively, and if you come up with important simplifications, don't be afraid to refactor.

The same also applies when you find something new. A couple of simple refactorings might make that new feature not only possible but also easy to achieve so it fits well within the model.

Refactorings alone might also lead to deeper knowledge, like when you do a refactoring that can open everything up and lead to one of those rare "eureka!" moments.

We will come back to refactoring shortly, but first I'd like to talk about something closely related, namely Test-Driven Development.

Test-Driven Development

I've often heard developers say that they can't use automatic unit testing because they don't have any good tools. Well, the mindset is much more important than the tools, although tools do help, of course.

I wrote my own tool (see Figure 1-6) a couple of years ago and used it for registering and executing tests of stored procedures, COM components, and .NET classes. Thanks to this tool, I could skip those forms with 97 buttons that have to be pressed in a certain order in order to execute the tests.

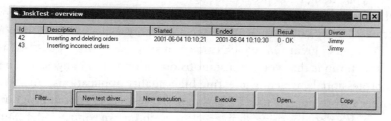

Figure 1-6   Screen shot of my old test tool called JnskTest

Later on, when NUnit [NUnit] (a derivate from the other xUnit versions) was released (see Figure 1-7), I started using that tool instead. Using NUnit is *way* more productive. For example, my tool didn't reflect on what the existing tests were. Instead you had to explicitly register information about them.

Note

Now I use another tool, called Testdriven.Net, but as I said, *what* tool you use is of less importance.

No matter what process you use, you can use automatic unit tests. For an even larger positive effect, I strongly recommend you find out if *Test-Driven Development* (TDD) is for you.

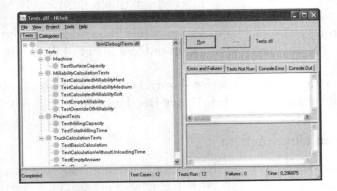

Figure 1-7   NUnit, the GUI version

The Next Level

TDD is about writing tests *before* writing the real code. In doing this, the tests will drive your design and programming.

TDD sounds dull and boring, and developers often expect it to be a pain in the backside. They couldn't be more wrong! In my experience, the opposite is true—it's actually great *fun*, which came as a surprise to me. I guess the reason that it is such fun is that you get instant feedback on your changes, and because we are professionals, we enjoy creating high-quality applications.

Another way to put it is that TDD isn't about testing. It's about programming and design. It's about writing simpler, clearer, and more robust code! (Sure, the "side-effect" of created unit tests is extremely important!)

Why TDD?

The reason I started with TDD in the first place was that I wanted to improve the quality of my projects. Improvement in quality is probably the most obvious and important effect. We don't want to create applications that crash when the customer uses them for the first time or applications that break down when we need to enhance them. It's just not acceptable anymore.

TDD won't automatically help you never release products with bugs again, but the quality will improve.

Note

The automatic tests themselves aren't the primary reason for TDD; they are nice side effects. If quality is everything, there are other formal methods, but for many scenarios they are considered too "expensive." Again, context is important.

You can see the effect of improved quality by writing tests *after* the real code. What I mean is that you don't have to apply TDD (which means writing tests *before* the real code), you just need a lot of discipline. On the other hand, using TDD gets the tests written. Otherwise, there is a very great risk that you won't write any tests when you're pressed for time, which always happens when it gets to a late stage in the projects. Again, TDD makes the tests happen.

The second effect you can expect when applying TDD is to see improved simplicity of design. In the words of two popular sayings, "Simple is beautiful" and "KISS." They are very important because, for example, complexity produces bugs.

Instead of creating loads of advanced blueprints covering every little detail upfront, when using TDD you will focus on the core customer requirements and just add the stuff the customer needs. You get more of a customer perspective than a technical perspective.

TDD is *not* about skipping design. On the contrary, you are doing design the whole time when using TDD.

In the past I've been *very* good at overcomplicating simple things. TDD helps me keep focused and not do anything other than what is really necessary *now*. This effect (getting improved simplicity of design) requires TDD. It's not enough to just write the tests afterwards.

Yet another effect of TDD is that you will get high productivity *all the way*. This might sound counterintuitive at first. When you start a new project, it feels very productive to get going and write the real code. At first you are very productive, but it's *very* common that the productivity completely drops near the end of the project. Bugs start cropping up; the customer decides on a couple of pretty substantial changes that upset everything; you find out that you have misunderstood some things...well, you get the picture.

Tests will force you to challenge the requirements and to challenge them early. Thereby, you will find out early if you have understood. You will also reveal lacking and contradictory requirements—again, early.

By the way, you shouldn't ask the customer if you should use TDD or not, at least not if you're asking for more payment/time/whatever at the same time. He will just tell you to do it right instead. When considering the project from start to finish, if using TDD incurs no extra cost, I believe you should just go ahead. The customer will be happy afterward when he gets the quality he expects.

Note

Let's for a moment skip TDD and focus only on automatic tests.

A colleague of mine has been *extremely* skeptical of the need for automatic unit tests (created before or after real code). He told me that during his two-decade career, automatic unit tests would not have helped him once. However, I think he changed his mind a bit recently. We were working together on a project where he wrote a COM component in C++ and I wrote tests as specifications and as just tests. When we were done, the customer changed one thing in the requirements. My colleague made a small change, but the tests caught a bug that occurred just four times in 1,000 executions. The bug was found after only seconds of testing, compared to hours if it had been done manually. And if it had been done manually, the bug would most probably not have been found at all, but would have shown itself during production.

The TDD Flow

Now I have tried to get you motivated to start with TDD, so let's have a closer look at how the process flows. (We'll get back to this in Chapter 3 when we will investigate it in a bit more depth with a real world demo.) Assuming you have a decent idea about the requirements, the flow goes like this:

First of all, you start writing a test. You make the test fail meaningfully so that you can be sure that the test is testing what you think. This is a simple and important rule, but even so, I have skipped over it several times and that is just asking for trouble.

The second step is to write the simplest possible code that makes the test pass.

The third step is to refactor if necessary, because you identify code that smells (for example, code duplication), and then you start all over again, adding another test.

If we use NUnit lingo, the first step should give you a red light/bar, and the second step should give you a green light/bar.

I mentioned refactoring previously and as the third step in the general process of TDD, and I think I should briefly explain the term a bit more.

Refactoring

Continuous learning was something we heard about in school all the time. It's very much true in the case of refactoring [Fowler R]—refactoring to get a better model, for example.

Refactoring is about making small, well-known changes step by step in order to improve the design of existing code. That is, to improve its maintainability without changing its observed behavior. Another way to say it is to change *how*, not *what*.

In a nutshell, what refactoring does is to take you from smelly code to nice code. It's as simple as that.

So you don't have to come up with a perfect design up-front. That is good news, because it can't be done anyway.

Why Use Refactoring?

None of us have any trouble in recognizing smelly code. What might be more troublesome is to know when to fix it. As I see it, you should deal with the problem as soon as it arises. You should use refactoring because without continuous maintenance of your code, it will start to degenerate and crumble.

Note

Mark Burhop said the following: "A good friend keeps a list of Software Development Laws. One goes something like "Code, left untouched, will develop bugs.""

Let's use the analogy of your home. Problems you choose to ignore, such as fixing windows, repairing the roof, painting the woodwork, and so on, ignored problems like these will grow in time. That's an immutable law. So sooner or later your house will fall to bits, and at that point it's worthless. Nobody wants *that* situation, right?

Software is different because it's not built of organic material and won't become affected from weather and wind if not changed. Still, we intuitively have a feeling for what's happening over time with software when refactoring isn't applied during bug fixes and when the software is extended.

How Should I Use Refactoring?

Refactoring can be used in all phases of the application lifecycle; for instance, during development of the first version of an application. But just assume we don't use refactoring, but an up-front, traditional design heavy process instead (now often referred to as Big Design Up-Front, BDUF). We will spend quite a lot of time on initial detailed design, creating loads of detailed UML diagrams, but as a result we will expect the development to go very smoothly and quickly. Even assuming that it does, there is still a risk that the code will be, well, smelly.

Instead, let's say we just accept the fact that we can't get it right up front the first time. In this case, a slightly different approach is to move some of the effort from initial detailed design over to development instead (and of course all development, especially in this case, *is design*) and to be prepared for doing refactoring continuously when we learn more. Learning more is exactly what we do during development, and as I see it, this approach results in higher quality code.

So instead of doing too much guessing, we do more learning and proofing!

Note

I was probably overly positive to BDUF so as to not distract you from the point that I was after regarding smelly code. Doing a lot of guesswork on day one will often lead to wasted time because it is just guesswork.

My friend Jimmy Ekbäck commented on this by saying, "BDUF can be even worse than wasted time because of incorrect guesses. BDUF can also lead to self-fulfilled prophesies."

Refactoring + TDD = True

In order to be able to use refactoring in a safe way, you *must* carry out extensive tests. If you don't, you will introduce bugs and/or you will prioritize, not making any changes simply for the sake of maintainability, because the risk of introducing bugs is just too large. And when you stop making changes because of maintainability, your code has slowly started to degrade.

Note

You will find much more coverage, with focus on hands-on examples, about both TDD and Refactoring in Chapter 3.

It's a good idea to use TDD and refactoring for bugfixing also. First expose the bug with a red test, then solve the bug so you get green, and then refactor.

Which Ingredient or a Combination?

Again, I'm sure many of you are wondering which way to go. For instance, should you focus on up-front design or TDD?

As I see it, you can mix up-front design and TDD successfully. For example, set up some up-front architecture, work with Domain-Driven Design, and for each piece of behavior build it with TDD (including refactoring). Then go back to your architecture and change it in accordance with what you have learned. Then work with Domain-Driven Design, and continue like that.

Note

I have to admit that I often fall back into the old habit of doing detailed up-front design. However, thinking about the problem in different ways is often the most efficient thing to do. A little bit top-down, a little bit bottom-up. A little bit inside out, a little bit outside in.

I think it's pretty well known that a *Big Design Up-Front* (BDUF) has some big problems. At the same time, most often we *know* some things from day one. It's a matter of balance.

Finally, a last remark regarding DDD and TDD: Domain Models are very suitable for TDD. Sure, you can also apply TDD with more database-oriented design, but I haven't been able to apply it as gracefully and productively as when I'm working with Domain Models.

Note

When I discussed TDD and/or DDD with Eric Evans he said the following, which I think is spot on:

"Myself, I actually play with the model while writing the tests. Writing the test lets me see what sort of client code different assignments of responsibility would produce, as well as the fine-tuning of method names and so on to communicate intention and have a good flow."

No matter if you focus on TDD or BDUF, there are lots of techniques that are useful anyway. The chapter will end with focusing on a couple of such things, such as operational aspects, but the first example is called Continuous Integration.

Continuous
Integration

Continuous Integration

I'm sure you all recognize how big a showstopper manual integration on a monthly basis, for example, can be—even if your team just consists of two developers on a project. The problem increases exponentially when you add more developers. Among other things, it costs lots of time, it is error prone, and you will find that it won't happen as planned. "Just one more day" will be a common sentence used in the project. My friend Claudio Perrone is just the right guy to describe the popular solution to this, known as continuous integration.

 ## The Integration Problem
By Claudio Perrone

Sooner or later, all the components that have been created and modified by different developers need to be built and assembled together to form a single system.

In the past, I've witnessed (and, yes, occasionally caused) spectacular delays in projects originated by last-minute integration efforts where unexpected defects were discovered in the final phases of a development cycle.

A build may fail for a variety of reasons, often in combination, such as

- Poorly tested components

- Wrong (but often plausible) assumptions about exception handling, null values, parameters, global variables, and so on

- Weak design

- Unpredicted behavior on different platforms

- Unexpected differences between release and debug builds

- Obfuscation issues

- Setup and permission issues

- Bugs in the underlying frameworks

Note that, despite all the best efforts, only some of these problems can be limited by the discipline and communication capabilities of the developers involved. The reality is that if the team does not integrate often and if the number of new classes in the system is sufficiently large, you may find yourself anxiously hunting combined bugs forever—an unpleasant scenario commonly known as "Integration Hell."

The Solution (Or at Least a Big Step in the Right Direction)

The key to significantly reducing integration problems is to generate your builds *automatically* and to use an *incremental* integration strategy where all the code is rebuilt and tested at least daily, if not continuously. The idea is that if your recently added code breaks a build, you either fix it immediately or roll back the changes to restore the system to the last known good state.

The fundamental parts that constitute a continuous integration system are as follows:

- A machine dedicated to the build process

- A source control system that acts as a central repository for all source code

- A monitoring service that checks the source control system for changes to the source code

- A scripting engine that, when triggered by the previous service, is able to create builds

- A reporting system that can give immediate feedback about the results of a build

There are several integration products available that you may want to investigate. Currently, my favorite is CruiseControl.NET [CC.NET], which I use in combination with NAnt, a very popular XML-based build engine. Both tools are open source. It takes quite an effort to configure CruiseControl.NET but, once up and running, it takes care of calling NAnt scripts whenever there is a change in the codebase. It notifies you of the progress and status of all current builds using a wide variety of client modules, including a little application that uses a Windows tray icon to show summary information at a glance through color coding and notification balloons.

Lessons Learned in My Organization

When we first contemplated the possibility of implementing a continuous integration system at InnerWorkings, most of us thought that it was a really great idea. Although we were already under severe scheduling pressure, we knew that it was definitely worth investing a few days to implement the system. If I think about it now, however, we certainly underestimated the profound impact that such a system would have on the quality of our products and the confidence of our team.

Today we have about 500 continuously integrated solutions, and the number is still increasing. A third of these solutions share a custom-built common framework, which is also integrated. Integration steps for all these solutions include compilation, obfuscation, packaging, testing, and deployment using different configurations and platforms.

Before we started this project, we were told that it would be impossible to integrate all of these solutions continuously. However, I'm convinced that it would have been impossible to do otherwise and that this effort constitutes a critical factor in our success.

Further Information

A good starting point for learning more about continuous integration is a paper written by Martin Fowler and Matthew Foemmel called "Continuous Integration" [Fowler/Foemmel CI].

◆

Thanks, Claudio! Now let's move on to some operational aspects.

Don't Forget About Operations

Not too long ago, I was talking to a team at a large Swedish company. I talked, for example, about the Valhalla framework and how it looked at that particular point in time.

They asked me how we had dealt with operational mechanisms, such as logging, configuration, security, and so on. When I told them that we hadn't added that yet, they first went quiet and then they started laughing out loud. They said they had spent years in their own framework with those aspects, and we hadn't even started thinking about it.

Luckily, I could defend myself to some extent. We had been thinking quite a lot about it, but we wanted to set the core parts of the framework before adding the operational mechanisms. After all, the core parts influence how the mechanism should look. I could also direct them to my last book [Nilsson NED] where I talked a lot in the initial chapters about mechanisms like those (such as tracing, logging, and configuration).

An Example of When a Mechanism Is Needed

Why are the operational aspects important? Let's take an example. Assume an application that is in production lacks tracing. (This isn't just fictional. I know that this operational aspect is forgotten pretty often. Even though for the last few years I have been talking myself blue in the face about this, I have old applications in production without tracing built-in myself.) When a weird problem occurs that isn't revealing too much about itself in the error log information, the reason for the problem is very hard to find and the problem is very hard to solve.

No Tracing in Place

You could always add tracing at that particular point in time, but it would probably take you a couple of days at least. If the problem is serious, the customer will expect you to find and solve the problem in less time than a couple of days.

A common—and most often pretty inefficient—way to approach this is to make ad-hoc changes and after each change cross your fingers and hope that the problem is gone.

What you probably do instead is add ad-hoc tracing here and there. It will make your code much uglier, and it will take some time before you track down the problem. The next time there is another problem, very little has changed. You will be back at square one.

What might also be possible is to run a debugger in the production environment. However, there are problems with this such as you might interfere too much with other systems or you might have obfuscated the code with some tool so that it's hard to debug.

It's also risky to change the code in production, even if the change is as small as adding tracing. Not a big risk, but it's there.

Note

If you have the possibility of using *Aspect-Oriented Programming* (AOP), it might not take more than a few minutes to add tracing afterward. We will discuss AOP quite a lot in Chapter 10, "Design Techniques to Embrace."

Tracing in Place

If you have a working tracing solution in place, you know how efficient it might be to find and solve the problem instead. The days-long delay is gone, and you are on the way to tracking down the problem in minutes.

So it's important to be careful and not think "You Aren't Going to Need It" (YAGNI) too often when it comes to operational mechanisms. Using YAGNI often will cost too much when it comes to adding the mechanism if (or rather when) you will need it. Remember, the idea with YAGNI is that the cost of adding something is pretty much the same now and later, in which case you can always wait until you really need it. When the cost is low now and high later, and there's a good chance you will need it, you should make a different decision.

Some Examples of Operational Mechanisms

Here I have listed a short number of operational mechanisms that can be considered for most enterprise scale applications:

- **Tracing**

  As we just discussed, it's nice to be able to listen to what is going on at the same time as users run scenarios in the system. This is not only a very efficient solution for tracking down bugs, but it can be used for investigating where the bottlenecks are located, for example.

- **Logging**

  Errors, warnings, and information messages must be logged. This is extremely important for investigating problems after they have occurred. We can't expect the users to write down the exact messages for us. It might also be that we want to collect information that we don't want to show to the users.

- **Config**

  Have you had to recompile old applications just because the database server was switched to a new machine with a new name? I have. Of course, that kind of information should be configurable and depending on the application, this might be the case for loads of information.

- **Performance monitoring**

  Getting performance monitoring based on Domain Model information and other parts of your application is extremely helpful for tracking down problems, but also for keeping a proactive eye on the system. By doing that, you can easily track that it now takes perhaps 30% longer to execute a certain scenario compared to a time two months ago.

- Security

These days, this one probably doesn't need any further explanation. We obviously need to carefully think through things like authentication and authorization. We also must protect our applications against attacks of different kinds.

- Auditing

As one part of the security aspects, it's important to have auditing so that it's possible to check afterwards who did what when.

It's Not Just Our Fault

In the defense of developers, I know I have asked operational people several times about their requirements regarding operational mechanisms, and they haven't said very much. I guess they haven't been spoiled with a lot of support from the applications.

That said, an appealing way of dealing with this is to, if you can, get some resources from the operations side early on to act explicitly as a stakeholder on the system, so that you create the operational mechanisms that are really needed. The ordinary customer of the system isn't a good requirement creator here. The operational mechanisms are typical examples of non-functional requirements, and the ordinary customers won't normally add much there.

The flexibility for your mechanisms might be important because different customers use different operational platforms. There are standards such as *Windows Management Instrumentation* (WMI), but it's wise to build in flexibility if you build a framework for this so you can easily switch to different output formats for the logging, for example. One customer uses CA Unicenter, another uses Microsoft Operations Manager (MOM), yet another might use some product that won't understand WMI, and so on.

Summary

We ended the chapter with a few words about operational aspects. We won't discuss that much more in this book. Instead, the focus will be about the core of the applications, the core business value.

The discussion in this chapter about what is important for modern software development is certainly not exhaustive. My hope was to briefly discuss a

Summary

couple of values worth considering for every developer. On the way we introduced Domain-Driven Design, Domain Models, Test-Driven Development, Patterns, and a lot of other concepts, both regarding architecture and regarding processes.

The three values I would like to stress again are balance, context-awareness, and continuous learning. Those are valuable values for developers and architects, and everybody else, too.

So with the scene set up, it's now time to discuss patterns of different types some more.

Chapter 2

A Head Start on Patterns

We are constantly facing new design problems. We always solve the problems, but sometimes we find that we have backed ourselves into a corner. Sometimes we find that the solution has serious drawbacks, and sometimes we create bad solutions. By reusing good, well-proven, and flexible solutions we minimize these risks and we reach the desired result faster. A tool to use for this is patterns. Thanks to the higher abstraction level that comes from patterns, we can also start and succeed with even larger design problems. Pattern awareness also leads to better understanding between developers—system development is very much about communication.

I've heard it many times. Patterns are academic nonsense, useless and elitist. If this is also how you feel, my aim in this chapter is to show you the opposite, because nothing could be more wrong. Patterns can be very pragmatic, highly useful in day-to-day work, and extremely interesting to all (or at least most) developers. Maybe you haven't noticed, but I have already discussed several patterns. One example is the Domain Model pattern [Fowler PoEAA] that I brought up in Chapter 1, "Values to Value." In this chapter, we will discuss three different categories of patterns: namely Design Patterns (generic and application-type specific), Architectural Patterns, and Domain Patterns.

Note

Please note that the categorizations here are a bit fuzzy, and not at all as important or interesting as the patterns themselves. So if the categorizations don't provide any help to you, don't let them get in the way for you.

Even if you are already pattern-conscious, I think you'll find this chapter interesting. I won't reuse old explanations, but will provide my own view of the patterns. For example, the discussion I'm going to use will be very Domain Model-focused, which is not typically the case when it comes to Design Patterns, for example. If nothing else, I hope you'll find the reflections here and there of interest.

Before getting started, though, I'd like to take you through a generic discussion of the concept of patterns and why you should learn about them.

A Little Bit About Patterns

Patterns provide simple, elegant solutions to recurring design problems. The key advantages patterns provide are flexibility, modularity, and creating understandable and clear design. Note that I skipped reusability, although it's a bit unfair. Patterns take away focus from code reuse and move the focus to knowledge reuse instead. So patterns are very much about reusability, too, but just not in the way we usually think about reuse.

> **Note**
>
> Gregory Young pointed out that many patterns are about reuse, through decoupling. The Dependency Injection pattern (which will be discussed in Chapter 10, "Design Techniques to Embrace") is a good example of that.

When you study patterns, you might think "OK, isn't that how we always do it?" An important point about patterns is that they aren't *invented*, but rather *harvested* or *distilled*. It's about *proven* solutions. But the solution part isn't the only piece of a pattern. They are described in three pieces: the *context*, the *problem*, and the *solution*.

Learning from your mistakes is very powerful, but from time to time it's nice to take a shortcut by studying other people's amassed knowledge, which is a good reason for learning patterns. Let's see if we can find other reasons.

Why Learn About Patterns?

The most obvious reason is probably that patterns are good abstractions that provide building blocks for system design.

If a development team is patterns-conscious, patterns become a very important part of the language. Instead of having to describe each and every design idea in minute detail, it's often enough to say a pattern name and everybody in the team can evaluate whether or not it's a good idea for that particular problem. Adding patterns to the team's language might be the single most important reason for embracing patterns because the common understanding, richness, and expressiveness of the language increase. Again, development is very much about communication.

Another reason I like patterns is that being able to utilize patterns is a long-lasting skill. As a comparison, I learned SQL in around 1988, and I can still make a good living from just working with that. The products and platforms I work with have changed several times, though the underlying concepts are the same. Patterns are similar. The *Design Patterns* book [GoF Design Patterns] came out in 1995, and it's still extremely relevant today. Also worth pointing out is that patterns are language-/product-/platform-agnostic. (Different platforms might have specific support for certain implementation variations, and it's also the case that the [GoF Design Patterns] have been written with object orientation as an assumption.)

If you study *Design Patterns* [GoF Design Patterns], you will find that the patterns there are very much in line with the principles of good object-oriented design. What is good object-oriented design, you might ask? Robert C. Martin discusses some such principles in *Agile Software Development: Principles, Patterns, and Practices* [Martin PPP]. Examples include the *Single Responsibility Principle* (SRP), the *Open-Closed Principle* (OCP) and the *Liskov Substitution Principle* (LSP).

More on Martin's Principles...

A bit of explanation of Martin's principles follows:

- Single Responsibility Principle (SRP)

  An item such as a class should just have one responsibility and solve that responsibility well. If a class is responsible both for presentation and data access, that's a good example of a class breaking SRP.

- Open-Closed Principle (OCP)

  A class should be closed for modification, but open for extension. When you change a class, there is always a risk that you will break something. But if instead of modifying the class you extend it with a sub-class, that's a less risky change.

- Liskov Substitution Principle (LSP)

  Assume that you have an inheritance hierarchy with Person and Student. Wherever you can use Person, you should also be able to use a Student, because Student is a subclass of Person. At first this might sound like that's always the case automatically, but when you start thinking about reflection (reflection is a technique for being able to programmatically inspect the type of an instance and read and set its properties and fields and call its methods, without knowing about the type beforehand), for example, it's not so obvious anymore. A method that uses reflection for dealing with Person might not expect Student.

  The reflection problem is a syntactical one. Martin uses a more semantical example of Square that is a Rectangle. But when you use SetWidth() for the Square, that doesn't make sense, or at least you have to internally call SetHeight() as well. A pretty different behavior from what Rectangle needs.

Sure, all these principles are debatable in certain contexts. They should be used as a guide only, not as the "only truth." For example, OCP can easily be over-applied. You might have come to a point where you understand better how a method should be implemented and want to modify it rather than extend it. And adding a method to a class could also be seen as an extension.

Patterns are not only great with up-front design, they are very usable (perhaps even more) during refactoring…*"My code is just becoming messier and messier. Ah, I need to use that pattern!"* It's like the chicken or the egg problem, but I decided to start with patterns in this book and discuss refactoring after that (in the next chapter).

Is There Something to Look Out for Regarding Patterns?

Honestly, I see little reason for not learning about patterns, but there is at least one very common negative effect to look out for. What I'm thinking about is that for developers who have just learned about patterns, it's very common that they feel compelled to squeeze in 17 patterns in each and every solution. Most often that effect won't stay around for very long.

What might stay around for a little longer is the risk of over-design. If not 17 patterns, there might at least be a lot of thought about how a problem should be solved. The initial solution doesn't feel right because it doesn't use a certain pattern.

Note

A friend of mine told me about a recent design problem he discussed with some developers at a company. It took him three minutes to come up with a very simple solution to the problem. (The problem itself was a simple one.) Yet the other developers weren't happy with the solution so they spent three days of hard thinking to get it just right.

Been there, done that. In my opinion, *Test-Driven Development* (TDD) is a good technique for avoiding that over-design problem. The design focus will be much more on solving the problem at hand and nothing else, and patterns will be introduced when needed via refactoring.

You might get the feeling that the patterns concept is the silver bullet. It's not—of course not—it's just another tool for the toolbox.

Patterns are often perceived individually as being pretty "simple," but they get very complex in context and combination with other patterns. I don't remember how many times I've heard people on the newsgroups say something like "I understand pattern X, but when I try to use it in my application together with pattern Y and pattern Z, it's extremely complex. Please help!" That isn't really a reason *not* to learn about patterns. This book will address that to some degree, but not here and now; first we will discuss some patterns in isolation.

I believe Joshua Kerievsky's *Refactoring to Patterns* [Kerievsky R2P] sets this straight by pointing out again and again that the way to most often use patterns isn't to use them in up-front design, but to refactor toward or to patterns.

Pattern Adoption

Gregg Irwin said this about pattern adoption:

"For me, many concepts, like patterns, are learned in stages:

1. You use it without being aware that you're using it
2. You hear about it, read up on it, and tinker a bit

3. You learn more and start using it explicitly, if naïvely

4. You get the fire and evangelize (optional)

5. Something "clicks"

6. You learn more and apply it "less naïvely" and more implicitly

7. Time passes and you see flaws

8. You question the concept (often because you misapplied it)

9. You either forget about it or add knowledge and experience
   (Repeat steps 5–9 as necessary)

10. You use it without being aware that you're using it"

OK, time to move over to the first pattern category. Let's see if we can create an "Aha!" and not just a "Huh?" for those of you who are pattern newcomers.

Design Patterns

When I say Design Patterns here, the first thoughts of many will go to the *Design Patterns* book [GoF Design Patterns], which has been mentioned a whole bunch of times by now. It's by no means the only book about Design Patterns, but it's considered the standard work on the subject.

Design Patterns are abstract and pretty low-level in that they are technical and general in regard to domain. It doesn't matter what tier or what type of system you are building, Design Patterns are still useful.

One way to describe Design Patterns is that they are about refining the subsystems or components. You will find when we move to the other two categories I'm about to discuss here that it's common that the patterns there use one or more Design Patterns or that some specific Design Patterns can be applied in a more specific way in those categories.

Note

While we're talking about low-level, here is a fun little story. I was asked what the difference was between me and a friend on a professional level. I said that my friend worked with low-level programming and I worked with high-level programming. The person asking didn't know anything about programming, but he got that look on his face you get when listening to someone blowing his own trumpet way too much.

The *Design Patterns* book [GoF Design Patterns] is pretty hard-going. Each time I read it I understand and learn more about it. For example, I have often thought, "That's not correct" or "That's not the best solution" or even "That's stupid." But after some deliberation, I decide that they are "right" each time.

So far there has been a lot of talk and little action. It's time to become concrete by giving an explanation of a Design Pattern. I have chosen one of my favorite Design Patterns called State, so here goes.

An Example: State Pattern

Problem-based teaching is a good pedagogic approach, so I'll use it here. The following is a problem.

Problem

A sales order can be in different states, such as "NewOrder," "Registered," "Granted," "Shipped," "Invoiced," and "Cancelled." There are strict rules concerning to which states the order can "go" from which states. For example, it's not allowed to go directly from Registered to Shipped.

There are also differences in behavior depending upon the states. For example, when Cancelled, you can't call AddOrderLine() for adding more items to the order. (That also goes for Shipped and Invoiced, by the way.)

One more thing to remember is that certain behavior will lead to state transformation. For example, when AddOrderLine() is called, the state transforms from Granted back to New Order.

Solution Proposal One

In order to solve this problem, I need to describe a state graph in code. In Figure 2-1 you find a very simple and classic state graph describing how state of the button is changed between Up and Down each time the user pushes the button.

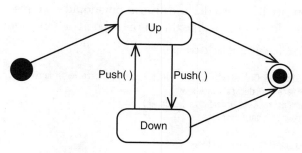

Figure 2-1 State graph for a button

Design
Patterns

If we apply this technique of a state graph on the Order, it could look like
Figure 2-2.

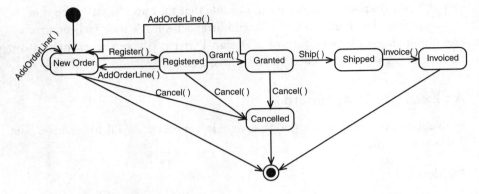

Figure 2-2 State graph for an Order

One obvious solution is probably to use an enum like this:

```
public enum OrderState
{
    NewOrder,
    Registered,
    Granted,
    Shipped,
    Invoiced,
    Cancelled
}
```

and then to use a private field for the current state in the Order class, like this:

```
private OrderState _currentState = OrderState.NewOrder;
```

Then, in the methods, you need to deal with two things on top of what the
methods should do. You must check if the method might be called at all in that
state, and you need to consider if a transition should take place and, if so, to
what new state. It could look like this in the AddOrderLine() method:

```
private void AddOrderLine(OrderLine orderLine)
{
    if (_currentState == OrderState.Registered || _currentState == OrderState.Granted)
        _currentState = OrderState.NewOrder;
    else if (_currentState == OrderState.NewOrder)
        //Don't do any transition.
    else
        throw new ApplicationException(...

    //Do the interesting stuff...
}
```

As you saw in the code snippet, the method got quite a lot of uninteresting code added just because of taking care of the state graph. An ugly if-statement is very fragile to changes in the future. Code similar to that will be sprinkled everywhere in the Order class. What we do is spread knowledge of the state graph in several different methods. This is a good example of subtle but evil duplication.

Even for simple examples like this, we should reduce the code duplication and fragmentation. Let's give it a try.

Solution Proposal Two

Proposal Two is just a slight variation. You can have a private method called _ChangeState(), which could, for example, be called from AddOrderLine(). _ChangeState() could have a long switch statement, like this:

```
private void _ChangeState(OrderState newState)
{
    if (newState == _currentState)
        return; //Assume a transition to itself is not an error.

    switch (_currentState)
    {
        case OrderState.NewOrder:
            switch (newState)
            {
                case OrderState.Registered:
                case OrderState.Cancelled:
                    _currentState = newState;
                    Break;

                default:
                    throw new ApplicationException(...
                    break;
            }
        case OrderState.Registered:
            switch (newState)
            {
                case OrderState.NewOrder:
                case OrderState.Granted:
                case OrderState.Cancelled:
                    _currentState = newState;
                    break;

                default:
                    throw new ApplicationException(...
                    break;
            }
        ...
        //And so on...
    }
}
```

Design
Patterns

The `AddOrderLine()` now looks like this:

```
public void AddOrderLine(OrderLine orderLine)
{
    _changeState(OrderState.NewOrder);

    //Do the interesting stuff...
}
```

I was quite lazy in the previous code and only showed the start of the structure of the huge switch statement, but I think it's still pretty obvious that this is a good example of smelly code, especially if you consider that this example was simplified and didn't discuss all aspects or all states that were really needed—not even close.

> ### *Note*
>
> As always, for some situations the example just shown was good enough and the "right" solution. I just felt I had to say that so as to not imply that there is only one solution to a problem that is always right.
>
> Also note that I will discuss some more about code smells in the next chapter.

OK, I've been there, done that in several projects. I can't say I like that solution very much. It seems fine at first, but when the problem grows, the solution gets troublesome. Let's try out another one.

Solution Proposal Three

The third solution is based on a table (some kind of configuration information) describing what should happen at certain stimuli. So instead of describing the state transformation in code as in proposals one and two, this time we describe the transformations in a table, Table 2-1.

Table 2-1 *State Transitions*

Current State	Allowed New State
NewOrder	Registered
NewOrder	Cancelled
Registered	NewOrder
Registered	Granted
Registered	Cancelled
...	...

Then your _ChangeState() method can just check if the new state that comes as a parameter is acceptable for when the current state is NewOrder, for example. For the current state NewOrder, only Registered and Cancelled are allowed as a new state.

You could also add another column as shown in Table 2-2.

Table 2-2 *State Transitions, Revised*

Current State	Method	New State
NewOrder	Register()	Registered
NewOrder	Cancel()	Cancelled
Registered	AddOrderLine()	NewOrder
Registered	Grant()	Granted
Registered	Cancel()	Cancelled
...		...

Now your _ChangeState() method shouldn't take the new state as a parameter, but rather the method name instead. Then _ChangeState() decides what the new state should be by looking in the table.

This is clean and simple. A big advantage here is that it's very easy to get an overview of the different possible state transformations. The main problem is probably that it's hard to deal with custom behavior depending upon the current state and then to go to one state of several possible states when a method executes. Sure, it's no harder than with proposal two, but it's still not very good. You could register information in the table about what delegates (a delegate is like a strongly typed function pointer) should be executed at certain transformations, and you could probably extend that idea to solve the other problems as well, but I think there is a risk that it gets a bit messy during debugging, for example.

Do we have more ideas? Let's apply some knowledge reuse and try out the Design Pattern called State.

Solution Proposal Four

The general structure of the State pattern is shown in Figure 2-3.

The idea is to encapsulate the different states as individual classes (see ConcreteStateA and ConcreteStateB). Those concrete state classes inherit from an abstract State class. Context has a state instance as a field and calls Handle() of the state instance when Context gets a Request() call. Handle() has different implementations for the different state classes.

Design
Patterns

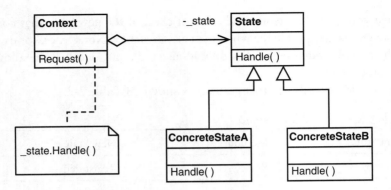

Figure 2-3   State pattern, general structure

That's the general structure. Let's see what this could look like if we apply it to the problem at hand. In Figure 2-4, you find a UML diagram for the specific example.

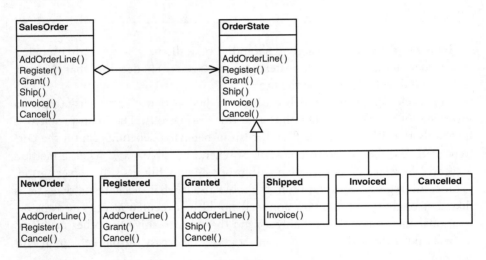

Figure 2-4   State pattern, specific example

Note

For this example, it might make sense to add another abstract class as the base class for NewOrder, Registered, and Granted. The new class would implement AddOrderLine() and Cancel().

In the specific example, the Order class is the Context from the general structure. Again, Order has a field of OrderState, although this time OrderState isn't an enum, but a class. For the sake of refactoring, your old tests might expect an enum, and then you can keep that enum as well (perhaps as a property which implementation inspects what is the current instance in the state inheritance hierarchy) and thereby not make changes to the external interface.

A newly created Order gets a new state instance of a NewOrder at instantiation and sends itself to the constructor, like this:

```
internal OrderState _currentState = new NewOrder(this);
```

Note that the field is declared as internal. The reason for this is so that the state class can change the current state by itself, so Order delegates the state transformations totally to the different state classes. (I could also let OrderState be an inner class of Order to avoid the need for internal.)

This time, the Register() method on Order is extremely simple. It could look like this:

```
public void Register()
{
    _currentState.Register();
}
```

The Register() method on NewOrder is also pretty simple. At least it can focus on its own state, and that makes the code clean and clear. It could look like this:

```
public void Register()
{
    _parent._Register();
    _parent._currentState = new Registered(_parent);
}
```

Before changing the state, there was kind of a callback to the parent (_parent._Register()) telling it to do its thing before the state was changed. (Note that the "callback" went to the internal method _Register() and not the public Register().) This is just one example of an option, of course. Other examples would be to put the code in the OrderState base class or in the NewOrder class itself. It should go wherever it's best located.

As you saw, if I want to do things before or after the state transformation, it's simple and very well encapsulated. If I want to disallow a certain transformation in the NewOrder class, I just skip implementing that method and use the implementation of the base class OrderState for that method. The implementation of the base class throws an exception saying it was an illegal state transformation, if that's the wanted behavior. Another typical default implementation is to do nothing.

> ## Note
>
> If you need more context-aware exceptions, you can of course implement the methods in the subclasses just as well, even if all they will do is raise exceptions.
>
> This also implies that instead of using a base class for OrderState you could use an interface instead. I guess that if the GoF book had been written today, many of the patterns would have used interfaces instead of (or at least together with) abstract base classes. The State pattern isn't the most typical example of this, but it still is a possible example.

More Comments

When using the State pattern, we were actually swapping a single field into a bunch of separate classes. That doesn't sound like a very good idea at first, but what we then get is the nice effect of moving the behavior to where it belongs and good alignment to the *Single Responsibility Principle* (SRP).

There are drawbacks, of course, and a typical one is that the program can potentially be flooded with small classes when we use a solution such as State.

Which solution you prefer is indeed up for debate, but I think the State pattern is one that should be seriously considered here. You might find that it solves your problem with the least amount of duplicated code and with the responsibility partitioned out into encapsulated and cohesive units, the concrete state classes. But watch out—the State pattern is also very easy to overuse, as is every tool. Use it wisely!

That was an example of a Design Pattern, a generic one. We'll come back to more Design Patterns of another family, but first a discussion about another category of patterns.

Architectural Patterns

A common association to the term "Architectural Patterns" is to think about some of the patterns discussed in Buschmann et al.'s *Pattern-Oriented Software Architecture* [POSA 1]. In that book there are a couple patterns gathered under the category called Architectural Patterns. Examples of the patterns are Pipes and Filters and Reflection.

Pipes and Filters are about channeling data through Pipes and processing the stream in Filters. Pipes and Filters have been picked up by the SOA community as a useful pattern for message-based systems.

Reflection is built into both Java and .NET, making it possible to write programs that read from and write to objects in a generic way by only using the metadata of the objects (not knowing anything about the type of the object beforehand).

If Design Patterns is about refining subsystems or components, Architectural Patterns is about the structuring into subsystems. To make it more concrete, let's take a common example, Layers [POSA 1].

An Example: Layers

Layers or layering is a basic principle when it comes to architecture, which means to factor out responsibilities into separate cohesive units (clusters of classes) and define the dependencies between those units. Most developers are reasonably familiar with this.

Because it's such a commonly used and well-understood pattern, we will just give a quick example of it here to give us a feeling of the pattern category.

Problem

Assume we have built a set of classes for a SalesOrder application, such as Customer, Order, Product, and so on. Those classes encapsulate the meaning they have for the Domain, and also how they are persisted/depersisted and presented. The current implementation is to persist to the file system and to present the objects as HTML snippets.

Unfortunately, we now find out that we need to be able to consume the objects as XML as well and to use a relational database for persistence.

Solution Proposal One: Apply Layers

The most common solution to this problem is probably to factor out some of the responsibilities of the classes. The new requirements made it obvious to us that the classes were clearly breaking the SRP.

We try to split the classes so that the responsibilities are cohesively dealt with from a technological point of view.

Therefore, the old classes will now only focus on the domain meaning (let's call the layer Domain layer). The presentation (or rather consumption) responsibilities are dealt with by another set of classes (another layer called the Consumer layer), and the persistence responsibilities are dealt with by yet another set of classes (the Persistence layer).

Three layers spontaneously felt like a typical solution here, one per responsibility category. The two new layers have two *implementations* each for dealing with both the old requirements and the new.

The dependencies between the layers are also defined, and in this case we decided that the consumption layer will depend on the domain layer, and the domain layer will depend on the persistence layer. That way, the Consumer layer is totally unaware of the Persistence layer, which was something we decided was good in this particular project.

We will get back to the subject of layering again in Chapter 4, "A New Default Architecture," and then approach it a bit differently.

Another Example: Domain Model Pattern

We have already discussed the Domain Model pattern [Fowler PoEAA] in Chapter 1 (and will do so much more throughout the book). I think about the Domain Model pattern as an example of an Architectural Pattern.

We're not going to discuss an example about the Domain Model pattern here and now because the whole book is about just that. Instead, we'll continue by focusing on another dimension of the patterns, regarding domain-dependence or not. Next up are Design Patterns for specific types of applications.

Design Patterns for Specific Types of Applications

Another set of Design Patterns isn't as generic as those discussed so far, but, for example, patterns for building enterprise applications.

Defining an enterprise application is tricky, but you can think of it as a large-scale information system with many users and/or a lot of data.

The main book dealing with the patterns in this category is Martin Fowler's *Patterns of Enterprise Application Architecture* [Fowler PoEAA].

The patterns here at first sight might not seem as cool or amazing as some of the Design Patterns, but they are extremely useful, cover a lot of ground, and contain a lot of experience and knowledge. As I said, they are less generic than the other Design Patterns and focused just on large-scale information systems.

They come into play for the chosen structure of the logic; for example, the Domain Model. The patterns here aren't so much about how *the Domain Model itself* (or any of the other models for structuring the main logic) should be structured, but more about the *infrastructure* for supporting the Domain Model.

To make it more concrete, I'd like to discuss an example, and I choose Query Objects [Fowler PoEAA].

An Example: Query Objects

Let's assume for a moment that you have a Domain Model for a SalesOrder application. There is a Customer class and an Order class, and the Order class in particular is composed of a number of other classes. This is simple and clear.

There are several different solutions from which to choose in order to navigate the Domain Model. One solution is to have a global root object that has references to root-like collections. In this case, a customer collection would be an example of one of these. So what the developer does is to start with the global root object and navigate from there to the customer collection, and then iterate the collection until what is needed is found, or perhaps navigate to the customer's sales orders if that's what's of interest.

A similar paradigm is that all collections are global so you can directly access the customer collection and iterate over it.

Both those paradigms are easy to understand and simple to use, but one drawback is that they are lacking somewhat from the perspective of a distributed system. Assume you have the Domain Model running at the client (each client has one Domain Model, or rather a small subset of the Domain Model instances, and no shared Domain Model instances) and the database is running at a database server (a pretty common deployment model). What should happen when you ask the root object to get the customer collection of one million customers? You can get all the customers back to the client so the client can iterate over the collection locally. Not so nice to wait for that huge collection to be transmitted.

Another option is to add an application server to the picture and ask it to only send over a collection *reference* to the client side, and then much less data is transmitted, of course. On the other hand, there will be an incredible amount of network calls when the client is iterating the list and asking for the next customer over the network one million times. (It will be even worse if the customer instances themselves aren't marshaled by value but only by reference.) Yet another option is to page the customer collection so the client perhaps gets 100 customers from the server at a time.

I know—all these solutions have one problem in common; you don't often want to look at all the customers. You need a subset, in which case it's time to discuss the next problem.

Problem

The problem is that the users want a form where they can search for customers flexibly. They want to be able to ask for all customers who

- Have a name with "aa" in it. (Hidden marketing for a Swedish car company.)

- Ordered something last month.

- Have orders with a total amount greater than one million.

- Have a reference person called "Stig."

But on the same form, they should also be able to ask for just customers in a certain part of Sweden. Again, the search form needs to be pretty flexible.

I'm going to discuss three different solution proposals, namely "filtering within Domain Model," "filtering in database with huge parameter lists," and "Query Objects."

Solution Proposal One: Filter Within Domain Model

Let's take a step back and admit that we *could* use any of the solutions already discussed so that the collection is materialized somewhere and then the filter is checked for every instance. All instances meeting the filter criteria are added to a new collection, and that is the result.

This is a pretty simple solution, but practically unusable in many real-world situations. You will waste space and time. Not only were there one million customers, but you also had to materialize the orders for the customers. Phew, that solution is just impossible to use and it's even worse when you scale up the problem....

Of course, the conclusion here depends to a large degree on the execution platform. Remember what I said about the deployment model—a subset of the Domain Model instances in each client, the database at a database server, no shared Domain Model instances.

If instead there was one shared set of Domain Model instances at an application server (which has its own problems—more about that in later chapters), this might have been a suitable solution, but only for server-side logic. For clients asking for a subset of the shared Domain Model instances, the clients must express their criteria somehow.

Solution Proposal Two: Filtering in Database with Huge Parameter Lists

Databases are normally good at storing and querying, so let's use them to our advantage here. We just need to express what we want with a SQL statement and then transform the result into instances in our Domain Model.

A SQL statement like the following could solve the first problem:

```
SELECT Id, CustomerName, …
FROM Customers
WHERE CustomerName LIKE '%aa%'
AND Id IN
```

```
        (SELECT CustomerId
        FROM ReferencePersons
        WHERE FirstName = 'Stig')
AND Id IN
        (SELECT CustomerId
        FROM Orders
        WHERE TotalAmount > 1000000)
AND Id IN
        (SELECT CustomerId
        FROM Orders
        WHERE OrderDate BETWEEN '20040601' AND '20040630')
```

Note

It's debatable whether I can combine the two subselects targeting Orders into a single subselect. As the requirement was stated, I don't think so (because the meaning would change slightly if I combined them).

Anyway, this isn't really important for the discussion here.

Here we just materialize the instances that are of interest to us. However, we probably don't want the layer containing the Domain Model to have to contain all that SQL code. What's the point of the Domain Model in that case? The consumer layer just gets two models to deal with.

So we now have a new problem. How shall the consumer layer express what it wants? Ah, the Domain Layer which is responsible for the mapping between the database and Domain Model can provide the consumer layer with a search method. Proposal number two is the following:

```
public IList SearchForCustomers
(string customerNameWithWildCards
, bool mustHaveOrderedSomethingLastMonth
, int minimumOrderAmount
, string firstNameOfAtLeastoneReferencePerson)
```

This probably solves the requirement for the first query, but not the second. We need to add a few more parameters like this:

```
public IList SearchForCustomers
(string customerNameWithWildCards
, bool mustHaveOrderedSomethingLastMonth
, int minimumOrderAmount
, string firstNameOfAtLeastoneReferencePerson
, string country, string town)
```

Do you see where this is going? The parameter list quickly gets impractical because there are probably a whole bunch of other parameters that are also needed. Sure, editors showing placeholders for each parameter helps when calling the method, but using the method will still be error-prone and impractical. And when another parameter is needed, you have to go and change all the old calls, or at least provide a new overload.

Another problem is how to express certain things in that pretty powerless way of primitive datatypes in a list of parameters. A good example of that is the parameter called mustHaveOrderedSomethingLastMonth. What about the month before that? Or last year? Sure, we could use two dates instead as parameters and move the responsibility of defining the interval to the consumer of the method, but what about when we only care about customers in a certain town? What should the date parameters be then? I guess I could use minimum and maximum dates to create the biggest possible interval, but it's not extremely intuitive that that's the way to express "all dates."

Note

Gregory Young commented on the problem of how to express presendence. Expressing this with a parameter list is troublesome:
(criterion1 and criterion2) or (criterion1 and criterion2)

I think we have quickly grown out of this solution, too. I came to the same conclusion back in the VB6 days, so I used an array-based solution. The first column of the array was the fieldname (such as CustomerName), the second column was the operator (such as Like from an enumerator) and the third column was the criterion such as "*aa*". Each criterion had one row in the array.

That solution solved some of the problems with the parameter list, but it had its own problems. Just because there was a new possible criterion added, I didn't have to change any of the old consumer code. That was good, but it was pretty powerless for advanced criterion, so I stepped back and exposed the database schema, for example, to deal with the criterion "Have any orders with a total amount larger than one million?" I then used the complete IN-clause as the criterion.

The array-based solution was a step in the right direction, but it would have become a little more flexible with objects instead. Unfortunately, it wasn't really possible to write marshal by value components in VB6. There were solutions to the problem, such as using a more flexible array structure, but the whole thing is so much more natural in .NET. Over to the Query Object pattern.

Solution Proposal Three: Query Objects

The idea of the Query Object pattern is to encapsulate the criteria in a Query instance and then send that Query instance to another layer where it is translated into the required SQL. The UML diagram for the general solution could look like that shown in Figure 2-5.

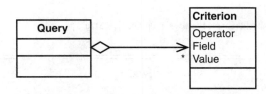

Figure 2-5 Class diagram for general Query Object solution

The criterion could use another query (even though it's not apparent in the typical description of this as in Figure 2-5), and that way it's easy to create the equivalent of a subquery in SQL.

Let's come up with a try for a Query Object language for applying on the problem. First though, let's assume that the Domain Model is as is shown in Figure 2-6.

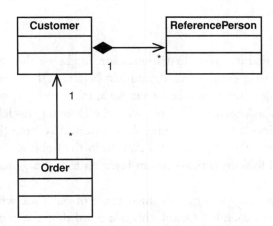

Figure 2-6 Domain Model to be used for the example

Let's see what it could look like our newly created naïve query language in C#:

```
Query q = new Query("Customer");
q.AddCriterion("CustomerName", Op.Like, "*aa*");
```

```
Query sub1 = new Query("Order");
sub1.AddCriterion("TotalAmount", Op.GreaterThan, 1000000);
q.AddCriterion(sub1);

Query sub2 = new Query("Order");
sub2.AddCriterion("OrderDate", Op.Between,
DateTime.Parse("2004-06-01"), DateTime.Parse("2004-06-30"));
q.AddCriterion(sub2);

q.AddCriterion("ReferencePersons.FirstName", Op.Equal, "Stig");
```

Note

The parameter to the Query constructor is not a table name but a Domain Model class-name. The same goes for the parameters to AddCriterion(); I mean it's not table columns, but class fields/properties. In that case, property names or field names are used in the Domain Model.

Also note that in this specific example, I didn't need a subquery for the criterion regarding the ReferencePersons because the Domain Model was navigable from Customer to ReferencePerson. On the other hand, subqueries were needed for the Orders for the opposite reason.

More Comments

If you are SQL-literate, your first impression might be that the SQL-version was more expressive, easier to read, and just better. SQL is certainly a powerful query language, but remember what we want to accomplish. We want to be able to work as much as possible with the Domain Model (within limits) and thereby achieve a more maintainable solution. Also note that the C# code just shown was needlessly talkative. Later on in the book we will discuss how the syntax could look by writing a thin layer on top of a general query object implementation.

So what we gained was further transparence of our code with regard to the database schema. Generally, I think this is a good thing. When we *really* need to, we can always go out of this little sandbox of ours to state SQL queries with the full power of the database and without a lifeline.

Another thing I'd like to point out is that creating a competent Query Object implementation will quickly become very complex, so watch out that you don't take on too much work.

A nice little side effect is that you can also use query objects pretty easily for local filtering, such as holding on to a cached list of all products. For the developer consuming the Domain Model, he or she just creates a Query Object as usual, but it is then used in a slightly different manner, without touching the database.

Domain
Patterns

> ### Warning
>
> I know, I know. Caching is just as cool and useful as it is dangerous. Watch out, it can backfire. You have been warned.

Some DDD-literate readers would probably prefer the Specification pattern [Evans DDD] as the solution to this problem. That provides a neat connection over to the third and final pattern category we are going to focus on: Domain Patterns.

Domain Patterns

Domain Patterns have a very different focus from the Design Patterns and the Architectural Patterns. The focus is totally on how to structure the Domain Model itself, how to encapsulate the domain knowledge in the model, and how to apply the ubiquitous language and not let the infrastructure distract away from the important parts.

There is some overlap with Design Patterns, such as the Design Pattern called Strategy, [GoF Design Patterns] which is considered to be a Domain Pattern as well. The reason for the overlap is that patterns such as Strategy are very good tools for structuring the Domain Model.

As Design Patterns, they are technical and general. As Domain Patterns, they focus on the very core of the Domain Model. They are about making the Domain Model clearer, more expressive, and purposeful, as well as letting the knowledge gained of the domain be apparent in the Domain Model.

When I ended the previous section, I mentioned that the Specification pattern as a Domain Pattern is an alternative to Query Objects pattern. I think that's a good way of explaining how I see what Domain Patterns are. Query Objects is a technical pattern where the consumer can define a query with a syntax based on objects, for finding more or less any of the objects in the Domain Model. The Specification pattern can be used for querying as well, but instead of using a generic query object and setting criteria, one by one, a specification is used as a concept that itself encapsulates domain knowledge and communicates the purpose.

For example, for finding the gold customers, you can use both query objects and specifications, but the solutions will differ. With Query Objects, you will express criteria about how you define gold customers. With a Specification, you will have a class that is perhaps called GoldCustomerSpecification. The criteria itself isn't revealed or duplicated in that case, but encapsulated in that class with a well-describing name.

One source of Domain Patterns is [Arlow/Neustadt Archetype Patterns], but I have chosen a Domain Pattern-example from another good source, Eric Evans' book *Domain Driven Design* [Evans DDD]. The chosen example pattern is called Factory.

Note

Pattern-aware readers might get confused because I talk about the Domain Pattern Factory here and the *Design Patterns* book [GoF Design Patterns] also has some Factory patterns. Again, the focus of Design Patterns is more on a technical level and the focus of Domain Patterns is on a semantic Domain Model level.

They are also different regarding the detailed intents and typical implementations. The Factory patterns of GoF are called Factory Method and Abstract Factory. Factory Method is about deferring instantiation of the "right" class to subclasses. Abstract Factory is about creating families of dependent objects.

The Factory pattern of DDD is straightforward implementation-wise and is *only* about capturing and encapsulating the creation concept for certain classes.

An Example: Factory

Who said that the software industry is influenced by industrialism? It's debatable whether it's good, but it is influenced. We talk about engineering as a good principle for software development; we talk about architecture, product lines and so on and so forth. Here is another such influence, the Factory pattern. But first, let's state the problem that goes with this example.

Problem

The problem this time is that the construction of an order is complex. It needs to be done in two very different flavors. The first is when a new order is created that is unknown to the database. The second is when the consumer asks for an old order to be materialized into the Domain Model from the database. In both cases, there needs to be an order instance created, but the similarity ends there as far as the construction goes.

Another part of the problem is that an order should always have a customer; otherwise, creating the order just doesn't make sense. Yet another part of the problem is that we need to be able to create new credit orders and repeated orders.

Solution Proposal One

The simplest solution to the problem is to just use a public constructor like this:

```
public Order()
```

Then, after having called this constructor, the consumer has to set up the properties of the instance the way it should be to be inserted or by asking the database for the values.

Unfortunately, this is like opening a can of worms. For example, we might have dirty tracking on properties, and we probably don't want the dirty tracking to signal an instance that was just reconstituted from persistence as dirty. Another problem is how to set the identification, which is probably not settable at all. Reflection can solve both problems (at least if the identifier isn't declared as readonly), but is that something the Domain Model consumer developer should have to care about? I definitely don't think so. There are some more esoteric solutions we could explore, but I'm sure most of you would agree that a typical and obvious solution would be to use parameterized constructors instead.

Because I have spent a lot of programming time in the past a long time ago with VB6, I haven't been spoiled by parameterized constructors. Can you believe that—not having parameterized constructors? I'm actually having a hard time believing it myself.

Anyway, in C# and Java and so on, we do have the possibility of parameterized constructors, and that is probably the first solution to consider in dealing with the problem. So let's use three public constructors of the Order class:

```
public Order(Customer customer);
public Order(Order order,
    bool trueForCreditFalseForRepeat);
public Order(int orderId);
```

The first two constructors are used when creating a new instance of an Order that isn't in the database yet. The first of them is for creating a new, ordinary Order. So far, so good, but I have delayed introducing requirements on purpose,

making it possible to create Orders that start as reservations. When that requirement is added, the first constructor will have to change to be possible to use for
two different purposes.

The second constructor is for creating either a credit Order or a repetition of an
old Order. This is definitely less clear than I would like it to be.

The last constructor is used when fetching an old Order, but the only thing
that reveals which constructor to use is the parameter. This is not clear. Another
problem (especially with the third constructor) is that it's considered bad practice to have lots of processing in the constructor. A jump to the database feels
very bad.

Solution Proposal Two

According to the book *Effective Java* [Bloch Effective Java], the first item (best
practice) out of 57 is to consider providing static Factory methods instead of
constructors. It could look like this:

```
public static Order Create(Customer customer);
public static Order CreateReservation(Customer customer);
public static Order CreateCredit(Order orderToCredit);
public static Order CreateRepeat(Order orderToRepeat);
public static Order Get(int orderId);
```

A nice thing about such a Factory method is that it has a name, revealing
its intention. For example, the fifth method is a lot clearer than its constructor
counterpart from solution 1, constructor three, right? I actually think that's the
case for all the previous Factory methods when compared to solution 1, and
now I added the requirement of reservations and repeating orders without getting into construction problems.

Bloch also discusses that static Factory methods don't have to create a new
instance each time they get involved, which might be big advantage. Another
advantage, and a more typical one, is that they can return an instance of any
subtype of their return type.

Are there any drawbacks? I think the main one is that I'm probably violating
the SRP [Martin PPP] when I have my creational code in the class itself. Evans'
book [Evans DDD] is a good reminder of that where he uses a metaphor of a
car engine. The car engine itself doesn't know how it is created; that's not its
responsibility. Imagine how much more complex the engine would have to be
if it not only had to operate but also had to create itself first. This argument is
especially valid in cases where the creational code is complex.

Add to that metaphor the element that the engine could also be fetched from
another location, such as from the shelf of a local or a central stock; that is, an

old instance should be reconstituted by fetching it from the database and mate-rializing it. This is totally different from creating the instance in the first place, both for a real, physical engine and for an Order instance in software.

We are close to the pattern solution now. Let's use a solution similar to the second proposal, but factor out the creational behavior into a class of its own, forgetting about the "fetch from database" for now (which is dealt with by another Domain Pattern called Repository, which we will discuss a lot in later chapters).

Solution Proposal Three

So now we have come to using the Factory pattern as the Domain Pattern. Let's start with a diagram, found in Figure 2-7.

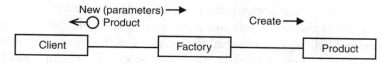

Figure 2-7 An instance diagram for the Factory pattern

The code could look like this from a consumer perspective to obtain a ready-made new Order instance:

```
anOrder = OrderFactory.Create(aCustomer);
aReservation = OrderFactory.CreateReservation(aCustomer);

aCredit = OrderFactory.CreateCredit(anOldOrder);
aRepeat = OrderFactory.CreateRepeat(anOldOrder);
```

This is not much harder for the consumer than it is using an ordinary con-structor. It's a little bit more intrusive, but not much.

In order for the consumer to get to an old Order, the consumer must talk to something else (not the Factory, but a Repository). That's clearer and expres-sive, but it's another story for later on.

To avoid the instantiation of orders via the constructor from other classes in the Domain Model if the Factory code is in an external class is not possible, but you can make it a little less of a problem by making the constructor internal, and hopefully because the Factory is there, the Domain Model developers them-selves understand that that's the way of instantiating the class and not using the constructor of the target class directly.

Domain Patterns

> ### Note
>
> Eric Evans commented on the previous paragraph with the following:
> "I hope someday languages will support concepts like this. (Just as they
> have constructors now, perhaps they will allow us to declare factories,
> etc.)"

More Comments

First of all, please note that sometimes a constructor is just what we want. For example, there might not be any interesting hierarchy, the client wants to choose the implementation, the construction is very simple, and the client will have access to all properties. It's important to understand *not* to just go on and create factories to create each and every instance, but to use factories where they help you out and add clarity to and reveal the intention of the Domain Model.

What is typical of the Factory is that it sets up the instance in a valid state. One thing I have become pretty fond of doing is setting up the sub-instances with Null Objects [Woolf Null Object] if that's appropriate. Take an Order, for example. Assume that the shipment of an Order is taken care of by a Transporter.

At first, the Order hasn't been shipped (and in this case we have not thought much about shipment at all), so we can't give it any Transporter object, but instead of just leaving the Transporter property as null, I set the property to the empty ("not chosen," perhaps) Transporter instead. In this way, I can always expect to find a description for the Transporter property like this:

```
anOrder.Transporter.Description
```

If Transporter had been null, I would have needed to check for that first. The Factory is a very handy solution for things like this. (You could do the same thing in the case of a constructor, but there might be many places you need to apply Null Objects, and it might not be trivial to decide on what to use for Null Objects if there are options. What I'm getting at is that the complexity of the constructor increases.)

You can, of course, have several different Factory methods and let them take many parameters so you get good control of the creation from the outside of the Factory.

Using Factories can also hide infrastructure requirements that you can't avoid.

It's extremely common to hear about Factories and see them used in a less semantic way, or at least differently so that all instances (new or "old") are created with Factories. In COM for example, every class has to have a class fac-tory, as do many frameworks. Then it's not the Domain Pattern Factory that is used: similar in name and in technique, different in intention.

Another example is that you can (indirectly) let the Factory go to the data-base to fetch default values. Again, it's good practice to not have much process-ing in constructors, so they are not a good place to have logic like that.

Note

Now we have a problem. It shouldn't be possible to set some properties from the outside; however, we need to get the values there. This is done when a Factory sets default values (and when a Repository fetches an old instance from the database). Perhaps this feels bad to you?

We'll get back to this later, but for now, remember that this is often a problem anyway because reflection can be used for changing the inner state, at least if that is allowed according to the security settings.

My philosophy on this is that you can't fully stop the programmers from doing evil when consuming the Domain Model, but you should make it hard to do stupid things by mistake, and you need to check that evil things haven't been done.

All in all, I don't think this is usually a real problem.

Overall, I think the usage of the Factory pattern clearly demonstrated that some instantiation complexity was moved from the Order into a concept of its own. This also helped the clarity of the Domain Model to some degree. It's a good clue that the instantiation logic is interesting and complex.

Summary

This was a quick introduction and my attempt to get you interested in patterns. Hopefully it worked, because I will use patterns as an important tool in the fol-lowing chapters.

Now it's time to dive into how to use TDD by discussing some examples.

Chapter 3

TDD and Refactoring

Test-Driven
Development
(TDD)

A good example is a powerful thing; I think we are in agreement on that. One way to describe *Test-Driven Development* (TDD) is to say that you use tests or *examples* for specifying the behavior. Those examples will serve you over and over again for many different purposes. They will serve you during development, for example, for finding lacking or incorrect requirements. When you refactor, the tests will be a safety net. After development they will serve you as quality documentation.

In this chapter we will not just talk about tests as examples; we will discuss TDD itself with some examples. I just think that's a good way of describing what it's all about.

After some initial discussion of TDD and the state-based style, my friend Claudio Perrone will discuss some techniques for creating examples the interaction-based way, writing tests by using stubs and mocks.

A key principle that is used during TDD is refactoring. Even refactoring is pretty example-centric. You can think of it as writing a first example of a piece of the solution, then using refactoring to refine that example until you're done. So you don't have to come up with a perfect design up front. That is good news, because it is close to impossible anyway.

Again, we will discuss refactoring with some examples, of course.

Let's start with some basics about TDD.

Test-Driven Development (TDD)

After having used TDD for a couple of years now, I'm still getting even fonder of the technique. I'm becoming more and more convinced that TDD is the single most important technique in becoming a better programmer. Strong words—any substance? You'll have to try it out on your own to know for yourself, of course, but let's have a look at what it's all about. Let's start with a short repletion from Chapter 1, "Values to Value," about the flow.

The TDD Flow

First, you start writing a test. You make the test fail meaningfully so that you can be sure that the test is testing what you think it should.

The second step is to write the simplest possible code that makes the test pass.

The third step is to refactor.

Then you start all over again, adding another test.

**Test-Driven
Development
(TDD)**

If we use xUnit lingo, the first step should give you a red light/bar, and the second step should give you a green light/bar. (Unfortunately, compilation errors and refactoring don't have colors yet.)

So the mantra is Red, Green, Refactor. Red, Green, Refactor…

Time for a Demo

I'm assuming that you are familiar with Testdriven.net [Testdriven.net], NUnit [NUnit], or some other similar tool (or pick up some such tool now and learn the basics on your own). So instead of a tool discussion, I'll focus on how to apply the concept of TDD.

I know, I know. There are an enormous number of good demonstration texts on how to use TDD, such as [Beck TDD], [Astels TDD], [Martin PPP]. Anyway, I'd like to have a go at demonstrating it myself. Rather than doing what is most common, I won't use a homemade toy example, but I'll use an example from a real-world application of mine.

A few years ago, I was asked by Dynapac to write an application that they could bundle with a new line of planers that they produced. The planers are used for removing old asphalt before paving out new. Asphalt milling is used to restore the surface of asphalt pavement to a specified profile. Bumps, ruts, and other surface irregularities are removed, leaving a uniform, textured surface.

The application would be used for calculating a number of different things, helping to optimize the usage of the planers. The application needed to be able to calculate the hardness of the old asphalt, the time needed to plane a certain project, the trucks needed to keep milling with the minimum cost, and lots of other things.

I'm going to use this real-world application to demonstrate how TDD can be used so you get a feeling for the flow. I'm going to focus on calculating the number of trucks.

It is important to have the correct number of trucks for transporting the old asphalt. If you have too few, the planer will have to stop every now and then or move slower. If you have too many, it's a waste of trucks and personnel. In both cases, the cost will increase for the project.

OK, let's do this the TDD way. I'll start out by writing the identified needed functionality in a text file like this:

```
Calculate millability
Calculate milling capacity
Calculate number of trucks needed
```

As I said, I'm going to focus on the calculation for the number of trucks now, so I put a marker in the file on that line so I know what I decided to start with. As soon as I (or more likely the customer) come up with another piece of functionality that I don't want to work on right now, I add it to the file. So that text file will help me to not forget about anything, while still enabling me to focus on one thing at a time.

Note

Tests and refactorings *could* be written to the same file, but I prefer not to. Instead I write tests tagged with the Ignore attribute for tests that I don't want to focus on now. Refactoring needs that I find, but I don't want to deal with now, are probably not worth being done, or they will be found again and dealt with then.

The next thing to do is to think about tests for the truck calculation. At first I thought it was very simple, but the more I thought about it, I found out it was actually pretty complex.

So let's start out by adding a simple test. Let the test check that when no input is given, zero trucks should be needed. First, I create a new project that I call Tests. I add a class that I call TruckCalculationTests, and I do the necessary preparations for making it a test fixture according to NUnit, such as setting a reference to nunit.framework, adding a using clause to NUnit.Framework, and decorating the class with [TestFixture]. Then I write a first test, which looks like this:

```
[Test]
public void WillGetZeroAsResultWhenNoInputIsGiven()
{
    TruckCalculation tc = new TruckCalculation();

    Assert.AreEqual(0, tc.NeededNumberOfTrucks);
}
```

As a matter of fact, when writing that extremely simple test, I actually made a couple of small design decisions. First, I decided that I need a class called TruckCalculation. Second, I decided that that class should have a property called NeededNumberOfTrucks.

Of course, the test project won't compile yet because we haven't written the code that it tests, so let's continue with adding the "real" project, so to speak. I add another project that I call Dynapac.PlanPave.DomainModel. In that project I add a class like this:

```
public class TruckCalculation
{
    public int NeededNumberOfTrucks
    {
        get {return -1;}
    }
}
```

What is a bit irksome is that I fake the return value to -1. The reason is to force a failure for my test. Remember, we should always start with an unsuccessful test, and for this specific test just returning zero would clearly not fail. It should fail *meaningfully*, but I can't come up with a really meaningful failure and still start out as simple (neither now nor when I wrote this in the real project), so this will have to do.

Then we go back to the Tests project and set a reference to the Dynapac.PlanPave.DomainModel project. We also add a using clause and build the whole solution. After that we execute the tests (or actually only the *test* at this point) in the Tests project. Hopefully we get a red bar. Then we go back to the property code and change it so it returns zero instead: re-execute the tests and a green bar.

Is there anything to refactor? Well, I'm pretty happy with the code so far. It's the simplest code I can think of right now that satisfies the tests (or—again—the *test*).

We have taken a small step in the right direction. We have started working on the new functionality for calculating number of trucks, and we have a first simple—but good—little test.

Let's take another small step. Again, we take the step by letting tests drive our progress. So we need to come up with another test. In the testing area, I need to show both a rounded result and a more exact result, at least to one decimal. The rounded result must always be rounded up because it's hard to create a half truck. (I know what you are thinking, but it's not in the customer requirements to deal with a mix of different-sized trucks.) That's a decent and necessary test, but I don't feel like dealing with it now. I want to take a more interesting step, so I add the rounding test with the Ignore attribute like this:

```
[Test, Ignore("Deal with a little later")]
public void CannotRoundDecimalTruckDown()
{
}
```

Instead, I'd like to take a step with the calculation. Heck, it can't be so hard to calculate this. I have to take transportation distance into account, as well as transportation speed, truck capacity, milling capacity, unloading time, loading time, and probably a couple of other things. Moving on and simplifying a bit, let's say that I don't care about transportation for now, nor the time for loading. I won't even care about other factors that are as yet unknown to me. The only things I care about now are milling capacity, truck capacity and time for unloading. So things are simple enough for the moment. I can write a test like this:

```
[Test]
public void CanCalculateWhenOnlyCapacityIsDealtWith()
{
    TruckCalculation tc = new TruckCalculation();

    tc.MillingCapacity = 20;
    tc.TruckCapacity = 5;
    tc.UnloadingTime = 30;

    Assert.AreEqual(2, tc.NeededNumberOfTrucks);
}
```

What I just did was to assume the milling capacity was 20 tons/hour and each truck can deal with 5 tons each time, which means 4 unloadings. I also assumed that unloading the truck takes 30 minutes, so each truck can only be used twice in one hour. That should mean that we need 2 trucks, so I test for that.

Note

The calculation might seem a bit strange so far because too few factors are taken into account and I just tried to get started with it. The important thing here isn't the calculation itself, but the process of how to move forward with TDD, so please don't let the calculation itself distract you.

When I try to compile the Tests project, it fails because the new test expects three new properties. Let's add those properties to the TruckCalculation class. They could look like this:

```
//TruckCalculation
public int TruckCapacity = 0;
public int MillingCapacity = 0;
public int UnloadingTime = 0;
```

Test-Driven
Development
(TDD)

Hmmm, that wasn't even properties, just public fields. We'll discuss this later. Now we can build the solution, and hopefully we'll now get a red bar.

Yes, expected and wanted. We need to make a change to NeededNumberOfTrucks, to make a real (or, at least, more real) calculation.

```
//TruckCalculation
    public int NeededNumberOfTrucks
    {
        get
        {
            return MillingCapacity /
            (TruckCapacity * 60 / UnloadingTime);
        }
    }
```

I now realize that this was perhaps too big a leap to take here, but I'm feeling confident now.

Let's build again and then re-execute the tests. Green bar; oops...**red.** How can that be? Ah, it wasn't the last test that was the problem; that test runs successfully. It's the old test that now fails. I get an exception from it. Of course, the first test doesn't give any values to the TruckCapacity and UnloadingTime properties, so I get a division by zero. A silly mistake to make, but I'm actually very happy about that red bar. Even that tiny little first test helped me by finding a bug just minutes (or even seconds) after I created the bug, and this extremely short feedback loop is very powerful.

I need to change the calculation a bit more:

```
//TruckCalculation
    public int NeededNumberOfTrucks
    {
        get
        {
            if (TruckCapacity != 0 && UnloadingTime != 0)
                return MillingCapacity /
                (TruckCapacity * 60 / UnloadingTime);
            else
                return 0;
        }
    }
```

So we build, run the tests, and get a green bar. Good—another step in the right direction, secured (at least to a certain degree) with tests.

Any refactorings? Well, I'm pretty sure several of you hate my usage of the public fields. I used to hate them myself, but I have since changed my mind. As long as the fields are both readable and writable and no interception is needed when reading or writing the values, the public fields are at least as good as properties. The good thing is that they are simpler; the bad thing is if you need to intercept when one of the values is set. I will refactor that later, if and when necessary, and not before.

> ## *Note*
>
> There is a difference between public fields and public properties when it comes to reflection, and that might create problems for you if you choose to switch between them.
>
> A reviewer pointed out another difference that I didn't think about: the fact that public properties can't be used as ref arguments, but that's possible with public fields.
>
> This whole discussion is also language dependent. In the case of C#/VB.NET, a public field and public property is used the same way by the consumer, but that's not the case with C++ and Java, for example.

Another thing I could refactor is to add a [SetUp] method to the test class that instantiates a calculation member on the instance level. That's right; don't forget about your tests when you think about refactoring. Anyway, I can't say I feel compelled to do that change either, at least not right now. It would reduce duplication a little bit, but also make the tests slightly less clear. In the case of tests, clarity is often a higher priority.

Yet another thing that I'm not very happy about is that the code for the calculation itself is a bit messy. I think a better solution would be to take away what I think will be the least common situation of zero values in a guard. In this way, the ordinary and real calculation will be clearer. This change is not extremely important and is more a matter of personal taste, but I think it makes the code a little more readable. Anyway, let's make the refactoring called Replace Nested Conditional with Guard Clauses [Fowler R]:

```
//TruckCalculation
    public int NeededNumberOfTrucks
    {
        get
        {
            if (TruckCapacity == 0 || UnloadingTime == 0)
                return 0;

            return MillingCapacity /
            (TruckCapacity * 60 / UnloadingTime);
        }
    }
```

> **Note**
>
> Just like pattern names, refactoring names can be used as a means of communication among developers.

Build the tests and then run them. We still see green bars, and the code is clearer, but we can do better. I think it's a good idea here to use Consolidate Conditional Expression [Fowler R] like this:

```
//TruckCalculation
    public int NeededNumberOfTrucks
    {
        get
        {
            if (_IsNotCalculatable())
                return 0;

            return MillingCapacity /
            (TruckCapacity * 60 / UnloadingTime);
        }
    }
```

And while I'm at it, the formula is a bit unclear. I reveal the purpose better if I change part of it into a property call instead by using Extract Method refactoring [Fowler R] like this:

```
    public int NeededNumberOfTrucks
    {
        get
        {
            if (_IsNotCalculatable())
                return 0;

            return MillingCapacity /
            _SingleTruckCapacityDuringOneHour;
        }
    }
```

That's fine for now, but it's time to add another test. However, I think this little introduction to writing a new class for calculating the needed number of trucks was enough to show the flow of TDD.

Some of you might dislike that you don't get help from intellisense (which helps you cut down on typing by "guessing" what you want to write) when writing tests first. I'm fond of intellisense too, but in this case I don't miss it. Remember, what we are talking about here is the interface, and it could be good to write it twice to get an extra check.

Also note that you should vary your speed depending upon how confident you are with the code you are writing at the moment. If it turns out that you are too confident and too eager so that you get into hard problems, you can slow down and write smaller tests and smaller chunks to get back to moving forward.

Design Effects

During the demo I said that writing the tests was very much a design activity. Here I have listed some of the effects I have found when designing with TDD instead of detailed up-front design:

- **More client control**

  I used to think that as much as possible should be hidden from the outside regarding configuration so that classes configure themselves. To use TDD, you need to make it possible for the tests to set up the instances the way they need them. This is actually a good thing because the classes become much easier to reuse. (Of course, watch out so you don't open up the potential for mistakes.)

- **More interfaces/factories**

  In order to make it possible (or at least easier) to use stubs or mock objects, you will find that you need to gather functionality via interfaces so you can pass in test objects rather than the real objects, which might be hard to set up in the test environment. If you come from a COM background, you will have learned the hard way that working with interfaces has many other merits.

Note

There will be more discussion about stubs and mocks later on in the chapter. For now, let's say that stubs are "stand-ins" that are little more than empty interfaces that provide canned values created for the sake of being able to develop and test the consumers of the stubs. Mocks are another kind of "stand-ins" for test purposes that can be set up with expectations of how they should be called, and afterward those expectations can be verified.

- **More sub-results exposed**

  In order to be able to move a tiny step at a time, you need to expose sub-results so that they are testable. (If I had continued the demo, you would have seen me expose more sub-results for the transportation and load time, for example.) As long as the sub-results are just read only, this is not such a big deal. It's common that you will need to expose sub-results in the user interface anyway. Just be careful that you don't expose too much of your algorithms. Balance this carefully against the ordinary target of information hiding.

- **More to the point**

  If I had started with detailed up-front design for the demo example, I'm pretty sure that I would have invented a truck class holding onto loads of properties for trucks. Because I just focused on what was needed to make the tests run, I skipped the truck class completely. All I needed that was closely truck-related was a truck capacity property, and I kept that property directly on the truck calculation class.

- **Less coupling**

  TDD yields less coupling. For instance, because UI is hard to test with automatic tests, the UI will more or less be forced not to intermingle with the Domain Model. The coupling is also greatly reduced thanks to the increased usage of interfaces.

As I have already stated, the design effects are not the only good things. There are loads of other effects, such as

- **Second version of API**

  When you use TDD, the API has already been used once when the time comes for your consumer to use it. Probably, the consumer will find that the API is better and more stable than it would have been otherwise.

- **Future maintenance**

  Maintenance goes like a dream when you have extensive test suites. When you need to make changes, the tests will tell you immediately if it breaks on consumers.

  If you don't have extensive test suites when you need to make changes, you *can* go ahead and create tests before making the changes. It's not much fun, and you probably won't be able to create high-quality tests long after the code was written, but it's often a better approach than just making the changes and crossing your fingers. You then have tests when it's time for the next change, and the next.

Despite using TDD, bugs will appear in production code. When it happens and you are about to fix the bug, the process is very similar to the ordinary TDD one. You start by writing a test that exposes the bug, and then write the code that makes the tests (the new and all the old tests) execute successfully. Finally, you refactor if necessary.

Test-Driven
Development
(TDD)

- **Documentation**

The tests you write are high-quality documentation. This is yet another good reason for writing them in the first place. Examples are really helpful in order to understand something, and the tests are examples both of what should work and what shouldn't.

Another way of thinking about the unit tests is that you reveal your assumptions, and that goes for the other developers, too. I mean, they reveal their assumptions about your class. If their tests fail, it might be because your class isn't behaving as is expected, and this is very valuable information to you.

- **A smarter compiler**

In the past I have tried hard to make the compiler help me by telling me when I do something wrong. Tests are the next level up from that. The tests are pretty good at finding out what the compiler misses. Another way of stating it is that the compiler is great at finding syntax problems, and the tests will find semantic problems.

It's even the case that you probably will value type safety a little less when you are using TDD because tests will catch type mistakes easily. That in its turn means that you can take advantage of a more dynamic style.

If you follow the ideas of TDD, you will also find that you don't need to spend nearly as much time with the debugger as you would otherwise have to.

Note

Even so, there might be situations where you need to inspect the values of variables, and so on. You can use `Console.WriteLine()` calls, and you can run the tests within the debugger. Personally I think it's a sign of too big leaps or too few tests when I get the urge to use those techniques.

- **Reusability chance in other tests**

  The tests you write during development will also come in handy for the integration tests. In my experience, many production time problems are caused because of differences in the production environment compared to what is expected. If you have an extensive set of tests, you can use them for checking the deployment of the finished application as well. You pay once, but reap the benefits many times over.

To summarize it all, test-friendly design (or testability) is a very important design goal nowadays. It's perhaps the main factor when you make design choices.

Problems

I have sounded like a salesman for a while. However, there are problems too. Let's have a look at the following:

- **UI**

  It is hard to use TDD for the UI. TDD fits easier and better with the Domain Model and the core logic, although this isn't necessarily a bad thing. It helps you be strict in splitting the UI from the Domain Model, which is a basic design best practice (so it should be done anyway, but TDD stimulates it). Ensure you write very thin UI and factor out logic from the forms.

- **Persistent data**

  Databases do cause a tricky problem with TDD because once you have written to the database in one test, the database is in another state when it's time for the next test, and this causes trouble with isolation. You could write your code to set up the database to a well-known state between each test, but that adds to the tester's burden and the tests will run much more slowly.

  You could also write tests so that they aren't affected by the changed state, which might reduce the power of the tests a bit. Yet another solution is to use stubs or mock objects to simulate the database apart from during the integration tests when a backup of the database is restored before the tests.

  Yet another way is to use transactions purely for the sake of testing. Of course, if your tests focus on the transactional semantics, this isn't a useful solution.

Note

We will discuss database bound testing more in Chapter 6, "Preparing for Infrastructure."

- **False sense of security**

   Just because you get a green bar doesn't mean that you have zero bugs—it just means that your tests haven't *detected* any bugs. Make sure that TDD doesn't lead you into a false sense of security. Remember that a green test doesn't prove the absence of bugs, only that that particular test executed without detecting a problem.

   On the other hand, just because your tests aren't perfect doesn't mean that you shouldn't use them. They will still help you quite a lot with improving the quality!

   As my friend Mats Helander once said, the value isn't in the green, but in the red!

- **Losing the overview**

   TDD can be seen as a bottom-up approach, and you must be aware that you might lose the overview from time to time. It's definitely a very good idea to visualize your code from time to time as UML, for example, so you get a bird's eye perspective. You will most certainly find several refactorings that should be applied to prepare your code for the future.

- **More code to maintain**

   The maintenance aspect is a double-edged sword. The tests are great for doing maintenance work, but you also have more code to maintain.

I just said that TDD is hard to apply for the UI and database, and that's just one more reason why the Domain Model pattern shines because you can typically run more meaningful tests without touching the database and the UI compared to when other logical structures have been used! That said, we will discuss both database testing and UI testing in later chapters.

Anyway, all in all I think TDD is a great tool for the toolbox!

The Next Phase?

That was an introduction to the basic concepts, but we have only scratched the surface a little bit. When you start applying TDD, it will probably work smoothly after you pass those first start-up problems.

Then after a while you will probably find that setting up some tests gets overly complex and too dependent on uninteresting parts—uninteresting for the test itself at least. That's a good sign that you have reached the next phase of TDD. My friend Claudio Perrone will talk more about that in the next section called mocks and stubs.

Mocks and Stubs

Mocks and Stubs

I said that we will talk about database testing later in the book. It's actually already time for the first incarnation of that. Here Claudio Perrone will discuss how you apply the technique of stubs and mocks in your testing. In the previous section, I talked about what is called state-based testing. Here Claudio will focus on interaction-based testing.

To not run in advance, Claudio will use a classic approach for his database-related examples before we really dive into using the Domain Model pattern in the next chapter.

Over to Claudio.

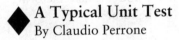 ### A Typical Unit Test
By Claudio Perrone

A common approach for testing the behavior of an object is to set it up with relevant context information, call one of its methods, and write a few assertions to check the return value or to verify that the method changed the *state* of the environment as expected.

The following example, which tests the SaveUser() method of the UserBC business component, illustrates this approach:

```
[Test, Rollback] //Automatic rollback
               //(using Services w/o components)
public void TestUserBCCanSaveUser ()
{
    // Setting up context information (preconditions)
    IUserInfo user = new UserInfo(
        "Claudio", "Perrone", "MyUniqueLogin", "MyPassword");
```

```
// I'm not testing yet, just clarifying initial state
Assert.IsTrue(user.IsNew);
Assert.AreEqual(NEW_OBJECT_ID, user.ID);
Assert.IsFalse(
    IsUserInsertedInDataBase(
    "Claudio", "Perrone", "MyUniqueLogin", "MyPassword"));

// Preconditions are ok - now exercising method to test
UserBC bcUser = new UserBC();
bcUser.SaveUser(user);

// Verifying post-conditions (state changed as expected)
Assert.IsFalse(user.IsNew);
Assert.IsTrue(user.ID != NEW_OBJECT_ID);
Assert.IsTrue(
    IsUserInsertedInDataBase(
    "Claudio", "Perrone", "MyUniqueLogin", "MyPassword"));
}
```

Note

The Rollback attribute is not provided with current NUnit yet (although it
is in their roadmap). I used a modified version written by Roy Osherove
to be found here: http://weblogs.asp.net/rosherove/archive/2004/07/12/
180189.aspx.

Because the UserBC business component takes a business entity and saves it to
the database, the test checks its behavior by creating the entity, passing it as a
parameter to the SaveUser() method, and verifying that the entity is persisted to
the data store.

Declaration of Independence

A potential problem with this testing style is that objects very rarely operate in
isolation. Other objects that our object under test depends on often carry out
part of the work.

To illustrate this issue with our example, we could implement the UserBC class
as follows (for convenience, all exception-handling code is omitted):

```
public class UserBC
{
    public void SaveUser(IUserInfo user)
    {
        user.Validate();
        UserDao daoUser = new UserDao();
```

```
        if (user.IsNew)
            daoUser.Insert(user);
        else
            daoUser.Update(user);
    }
}
```

Mocks and
Stubs

In this case, UserBC delegates the user validation to the UserInfo business entity. If one or more business rules are broken, UserInfo will throw a custom exception containing a collection of validation errors. UserBC also delegates the persistence of the business entity to the UserDao data access object that has responsibility for abstracting all database implementation details.

As IUserInfo is an explicit parameter of the SaveUser() method, we can argue that UserBC explicitly declares a dependency on the IUserInfo interface (implemented by the UserInfo class). However, the dependency on UserDao is somewhat hidden inside the implementation of the UserBC class.

To complicate matters further, dependencies are *transitive*. If UserBC depends on UserInfo and, for example, UserInfo needs a set of BusinessRule objects to validate its content, UserBC depends on BusinessRule. A bug in a BusinessRule object could suddenly break our test and several others at the same time.

Indeed, the complex logic handled by a Domain Model is often implemented through a chain of objects that forward part of the behavior to other collaborating objects until the required result is created. Consequently, unit tests that aim at verifying the behavior of an object with many dependencies might fail if one of the objects in the chain has bugs. As a result, it is sometimes difficult to identify the cause of an error, as the tests are essentially small-scale integration tests, rather than "pure" unit tests.

Working with Difficult Team Members

There is another problem related to collaborators that is very common in this world of distributed applications. How can we test an object's behavior when the method we try to exercise depends on components or conditions that are difficult to recreate? For example, we might have components that

- Have not yet been implemented

- Are difficult to set up or test (for example, user interface components or messaging channels)

- Are too slow (such as data access layer components, service agents, or distributed components)

- Contain behavior that is difficult to reproduce (such as intermittent network connectivity or concurrency issues)

Replacing Collaborators with Testing Stubs

A viable solution to the previous problems is to replace some or all of the collaborators with *testing stubs*. A testing stub is a simulation of a real object used for testing purposes. It provides a mechanism to set up expected values to supply to the code being tested.

Let's go back to our example. In this case, we have two close collaborators in the SaveUser() method—UserInfo and UserDao. UserInfo is easy to substitute, as our test simply needs to provide an object that implements the IUserInfo interface and does not throw exceptions when its Validate() method is called (unless, of course, we want to test the behavior of the SaveUser() method when a validation exception occurs).

**Mocks and
Stubs**

UserDao is much more difficult to replace because the construction of the object is embedded inside the UserBC class. We really want to substitute this collaborator, however, because its access to the database will slow down the execution of our tests. Additionally, checking values in the database is time consuming and possibly of value only when testing UserDao in isolation or within an integration test. One viable solution is to extract the interface from UserDao and add a constructor to the UserBC class that sets an explicit dependency on IUserDao.

The required code is very simple, with very low probability of introducing bugs. In some cases, you may even consider writing it in addition to the existing constructor(s) for testing purposes only.

```
public class UserBC
{
    private IUserDao _daoUser;

    // Default constructor
    public UserBC()
    {
        _daoUser = new UserDao();
    }

    // Constructor used by testing code
    public UserBC(IUserDao daoUser)
    {
        _daoUser = daoUser;
    }

    public void SaveUser(IUserInfo user)
    {
        user.Validate();

        if (user.IsNew)
            _daoUser.Insert(user);
        else
            _daoUser.Update(user);
    }
}
```

Now we can easily create a couple of stubs that implement IUserInfo and IUserDao. Their implementation is trivial, so let's examine UserDaoStub only.

```
public class UserDaoStub : IUserDao
{
    private IUserInfo _userResult = null;

    // Note: Test will need to set the expected value
    // to be returned when Insert is called
    public IUserInfo UserResult
    {
        get { return _userResult;}
        set { _userResult = value;}
    }

    public void Insert(IUserInfo user)
    {
        // Note: Before calling this method our test will need to
        // set up the UserResult property with the expected values
        user.ID = UserResult.ID;
        user.Name = UserResult.Name;
        // etc
    }
    . . .

}
```

There are a few important aspects to consider at this point.

First, our initial test was setting a couple of expectations about the state of the IUserInfo object as a result of calling the SaveUser() method. If we modify our test so that it uses a UserDaoStub object, we will also need to set up the expected result by setting the UserResult property before the Insert() method is executed.

A second aspect to consider is that the dependency on the database is now completely removed and our initial test is now much faster.

Because SaveUser() delegates most of its behavior, however, such a test provides virtually no value. Actually, on second thought, I would also add that we are committing the deadly (but unfortunately common) sin of putting assertions on values returned from our stubs. So we are effectively testing our stubs rather than UserBC!

On the other hand, it's a different story if we want to know how our UserBC class reacts when the data access layer throws an exception such as DalUnique-ConstraintException—a situation that could occur if the user login already exists on the database.

The Insert() method in the stub class now becomes

```
//UserDaoStub
public void Insert(IUserInfo user)
{
```

```
if (ThrowDalUniqueConstraintExceptionOnInsert)
    throw new DalUniqueConstraintException();

user.ID = UserResult.ID;
user.Name = UserResult.Name;
// etc
}
```

Assume we'd like the UserBC to catch the DalUniqueConstraintException and throw a proper business exception to maintain the abstraction of the layers. The following test illustrates this scenario:

Mocks and
Stubs

```
[Test] // Note no database is needed anymore!
[ExpectedException(
            typeof(BusinessException),
            "The provided login already exists.")]
public void TestUserBCSaveUserThrowsBusinessException()
{
    // Setting stubs to remove all dependencies
    IUserInfo user = new UserInfoStub (
        "Claudio", "Perrone", "Login", "MyPassword");

    UserDaoStub daoUser = new UserDaoStub();
    daoUser.ThrowDalUniqueConstraintExceptionOnInsert = true;

    // Executing test - it should throw a business exception
    UserBC bcUser = new UserBC(daoUser);
    bcUser.SaveUser(user);
}
```

As you might expect, the test is very fast, doesn't require access to the database or other collaborators, and allows us to quickly verify the functionality of the class under test in a condition that is potentially hard to recreate. Simulating other conditions becomes a very simple exercise.

This brings us to an important lesson about stubs. Using testing stubs allow us to isolate the code under test and to observe how it *reacts* to the external conditions simulated by the faked collaborators.

Replacing Collaborators with Mock Objects

A notable variation to stubs is the concept of *mock object*. A mock object is a simulation of a real object. It replaces a collaborator and provides expected values to the code under test. In addition, it supplies a mechanism to set up expectations about how it should be used and can provide some self-validation based on those expectations.

To illustrate what this means, let's create a test that focuses on the interaction of UserBC with the collaborating objects. This time we will use a popular .NET mock objects framework called NMock [NMock]. A nice feature of this open source framework is that it uses reflection to generate mocks dynamically from existing classes or interfaces at run time.

```
[Test]
public void TestUserBCSaveUserInteractsWell()
{
    // (1 - Setup) Create mocks dynamically based on interface
    DynamicMock mockUser =
        new NMock.DynamicMock(typeof(IUserInfo));
    DynamicMock mockUserDao =
        new DynamicMock(typeof(IUserDao));

    // Set up canned values (same as stubs)
    mockUser.SetupResult("FirstName", "Claudio",
        typeof(string));
    . . .
    mockUser.SetupResult("ID", NEW_OBJECT_ID, typeof(int));
    mockUser.SetupResult("IsNew", true, typeof(bool));

    // Generate mock instances (need to cast)
    IUserInfo user = (IUserInfo) mockUser.MockInstance;
    IUserDao daoUser = (IUserDao) mockUserDao.MockInstance;

    // (2 - Expectations) How we expect UserBC to deal with
    //                    mocks
    mockUser.Expect("Validate");
    mockUserDao.Expect("Insert", user);
    mockUserDao.ExpectNoCall("Update", typeof(IUserInfo));

    // (3 - Execute) Executing method under test
    UserBC bcUser = new UserBC(daoUser);
    // Unexpected calls on the mocks will fail here
    // (e.g. calling Validate twice)
    bcUser.SaveUser(user);

    // (4 - Verify) Checks that all expectations have been met
    mockUser.Verify();
    mockUserDao.Verify(); // Note: No need for assertions
}
```

Note

NMock either produces a class that implements an interface or generates a subclass of a real class. In both cases, we then use polymorphism to replace the real class with an instance of the generated class. Although really powerful, this approach presents some notable limitations. For example, it is not possible to create mocks of sealed classes, and mocked methods must be marked as virtual.

An interesting alternative to NMock is a commercial framework called POCMock [POCMock] from Pretty Objects. In this case, mocks are created by replacing collaborators statically.

As you can see, there is no need for assertions in our test because they are located inside the mock objects and are designed to ensure that the mocks are called as expected by the code under test. For example, calling Validate() twice would immediately throw an exception even before the call to Verify() is made.

This example leads us to the following observation: As mock objects verify whether they are used correctly, they allow us to obtain a finer understanding of how the object under test *interacts* with the collaborating objects.

Design Implications

When I first learned about mock objects, I thought that it was particularly tricky to come up with an easy mechanism to replace my collaborators. The fundamental problem was that my code was coupled with the concrete implementation of those collaborators rather than their interfaces. The "aha!" moment came when I discovered two key mechanisms called *Dependency Injection* and *Service Locator*.

The first principle, Dependency Injection, suggests that a class explicitly declares the interfaces of its collaborators (for example, in the constructor or as parameters in a method) but leaves the responsibility for the creation of their concrete implementation to the container. Because the class is not in control of the creation of its collaborators anymore, this principle is also known as *Inversion of Control*.

The second principle, Service Locator, means that a class internally locates its concrete collaborators through the dependency on another object (the locator). A simple example of a locator could be a factory object that uses a configuration file to load the required collaborators dynamically.

Note

There will be much more coverage about Dependency Injection, Inversion of Control, and Service Locator in Chapter 10, "Design Techniques to Embrace."

Consequences

Mock objects and stubs permit you to further isolate the code that needs to be tested. This is an advantage, but can also be a limitation, as tests can occasionally hide integration problems. While tests tend to be quicker, they are often coupled too closely with the system under test. Consequently, they tend to become obsolete as soon as a better implementation for the system under test is found.

Refactoring activities aimed at introducing mocks tend to decouple objects from a particular implementation of their dependencies. Although it is generally achievable to create mocks from classes containing virtual methods, it is usually recommended to use interfaces whenever possible. As a result, it is not rare to observe that systems designed to be tested using mock objects contain a significant number of interfaces introduced for testing purposes only.

Further Information

For a more in-depth discussion of the differences between mock objects and stubs (and state-based versus interaction-based testing), see Martin Fowler's "Mocks Aren't Stubs" [Fowler Mocks Aren't Stubs].

◆

Thanks Claudio! We are strengthened with yet another tool; can we resist getting yet one more? Next up is refactoring.

Refactoring

I mentioned refactoring previously as the third step in the general process of TDD, and I think I should briefly explain the term a bit more. Refactoring is about making small, well-known changes step-by-step in order to improve the design of existing code. That is, you make changes to improve the maintainability of the code without changing its observed behavior. Another way to say it is to change *how*, not *what*.

The term "refactoring" has become something of a buzzword; it's much overused and also misused. For instance, instead of saying that we are going to make loads of significant and ground-breaking changes to our code base, we say that we will refactor it. That's not, however, the central meaning of the term.

We talked quite a lot about what refactoring is and why you should use it in Chapter 1. In this section about refactoring, we'll take a look at how it's used.

We will start with some basic refactorings for routine cleaning. Then we'll talk briefly about how productivity could gain from new tooling support. Finally, we'll refactor to, toward, or from patterns for preventing the occurrence of maintainability issues.

Let's Clean Some Smelly Code

We did discuss some refactorings in the previous TDD example, but I think it's time to have a look at another refactoring example. Let's start with the following piece of code, a Person class:

```
public class Person
{
      public string Name = string.Empty;
      public DateTime BirthDate = DateTime.MinValue;
      public IList Children = new ArrayList();

      public int HowOld()
      {
            if (BirthDate != DateTime.MinValue &&
                  BirthDate < DateTime.Now)
            {
                  int years = DateTime.Now.Year -
                        BirthDate.Year;
                  if (DateTime.Now.DayOfYear <
                        BirthDate.DayOfYear)
                        years--;

                  return years;
            }
            else
                  return 0;
      }
}
```

Refactoring

Smelly Code

I have talked about smelly code many times already by now, and code smells will be the focus of our refactoring efforts for the coming pages. Therefore, I'd like to point out that Martin Fowler and Kent Beck presents a list of code smells in the *Refactoring* book [Fowler R].

A typical example, and also the first one, is the code smell called Duplicated Code.

Routine Cleanings

The class we just saw, Person, is a nice little class that probably solves the problem at hand. Deducing from the nature of the class, the requirement was to track names and birthdates of certain persons, who their children are and how old these people are. Again, let's assume that the requirements are fulfilled. That's a good thing, but we have started to add to our technical debt because the code is a bit messy, and that's where refactoring comes in. We'll clean up the code with a couple of examples which I have called "Routine Cleanings," each of which is based on Fowler's work [Fowler R].

Routine Cleaning Example One: Encapsulate Field The target of the first example is the Name-field. It's currently a public string and that might be too much for some to take. Let's transform it from this:

```
public string Name = string.Empty;
```

into something like this:

```
//Person

private string _name = string.Empty;
public string Name
{
     get {return _name;}
}

public Person(string name)
{
     _name = name;
}
```

I said that the requirements were fulfilled before, didn't I? Well, they were, kind of; it was possible to set the Name and read it. However, the requirements could be fulfilled even more successfully. The read-only aspect of the Name field wasn't addressed before, but it is now.

Are we done, or could we do better? Well, I think it could be even better to use a public readonly field instead, like this:

```
//Person
public readonly string Name;
public Person(string name)
{
     Name = name;
}
```

I think that was even clearer, but unfortunately, there are drawbacks as well. The one I'm thinking about is that it's not possible to set the Name via reflection, which is important for many tools, such as many *Object Relational* (O/R) Mappers. In this case, I need the option of setting the Name via reflection, so I decide to go for the get-based version instead.

That reminds me...does all my consumer code still run? After all, the observable behavior of the code has actually changed slightly because I require the Name to get its value via the constructor. I get compiler errors, so that's simple to sort out; but are we done?

Nope, we aren't done. Assume the following snippet:

```
//Some consumer
public void SetNameByReflection()
{
    Person p = new Person();

    FieldInfo f = typeof(Person).GetField("Name",
            BindingFlags.Instance | BindingFlags.Public);

    f.SetValue(p, "Jimmy");

    ...
```

That snippet sets the Name field via reflection (you might wonder why, but that's not important here). This won't work any longer, but the compiler won't detect the problem. Hopefully we have written automatic tests that will detect the problem.

So the lesson learned is that refactoring requires automatic tests! As a matter of fact, refactoring and TDD are symbiotic. As I said at the start of this chapter, the TDD mantra is Red-Green-Refactor, Red-Green-Refactor....

(Well, refactoring doesn't require TDD; it requires automatic tests. On the other hand, using TDD is a great way of getting those automatic tests to be written at all.)

Routine Cleaning Example Two: Encapsulate Collection   The second problem I'd like to address is the public list of children, which looked like this:

```
public IList Children = new ArrayList();
```

This solution means that the consumer can add to and delete from the list without the parent knowing about it. (To be fair, that's not a violation to any requirements here, but I still dislike it.) It's also possible to add strings and ints instead of Person-instances. It's even the case that the consumer can swap the whole list.

A typical solution is to create a type safe Children list class, with an Add() method that only accepts Person-instances. That addresses the problem of lack of type safety. It could also address the problem of letting the parent know about the adds and deletes, but it won't address the problem of swapping the whole list. That can be solved with Encapsulate Field refactoring for the list itself.

The problem with this solution is that you have to write some dummy code that you don't really want to have for getting that type safe list. It's certainly doable, but it's not the style I currently prefer. If we target a platform with generics (such as .NET 2.0), we can avoid the lack of type safety in a nicer way.

That said, with or without generics, I prefer the style of Encapsulate Collection refactoring. First, you use Encapsulate Field refactoring so that you get the following code:

Refactoring

```
//Person
private IList _children = new ArrayList();
public IList Children
{
        get {return _children;}
}
```

At least the consumer can't swap the whole list any longer, but the consumer can still add whatever he wants to the list and delete items as well. Therefore, the next step is to hand out a wrapped list to the consumer like this:

```
get {return ArrayList.ReadOnly(_children);}
```

Finally, we need to give the consumer a way of adding elements, so I add an AddChild() method to the Person class like this:

```
//Person
public void AddChild(Person child)
{
        _children.Add(child);
}
```

Then we have the type safety as well, and the parent knows about when new instances are added so it can intercept that action (if it's needed, which—to be fair—it actually isn't in this particular example).

Unfortunately, this has changed the visible behavior of the Person class, and that has to be weighed in as a factor as to whether you can go ahead or not. In this case, most of the needed consumer changes aren't found by the compiler. Luckily, we have some automatic tests in place, standing in sort of as a second compiler layer, detecting the problem. The test that looked like this helped out:

```
[Test]
public void CanCalculateNumberOfKids()
{
        Person p = new Person("Stig");
```

```
    p.Children.Add(new Person("Ulla"));
    p.Children.Add(new Person("Inga"));
    Assert.AreEqual(2, p.Children.Count);
}
```

Refactoring

Note

To be very clear, as you saw here, the test didn't point out the real consumer code that needed to be changed. It was just some test code of the Person-class. Tests of the consumer are needed to point out necessary changes of the consumer code itself.

The `p.Children.Add()` lines are easily changed so that I get this instead:

```
[Test]
public void CanCalculateNumberOfKids()
{
    Person p = new Person("Stig");

    p.AddChild(new Person("Ulla"));
    p.AddChild(new Person("Inga"));
    Assert.AreEqual(2, p.Children.Count);
}
```

It's kind of unfortunate that the IList has an Add() method even though it has been wrapped as a read-only list, but tests easily catch the problem. To solve that, I can change Children to be an ICollection instead.

Is there any more to do? We need to do something about the HowOld() method. It's not overly clear, is it?

Routine Cleaning Example Three: Extract Method   Perhaps you have another, much better solution to the problem at hand? *Before* thinking about a better solution, I'd like to simplify the code, making it easier to read and understand. Refactoring is in itself actually a way of trying to understand the code. That's a nice side effect, and the better we understand it, the easier we can find simplifications and better solutions.

This is what we have:

```
//Person
public int HowOld()
{
    if (BirthDate != DateTime.MinValue &&
                BirthDate < DateTime.Now);
    {
```

```
            int years = DateTime.Now.Year - BirthDate.Year;

            if (DateTime.Now.DayOfYear < BirthDate.DayOfYear)
                years--;

            return years;
        }
    else
            return 0
}
```

Refactoring

First, there are two different situations that will return 0. That's not good. I prefer to throw an exception in the incorrect case.

Next, I'd like to take out that non-intuitive logical expression by using the Extract Method refactoring to get an explaining method name instead. So we go from

```
if (BirthDate != DateTime.MinValue &&
    BirthDate < DateTime.Now)
```

to

```
if (_CorrectBirthDate())
```

Almost no matter what the logical expression was, its intention in the context of the How0ld() method is now much clearer.

Another style now comes to mind, that of Guard clauses, which means that I should take away the unusual, almost never happens situation first. In this way, I am letting go of the else clause, and the code now reads like this:

```
if (! _CorrectBirthDate())
    throw new ArgumentException("Incorrect birthdate!");
```

Hmmm... Perhaps it's even better to change it to

```
if (_IncorrectBirthDate())
    throw new ArgumentException("Incorrect birthdate!");
```

I think this is slightly clearer and more fluent.

What's left is the calculation itself when we have the unusual situation taken care of. It looks like this:

```
int years = DateTime.Now.Year - BirthDate.Year;
if (DateTime.Now.DayOfYear < BirthDate.DayOfYear)
    years--;

return years;
```

Yet again I use the Extract Method refactoring, moving the calculation to another private method called _NumberOfYears(). The complete HowOld() method then looks like this:

```
//Person
public int HowOld()
{
    if (_IncorrectBirthDate())
        throw new ArgumentException("Incorrect birthdate!");

    return _NumberOfYears();
}
```

Sure, we could find more to do (for example in the newly created private method _NumberOfYears() or factoring out some logic from the class itself), but you get the message by now.

It's important to stress that we should re-execute the tests after each step to confirm that we didn't introduce any errors, according to the tests at least.

What we did, though, was time-consuming and error prone. If you use lots of discipline, it is possible to deal with the error proneness, but it's still time-consuming. Having the concepts in place, but finding out that they are time-consuming to apply is a *perfect* situation for using the support of a tool, if you ask me.

Cleaning Tool

There are several different refactoring tools around. If we focus on .NET, we have, for example, ReSharper [ReSharper] and Refactor! [Refactor!], which are add-ins to Visual Studio .NET. In the 2005 edition of Visual Studio .NET, there is also built-in refactoring support in the IDE.

Those refactoring tools make the changes similar to what we just made in order to help us become more productive. The value of this should certainly not be underestimated. As a matter of fact, when you get used to a refactoring tool, there's no way you will want to give it up!

The tools not only help you make the changes you want, they can also tell you about when and what changes need to be made. In this way, the tools free you to some small degree from some of the discipline of having to think about refactoring by providing a visual reminder.

Note

Do you remember that I said that a failing test is red and a test that executes successfully is green, but that a need for refactoring doesn't have a color? As a matter of fact, the refactoring tool ReSharper uses orange to tell you that refactoring is needed (according to ReSharper, that is). So before starting a new iteration, you should also see to it that you change the orange into green by cleaning up the code before moving on. Of course, this won't make it possible for you to stop thinking about what code is smelly yourself; it's just a help.

Refactoring

When you see a developer in the flow with a good refactoring tool in his hands, the speed at which he moves is just amazing, and without creating bad code. It's rather the opposite regarding the code quality!

So far we have mostly dealt with simple stuff. There's nothing wrong with that, of course, but from time to time you just aren't happy with the code even after cleaning up the small things. It might also be that you have a situation where there is a steady stream of new problems that needs to be cleaned up.

Prevent Growing Problems

Perhaps you think that using patterns is the natural solution to that problem. The problem with patterns is that they are traditionally used for up-front design, which often means too much guesswork (whereas refactoring, as we have discussed, is used later on during development). Should you choose patterns *or* refactoring?

Before discussing that any further, I think a short example of another pattern is in order. I'd like to discuss the Template Method pattern [GoF Design Patterns]. The idea is that you define the overall algorithm, or template method, in a base class like this:

```
public abstract class TotalBase
{
    public void TotalAlgorithm()
    {
        _DoSomeStuff();

        VariationPoint();

        _DoSomeMoreStuff();
    }

    protected abstract void VariationPoint();
}
```

Now the subclasses can inherit from TotalBase and provide a custom implementation of the VariationPoint() method. It could look like this:

```
public class TotalSub : TotalBase
{
    protected override void VariationPoint()
    {
        Console.WriteLine("Hello world!");
    }
}
```

The consumer code isn't aware of how the algorithm is created. It doesn't even know about the base class, only the subclass. The consumer code could look like this:

```
//Some consumer
TotalSub t = new TotalSub();
t.TotalAlgorithm();
```

Note that you decide in the base class if the hook should be optional or mandatory. In the previous example, I used a mandatory one because I used abstract for the VariationPoint() method. With virtual, it would have been optional instead, such as when you want to make it optional for subclasses to define a piece of the total template method.

Let's say we decide up front to use Template Method, which then gives us the problem of deciding where we should make variations possible or forced. That's a very tough decision.

Nevertheless, patterns are extremely useful, and we don't *have* to choose; we can use both patterns *and* refactoring. As a matter of fact, I think that's the way to go. Refactoring toward, to, or from patterns! This is what Kerievsky talks about in his book *Refactoring to Patterns* [Kerievsky R2P].

Let's see this in action with a fourth example, which will connect to the pattern we just talked about.

Prevent Growing Problems Example One: Form Template Method Let's assume that we have written a batch monitor in which we can hook in different programs. For a program to be a batch program, it has to adjust to some rules, and those are basically to tell the batch monitor (by some custom logging routines) when the program starts and finishes.

After a while, we will probably have written a couple of batch programs, and we will also have decided to reuse a base class for each batch program so that we don't have to write the log code over and over again. An example of the Execute() method in a subclass might look like this:

```
//A subclass to the batchprogram baseclass
public void Execute()
{
    base.LogStart();
```

```
    _DoThis();
    _DoThat();

    base.LogEnd();
}
```

What is smelly here? As you see, the subclass is responsible for calling up to the base class at certain points in the execution of the Execute() method. I think that's too loose a contract for the subclass; the developer of the subclass has to remember to add those calls and to do it at the right places. Another thing that smells here (which is more obvious in a more realistic example where there are many log spots, such as after introduction, after first phase, after second phase and so on) is that within the core method, there's a lot of infrastructure code, that is, the log calls. Because of that, the calls to the interesting methods, such as _DoThis() and _DoThat(), aren't as obvious as they should be.

As I see it, this code snippet is crying out for Template Method. So let's use the refactoring called Form Template Method [Kerievsky R2P].

The basic idea is to not have a public Execute() in the subclasses any longer, but to move that responsibility to the superclass. First let's move that Execute() method to the superclass. It could then look like this:

```
//The batchprogram baseclass
public void Execute()
{
    _LogStart();

    DoTheWork();

    _LogEnd();
}
```

The _LogStart() and _LogEnd() methods are now private instead of protected. The DoTheWork() method is defined in the following way in order to force the subclasses to implement it:

```
protected abstract void DoTheWork();
```

Finally, the DoTheWork() implementation in the subclass could look like this:

```
//A subclass to a batchprogram baseclass
protected override void DoTheWork()
{
    _DoThis();
    _DoThat();
}
```

This is pretty much the other way around. Instead of the subclass calling up to the superclass, now the superclass calls down to the subclass. *If* the variation points are good, then this is a very powerful solution, yet clean and simple! The subclass can totally forget about the infrastructure (such as logging) and focus on the interesting and specific stuff, which is to implement DoTheWork(). (Again, remember that this was a scaled-down version. In the real-world case that this was based on, there were several methods that the subclasses could implement, not just one.)

Another problem where it is hard to know whether to use the solution up front or not is the State pattern [GoF Design Patterns]. It's often a matter of over-design if you apply it from the beginning. Instead, it's often better to wait until you know that it's a good idea because you have the problem. But I talked quite a lot about the State pattern in Chapter 2, "A Head Start on Patterns," so I'm sure you have a good feeling for how to approach it.

So we have discussed refactoring *to* patterns a bit now. I mentioned refactoring *from* patterns as well, so let's take one such example.

Prevent Growing Problems Example Two: Inline Singleton More and more often the Singleton pattern [GoF Design Patterns] is considered a worst practice. The reason for that is you create global instances, which are often a problem in themselves. Another problem is that singletons often make the tests harder to write (remember, testability is crucial), and the interaction with the singletons isn't very clear in the code.

Let's assume you have a code snippet that goes like this:

```
public void DoSomething()
{
    DoThis();
    DoThat();
    MySingleton.Instance().Execute();
}
```

The refactoring called Inline Singleton [Kerievsky R2P] doesn't go "exactly" like this, but this is a variant.

Instead of letting the DoSomething() method call the global variable (the singleton itself), the DoSomething() method could ask for the instance as a parameter.

Another typical solution is for DoSomething() to expect to find the instance as a private member that has been injected at construction time or via a setter before the call to DoSomething() is made. Then DoSomething() goes like this:

```
public void DoSomething()
{
    DoThis();
    DoThat();
    _nowMyPrivateMember.Execute();
}
```

So the singleton is gone, and testability is much better!

> **Note**
>
> To be fair, singletons can be used without affecting testability in the previous code if the singleton is injected by the consumer. Then you can use a test object during testing, and the real singleton during runtime.

Problems? Well, the most apparent problem is that if you need the value way down in the call stack, the parameter is sent a long way before it's used. On the other hand, it's very clear where the value is used, and this might be a sign of smelly code in itself that might need some refactoring. So singletons might actually hide smelly code.

It's also the case that Dependency Injection (which will be discussed in Chapter 10) will gracefully reduce the problem of too many singletons.

Summary

As a summary, I'd like to stress the point of TDD + Refactoring == true. They are so very much in symbiosis.

In order to be able to use refactoring in a safe way, you *must* carry out extensive tests. If you don't, you will introduce bugs and/or you will prioritize not making any changes simply for the sake of maintainability, because the risk of introducing bugs is just too large. And when you stop making changes because of maintainability, your code has slowly started to degrade.

At the same time, in order to use TDD, you will have to carefully guard your code and keep it clean all the time by applying refactoring. Also, isolate your unit tests with the help of stubs and mocks. If you don't also guard the test code, *that* code has started to degrade.

TDD + Refactoring is a totally different way of writing code compared to what most of us learned in school. If you give it a *real* try, it will totally rock your world, and you won't go back.

With these tools on the belt, we are ready for an architecture discussion.

PART II

Applying DDD

In this part, it's time to apply DDD. We also prepare the Domain Model for the infrastructure, and focus on rules aspects.

This part is the most important—the core.

Chapter 4

A New Default Architecture

In the past, I've been pretty data-centric in my application architectures. Lately, this has gradually changed and my current default architecture is based on a Domain Model. This is why the title of this chapter is "A New Default Architecture."

New to whom, you might wonder. It depends. When you describe Domain Model to some, they will say "Yes? Isn't that how it's always done?" At the same time, another large group of developers will say "Hmmm... Will that work in reality?"

No matter in which of those two groups you belong, we are just about to start a journey together exploring the Domain Model, and especially how to build it in the spirit of *Domain-Driven Design* (DDD).

We will start the journey with a short discussion about Domain Models and DDD. To become more concrete, we will discuss a list of requirements of an example application and sketch possible solutions to different features. To get a better feeling of the requirements, we will also use another view and sketch an initial UI. The chapter will end with a discussion about execution styles for Domain Models.

Let's get started.

The Basis of the New Default Architecture

As I just said, my new default architecture is based on a Domain Model. We discussed Domain Models a lot in Chapter 1, "Values to Value," but let's discuss it here, also.

> **Note**
>
> Paul Gielens said that a warning is in place regarding the word "Default" in the name of this chapter. The risk is that some readers will get the feeling that this is *the* way to approach all systems. Let me stress that this is definitely not the case; this book is not aiming to be a template or something like that. Absolutely not! It's in the spirit of DDD to let the *business problem* govern what your solution looks like!

When one says "Domain Model" in the context of architecture, what is usually meant is usage of the Domain Model pattern [Fowler PoEAA]. It's like old school object-orientation, in that you try to map a simplified view (or more correctly stated, the chosen abstraction) of the reality from your problem domain as closely as possible with an object-oriented model. The final code will be very close to the chosen abstractions. That goes for both state and behavior, as well as for possible navigation paths and relationships between objects.

> **Note**
>
> Someone (unfortunately, I don't remember who) called the application of the Domain Model pattern in C# "programming C# as if it was SmallTalk." To some, that might not sound positive at first, but it was said and meant as a very positive thing.

The Domain Model is not the silver bullet, but it certainly comes with several positive properties, especially for large-scale and/or complex applications that are long lasting. And as Martin Fowler says [Fowler PoEAA], if you start using Domain Model for one project, you will probably find yourself wanting to use it even for small, simple applications later.

How to Recognize If an Application Will Be Long Lasting

Speaking of long-lasting applications, I especially remember one particular application I was asked to build. A global data communication service provider asked me to build a preliminary help desk application to be used at their new office in Sweden. Time was tight—they needed it the next day so that they weren't sitting there with paper and pen in their high-tech office when the press came to the opening day. Because it was going to be exchanged for a company policy standard application just a few weeks later, however, they told me that building it well wasn't important.

Yep, you guessed right. The quick-and-dirty application I built was still being used in production five years later. Sure, we improved it a lot, but I couldn't convince them to change from the platform I started using to something more suitable for a mission-critical application.

From Database Focus to Domain Model Focus

My move from database focus to Domain Model focus was mainly because I changed my emphasis from efficiency to maintenance. It's not that my new design style has to sacrifice efficiency, but I try to avoid those premature optimizations of every little detail that often cost more than they are worth. Instead, I try to create as clear a Domain Model as possible, which makes it easier to do optimizations when really needed. It's not that I'm forgetting about the database—it's just not my first focus. I try to find suitable compromises, so I do think it's important to deal with the database neatly.

The Basis
of the New
Default
Architecture

A Domain Model-focused design is more maintainable in the long run because of its increased clarity and an implementation that is more true to the abstractions of the domain. Another very important reason is that a powerful Domain Model is a good tool for decreasing duplication of logic. (Those are all properties of object-orientation as well. I see Domain Model as a style where object-orientation is used in a pure way, pushing the limits to write maintainable code. Oh, and to increase testability.)

When you hear the words "Domain Model pattern" [Fowler PoEAA], it might mean something very specific to you, but of course there are a lot of variations on how to apply that pattern. Let's call the variations different styles.

More Specifically, a DDD Focus

This leads me on to what I consider the main inspiration of my current favorite Domain Model style, that of DDD by Eric Evans [Evans DDD].

As you already know from the lengthy discussion in Chapter 1, DDD is several different things; for example, it is a set of patterns for helping out with structuring the Domain Model. We will get started in applying those tools really soon.

But before focusing on the details, I'd like to take a quick look at layering according to DDD.

Layering According to DDD

In my previous book [Nilsson NED], I talked a lot about a rigorous layering scheme, and I think I need to say at least a few words about how I think about layering today.

In one way, I still stress layering a lot. Because I'm very much into DDD, I try hard to move Infrastructure, such as persistence, into a layer of its own, away from the core Domain layer.

On the other hand, I'm more relaxed about layering and focus a lot of the efforts on a single one: the Domain layer. I won't split that layer, the Domain Model, into finer layers; I let it be pretty coarse-grained. (As a matter of fact, some of the DDD patterns come in handy for some of the problems I previously used layering for.)

The Basis
of the New
Default
Architecture

We have discussed two layers so far: Infrastructure and Domain. On top of these there might be an Application layer providing some coordination, but it's very thin, only delegating to the Domain layer. (See Service Layer pattern [Fowler PoEAA], which is like scenario classes, delegating all the work to the Domain Model.)

Finally, we have the UI layer on top.

I drew a simplified layering schema example in Figure 4-1.

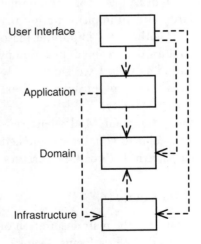

Figure 4-1   Typical layering for DDD projects

> **Note**
>
> Again, please don't automatically do anything regarding layering just because you read about it in a book! You should challenge every decision!

I think there are few things to note regarding how I use layering now compared to my old style. First of all, the Application layer isn't mandatory; it is only there if it really adds value. Since my Domain layer is so much richer than before, it's often not interesting with the Application layer.

Another difference is that instead of all calls going down, the Infrastructure layer might "know" about the Domain layer and might create instances there when reconstituting from persistence. The point is that the Domain Model should be oblivious of the infrastructure.

> **Note**
>
> It is also important to note we didn't take into account *partitioning*, or slicing the pieces in the other dimension compared to layering. This is important for large applications. We get back to this in Chapter 10, "Design Techniques to Embrace."

It's time to start our journey and to try out some of the concepts we have been discussing in this and earlier chapters, with a strong focus on the Domain layer. I think a good way of doing that is to set up an example.

A First Sketch

To make it a bit more concrete, let's use a list of problems/features to discuss how some common design problems of an ordering application could be solved.

I know, I know. The answer to how I would deal with the feature list with my current favorite style of a Domain Model depends on many factors. As I said before, talking about a "default architecture" is strange because the architecture must first and foremost depend on the problem at hand.

However, I still want to discuss a possible solution here. It will be very much a sketched summary, with details following in later chapters. What I will be discussing here will be kind of a first rough attempt, and I will leave it like that, letting the design evolve in later chapters.

Problems/Features for Domain Model Example

I will reuse this list of requirements in later chapters for discussing certain concepts. Let's dive in and examine the details for each problem/feature in random order.

1. List customers by applying a flexible and complex filter.

   The customer support staff needs to be able to search for customers in a very flexible manner. They need to use wildcards on numerous fields such as name, location, street address, reference person, and so on. They also need to be able to search for customers with orders of a certain kind, with orders of a certain size, with orders for certain products, and so on. What we're talking about here is a full-fledged search utility. The result is a list of customers, each with a customer number, customer name, and location.

2. List the orders when looking at a specific customer.

   The total value for each order should be visible in the list, as should the status of the order, type of order, order date, and name of reference person.

3. An order can have many different lines.

   An order can have many order lines, where each line describes a product and the number of that product that has been ordered.

4. Concurrency conflict detection is important.

   It's alright to use optimistic concurrency control. That is, it's accepted that when a user is notified after he or she has done some work and tries to save, there will be a conflict with a previous save. Only conflicts that lead to real inconsistencies should be considered conflicts. So the solution needs to decide on the versioning unit for customers and for orders. (This will slightly affect some of the other features.)

5. A customer may not owe us more than a certain amount of money.

   The limit is specific per customer. We define the limit when the customer is added initially, and we can change the limit later on. It's considered an inconsistency if we have unpaid orders of a total value of more than the limit, but we allow that inconsistency to happen in one situation, that is if a user decreases the limit. Then the user that decreases the limit is notified, but the save operation is allowed. However, an order cannot be added or changed so that the limit is exceeded.

6. An order may not have a total value of more than one million SEK (SEK is the Swedish currency, and I'm using it for this example).

   This limit (unlike the previous one) is a system-wide rule.

7. Each order and customer should have a unique and user-friendly number.

   Gaps in the series are acceptable.

8. Before a new customer is considered acceptable, his or her credit will be checked with a credit institute.

   That is, the limit discussed in step 5 that is defined for a customer will be checked to see if it's reasonable.

9. An order must have a customer; an order line must have an order.

   There must not be any orders with an undefined customer. The same goes for order lines: they must belong to an order.

10. Saving an order and its lines should be atomic.

   To be honest, I'm not actually sure that this feature is necessary. It might be alright if the order is created first and the order lines are added later, but I want the rule for this example so that we have a feature related to transactional protection.

11. Orders have an acceptance status that is changed by the user.

   This status can be changed by users between different values (such as to approved/disapproved). To other status values, the change is done implicitly by other methods in the Domain Model.

So we now have a nice, simple little feature list that we can use for discussing solutions from an overview perspective.

Note

You might get the feeling that the feature list is a bit too data focused. In some cases, what might seem data focused will in practice be solved with properties that have some behavior attached.

But the important thing to note here is that what we want is to apply the Domain Model. The main *problem* with that is how to deal with data if we use a relational database. Therefore, it's more important to focus a bit more on the data than normal when it comes to object-orientation.

With the problems/features in place, it's time to discuss a possible solution for how to deal with them.

Dealing with Features One by One

What does all this come down to? Let's find out by examining how I would typically solve the problems/features listed earlier in this chapter. I will focus solely on the Domain Model so that we concentrate on the "right" things for now and try to catch and form the Ubiquitous Language without getting distracted by the infrastructure or other layers.

Still, it can be good to have *some* idea about the technical environment as well. We keep down the technical complexity and decide that the context is a Rich GUI application executing at the client desktops together with the Domain Model and a physical database server with a relational database, all on one LAN.

A First
Sketch

> ### Note
>
> I'm going to mention loads of patterns everywhere, but please note that we will come back to those in later chapters and talk and show a lot about them. (See Appendix B.)

Without further ado...

1. List Customers by Applying a Flexible and Complex Filter

The first requirement is pretty much about data and a piece of search behavior. First, let's sketch what the Customer class and surroundings (without the Order for now) could look like (see Figure 4-2).

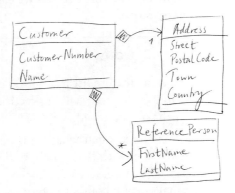

Figure 4-2   The Customer class and surroundings

> **Note**
>
> Believe it or not, there's a reason for using hand-drawn figures. I'm showing early sketches, just a quick idea of what I think I can start with. The code is the executable, crisp artifact. The code is the most important representation of the real model.

As you see, I used a simple (naïve) Customer class and let it be a composition of Address and ReferencePersons. I prefer to not put this kind of search behavior directly on the Customer class itself, so at this point I only have data on the classes shown in Figure 4-2.

A First
Sketch

> **Note**
>
> I could use the Party Archetype pattern [Arlow/Neustadt Archetype Patterns] instead or other types of role implementations, but let's use simple structures for now.

We could solve the first requirement by using a Query Object [Fowler PoEAA], which I talked about in Chapter 2, "A Head Start on Patterns," but in practice I have found that it's nice to encapsulate the use of Query Objects a bit if possible. There are often a lot of things to define regarding the result of queries that aren't just related to the criteria. I'm thinking about sort order, other hidden criteria, optimizations, where to send the Query Object for execution, and so on. I therefore prefer to use a Repository [Evans DDD] for encapsulating the query execution a bit. It also cuts down in code verbosity for the consumers and increases the explicitness in the programming API.

In Chapter 2, we discussed the Factory pattern [Evans DDD] and said it was about the start of the lifecycle of an instance. The Repository takes care of the rest of the lifecycle, after the creation until the "death" of the instance. For example, the Repository will bridge between the database and the Domain Model when you want to get an instance that has been persisted before. The Repository will then use the infrastructure to fulfill its task.

I could let the method on the Repository take a huge list of parameters, one for each possible filter field. That is a sure sign of smelly code, however: code that's not going to be very clear or easy to maintain. What's more, a parameter of string type called "Name" is hard to understand for the Repository regarding how the parameter should be used, at least if the string is empty. Does it mean that we are looking for customers with empty names or that we don't care about the names? Sure, we can invent a magic string that means that we are looking for customers with empty names. Or slightly better, we force the user to add an asterisk if he or she isn't interested in the name. Anyway, neither is a very good solution. On the other hand, going for a Query Object [Fowler PoEAA], especially a domain-specific one, or the Specification pattern [Evans DDD] is to start by going too far, too quickly, don't you think? Let's go for the simplest possible and only consider two of all possible criteria for now. See Figure 4-3 for an example of how this could be done.

A First Sketch

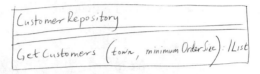

Figure 4-3   A `CustomerRepository` for dealing with flexible criteria

Note

Of course, we might use a Query Object, for example, inside the Repository.

DDD and TDD are a great combination. You get instant feedback, and trying out the model with test code is a great way of gaining insight. With that said, I'm not going the TDD route here and now. I will explain the model sketch with some tiny tests here, but only as a way of providing another view of the solution idea. In the next chapter, we will take a step back and more thoroughly and true to TDD try out and develop the model.

So to fetch all customers in a certain town (Ronneby), with at least one order with a value of > 1,000 SEK, the following test could be used:

```
[Test]
public void
    CanGetCustomersInSpecificTownWithOrdersOfCertainSize()
{
    int numberOfInstancesBefore = _repository.GetCustomers
        ("Ronneby", 1000).Count;

    _CreateACustomerAndAnOrder("Ronneby", 20000);

    Assert.AreEqual(numberOfInstancesBefore + 1
        , _repository.GetCustomers ("Ronneby", 1000).Count);
}
```

As you saw in the example, the Repository method GetCustomers() is used to fetch all the customers that fulfill the criteria of town and minimum order size.

2. List the Orders When Looking at a Specific Customer

I could go for a bidirectional relationship between Customer and Order. That is, each Customer has a list of Orders, and each Order has one Customer. But bidirectionality costs. It costs in complexity, tight coupling, and overhead. Therefore, I think it's good enough to be able to get to the Orders for a Customer via the OrderRepository. This leads to the model shown in Figure 4-4.

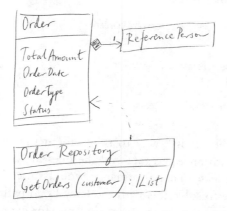

Figure 4-4 OrderRepository, Order, and surroundings

So when the consumer wants to look at the Orders for a certain Customer, he has to ask the OrderRepository like this:

```
[Test]
public void CanGetOrdersForCustomer()
{
    Customer newCustomer = _CreateACustomerAndAnOrder
        ("Ronneby", 20000);

    IList ordersForTheNewCustomer =
        _repository.GetOrders(newCustomer);

    Assert.AreEqual(1, ordersForTheNewCustomer.Count);
}
```

I could let the Customer have an OrderList property and implicitly talk to the Repository, but I think the explicitness is better here. I also avoid coupling between the Customer and the OrderRepository.

The total value of each order is worth a separate mention. It's probably trickier than first expected as the calculation needs all orderLines of the order. Sure, that's not tricky, but it does alarm me. I know this is premature, but I can't help it (because loading the orderLines will be expensive when you just want to show a pretty large list of orders for a certain customer, for example). I think one helpful strategy is that if the orderLines aren't loaded, a simple amount field, which probably is stored in the Orders table, is used for the TotalAmount property. If orderLines *are* loaded, a complete calculation is used instead for the TotalAmount property.

This isn't something we need to think about right now. And no matter what, for consumers, it's as simple as this:

```
[Test]
public void CanGetTotalAmountForOrder()
{
    Customer newCustomer = _CreateACustomerAndAnOrder
        ("Ronneby", 420);

    Order newOrder = (Order)_repository.GetOrders
        (newCustomer)[0];

    Assert.AreEqual(420, newOrder.TotalAmount);
}
```

A First Sketch

In my opinion, the "right" way to think about this is that lines are there because we work with an Aggregate and the lines are an intimate part of the order. That might mean that performance would suffer in certain situations. If so, we might have to solve this with the Lazy Load pattern [Fowler PoEAA] (used to load lists from the database just in time, for example) or a read-only, optimized view.

But, as I said, that's something we should deal with when we have found out that the simple and direct solution isn't good enough.

3. An Order Can Have Many Different Lines

Feature 3 is pretty straightforward. Figure 4-5 describes the enhanced model.

Note that I'm considering a unidirectional relationship here, too. I can probably live with sending both an Orderline and its Order if I know that I need both for a certain piece of logic. The risk of sending an order together with a line for another order is probably pretty small.

```
[Test]
public void CanIterateOverOrderLines()
{
    Customer newCustomer = _CreateACustomerAndAnOrder
        ("Ronneby", 420);

    Order newOrder = (Order)_repository.GetOrders
```

```
    (newCustomer)[0];

foreach (OrderLine orderLine in newOrder.OrderLines)
    return;

    Assert.Fail("I shouldn't get this far");
}
```

Also note the big difference in the model shown in Figure 4-5 compared to how a relational model describing the same thing would look. In the relational model, there would be a one-to-many relationship from Product to OrderLine and many-to-one, but so far we think that the one-to-many relationship isn't really interesting in this particular Domain Model.

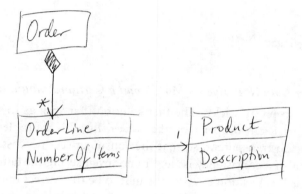

Figure 4-5   Order and OrderLines

4. Concurrency Conflict Detection Is Important

Hmmm...feature 4 is tricky. I think a reasonable solution here is that Customer is on its own, and Order together with OrderLines is a concurrency unit of its own. That fits in well with making it possible to use the Domain Model for the logic needed for features next. I use the pattern called Aggregate [Evans DDD] for this, which means that you decide what objects belongs to the certain clusters of objects that you typically work with as single units, loading together (by default, at least for write scenarios), evaluating rules for together, and so on.

It's important to note, though, that the Aggregate pattern isn't first and foremost a technical pattern, but rather should be used where it adds meaning to the model.

Concurrency unit is one thing Aggregate is used for. (See Figure 4-6.)

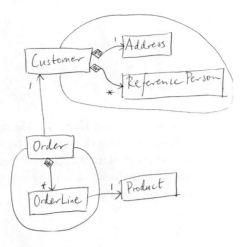

A First
Sketch

Figure 4-6   Aggregates

5. A Customer May Not Owe Us More Than a Certain Amount of Money

Feature 5 is also pretty tricky. The first solution that springs to mind is probably to add a TotalCredit property on the Customer. But this is problematic because
it's then a bit too transparent, so that the consumer sees no cost at calling the
property. It's also a consistency issue. I'm not even seeing the Customer Aggregate
as having the Orders, so I don't expect the unit to be the correct one for assuming
consistency handling directly in the Domain Model, which is a good sign that I
should look for another solution.

I think I need a Service [Evans DDD] in the Domain Model that can tell me
the current total credit for a customer. You'll find this described in Figure 4-7.

The reason for the overload to GetCurrentCredit() of TotalCreditService is that I
think it would be nice to be able to check how large the current credit is without
considering the current order that is being created/changed. At least that's the
idea. Let's see how the service could look in action (and skipping the interaction
here between the different pieces).

```
[Test]
public void CanGetTotalCreditForCustomerExcludingCurrentOrder()
{
    Customer newCustomer = _CreateACustomerAndAnOrder
        ("Ronneby", 22);

    Order secondOrder = _CreateOrder(newCustomer, 110);

    TotalCreditService service = new TotalCreditService();
```

```
Assert.AreEqual(22+110
    , service.GetCurrentCredit(newCustomer));
Assert.AreEqual(22,
    service.GetCurrentCredit(newCustomer, secondOrder));
}
```

I think you can get a feeling about the current idea of the cooperation between the Order, the Customer, and service from Figure 4-7 and the previous snippet.

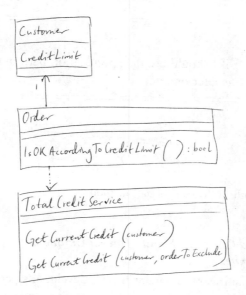

Figure 4-7   TotalCreditService

6. An Order May Not Have a Total Value of More Than One Million SEK

Because I established with the concurrency conflict detection feature that an Order including its OrderLines is a concurrency conflict detection unit of its own or—more conceptually—an Aggregate, I can deal with this feature in the Domain Model. An Aggregate invariant is that the Order value must be one million SEK or less. No other user can interfere, creating a problem regarding this rule for a certain order, because then I or the other user will get a concurrency conflict instead. So I create an IsOKAccordingToSize() method on the Order that can be called by the consumer at will. See Figure 4-8 for more information.

A simple test for showing the API could look like this:

```
[Test]
public void CanCheckThatAnOrdersTotalSizeIsOK()
{
```

```
Customer newCustomer = _CreateACustomerAndAnOrder
    ("Ronneby", 2000000);

Order newOrder = (Order)_repository.GetOrders
    (newCustomer)[0];

Assert.IsFalse(newOrder.IsOKAccordingToSize());
}
```

**A First
Sketch**

Note

I need to consider if I should use the Specification pattern [Evans DDD]
for this kind of rule later on.

Figure 4-8   Order with IsOKAccordingToSize() method

7. Each Order and Customer Should Have a Unique and User-friendly Number

As much as I dislike this requirement from a developer's perspective, as important and common it is from the user's perspective. In the first iteration, this
could be handled well enough by the database. In the case of SQL Server, for
example, I'll use IDENTITYs. The Domain Model doesn't have to do anything
except refresh the Entity after it has been inserted into the table in the database.
Before then, the Domain Model should probably show 0 for the OrderNumber and
CustomerNumber (see Figure 4-9).

Figure 4-9   Enhanced Order and Customer

Hmmm…I already regret this sketch a bit. This means that I allocate an OrderNumber as soon as the Order is persisted the first time. I'm not so sure that's a good idea.

I'm actually intermingling two separate concepts, namely the Identity Field pattern [Fowler PoEAA] for coupling an instance to a database row (by using the primary key from the database row as a value in the object) and the ID that has business meaning. Sometimes they are the same, but quite often they should be two different identifiers.

It also feels strange that as soon as a customer is *persisted* it gets a user-friendly number kind of as a marker that it is OK. Shouldn't it rather be when a customer is operational in the system (after credit checks and perhaps manual approval)? I'm *sure* we'll find a reason to come back to this again in later chapters.

8. Before a New Customer Is Considered OK, His or Her Credit Will Be Checked with a Credit Institute

So we need another Service [Evans DDD] in the Domain Model that encapsulates how we communicate with the credit institute. See Figure 4-10 for how it could look.

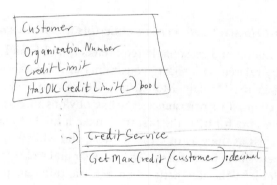

Figure 4-10 CreditService

Again, the idea is a matter of cooperation between an Entity (Customer in this case) and a Service for letting the Entity answer a question. Let's see how the cooperation could be dealt with in a test. (Also note that the real service will probably use the OrganizationNumber of the Customer, which is not the same as the CustomerNumber, but the official identification provided by the authorities for registered companies.)

```
[Test]
public void CantSetTooHighCreditLimitForCustomer()
{
```

```
Customer newCustomer = _CreateACustomer("Ronneby");

//Inject a stubbed version of CreditService
//that won't allow a credit of more than 300.
newCustomer.CreditService = new StubCreditService(300);

newCustomer.CreditLimit = 1000;

Assert.IsFalse(newCustomer.HasOKCreditLimit);
}
```

A First
Sketch

Note

Gregory Young pointed this out as a code smell. The problem is most likely to be that the operation isn't atomic. The value is first set (and therefore the old value is overwritten) and then checked (if remembered). Perhaps something like `Customer.RequestCreditLimit(1000)` would be a better solution. We get back to similar discussions in Chapter 7, "Let the Rules Rule."

9. An Order Must Have a Customer; an Orderline Must Have an Order

Feature 9 is a common and reasonable requirement, and I think it's simply and best dealt with by referential integrity constraints in the database. We can, and should, test this in the Domain Model, too. There's no point in sending the Domain Model changes to persistence if it has obvious incorrectness like this. But instead of checking for it, as the first try I make it kind of mandatory thanks to an `OrderFactory` class as the way of creating `Order`s, and while I'm at it I deal with `OrderLine`s the same way so an `OrderLine` must have `Order` and `Product` (see Figure 4-11).

Let's take a look at the interaction between the different parts in a test as usual.

```
[Test]
public void CanCreateOrderWithOrderLine()
{
    Customer newCustomer = _CreateACustomer("Karlskrona");

    Order newOrder = OrderFactory.CreateOrder(newCustomer);

    //The OrderFactory will use AddOrderLine() of the order.
    OrderFactory.CreateOrderLine(newOrder, new Product());

    Assert.AreEqual(1, newOrder.OrderLines);
}
```

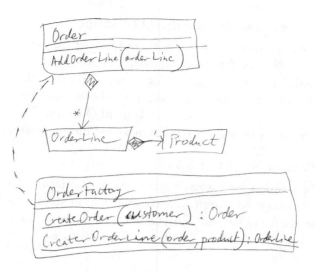

Figure 4-11 OrderFactory and enhanced Order

Hmmm... This feels quite a bit like overdesign and not exactly fluent and smooth, either. Let's see what we think about it when we really get going in the next chapter.

While we are discussing the OrderFactory, I want to mention that I like the idea of using Null Objects [Woolf Null Object] for OrderType, Status, and ReferencePerson. (That goes both for the Domain Model and actually also for the underlying relational database.) The Null Object pattern means that instead of using null, you use an empty instance (where empty means default values for the members, such as string.Empty for the strings). That way you can always be sure to be able to "follow the dots" like this:

```
this.NoNulls.At.All.Here.Description
```

When it comes to the database, you can cut down on outer joins and use inner joins more often because foreign keys will at least point to the null symbols and the foreign key columns will be non-nullable. To summarize, null objects increase the simplicity a lot and in unexpected ways as well.

As you saw in Figure 4-11, I had also added a method to the Order class, AddOrderLine(), for adding OrderLines to the Order. That's part of an implementation of the Encapsulate Collection Refactoring [Fowler R], which basically means that the parent will protect all changes to the collection.

On the other hand, the database is the last outpost, and I think this rule fits well there, too.

A First
Sketch

10. Saving an Order and Its Lines Should Be Atomic

Again, I see Order and its OrderLines as an Aggregate, and the solution I plan to use for this feature will be oriented around that.

I will probably use an implementation of the Unit of Work pattern [Fowler PoEAA] for keeping track of the instances that have been changed, which are new, and which are deleted. Then the Unit of Work will coordinate those changes and use one physical database transaction during persistence.

11. Orders Have an Acceptance Status

As we specified, orders have an acceptance status (see Figure 4-12). Therefore, I just add a method called Accept(). I leave the decision about whether or not to internally use the State pattern [GoF Design Patterns] for later. It is better to make implementation decisions like this during refactoring.

Figure 4-12   Order and Status

When we discuss other states for Order, we add more methods. For now, nothing else has been explicitly required so we stay with just Accept().

The current idea could look like this:

```
[Test]
public void CanAcceptOrder()
{
    Customer newCustomer = _CreateACustomer("Karlskrona");
    Order newOrder = OrderFactory.CreateOrder(newCustomer);

    Assert.IsFalse(newOrder.Status == OrderStatus.Accepted);

    newOrder.Accept();

    Assert.IsTrue(newOrder.Status == OrderStatus.Accepted);
}
```

The Domain Model to This Point

So if we summarize the Domain Model just discussed, it could look like Figure 4-13.

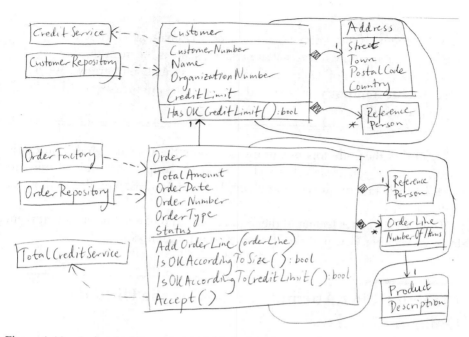

Figure 4-13   A sketched Domain Model for how I now think I will approach the feature list

A First
Sketch

Note

The class ReferencePerson is in two different Aggregates in Figure 4-13, but the instances aren't. That's an example of how the static class diagram lacks in expressiveness, but also an example that is simply explained with a short comment.

What's that? Messy? OK, I agree, it is. We'll partition the model better when we dive into the details further.

Note

The model shown in Figure 4-13 and all the model fragments were created up-front, and they are bound to be improved a lot when I move on to developing the application.

> Another note is that I only showed the core Domain Model and not things that are more infrastructure related, such as the mentioned Unit of Work [Fowler PoEAA]. Of course, that was totally on purpose. We'll get back to infrastructure later in the book. Now I'm focusing on the Domain Model.

I said that there are lots of variations of how the Domain Model pattern is used. To show you some other styles, I asked a couple of friends of mine to describe their favorite ways of applying Domain Models. You'll find those in Appendix A.

To give us a better feeling of the requirements, I'd like to take a look at them from yet another view and sketch a few forms for an upcoming UI.

Making
a First
Attempt at
Hooking
the UI to
the Domain
Model

Making a First Attempt at Hooking the UI to the Domain Model

I once started describing a new architecture from the bottom up. I mean, I started describing it from the database. One of the readers told me in no uncertain terms that I should start talking about what the architecture looked like from the UI programmer's point of view. If it wasn't good in that perspective, there was no point reading on. I decided that that way of thinking had its merits, so it's now time to have a first look at the Domain Model we just sketched from a UI programmer's viewpoint.

A Basic Goal

I want you to consider whether you think we are fulfilling one of my basic goals, which is providing "simplicity to the left" (or "simplicity to the top," depending upon how you visualize the layers in a layered architecture). What I mean is providing a simple API for the UI programmer so he or she can easily see, breathe, and understand the model, and can focus on UI matters and not have to think about complex protocols for the Domain Model.

Skipping data binding is not a basic goal, not at all, but I will skip data binding here in the first discussion about the UI. Data binding won't be the focus at all in this book, but we'll touch some more on that in later chapters.

The Current Focus of the Simple UI

I think the Domain Model might be somewhat abstract at the moment, but discussing it from a UI point of view might change this a bit. The scenarios I think we should try out are the following:

- List orders for a customer

- Add an order

Again, I won't use ordinary databinding right here, but just simple, direct code for hooking the UI to the Domain Model.

List Orders for a Customer

Making
a First
Attempt at
Hooking
the UI to
the Domain
Model

I need to be able to list orders for a customer. When the Domain Model is built later on, I just need to add a "view" on top of the Domain Model and fake some Orders. I'm thinking about a form that looks something like the one in Figure 4-14.

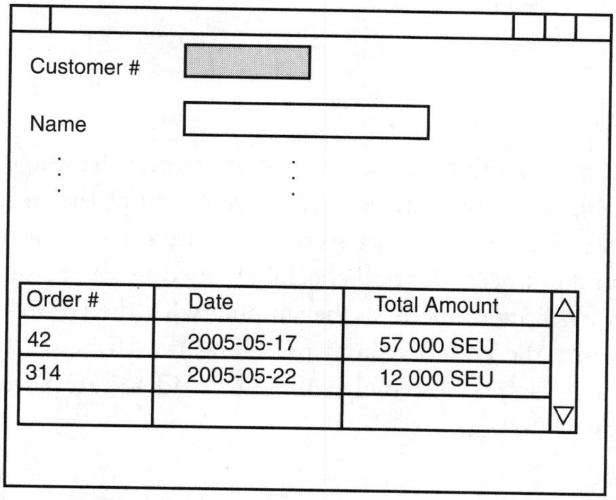

Figure 4-14 List orders for a customer

Note

You might think that I'm fighting the tool (VS.NET or similar form editors), but because I'm in extremely early sketch mode, I decided to visualize the form ideas with pen and paper. (But for this book, I'll provide images that were rendered in a graphics program.)

This is plain and simple. To make this possible to test and show, we need to write a function that could be called from Main() for faking a customer and some orders.

The user will probably choose a customer from a customer list form, and we provide the customer instance to the constructor of the form to show details of a single customer (let's call the form CustomerForm). The form stores the customer instance in a private field called (_customer).

Then the code in _PaintCustomer() method of the form could look like this:

Making
a First
Attempt at
Hooking
the UI to
the Domain
Model

```
//CustomerForm
private void _PaintCustomer()
{
    //Get the data:
    IList theOrders = _orderRepository.GetOrders(_customer);

    //Paint the customer:
    txtCustomerNumber.Text =
        _customer.CustomerNumber.ToString();
    txtName.Text = _customer.Name;

    //Paint the orders:
    foreach (Order o in theOrders)
    {
        //TODO...
    }
}
```

Something that is worth pointing out is that I expect the usage of Null Object [Woolf Null Object] in the previous code when I paint the orders. Because of that, all orders will have a ReferencePerson (an empty one), even if it hasn't been decided yet, so I don't need any null checks. In my opinion, this is an example of a detail that shows how to increase the simplicity for the UI programmer.

Having to write the code by hand for filling the UI was a bit tedious. But looking back at it, isn't it extremely simple to read so far? Sure, we are trying out simple things, but still.

Add an Order

The other form example is one for making it possible to add an order. I'm envisioning that you have first selected the customer and then you get a form like the one shown in Figure 4-15.

To make this happen, first an Order is instantiated, and then the order is sent to the constructor of the form.

The code for _PaintOrder() could then look like this:

```
//OrderForm._PaintOrder()
txtOrderNumber.Text = _ShowOrderNumber(_order.OrderNumber);
```

```
txtOrderDate.Text = _order.OrderDate.ToString();
//And so on, the code here is extremely similar in
//principle to the one shown above for _PaintCustomer().
```

To avoid having a zero value for txtOrderNumber, I used a helper (_ShowOrderNumber()) that perhaps shows "New" instead of 0.

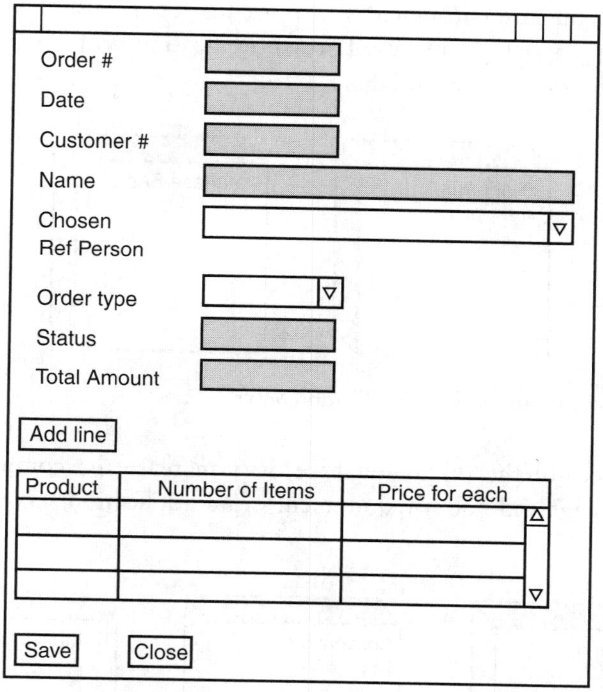

Figure 4-15   Form for adding an order

Making
a First
Attempt at
Hooking
the UI to
the Domain
Model

What Did We Just See?

One way of describing this type of UI is to use the pattern Fowler calls Separated Presentation [Fowler PoEAA2]. The idea is to separate the logic from the code that manipulates the presentation. It's a basic principle that has been recommended for a long time; however, it's *very* often abused. We get it at least to a degree more or less automatically and for free because we use DDD.

Again, this section was mostly to give us a better feeling about the requirements by thinking about them from another perspective, the UI. From now on, we won't discuss much about UI-related things until we get to Chapter 11, "Focus on the UI."

Now let's move on to yet another view regarding the requirements.

Yet Another Dimension

So far in this chapter, I have mostly talked about the logical structure of the Domain Model, which is just one dimension of the picture, of course. There are others. I'd also like to discuss different execution styles for a while. Let's start with the deployment environment set up for the feature list. There, I said that we are creating a rich client (WinForms) application without an Application Server. It could look similar to Figure 4-16.

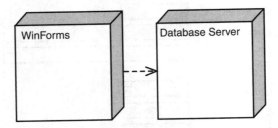

Figure 4-16   WinForms and no Application Server

For the sake of the discussion here, let's increase the complexity quite a bit for a moment and add a requirement of an application server as shown in Figure 4-17.

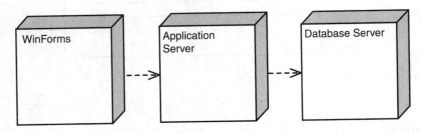

Figure 4-17   WinForms and Application Server

The first question is on what tier(s) should the Domain Model execute? Should it only execute on the Application Server and then you give out dumb data structures, Data Transfer Objects (DTO) [Fowler PoEAA] to the Consumer tier? Or should the Domain Model only execute on the consumer side, and you fill it by asking for DTOs from the Application server? Or perhaps you want the Domain Model to execute on both tiers? Perhaps two different Domain Models?

> **Note**
>
> It's important to think about the purpose of the application server, that it's really needed and that you really need to distribute the Domain Model. Remember Fowler's First Law of Distributed Object Design: Don't distribute your objects! [Fowler PoEAA]

Let's assume for a second that the Domain Model should (at least) execute at the Application server. Should it then be a shared Domain Model instantiation, so that there is a single instance for representing a single customer to be used by all users? Or should it be one Domain Model instantiation per user or per session so that there are several instances representing a certain customer at a certain point in time?

The third question is, should the Domain Model instantiation be stateful between calls, or should it go away after each call?

Fourth, should we try to build up a complete Domain Model instantiation by fetching as much data as possible at each request, and never let go of instances?

We have lots of questions and, as always, the answers depend on the situation. One problem with the discussion is that I haven't (in a DDD-ish manner) decided too much about the infrastructure.

Anyway, I'd like to say a few words about how I usually prefer to deal with this.

> **Note**
>
> What I mean with the term "Domain Model instantiation" is a set of instances of the Domain Model instead of its classes. Of course, we are sharing the classes between users much more often than the instances. Yet I think this term adds clarity to the discussion.

Location of the Domain Model

First, if I'm in control of both the consumer and the Application Server, I think it *might* be fine to expose and use the Domain Model both at the consumer and the Application Server. If we don't use it at both places, there is a risk of unnecessary work and less power because then we might create two similar, but slightly different, Domain Models, one being for the consumer and one for the

Application Server. We also need adapters that can transform between the two Domain Models. (The most important thing here is probably to be very aware of which situation you have—one model or two. If you think it's one but it's actually two in reality, you will run into subtle problems.)

It's important to mention, for complex scenarios I'm fond of Presentation Model [Fowler PoEAA2] as the UI-optimized view or version of the Domain Model.

Isolating or Sharing Instances

Yet Another Dimension

At the application server, should we have shared Domain Model instantiaton, per user or per session? Well, I like the idea of a shared Domain Model instantiation in theory, but in practice I prefer to stay away from it most often. It gets much more complex than what you would first expect, so I go for a Domain Model instantiation per user instead or actually usually per session. It's much simpler.

One of the main problems with a shared set of instantiated domain objects occurs if it has to execute in a distributed fashion, perhaps on two application servers in a "shared nothing" cluster. We then have the problem of distributed caching, and that's a tricky problem (to make an understatement), at least if you need real-time consistency. It is so tricky that I have given up on it for now as far as finding a general solution that can scale up well. However, for specific situations, we can find good enough solutions. Of course, if we have all Domain Model instances in memory, there are probably fewer situations where we need to scale out, at least for efficiency reasons. Still, *if* we do have the problem, it's a tough one to solve in a good way.

Note

The term "shared nothing" cluster needs a short explanation. What I'm aiming at is that the application servers aren't sharing either CPU, disk, or memory. They are totally independent of each other, which is beneficial for scalability.

To read much more about this I recommend Pfister's *In Search of Clusters* [Pfister Wolfpack].

Stateful or Stateless Domain Model Instantiation

At the application server I don't let the Domain Model instantiation be stateful, and I toss it out between requests. On the consumer side, on the other hand, I try to keep the Domain Model instantiation around between requests, but often not after the use case is done.

Complete or Subset Instantiation of the Domain Model

Finally, I don't try to instantiate the complete Domain Model. At the consumer that would just be plain stupid in cases where the database is moderately large or bigger. Instead, I use the old way of thinking that says fetch what you need and nothing else. And when I'm done with it, I toss it out, making room for other data, and don't hold on to old data for too long. On the other hand, when it comes to static data, it's different. We should try to cache read-only data as much as possible.

Yet Another
Dimension

Note

There is an open source project called Prevayler [Prevayler] (and there are others that are similar) that supports Domain Model instantiations that are stateful, shared, and complete. So that means more or less that the Domain Model and the database are the same thing. For that to be possible, we need large amounts of RAM, but that's less of a problem today because memory prices are falling, and 64-bit machines are becoming commonplace.

The idea is that it writes to a sequential log file each time there is a change to the database. If the power goes, the Domain Model instantiation can come back by reading an image created at a certain point in time and reading through the log file. This is pretty simple and extremely efficient execution-wise because all data is in memory.

What we have then is basically an object database, but a simple one because there is no need for faulting or other such things. All instances are in memory all the time, and there is no need for O/R Mapping from/to a relational database, not even from/to an object database. There is just the Domain Model instantiation.

OK, from now on in this book I will leave the added complexity because of the application server and just assume that we work with the rich client including the Domain Model or a web application, which again talks directly to the Domain Model.

One reason for this decision is that I think the classic way of using application servers is in a way disappearing, or at least changing. What's the driving force regarding that? Perhaps SOA, but that's another story (which we talk a bit about again in Chapter 10).

Summary

I know, you wanted the chapter to go on forever, but sadly it's come to an end. We've covered a lot of ground, discussed a "new" default architecture based on Domain Models to quite an extent, and also sketched how it can be used for an example. Now it's time to dig deeper into the Domain Model and investigate it further and also make lots of changes to the initial sketch discussed in this chapter.

Chapter 5

Moving Further with Domain-Driven Design

Some of you might be really eager by now and might be saying something like "Come on, let's see the tools and tricks that will show us how to implement a Domain Model and its surroundings."

Sorry, but that's not how to proceed. On the contrary, I want to create the Domain Model without thinking about the tools and infrastructure. That means good old OO that I used to laugh about for real-world applications. As you know by now, I have since then changed my mind. It's pretty much a matter of design.

Refining the Domain Model Through Simple TDD Experimentation

So far the book has been pretty general and abstract with only sketches of models. It's time to change that now. From here on I will talk about how the problems could be solved in reality.

In this chapter, we will discuss how to develop and refine the Domain Model that was sketched in the previous chapter. We will move slowly by applying TDD when we let the model evolve. Please be prepared that the discussion will be a bit "moving around" and the progress a bit slow. (We will change this way of discussing the development by the next chapter.)

Let's get started with the theme for this chapter; refining the Domain Model.

Refining the Domain Model Through Simple TDD Experimentation

Do you remember the very early sketch we had when we left Chapter 4, "A New Default Architecture"? You'll find it again in Figure 5-1.

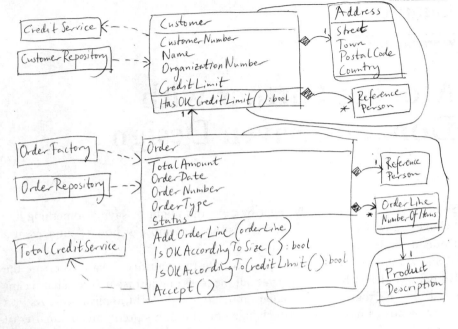

Figure 5-1   Early sketch from Chapter 4

I went a bit overboard, providing too many details in the sketch which I normally wouldn't have. Anyway, it's better now than never to really learn some of the details of the requirements. Let's start implementing this now in a TDD-ish manner and see what issues we need to address and resolve, and by doing so we'll evolve the model as we go.

I typically attack feature by feature, but considering that we talked about some UI sketches in the last chapter, I think I'll start by trying to make it possible to support those UI sketches and later on summarize what features we covered.

Starting with the Creation of *Order* and *OrderFactory*

We'll start out by creating the Order class and the OrderFactory. I'll skip thinking about everything at first except for what is shown in Figure 5-2.

Note

The first few steps are necessary to properly create the domain objects. We must complete these steps before we can get to the interesting and crucial part, namely testing and implementing the logic that our model facilitates.

Figure 5-2   First part to implement, parts of Order and OrderFactory

I'll get started on writing a first test for this. I'll test so as to make sure that I don't get null back when I ask the factory to create a new order. Here goes:

```
[Test]
public void CanCreateOrder()
{
    Order o = OrderFactory.CreateOrder(new Customer());

    Assert.IsNotNull(o);
}
```

> ### Note
>
> You might wonder why I name my tests the way I do? The early convention for naming xUnit tests was to prefix them with "Test," but that's not necessary with NUnit, for example, because it will understand the attribute Test instead. This means we are free to name the tests the way we want. This also means we get the tech-talk out of the way and can focus the discussion on domain concepts and design.
>
> I like naming the tests as statements of what the tests intend to verify. That way, the collection of test names becomes a list of what should be possible and what should not.

At first, the test looks extremely simple. To make the test compile, I need to create an empty Order class. That's fine for now. Next, I need to create an OrderFactory class with a single method, but our problems start cropping up already when writing that method. One of the rules defined in Chapter 4 was that an Order always has to have a certain Customer, and this is solved by giving that responsibility to the OrderFactory, giving the Order a Customer at creation time. Therefore, the CreateOrder() method of the OrderFactory needs to receive a Customer instance as a parameter (which you can see in the test code). No rocket science there, but we have just started working on the Order Aggregate and we would like to forget about everything else right now.

The first solution that springs to mind (which is also visible in the test I wrote previously) would be to also just create an empty Customer class. After all, I will need it really soon, and I'm not going to interact with it in this test, so there isn't a lot of coupling added between the building bricks—at least not yet. On the other hand, it feels like we are touching on too many things in this first little test. That's a typical smell, so let's try to avoid that if possible.

The second solution I thought about would be to mock the Customer and thereby create looser coupling between the Aggregates, at least in this test. I certainly do like the idea of mocks, but it feels a little bit like overkill here. After all, I'm not going to interact with the Customer at all; I just need the Customer more or less as a placeholder.

The third solution could be to create an interface called ICustomer (or something similar, or let Customer be an interface) and then create a stub implementation of the interface. Again, that feels like overkill right now, and what would the purpose be when moving forward? To be able to swap ICustomer implementations? Is that really something I expect? No, I don't, so until proven wrong, I decide that this isn't the solution I am going to start with.

Refining the
Domain Model
Through
Simple TDD
Experimentation

The fourth solution could be to skip the Customer parameter. I could do that temporarily in order to get going and then change the test when I add the Customer parameter later on. I could also decide that I probably don't want gluing the Order and the Customer together to be a responsibility of the factory. Could it have been a premature design decision that TDD revealed in a few seconds?

Not binding the Order and Customer together in the factory would actually add flexibility to the UI design so that I don't first have to start with choosing the customer. Instead, I could start by letting the user fill in other information about the new order and then ask the user who the customer is. On the other hand, flexibility somewhere usually means complexity somewhere else. For example, assume prices are customer dependent; what price should be used when I add OrderLines to the Order without a defined Customer? What should happen later? It's certainly not impossible to solve, but we shouldn't introduce complexity if we can avoid it.

Another drawback with the fourth solution is that the Order I get back from the factory isn't really in a valid state. The rule was that every Order should have a Customer. Sure, the order isn't persisted in the factory, but it's still not in a valid state. The consumer must do something to transform the order to a valid state after the factory has executed.

A fifth solution could be to use object as the type for the parameter to CreateOrder(), but that's not very purposeful, and it adds to the casting needs. The same goes if you invent some generic interface that all your Domain Model classes should implement, like IEntity, and then use that as a parameter. What we are discussing now is using a sledgehammer to crack a nut.

You probably think that I'm violating the principles of TDD here by thinking too much instead of trying it out with tests, code, and refactoring. On the other hand, during the time it takes you to write the name of the test, lots of ideas and thoughts (and decisions) will flee through your mind very fast and semi-consciously. (This, of course, depends on your experience with the problem at hand.)

Anyway, let's not think too much and instead decide on one solution to try out. I'll grab the first one. Adding an empty Customer class with a public default constructor is actually very quick and easy to do, so let's do that. Now the test compiles, and I get a red bar because I only wrote the signature and only returned null from the CreateOrder() method in OrderFactory.

It's time to implement CreateOrder(). The first try could look like this:

```
//OrderFactory
public static Order CreateOrder(Customer customer)
{
    return new Order();
}
```

For that to compile, I must have an accessible default constructor of the Order. It could be public, but instead I decide to let it be internal in order to hinder the consumer of the Order class instantiating it except via the OrderFactory. Sure, this isn't the perfect protection, but at least direct instantiation by mistake will only happen inside the Domain Model, and that's a step in the right direction in my opinion.

Refactoring time? Well, what value does the factory really add? Not anything yet. It just adds a bit of complexity. I really should have at least started without the factory, because it shouldn't be around if it doesn't add value. Now I still think there are quite a lot of things it will deal with, such as snapshotting the customer, adding null objects, creating different kinds of orders, and a few other things.

But the code so far just feels silly now with a factory, don't you think? It *might* add value later on, but now it's less simple than it could be. Let's change it directly to use the simplest possible construction for this: direct use of a constructor.

Refining the Domain Model Through Simple TDD Experimentation

Note

It feels strange to refactor *away* from a factory. But it's just a sign that I got carried away and started out with a too detailed design from the beginning.

Also worth pointing out is that I had a CreateOrderLine() method in the sketch in Chapter 4, but life is simpler without it.

```
[Test]
public void CanCreateOrder()
{
    Order o = new Order(new Customer());

    Assert.IsNotNull(o);
}
```

Any other tests to write? Sure, what we have been discussing all along is how to deal with the customer parameter. So in my opinion an interesting test would be to check that a newly created order has a customer. I currently don't have verification of that. Let's add a test for doing so.

```
[Test]
public void CanCreateOrderWithCustomer()
{
    Order o = new Order(new Customer());

    Assert.IsNotNull(o.Customer);
}
```

Refining the
Domain Model
Through
Simple TDD
Experimentation

This test tells me that I need to add a Customer field or property on the Order. (I think it will be needed not only for my test, but also for some of the requirements.)

In order to cut down the complexity, I decide on a read-only property like this in the Order class:

```
//Order
public readonly Customer Customer;
```

If there is no way to change the Customer of the Order, we can expect it to be ever-present (and never-changing), and that will simplify the other rules. If you don't need the flexibility...

Now everything compiles and life is good, and we do get a red bar. That's easily fixed by modifying the constructor so it uses the customer parameter. The constructor now looks like this, and we get a green bar:

```
//Order
public Order (Customer customer)
{
    Customer = customer;
}
```

Some Domain Logic

In Figure 5-2, I mentioned that I should also add OrderDate to the Order. What could the semantics around that one be? The order should probably get an initial

OrderDate when first created and then a final OrderDate when the order gets the status of Ordered (or something like that). Let's express that in a test:

```
[Test]
public void OrderDateIsCurrentAfterCreation()
{
    DateTime theTimeBefore = DateTime.Now.AddMilliseconds(-1);

    Order o = new Order(new Customer());

    Assert.IsTrue(o.OrderDate > theTimeBefore);
    Assert.IsTrue(o.OrderDate
        < DateTime.Now.AddMilliseconds(1));
}
```

The idea with the test is to set up an interval of spots in time and then check that the OrderDate is within this interval.

As usual, this won't compile. I need to add a public OrderDate property. This time, I'm using a private field + a public getter since I'm going to change the OrderDate value later on in the lifecycle. And this time, I let the constructor of the Order set the OrderDate field without adding another parameter to the constructor. For clarity, here's the piece:

```
//Order
private DateTime _orderDate;

public Order (Customer customer)
{
    Customer = customer;
    _orderDate = DateTime.Now;
}

public DateTime OrderDate
{
    get {return _orderDate;}
}
```

We get a green bar.

I started this section with a diagram describing a subset of the model in Figure 5-2. The model has evolved slightly, as shown in Figure 5-3 where I visualize the code.

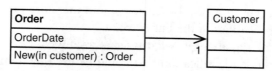

Figure 5-3   First part to implement, Order, revised

> ### Note
>
> You might wonder why I draw figures by hand sometimes and with a UML tool sometimes. The reason is that I wanted to illustrate that upfront, I just sketch quickly as a help with the thought and communication process. When I have implemented the thing, then I may visualize the implementation with a UML tool.

When you compare Figure 5-3 with Figure 5-2, the visible differences aren't that big. It's actually just that I had to implement a first version of the Customer class and the relationship from Order to Customer. That's not a real change to the model; only to the subset diagram.

> ### Note
>
> I also show the constructor in Figure 5-3 to give a more detailed view of how the classes work.

Refining the Domain Model Through Simple TDD Experimentation

It's time for refactoring before moving on to the next step. First, I wanted the call to the constructor of the Order to be moved out to the [SetUp], but then I would have to change the last test slightly regarding the time interval, and that would make it a little less to the point. Moreover, the three tests shown so far are just about the creation, so I like having the calls in the test methods themselves. Let's leave refactoring for the time being and move on with refining the Domain Model.

Second Task: The *OrderRepository* + *OrderNumber*

In the previous section, we talked about what the OrderFactory could look like in order to serve our need to create new Order instances from scratch, but then decided to skip the factory for now. In my opinion, the next problem naturally is how the OrderRepository should work out.

In Chapter 4, I discussed GetOrders() of the OrderRepository. Right now, I think the most important, typical method is GetOrder(), and therefore I'd like to start with that one and the identifier of the Entity Order.

While we're talking about it, what is OrderNumber? Well, typically an order has some form of unique identification that could be used by humans for identifying one particular order. One common solution is to just assign a new number to each order from an ever-increasing sequence of numbers. In Figure 5-4, I show the Order class again after modification and the newly added method in the OrderRepository class.

I know, I was supposed to talk about the OrderRepository, but I think it is important to do something about the OrderNumber first. Do we have to give the Order its identity when it is created? I think it's correct to say that the OrderNumber is 0 until the order is saved (meaning that the status is Ordered) for the first time. Until it is, we don't want to waste an OrderNumber on something that just *might* become a real order.

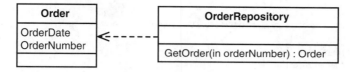

Figure 5-4   Order and OrderRepository

Refining the
Domain Model
Through
Simple TDD
Experimentation

Note

This depends very much on the requirements (whether it's good or bad), but I get a growing feeling that we are mixing two different things here—the business identification and the persistence identification. We'll come back to that in a later chapter.

I also strongly dislike the coupling between persistence and business rules. I mean that the moment the order is persisted, it's also "Ordered." We'll leave that for now and come back to it in Chapter 7, "Let the Rules Rule," when we focus on business rules.

So as usual we can then write a very simple test like this:

```
[Test]
public void OrderNumberIsZeroAfterCreation()
{
    Order o = new Order(new Customer());

    Assert.AreEqual(0, o.OrderNumber);
}
```

Guess what? This won't compile, so I add a new read-only property called OrderNumber to the Order class and let it use a private _orderNumber field.

This way we dealt with OrderNumber from the constructor perspective. If the OrderNumber property is read-only, however, how can we give it the value when using the OrderRepository for finding and reconstituting an old Order? To make the whole issue clear, let's take a step back and write a test and a [Setup] method (after having declared OrderRepository with the name _repository):

```
[SetUp]
public void SetUp()
{
    _repository = new OrderRepository();
}


[Test]
public void OrderNumberCantBeZeroAfterReconstitution()
{
    int theOrderNumber = 42;
    _FakeAnOrder(theOrderNumber);

    Order o =
    _repository.GetOrder(theOrderNumber));

    Assert.AreEqual(theOrderNumber, o.OrderNumber);
}
```

Refining the Domain Model Through Simple TDD Experimentation

As usual, the whole thing won't compile. I don't have an OrderRepository class, so I write one with just a signature for the GetOrder() method and no code. The test code still won't compile, so I have to stub the _FakeAnOrder() in the test class. I get a red bar.

I'm just getting further and further away from the problem I thought I wanted to focus on. To be able to write the _FakeAnOrder() method, I need to make it possible for the Repository to know about an Order. I could go ahead and implement a new method in the OrderRepository that is only there for supporting other tests, but I think this is a good sign of my needing to write another test instead. I need to test saving Orders, or at least make the Repository aware of Orders.

Note

I have to admit that I have quite a lot of ideas about how the saving should really happen, but I'll move on slowly here and write simple code that I will refactor a lot now. Please don't get upset about this; it's not the final solution.

So, I add the Ignore attribute to the OrderNumberCantBeZeroAfterReconstitution() test so that it won't give me a red bar right now. Then I write another test that looks like this:

```
[Test]
public void CanAddOrder()
{
    _repository.AddOrder(new Order(new Customer()));
}
```

As usual, it won't compile. I need to add the AddOrder() method to the OrderRepository. And as usual, I just add the signature, but this is not enough to get a red bar. As a matter of fact, there is no test code at all in the CanAddOrder() method. The reason is that I'm not keen on the idea of letting the Repository publish any methods for the sole purpose of an external test class for checking the inner state of the Repository. Sure, I could use the GetOrder() method, but then it's the chicken or the egg scenario. The implementation of this method is far from even being started yet.

Instead, I take a step back and add a private IList to the Repository for holding on to the orders. I don't publish anything about the IList to the outside; it's very much an implementation detail, and I already think I will have to get rid of it really soon. Instead I use another assertion, not a xUnit one, but an assertion from the Diagnostics namespace for checking what I think should be checked. What the Assert() does is check that the statement is true. If not, the developer will be notified. The AddOrder() method could look like this:

Refining the Domain Model Through Simple TDD Experimentation

```
//OrderRepository
public void AddOrder(Order order)
{
    int theNumberOfOrdersBefore = _theOrders.Count;

    //TODO Add here...

    Trace.Assert(theNumberOfOrdersBefore
        == _theOrders.Count - 1);
}
```

Need for Another Assert Lib?

You should think twice before using the ordinary Diagnostics assertions. One problem with that is that it won't integrate well with NUnit. Another problem is that I can't customize it for how it should act in different situations like development, continuous integration, beta testing, and during production. I discussed this some more in my earlier book [Nilsson NED].

You might also wonder why I didn't make sure that the test could be expressed somehow in a NUnit test. I could expose the necessary state that the test needs, but I prefer not to if I don't have to. If I did, it would make it harder to refactor the Repository class, and—again—I'm sure I need to do that.

The technique I used earlier is to some extent inspired by *Design By Contract* by Bertrand Meyer [Meyer OOSC]. Even though it's not formalized at all, the assertion expresses what the AddOrder() ensures, that is its assurances for post-conditions.

What could be the pre-conditions that the AddOrder() requires? Perhaps that the order isn't known to the Repository before? No, I dislike seeing that as an error. That _theOrders isn't null? But the method would throw an exception if it is. It's also the case that the whole thing about _theOrders is a very temporary solution, as you will soon see. Let's leave this alone for now.

Refining the Domain Model Through Simple TDD Experimentation

So let's create MyTrace.Assert(), which will just throw an exception if it receives false as the parameter. That way, it at least integrates well with NUnit/Testdriven.net.

Compile, test, and red bar. Good. So let's swap the TODO-comment for the add call:

```
//OrderRepository
public void AddOrder(Order order)
{
    int theNumberOfOrdersBefore +1 = _theOrders.Count;

    _theOrders.Add(order);

    MyTrace.Assert(theNumberOfOrdersBefore
        == _theOrders.Count);
}
```

And we now have a green bar. We are writing some strange code here and there, but we are moving forward, and we are creating tests that aren't weird at all along the way, so let's continue.

Note

I could have also worked with a mock to verify that the System Under Test (SUT) worked as expected, but you can probably envision how from Chapter 3, "TDD and Refactoring," so let's move forward.

Now it's time to go back to the `OrderNumberCantBeZeroAfterReconstitution()`, and what I stumbled on the last time was the help method for the test that I called `_FakeAnOrder()`. It could look like this:

```
//A test class
public void _FakeAnOrder(int orderNumber)
{
    Order o = new Order(new Customer());

    _repository.AddOrder(o);
}
```

Ouch, we are now experiencing another problem. Do you see it? Yep, how can we get the faked `OrderNumber` into the order instance? The `OrderNumber` property was read-only (which makes sense), so using that one won't work.

As a matter of fact, this is a generic problem. It can be expressed like this: How can we from the outside (such as in a Repository) set values in instances that are being reconstituted from persistence?

Reconstituting an Entity from Persistence: How to Set Values from the Outside

I mentioned the generic problem of setting values in an instance that is being recreated by reading it back from the database. In the case of `OrderNumber` it's obviously a problem because the `OrderNumber` will never change by letting the consumer interact with the property directly, but it's more or less the same with other attributes. Let's for the moment assume that `OrderDate` is read/write. If the consumer sets a new `OrderDate`, there might need to be some checks kicking in. It's probably not interesting to execute these checks when the `OrderDate` is getting a value at the time an `order` is being read from the database and reconstituted as an instance.

There are several possible ways in which to deal with this problem. Let's see what we can come up with.

Use a Specific Constructor

We could have a specific constructor that could be used just for this reconstitution. It could look like this:

```
//Order
public Order(int orderNumber, DateTime orderDate,
    Customer customer)
```

It works, but it's not very clear to consumers of the Order that they aren't supposed to use that constructor. Well, I could let it be internal, of course, to lessen the problem quite a lot!

The intention of the constructor could become slightly clearer if you use a static named method as a factory like this:

```
//Order
public static Order ReconstituteFromPersistence(int orderNumber
    , DateTime orderDate, Customer customer)
```

This not only makes the purpose of the method slightly clearer, but also the fact that the consumer should not mess with this method. Still, it's possible for the consumer to use the method by mistake, but—again—that could be dealt with by using an internal method instead. It's also problematic when the class gets more real world-ish, when instead there are perhaps 50 properties that should be set at reconstitution. If this is the case, the parameter list became unwieldy a long time ago.

Use a Specific Method, Typically in a Specific Interface

Another option is to decide on a method that the Order class has to implement, and typically this method should just be reachable via a specific interface. Consequently, there is much less of a risk that the consumer will mess with the method by mistake. If the consumer wants to do evil things, he can, but that's more or less always a problem. If it's possible to set values in the instance from the outside, the consumer can do it too. That is actually not necessarily a bad thing. Instead you should take a reactive approach and decide that the possible usage didn't create a problem.

So what could this look like? One approach could be to have a method like this on the Order:

```
//Order
public void SetFieldWhenReconstitutingFromPersistence
    (int fieldKey, object value)
```

It's definitely a bit messy. Now we have to set up a map of field keys, which must be maintained from now on, both as the map and as regards the SetFieldWhenReconstitutingFromPersistence() code itself.

A similar solution (still without a nice maintainability story) would be to swap the fieldKey parameter for a fieldName parameter instead.

Use Reflection Against the Private Fields

I could use reflection, but there are pros and cons to this, as usual. The drawbacks are that reflection is slow (at least compared to ordinary access, but is it *too* slow?), we can't close down privileges for the user, and we must know about the internal structure such as field names from the outside. (The last thing could be dealt with in part by adding private properties that are only there to be used for the reflection or by setting up naming rules so that if the property is called Name, there should be a private field called _name. It might become slightly more robust, but the basic problem is still there.)

The most important advantage is that it's not intrusive. You can create your Domain Model just the way you want it, without having to add infrastructure-specific and obscure constructions.

Note

Well, there are small details, such as that Customer can't be readonly. We'll get back to this in depth in later chapters.

Refining the
Domain Model
Through
Simple TDD
Experimentation

A Totally Different Solution...

We could go for a completely different solution: for example, keeping the values outside the instance all the time in a "safe place" so that the instance is just like a Proxy [GoF Design Patterns]. It really is a totally different solution, along with its ups and downs. However, I really don't like making such a big, specific decision right now. It would also mess up the Domain Model classes with stuff that has nothing to do with the domain. Let's continue as simply as possible.

All this has quite a lot of infrastructure flavor, hasn't it? I'd like to postpone the decision regarding how to set values from the outside until later, when I start thinking about what infrastructure to use for supporting my Domain Model. On the other hand, I need to make some sort of decision now in order to move on with the tests. What's the simplest mechanism that could possibly work for now? Unfortunately, there is no really simple solution that I can come up with now. That's a good sign that I should probably go back and rethink the whole thing.

Note

It's pretty ironic that we ended up in this long discussion just because I started to work with the semantics around OrderNumber. But we are here now, so let's end the discussion.

For now, I decide to use reflection against the private fields. I write a helper method in the OrderRepository (which probably should be factored out later) that looks like this:

```
//OrderRepository
public static void SetFieldWhenReconstitutingFromPersistence
    (object instance, string fieldName, object newValue)
{
    Type t = instance.GetType();
    System.Reflection.FieldInfo f = t.GetField(fieldName
        , BindingFlags.Instance | BindingFlags.Public
        | BindingFlags.NonPublic);
    f.SetValue(instance, newValue);
}
```

At last, we can move on again. What a long discussion just because OrderNumber was read-only. Remember, however, that this was actually a generic discussion about how to let the Repositories set values when reconstituting instances from persistence without running into problems with read-only properties and code in setters.

Refining the
Domain Model
Through
Simple TDD
Experimentation

Do you remember the test called OrderNumberCantBeZeroAfterReconstitution()? It's repeated here:

```
[Test]
public void OrderNumberCantBeZeroAfterReconstitution()
{
    int theOrderNumber = 42;
    _FakeAnOrder(theOrderNumber);

    Order o =
    _repository.GetOrder(theOrderNumber);

    Assert.IsTrue(o.OrderNumber != 0);
}
```

I added the Ignore attribute before so that the test wouldn't be executed. Now I take away the Ignore attribute, and I get a red bar.

Time to change the _FakeAnOrder(). I make sure that the new order gets the OrderNumber of 42, like this:

```
//A test class
public void _FakeAnOrder(int orderNumber)
{
    Order o = new Order(new Customer());

    OrderRepository.SetFieldWhenReconstitutingFromPersistence
        (o, "_orderNumber", orderNumber);

    _repository.AddOrder(o);
}
```

Still a red bar, but it's due to something else this time. I'm afraid that I created a situation for myself when there were several reasons for red bars, which is not recommended. I took too big a leap in my TDD approach.

Anyway, the problem is that I haven't implemented OrderRepository.GetOrder(). It's just an empty method (returning null). For the moment, we have the orders in an IList so we can just iterate over the items in the list, checking them one by one. It could look like this:

```
//OrderRepository
public Order GetOrder(int orderNumber)
{
    foreach (Order o in _theOrders)
    {
        if (o.OrderNumber == orderNumber)
            return o;
    }
    return null;
}
```

I know, it's a naïve implementation, but that's just what I want right now. And guess what? Green bars.

So we are back on dry ground, but my whole being is screaming for refactoring the SetFieldWhenReconstitutingFromPersistence() method. The SetFieldWhenReconstitutingFromPersistence() method just doesn't belong in the OrderRepository. I create a RepositoryHelper class for now and move the SetFieldWhenReconstitutingFromPersistence() method there. Still a green bar after I changed the call to SetFieldWhenReconstitutingFromPersistence().

Let's have a look at how the Domain Model diagram looks now. You'll find the revised diagram in Figure 5-5.

Refining the
Domain Model
Through
Simple TDD
Experimentation

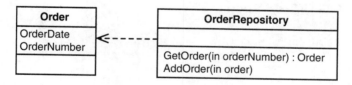

Figure 5-5   Order and OrderRepository, revised

I have the growing feeling that the whole thing isn't as good as I want it, but I can't put my finger on why. I'm sure it will appear more clearly when I move on, so that's what I'd like to do now. What's next on the list? Perhaps fetching the list of orders for a certain customer.

Fetching a List of Orders

So what we are talking about is another method in the OrderRepository called GetOrders(), which takes a customer as parameter for a start. When we have found some Orders, the second part of the problem is to show some values such as OrderNumber and OrderDate. In Figure 5-6, you find a diagram showing what I think we will be creating in this section.

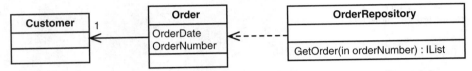

Figure 5-6   Order, Customer, and OrderRepository for listing orders

**Refining the
Domain Model
Through
Simple TDD
Experimentation**

> ### *Note*
>
> Did you notice how different the multiplicity in the UML diagram in Figure 5-6 is compared to how it would be expressed in a database diagram? If you come from a database background, I think differences such as no navigable relationship from Customer to Order might surprise you, and the multiplicity is one to one for the relationship that is there because it is from Order to Customer.

It's time for another test. Again, I need to fake Orders in the OrderRepository for the test to run. Here goes:

```
[Test]
public void CanFindOrdersViaCustomer()
{
    Customer c = new Customer();

    _FakeAnOrder(42, c, _repository);
    _FakeAnOrder(12, new Customer(), _repository);
    _FakeAnOrder(3, c, _repository);
    _FakeAnOrder(21, c, _repository);
    _FakeAnOrder(1, new Customer(), _repository);

    Assert.AreEqual(3, _repository.GetOrders(c).Count);
}
```

As you saw, I changed _FakeAnOrder() so it now also takes Customer and OrderRepository as parameters. That's a simple change, of course. Another pretty simple thing is needed for making the solution compile and that is adding the GetOrders() method. It could look like this (after you first took that mandatory tour of red, of course):

```
//OrderRepository
public IList GetOrders(Customer customer)
{
    IList theResult = new ArrayList();

    foreach (Order o in _theOrders)
    {
        if (o.Customer.Equals(customer))
            theResult.Add(o);
    }
    return theResult;
}
```

I'm not sure I really like the previous code. I'm thinking about the check for equality. Assume that I have two Customer instances (not two variables pointing to the same instance, but two separate instances), both with the same CustomerNumber. Will the call to Equals() then return true or false? It depends on whether Equals() has been overridden or not and whether or not the overridden implementation uses the CustomerNumber for deciding on equality.

> ### Note
>
> Readers that are familiar with the concept of the Identity Map pattern [Fowler PoEAA] and who see it as a must will probably wonder why we are having this discussion at all. The idea with Identity Map is that you will *not have* two separate instances for a single customer. The Identity Map will take care of that for you.
>
> The language itself, C# for example, won't take care of this for you. But when we discuss persistence solutions in Chapter 8, "Infrastructure for Persistence," and Chapter 9, "Putting NHibernate into Action," we'll cover this. Until then, we are on our own.

It's Time to Talk About Entities

Well, we have already touched on this subject several times in this chapter since Order and Customer are examples of Entities, but let's take a step back and focus on the concept.

It is important for us to keep track of some things in the domain over time. No matter whether a customer changes name or address, it's still the same customer, and it's something we are interested in keeping track of. On the other hand, if a customer's reference person changes, it is probably not anything we care to keep track of. A customer is a typical example of an Entity [Evans DDD]. Again, an Entity is something we keep track of by identity rather than all its values.

To take an extreme example of something that isn't an Entity, let's think about the integer 42. I don't care about the identity of 42 at all; I only care about the value. And when the value changes, I no longer think it's the 42 that has changed—it's a totally new value with no connection to the old one. Forty-two is a Value Object [Evans DDD] and not an Entity.

If we take that extreme example over to our domain, we might be able to say that it isn't interesting for us to track ReferencePerson of a Customer by identity. It's only interesting for us to track it by value. We'll get back to Value Objects later on in this chapter.

> ### Note
>
> Of course, what should be tracked by identity and what should just be thought of as values is highly dependent on the domain. Let's take an example. As I said above, I believe that ReferencePerson in this application can be dealt with as a Value Object, but if the application is for, let's say, a sales support application for salesmen, perhaps they see ReferencePerson as an Entity instead.

Back to the Flow Again

Unfortunately, the test CanFindOrdersViaCustomer() won't execute successfully after I override Equals. The reason is that all customers used in the test have the same CustomerNumber, that being zero, and therefore I find five Orders that have the right Customer, not three. We need to change the test a little bit. I create another little helper method called _FakeACustomer() like this:

```
//A test class
private Customer _FakeACustomer(int customerNumber)
{
    Customer c = new Customer();

    RepositoryHelper.SetFieldWhenReconstitutingFromPersistence
        (c, "_customerNumber", customerNumber);

    return c;
}
```

Note

_FakeACustomer() should associate the customer with the CustomerRepository (or rather the Unit of Work, when that comes in to play). Let's skip this for now because it won't affect the flow now.

Then I change the test CanFindOrdersViaCustomer(), so I use _FakeACustomer() instead of just calling the constructor of the Customer directly. The code looks like this after the change.

```
[Test]
public void CanFindOrdersViaCustomer()
{
    Customer c = _FakeACustomer(7);

    _FakeAnOrder(42, c, _repository);
    _FakeAnOrder(12, _FakeACustomer(1), _repository);
    _FakeAnOrder(3, c, _repository);
    _FakeAnOrder(21, c, _repository);
    _FakeAnOrder(1, _FakeACustomer(2), _repository);

    Assert.AreEqual(3, _repository.GetOrders(c).Count);
}
```

We are back to green bar again.

I think it is time to sum up where we are with a figure. Since Figure 5-6, we have also added CustomerNumber to the Customer class, as you can see here in Figure 5-7.

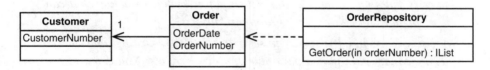

Figure 5-7 Order, Customer, and OrderRepository for listing orders, revised

The Bird's-Eye View

What is it that we have tried to accomplish so far? To a guy like me who has spent over a decade working with databases and database-focused applications, the code looks pretty strange when you think about it. For instance, there are no jumps to a database at all. Sure, it feels nice to leave that for now when focusing on the Domain Model and writing tests, but I also want to have the possibility of writing tests without touching the database later on.

What have the tests bought us thus far? Well for starters, we've used the tests as a means to discover and nail down the behavior and specification that we want the Domain Model to implement. By starting out with Fake/naïve implementation, we've been able to concentrate our energy on inventing the API. We are also trying hard to come up with, and playing with, the Ubiquitous Language. Finally, our tests have now given us a solid foundation in which we can transition the code from our naïve implementation to the "real thing."

I also believe we have respected the eventual target with the design choices. We have also created an abstraction layer in the form of repositories so we can defer dealing with the database (which is worth deferring).

So, specifically what we have done was write a first fake version of the OrderRepository...! We have also given the OrderRepository several different responsibilities. That might be the reason for my uneasiness with the design. I don't want to focus on infrastructure at all right now—I want to postpone it until later on. However, because I noticed that what I'm currently working on is infrastructure within the Domain Model, let's wait with the feature list for a while and consider some refactoring to get a nicer solution with the faking of the OrderRepository.

**Refining the
Domain Model
Through
Simple TDD
Experimentation**

Note

I'm trying to use "stub," "fake" and "mock" with specific, explicit meanings. Here's a quote from Astels [Astels TDD]:

"Stubs: A class with methods that do nothing. They are simply there to allow the system to compile and run.

Fakes: A class with methods that return a fixed value or values that can either be hardcoded or set programmatically.

Mocks: A class in which you can set expectations regarding what methods are called, with which parameters, how often, etc. You can also set return values for various calling situations. A mock will also provide a way to verify that the expectations were met."

But that's not the only definition. It's discussed a little differently by Meszaros [Meszaros XUnit]:

*"A **Test Stub** is an object that is used by a test to replace a real component on which the SUT depends so that the test can control the indirect inputs of the SUT. This allows the test to force the SUT down paths it might not otherwise exercise.*

> "A *Fake Object* is an object that replaces the functionality of the real depended-on component in a test for reasons other than verification of indirect inputs and outputs. Typically, it will implement the same or a subset of the functionality of the real depended-on component but in a much simpler way.
>
> "A *Mock Object* is an object that is used by a test to replace a real component on which the SUT depends so that the test can observe its indirect outputs. Typically, the Mock Object fakes the implementation by either returning hard-coded results or results that were pre-loaded by the test."

Faking the *OrderRepository*

My first thought was that I should fake some of the inner parts of OrderRepository so that the same OrderRepository could be used in different cases and get an instance like a DataFetcher in the constructor, which will do the right thing. When I think about it more, it feels a bit like overkill. More or less the whole OrderRepository will have to be swapped if I decide to let the OrderRepository talk to a relational database instead of just being a fake. The whole class will have to be swapped.

Refining the Domain Model Through Simple TDD Experimentation

Perhaps an interface like the one shown in Figure 5-8 is what I need for now.

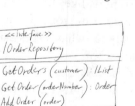

Figure 5-8   IOrderRepository, first proposal

Instinctively, I like this a lot. It might be because of my COM heritage or because many authors (such as [Szyperski Component Software], [Johnson J2EE Development without EJB] and [Löwy Programming .NET Components]) clearly state that programming against interfaces is preferable to programming against concrete classes.

Still—and I have already touched on this—I do have concrete classes (Customer and Order) within the signatures of the interface. Again, I leave it like this for now because I don't currently see any value in creating interfaces for those classes.

Another thing that comes to mind is that it might be nice to create a more generic Repository interface. It could look like what is shown in Figure 5-9.

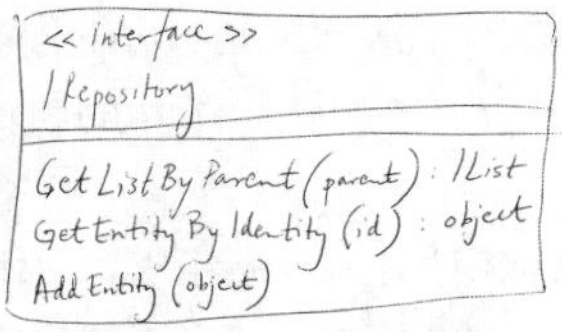

<< Interface >>
IRepository

GetListByParent (parent) : IList
GetEntityByIdentity (id) : object
AddEntity (object)

Figure 5-9 `IOrderRepository` (or rather `IRepository`), second proposal

This might grow on me, but right now I prefer the more specific interface in Figure 5-8, as it clearly states exactly what is needed. The generic `IRepository` requires more casts when being used and might be incorrectly trying to gather all upcoming Repositories in one and the same shape.

Another solution might be to use generics in the `IRepository`-interface + a base class and thereby at least get the type safety (and avoid code duplication) and avoid extra type casts. One problem then is that I might add a `Delete()` method to the Repository, even though not all Repositories will need it. And even with generics, the `GetListByParent(parent)` is troublesome because what if an Entity has several parents? Well, it's an early sketch and that can be solved of course. But I can't help thinking that it's better to let the code "speak as clearly as possible for now" and skip generalizations like that. It's just not feeling important yet. As usual, no decisions are carved in stone. I can challenge the decisions again later on when I can more easily see what pieces can be generalized, but for now, I'll stay with `IOrderRepository`.

Because of that, I rename the `OrderRepository` class to `OrderRepositoryFake` and let the class implement the `IOrderRepository`. I also need to change the `[SetUp]` code in my test class. It currently looks like this:

```
//A test class, the [SetUp]

_repository = new OrderRepository();
```

It could now look like this:

```
//A test class, the [SetUp]

_repository = new OrderRepositoryFake();
```

The declaration of `_repository` must use `IOrderRepository` as the type.
And the tests still work.

I guess pure XPers would groan a little bit at the refactoring I just did. I actually didn't have to make that change now; it was a change for preparing for the future, when I need a real Repository instead of the faked one. OK, I can agree with that, but I can't help thinking a little bit about the future (read: later chapters) when I will be hooking in infrastructure.

I cross my fingers that this preparation will prove to be good. I fell back into old habits of early guessing.... On the other hand, we are of course free to choose *our own balance* and don't have to stick to XP dogma!

A Few Words About Saving

I mentioned saving data previously. AddOrder() isn't really saving; it just adds the Order to the Repository. Or should it mean saving also? No, I don't think I want that behavior. What I want from AddOrder() is that the Repository (and the underlying infrastructure) from that point should know about the instance and deal with it when I ask for a PersistAll().

I need to ask the infrastructure to deal with the save functionality. The question for now is if I want to state the PersistAll() to the Repository instance or to something at a higher level that monitors instances for all the Repositories. Again, I think I'm drifting away from the Domain Model and into the infrastructure part. I'm glad the question was raised, but parts of the discussion will have to wait until the next chapter. There is a great deal that we need to discuss as far as that is concerned. For now, I'm happy with AddOrder() as a way of letting the Repository know about the instance. As far as the tests that have been written so far are concerned, it doesn't really matter that the instance is transient (but prepared for being persisted) and not persistent at that point in time.

OK, I'm as eager as you are to get writing some more tests. What's on the list? Well, I have dealt with most of it in feature 2, "List the orders when looking at a specific customer." What I haven't dealt with there is showing the total amount for each order, type of order, and reference person.

Let's take them one by one, starting with total amount for each order.

Total Amount for Each Order

At first this seems like a trivial task. I need to create an OrderLine class that I hook into the Order class as a list. Then I can just iterate over the OrderLine collection and calculate the total amount. I could actually do that from the consumer code, of course, but I don't want to. That would reveal the algorithm to the consumer, and it's not all that clear or purposeful either. In reality, the algorithm will become much harder when we move further, adding discounts of many different kinds, for example. Instead, I want a read-only property called TotalAmount on the Order class. Again, it could internally iterate over the OrderLine collection and calculate the value.

But this is getting to be too much for me, the "premature optimizer guy" that I am (even though I'm trying hard not to be). Instantiating all orderLines for each order for a customer just to be able to show the TotalAmount of the orders sets off the alarm bells. This might not be a problem depending upon the execution environment and chosen infrastructure. On the other hand, in the case of a distributed system, it is a problem, and potentially a big one that can hurt the database server, the network, and the garbage collector.

I must admit I have to force myself not to deal with this optimization right away. It's simple to fix it directly, but it's not really important right now when I'm crunching what the Domain Model should look like. It's much more important right now to design for simplicity and clarity, and get back later with a profiler to see if it's a *real* performance problem. So I start with the simplest solution and can then refactor the TotalAmount property later on if the performance characteristics aren't good enough.

Ah, I made it! I skipped an optimization now. And it feels so good for the moment.

Refining the Domain Model Through Simple TDD Experimentation

Let's take a step back now that we have thought a bit about the TotalAmount. It's time to write a test (better late than never). I start with the simplest possible one I can come up with.

```
[Test]
public void EmptyOrderHasZeroForTotalAmount()
{
    Order o = new Order(new Customer());

    Assert.AreEqual(0, o.TotalAmount);
}
```

It's simple to make that test compile. I just add a public read-only property called TotalAmount to the Order class and let it return -1. It compiles and I get red. I change it so that the property returns 0 and I have a green bar.

I could leave that for now, but because I have the context set up for me now, I continue a little bit. Here's another test:

```
[Test]
public void OrderWithLinesHasTotalAmount()
{
    Order o = new Order(new Customer());

    OrderLine ol = new OrderLine(new Product("Chair", 52.00));
    ol.NoOfUnits = 2;

    o.AddOrderLine(ol);

    Assert.AreEqual(104.00, o.TotalAmount);
}
```

Ouch, there was a lot of design done in that single test, and I now need to create two classes and new methods at old classes to just make it compile. I think I'd better comment out that test for the moment and start a little more simply, focusing on the OrderLine class.

First of all, I want the OrderLine to get the price from the chosen product as a default. Let's write a test.

```
[Test]
public void OrderLineGetsDefaultPrice()
{
    Product p = new Product("Chair", 52.00);

    OrderLine ol = new OrderLine(p);

    Assert.AreEqual(52.00, ol.Price);
}
```

Even that is a pretty large jump that requires some code to be written, but I'm feeling confident right now, so let's write a Product class. The second argument in the constructor should be the unit price. The Product class should also have two read-only properties: Description and UnitPrice.

I also wrote an OrderLine class with two members: Product and Price. It looks like this:

```
public class OrderLine
{
    public decimal Price = 0;
    private Product _product;

    public OrderLine(Product product)
    {
        _product = product;
    }

    public Product Product
    {
        get {return _product;}
    }
}
```

The test now compiles, but it's red. I need to change the constructor so that I grab the price from the Product and put it into the OrderLine itself. The constructor now looks like this:

```
//OrderLine
public OrderLine(Product product)
{
    _product = product;
    Price = product.UnitPrice;
}
```

We are back to green again. I write a test proving that I can override the default price in the OrderLine, but it's not very interesting, so let's leave it out here.

The next test I'd like to write is a calculation of the TotalAmount of one orderLine. The test could be like this:

```
[Test]
public void OrderLineHasTotalAmount()
{
    OrderLine ol = new OrderLine(new Product("Chair", 52.00));
    ol.NumberOfUnits = 2;

    Assert.AreEqual(104.00, ol.TotalAmount);
}
```

Two more design decisions there. I need a NumberOfUnits field and a TotalAmount on the OrderLine. I let the NumberOfUnits be a public field, and I write the TotalAmount as a read only property returning 0. It compiles, but is red. I then change the TotalAmount into this:

Refining the
Domain Model
Through
Simple TDD
Experimentation

```
//OrderLine
public decimal TotalAmount
{
    get {return Price * NumberOfUnits;}
}
```

Green again.

Let's have a look at what we just did. In Figure 5-10, you find a diagram with OrderLine and Product.

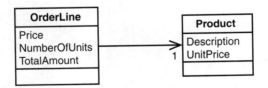

Figure 5-10   OrderLine and Product

It's time to go back to the test I commented out before. You'll find it again here, but I made it a little bit "bigger" this time, dealing with two OrderLines.

```
[Test]
public void OrderWithLinesHasTotalAmount()
{
    Order o = new Order(new Customer());

    OrderLine ol = new OrderLine(new Product("Chair", 52.00));
```

```
ol.NoOfUnits = 2;
o.AddOrderLine(ol);

OrderLine ol2 = new OrderLine(new Product("Desk", 115.00));
ol2.NoOfUnits = 3;
o.AddOrderLine(ol2);

Assert.AreEqual(104.00 + 345.00, o.TotalAmount);
}
```

In order to get this to compile, I need to add AddOrderLine() and TotalAmount to Order. I let the read-only property TotalAmount just return 0 for the moment. And I set [Ignore] on OrderWithLinesHasTotalAmount() test. Instead, I write another test to focus on AddOrderLine(). That test could look like this:

```
[Test]
public void CanAddOrderLine()
{
    Order o = new Order(new Customer());

    OrderLine ol = new OrderLine(new Product("Chair", 52.00));
    o.AddOrderLine(ol);

    Assert.AreEqual(1, o.OrderLines.Count);
}
```

Refining the
Domain Model
Through
Simple TDD
Experimentation

For this to compile, I need to add both AddOrderLine() and an OrderLines property to the Order. Because the test will fail meaningfully if either of them isn't working, I get started by writing OrderLines the way I think I want it, but don't finish AddOrderLine(). You can find the code here:

```
//Order
private IList _orderLines = new ArrayList();

public IList OrderLines
{
    get {return ArrayList.ReadOnly(_orderLines);}
}

public void AddOrderLine(OrderLine orderLine)
{
}
```

It compiles and is red. I add a line to the AddOrderLine() method like this:

```
//Order
public void AddOrderLine(OrderLine orderLine)
{
    _orderLines.Add(orderLine);
}
```

It compiles and is green.

It's time to delete the Ignore attribute from the test called OrderWithLinesHasTotal-Amount(). The test is red because TotalAmount of the Order just returns 0.

I rewrite the TotalAmount property like this:

```
//Order
public decimal TotalAmount
{
    get
    {
        decimal theSum = 0;
        foreach (OrderLine ol in _orderLines)
            theSum += ol.TotalAmount;

        return theSum;
    }
}
```

Simple, straightforward, and green. And did you notice that I resisted the urge to optimize it? I just wrote it the simplest way I could think of, and I even almost did it without groaning. After all, I currently see the Order and its OrderLines as the Aggregate and therefore as the *default* load unit as well.

Historic Customer Information

I think it's time for some refactoring. Any smells? One thing I didn't like much was that Order has a relationship with Customer. Sure, an Order has a Customer, that's fine, but if I look at an Order one year later, I probably want to see the Customer information as it was when the Order was created, not as it is now.

The other problem is that the constructor takes a Customer as a parameter. That means that the Order might get into the persistent object graph directly, without a call to IOrderRepository.AddOrder(), and this might not be such a good idea. (Well, it depends on your infrastructure as well, but it's not obvious that there is a boundary.) AddOrder() is the way of saying that this order should get persisted when it's time for saving.

None of these problems are at all hard to deal with, but how do I communicate this clearly? I write a test, to try out a proposal:

```
[Test]
public void OrderHasSnapshotOfRealCustomer()
{
    Customer c = new Customer();
    c.Name = "Volvo";

    Customer aHistoricCustomer = c.TakeSnapshot();

    Order o = new Order(aHistoricCustomer);

    c.Name = "Saab";
```

```
    Assert.AreEqual("Saab", c.Name);
    Assert.AreEqual("Volvo", o.Customer.Name);

}
```

But I'm not so sure about this solution... Currently, the Customer is a pretty small type, but it will probably grow a lot. Even though it's small now, is it really interesting to keep track of what reference people the Customer had at that point in time?

I think creating another type with only the properties that are interesting might be a good solution here because it will also create an explicit boundary between the Aggregates, but especially because that's what the underlying model indicates. Let's create a CustomerSnapshot (somewhat inspired by [Fowler Snapshot] regarding the purpose, but different in implementation) that only has the minimum amount of properties, and let it be a value object. The test only has to be transformed very slightly (after I have corrected two compile errors: the type for the Customer property and the parameter to the constructor):

Refining the
Domain Model
Through
Simple TDD
Experimentation

```
[Test]
public void OrderHasSnapshotOfRealCustomer()
{
    Customer c = new Customer();
    c.Name = "Volvo";

    CustomerSnapshot aHistoricCustomer = c.TakeSnapshot();

    Order o = new Order(aHistoricCustomer);

    c.Name = "Saab";

    Assert.AreEqual("Saab", c.Name);
    Assert.AreEqual("Volvo", o.Customer.Name);

}
```

Another thing to consider is whether the consumer or the Order constructor is responsible for creating the snapshot. Previously, I let the consumer be responsible. Let's change that so that the constructor again takes a Customer instance as the parameter, as follows:

```
[Test]
public void OrderHasSnapshotOfRealCustomer()
{
    Customer c = new Customer();
    c.Name = "Volvo";

    Order o = new Order(c);

    c.Name = "Saab";
```

```
        Assert.AreEqual("Saab", c.Name);
        Assert.AreEqual("Volvo", o.Customer.Name);
}
```

And the constructor of the Order looks like this:

```
//Order
public Order(Customer customer)
{
    Customer = customer.TakeSnapshot();
}
```

Another thing to consider is if it's the correct place in time to take the snap-shot when the customer instance is created. Isn't that too early? What if the customer changes? Perhaps we should take the snapshot at a transition for when the customer accepts the order? Lots of interesting and important questions, but I start like this now.

Let's just conclude this section with an update of the Customer. See Figure 5-11.

Refining the Domain Model Through Simple TDD Experimentation

Customer
TakeSnapshot() : CustomerSnapshot

Figure 5-11   An added method for taking a snapshot of Customer

It's refactoring time again, I think. Hmmm…I'm not totally happy with the fact that I send a Customer *instance* to GetOrders() when finding Orders. It's actually just the ID of the customer that is important for the functionality, and it feels a bit strange to use a current customer for fetching orders with historic customer information. Anyway, I'd like to think about it some more.

Another question is what we should call the property of the Order for see-ing the historic customer information of that order. Right now it's called Order. Customer, but that says nothing about the time aspect of the Customer information. Perhaps Order.CustomerSnapshot is better. I think it is, I make that change, and you can see the new Order-class in Figure 5-12.

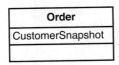

Order
CustomerSnapshot

Figure 5-12   Changed name of Customer property

Yet another thing is that Customers are instantiated directly and not with a CustomerFactory. It's absolutely OK for now, I think. We add factories when needed, not before!

Perhaps I should add that `OrderFactory` back again, add a method to it for `CreateOrderLine()`, and let it take both a `Product` and an `Order` as parameter (or at least an `Order`). On the other hand, it feels good to be able to work with an `OrderLine` without making it persistent (which will happen when I add the order line to a persistent order). Let's see if this might need to be changed later on, but this has raised another concern. I think I need to discuss the life cycle of an instance right here.

The Life Cycle of an Instance

In the previous section, I said that an order line becomes persistent when I add it to a persistent order, and this needs explaining. What I mean is that an instance starts its life as transient when you do the following, for example:

```
Product p = new Product();
```

Then the `Product` is transient. It is not fetched from the database as it has never become persistent. If we want it to become persistent (and stored to the database at next call to `PersistAll()`), we need to ask a Repository for help by calling `AddProduct()`. Depending upon the infrastructure that is used, the Repository makes the infrastructure aware of the product.

Then again, when I ask the Repository for help with reconstituting an instance from the database, that fetched instance is persistent when I get it. All changes I make to it will be stored at next `PersistAll()`.

But what about `OrderLine`? I didn't ask the Repository to `AddOrderLine()`, but I did ask the Aggregate root `Order` to `AddOrderLine()`, and because of that the order line is made persistent, too. Within Aggregates, I think the persistence aspect should be cascaded.

Let's summarize what I think the semantics are for the life cycle that I need in my Domain Model. They are shown in Table 5-1.

Table 5-1 *Summary of the semantics for the life cycle of the Domain Model instances*

Operation		Result Regarding Transient/Persistent
Call to new	→	Transient
Repository.Add(instance) or persistentInstance.Add(instance)	→	Persistent in Domain Model
x.PersistAll()	→	Persistent in Database
Repository.Get()	→	Persistent in Domain Model (and Database)
Repository.Delete(instance)	→	Transient (and instance will get deleted from database at x.PersistAll)

In Figure 5-13, you'll find the life cycle described as a state diagram.

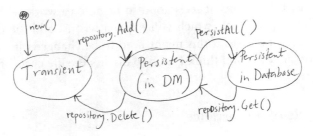

Figure 5-13   The life cycle of an instance

Note

Evans talks a lot about this too… [Evans DDD]. There is a splendid explanation for this, so be sure to read it. The same goes for Jordan/Russell [Jordan/Russell JDO]. JDO has more complex (and flexible) semantics, but of course I might discover later that the simple semantics I sketched previously are not enough.

Don't mix this up with how the infrastructure (for example NHibernate) sees the transient/persistent. What I talk about here is the way *I* want the life cycle semantics for my Domain Model instances. It's then up to the infrastructure to help me with the wanted semantics behind the scenes. This will be discussed a lot more in later chapters.

Talking about the infrastructure, the hawk-eyed reader might wonder what I meant with x.PersistAll() in Table 5-1. I tried to symbolize that unknown infrastructure with x. Again, we can forget about that for now.

Back to feature 2, listing orders for a customer. The next sub-feature was that an order must have an ordertype.

Type of Order

A simple solution here would be to add an OrderType instance to each Order, as shown in Figure 5-14.

Figure 5-14   Order and OrderType

I considered whether the OrderType is really an Entity [Evans DDD], and I don't think it is—it is a Value Object [Evans DDD]. The set of possible values are "global" for the whole application and are very small and static.

I'm probably on the wrong track here. Sure, I could implement OrderType as a Value Object, but much is pointing in the direction that an enum is good enough, and especially good enough for now, so I define an OrderType enum and add such a field to the Order.

Reference Person for an Order

It's time to talk about ReferencePerson of an Order again. There I think we have an example of a Value Object [Evans DDD], although it is a bit different than the OrderType (which was a value object candidate) because reference people aren't global for the whole system but rather specific per Customer or Order. (Well, that's a good indication that ReferencePerson shouldn't be an enum.)

In Figure 5-15, you can see the ReferencePerson "in action."

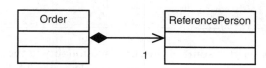

Figure 5-15   Order and ReferencePerson

When we go for a Value Object pattern [Evans DDD], it might feel obvious that we should use a struct in .NET instead of a class, but there are recommendations for size regarding when to use a struct and when not to, and you'll get more problems with infrastructure when it comes to structs. It's also the case that you will see more boxing when using structs, so the decision isn't clear-cut. I'm actually leaning to using classes, but most often I'm making them immutable. If you go that route, you need to use all the values of the class for when you are overriding the Equals().

This is what the Equals() could look like for the Value Object ReferencePerson. (Note that I'm comparing all the fields of the Value Object, unlike how I did it with the Entity before. Also note that, Identity Map or not, overriding Equals() for Value Objects is needed.)

```
//ReferencePerson
public override bool Equals(object o)
{
    if (o == null)
        return false;

    if (this.GetType() != o.GetType())
        return false;
```

```
ReferencePerson other = (ReferencePerson) o;

if (! FirstName.Equals(other.FirstName))
    return false;
if (! LastName.Equals(other.LastName))
    return false;

return true;
}
```

Note

Ingemar Lundberg commented on the previous listing with a more condensed version:

```
//ReferencePerson.Equals()
ReferencePerson other = o as ReferencePerson;
return other != null
    && this.GetType() == other.GetType()
    && FirstName.Equals(other.FirstName)
    && LastName.Equals(other.LastName);
```

Refining the Domain Model Through Simple TDD Experimentation

So we have now written some of the core functionality in the Domain Model. In Figure 5-16, you can see how the developed Domain Model looks for the moment.

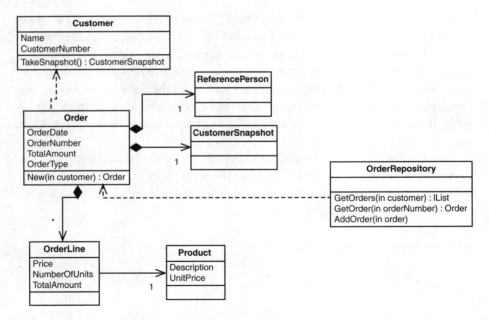

Figure 5-16   Implementation of the Domain Model so far

OK, I think that will do for now and we need a break. The break will also mean a change. When we get back to refining the Domain Model in later chapters, I won't use such a TDD-ish way of describing all the tiny design decisions as we go. It will be a more condensed description.

But let's end the chapter with a discussion about another style of API.

Fluent Interface

So far we have sketched out a pretty basic and primitive API for our Domain Model. Creating an order with two products could look like this (assuming we are already holding on to a specific customer):

```
Order newOrder = new Order(customer);
OrderLine orderLine;

orderLine = new OrderLine(productRepository.GetProduct("ABC"));
orderLine.NumberOfUnits = 42;
newOrder.AddOrderLine(orderLine);

orderLine = new OrderLine(productRepository.GetProduct("XYZ"));
orderLine.NumberOfUnits = 3;
newOrder.AddOrderLine(orderLine);
```

Fluent
Interface

I think it's pretty easy to follow. But it's a bit verbose and not as fluent as it could be. A simple way of shortening it would be to add numberOfUnits to the constructor of OrderLine, taking it down to three statements, like this:

```
Order newOrder = new Order(customer);

newOrder.AddOrderLine(new OrderLine
    (42, productRepository.GetProduct("ABC")));

newOrder.AddOrderLine(new OrderLine
    (3, productRepository.GetProduct("XYZ")));
```

But it's still not very fluent. Martin Fowler's "FluentInterface" [Fowler FluentInterface] is good inspiration. Let's see if we can sketch the API to be a bit more fluent. Perhaps something like this:

```
Order newOrder = new Order(customer)
    .With(42, "ABC")
    .With(3, "XYZ");
```

It's both shorter and clearer. In my sketch, I kept the first line because I think that is pretty clear. Then the With() method takes the numberOfUnits as parameter and a product identification so that With() internally can use the productRepository for finding the product. (Let's assume for now that With() can find the productRepository at a well known place.)

With() also returns the order, and therefore we can chain several statements after each others.

Let's try out a variation. Assume that we can't create the whole order in one swoop, but want to add an orderLine as the result from a user action. Then we might prefer something like this for adding an orderLine:

```
newOrder.AddOrderLine("ABC").NumberOfUnits = 42;
```

This time AddOrderLine() returns the orderLine and not the order. We could take that further if we want to be able to set more values of the orderLine by changing NumberOfUnits into a method instead that returns the orderLine again, but you get the point.

The important thing to take away from this section is how much better your API can become if you play with it a bit.

Summary

Summary

So we spent the whole chapter discussing some initial parts of the model, but with a fairly detailed discussion. As I see it, detailed model discussions are best done with code and TDD instead of UML sketches, and this chapter followed that idea.

I think it's a good idea to summarize where we are in the feature list before we leave the chapter. So far we have dealt with features 2, 3, 7 and 9. Not that much, but clear progress. And the progress is secured with quite a lot of tests. Good.

We'll continue the work with refining the Domain Model in Chapter 7. The focus will shift a bit in the next chapter. As you might have noticed, we sniffed on infrastructure related discussions several times in this chapter, so let's take on those problems next by preparing for adding infrastructure.

Chapter 6

Preparing for Infrastructure

It's time to continue the exploration of applying DDD to our problem domain. There is no specific next step, but you may be wondering when I will start dealing with the infrastructure. For instance, we haven't yet made it possible to persist or depersist (materialize or reconstitute) the orders to or from a database. As a matter of fact, we haven't even thought about, let alone decided on, using a database.

This is intentional. We want to delay making this decision a bit longer, at least if we are feeling safe and familiar with existing infrastructural options. If this is our first DDD-ish project, this might not be the case, of course, but let's pretend.

The reason I want to delay the binding to a relational database is that in doing so we will focus on the Domain Model with as few distractions as possible. Hey, I'm an old database guy, so it's OK for me to talk about the database as a distraction. I would never dare to say that if I came from the OO side.

Seriously, I'm not saying that the database interaction isn't important; on the contrary, I *know* that it is important. But staying away from the database a bit longer makes trying out and exploring both small and large model changes more productive for us.

It's also much easier to write the tests, because changes done in tests won't be persistent between executions. The test executions themselves will also execute much faster, making it much more manageable for the developers to run the tests after each code change.

There are also problems with this approach. I have already said that we assume we have good control of dealing with the probable upcoming database interaction, so this is not where the problem lies. Instead, there's a good chance that you will want to write some UI prototypes early on, not only for your own sake as a way of challenging your Domain Model, but also as a way to dialogue with the customer. If these prototypes have "live" data that the user can interact with, add to, and so on, they will be more useful than what is common for early prototypes.

As you might recall, we ended Chapter 5, "A New Default Architecture," with a preliminary discussion about adding early UI examples. Users will find these examples even more interesting to try out if the data is also around after a restart. (Sure, this can easily be done if you start using the planned persistence solution directly. However, we expect that this will increase the overhead during early refactoring attempts, so what we want is to create an inexpensive "illusion.")

> ### Note
>
> Watch out so that your customer (or your boss) doesn't think that the whole application is done after only having seen one or two prototypes. Been there, done that.

The second thing I'm after at this point is to be able to write tests for save scenarios here, again without dealing with a real database. You might ask what the point of this is. Again, I'd like to focus on the model, the semantics "around" it, and so on.

I could certainly deal with this problem on an individual basis in the repositories, as I have done so far, but I see value in having consistency and just applying one solution to all the repositories. I also want a solution that scales up to early integration testing, and most importantly I want to write real repositories now and not stupid, temporary code that should be thrown away!

So even though I started out saying that it's too early for infrastructure, this chapter will deal with *preparation* for the infrastructure, and in such a way that we won't have to redo work when we add infrastructure. What we want is to write infrastructure-agnostic code.

POCO as a
Lifestyle

POCO as a Lifestyle

What I also just said between the lines is that I'd really like to try to keep the main asset of my applications as free from infrastructure-related distractions as possible. The *Plain Old Java Object* (POJO) and *Plain Old CLR Object* (POCO) movement started out in Java land as a reaction against J2EE and its huge implications on applications, such as how it increased complexity in everything and made TDD close to impossible. Martin Fowler, Rebecca Parsons, and Josh MacKenzie coined the term POJO for describing a class that was free from the "dumb" code that is only needed by the execution environment. The classes should focus on the business problem at hand. Nothing else should be in the classes in the Domain Model.

Note

This movement is one of the main inspirations for lightweight containers for Java, such as Spring [Johnson J2EE Development without EJB].

In .NET land it has taken a while for Plain Old... to receive any attention, but it is now known as POCO.

POCO is a somewhat established term, but it's not very specific regarding persistence-related infrastructure. When I discussed this with Martin Fowler he said that perhaps *Persistence Ignorance* (PI) is a better and clearer description. I agree, so I'll change to that from now on in this chapter.

PI for Our Entities and Value Objects

So let's assume we want to use PI. What's it all about? Well, PI means clean, ordinary classes where you focus on the business problem at hand without adding stuff for infrastructure-related reasons. OK, that didn't say all that much. It's easier if we take a look at what PI is *not*. First, a simple litmus test is to see if you have a reference to any external infrastructure-related DLLs in your Domain Model. For example, if you use NHibernate as your O/R Mapper and have a reference to nhibernate.dll, it's a good sign that you have added code to your Domain Model that isn't really core, but more of a distraction.

What are those distractions? For instance, if you use a PI-based approach for persistent objects, there's no *requirement* to do any of the following:

- Inherit from a certain base class (besides `object`)

- Only instantiate via a provided factory

- Use specially provided datatypes, such as for collections

- Implement a specific interface

- Provide specific constructors

- Provide mandatory specific fields

- Avoid certain constructs

POCO as a Lifestyle

There is at least one more, and one that is so obvious that I forgot. You shouldn't have to write database code such as calls to stored procedures in your Domain Model classes. But that was so obvious that I didn't write specifically about it.

Let's take a closer look at each of the other points.

Inherit from a Certain Base Class

With frameworks, a very common requirement for supporting persistence is that they require you to inherit from a certain base class provided by the framework.

The following might not look too bad:

```
public class Customer : PersistentObjectBase
{
    public string Name = string.Empty;
    …

    public decimal CalculateDepth()
    …

}
```

Well, it *wasn't* too bad, but it did carry some semantics and mechanisms that aren't optimal for you. For example, you have used the only inheritance possibility you have for your Customer class because .NET only has single inheritance. It's certainly arguable whether this is a big problem or not, though, because you can often design "around" it.

It's a worse problem if you have developed a Domain Model and now you would like to make it persistent. The inheritance requirement might very well require some changes to your Domain Model. It's pretty much the same when you start developing a Domain Model with TDD. You have the restriction from the beginning that you can't use inheritance and have to save that for the persistence requirement.

Something you should look out for is if the inheritance brings lots of public functionality to the subclass, which might make the consumer of the subclass have to wade through methods that aren't interesting to him.

It's also the case that it's not usually as clean as the previous example, but most of the time PersistentObjectBase forces you to provide some method implementations to methods in PersistentObjectBase, as in the Template Method pattern [GoF Design Patterns]. OK, this is still not a disaster, but it all adds up.

Note

This doesn't necessarily have to be a requirement, but can be seen as a convenience enabling you to get most, if not all, of the interface implementation that is required by the framework if the framework is of that kind of style. We will discuss this common requirement in a later section.

This is how it was done in the Valhalla framework that Christoffer Skjoldborg and I developed. But to be honest, in that case there was so much work that was taken care of by the base class called EntityBase that implementing the interfaces with custom code instead of inheriting from EntityBase was really just a theoretical option.

Only Instantiate via a Provided Factory

Don't get me wrong, I'm not in any way against using factories. Nevertheless, I'm not ecstatic at being *forced* to use them when it's not my own sound decision. This means, for instance, that instead of writing code like this:

```
Customer c = new Customer();
```

I *have* to write code like this:

```
Customer c = (Customer)PersistentObjectFactory.CreateInstance
    (typeof(Customer));
```

POCO as a
Lifestyle

Note

I know, you think I did my best to be unfair by using extremely long names, but this isn't really any better, is it?

```
Customer c = (Customer)POF.CI(typeof(Customer));
```

Again, it's not a disaster, but it's not optimal in most cases. This code just looks a lot weirder than the first instantiation code, doesn't it? And what often happens is that code like this increases testing complexity.

Often one of the reasons for the mandatory use of a provided factory is that you will consequently get help with dirty checking. So your Domain Model classes will get subclassed dynamically, and in the subclass, a dirty-flag (or several) is maintained in the properties. The factory makes this transparent to the consumer so that it instantiates the subclass instead of the class the factory consumer asks for. Unfortunately, for this to work you will also have to make your properties virtual, and public fields can't be used (two more small details that lessen the PI-ness a little). (Well, you *can use* public fields, but they can't be "overridden" in the generated subclass, and that's a problem if the purpose of the subclass is to take care of dirty tracking, for example.)

> ### Note
>
> There are several different techniques when using Aspect-Oriented Programming (AOP) in .NET, where runtime subclassing that we just discussed is probably the most commonly used. I've always seen having to declare your members as virtual for being able to intercept (or advice) as a drawback, but Roger Johansson pointed something out to me. Assume you want to make it impossible to override a member and thereby avoid the extra work and responsibility of supporting subclassing. Then that decision should affect both ordinary subclassing and subclassing that is used for reasons of AOP. And if you make the member virtual, you are prepared for having it redefined, again both by ordinary subclassing and AOP-ish subclassing.
>
> It makes sense, doesn't it?

Another common problem solved this way is the need for Lazy Load, but I'd like to use that as an example for the next section.

POCO as a Lifestyle

Use "Specially" Provided Datatypes, Such as Collections

It's not uncommon to have to use special datatypes for the collections in your Domain Model classes: special as in "not those you would have used if you could have chosen freely."

The most common reason for this requirement is probably for supporting Lazy Load, [Fowler PoEAA], or rather *implicit* Lazy Load, so that you don't have to write code on your own for making it happen. (Lazy Load means that data is fetched just in time from the database.)

But the specific datatypes could also bring you other functionality, such as special delete handling so that as soon as you delete an instance from a collection the instance will be registered with the Unit of Work [Fowler PoEAA] for deletion as well. (Unit of Work is used for keeping track of what actions should be taken against the database at the end of the current logical unit of work.)

> ### Note
>
> Did you notice that I said that the specific datatypes could *bring* you *functionality*? Yep, I don't want to sound overly negative about NPI (Not-PI).

You could get help with bi-directionality so that you don't have to code it on your own. This is yet another example of something an AOP solution can take care of for you.

Implement a Specific Interface

Yet another very regular requirement on Domain Model classes for being persistable is that they implement one or more infrastructure-provided interfaces.

This is naturally a smaller problem if there is very little code you have to write in order to implement the interface(s) and a bigger problem if the opposite is true.

One example of interface-based functionality could be to make it possible to fill the instance with values from the database without hitting setters (which might have specific code that you don't want to execute during reconstitution).

Another common example is to provide interfaces for optimized access to the state in the instances.

Provide Specific Constructors

Yet another way of providing values that reconstitute instances from the database is by requiring specific constructors, which are constructors that have nothing at all to do with the business problem at hand.

It might also be that a default constructor is needed so that the framework can instantiate Domain Model classes easily as the result of a Get operation against the database. Again, it's not a very dramatic problem, but a distraction nonetheless.

POCO as a Lifestyle

Provide Mandatory Specific Fields

Some infrastructure solutions require your Domain Model classes to provide specific fields, such as Guid-based Id-fields or int-based Version-fields. (With Guid-based Id-fields, I mean that the Id-fields are using Guids as the datatype.) That simplifies the infrastructure, but it might make your life as a Domain Model-developer a bit harder. At least if it affects your classes in a way you didn't want to.

Avoid Certain Constructs/Forced Usage of Certain Constructs

I have already mentioned that you might be forced to use virtual properties even if you don't really want to. It might also be that you have to avoid certain constructs, and a typical example of this is read-only fields. Read-only (as when the keyword readonly is used) fields can't be set from the outside (except with constructors), something that is needed to create 100% PI-Domain Model classes.

Using a private field together with a get-only property is pretty close to a read-only field, but not exactly the same. It could be argued that a read-only field is the most intention-revealing solution.

Note

Something that has been discussed a lot is whether .NET attributes are a good or bad thing regarding decorating the Domain Model with information about how to persist the Domain Model.

My opinion is that such attributes can be a good thing and that they don't really decrease the PI level if they are seen as default information that can be overridden. I think the main problem is if they get too verbose to distract the reader of the code.

PI or not PI?

PI or not PI—of course it's not totally binary. There are some gray areas as well, but for now let's be happy if we get a feeling for the intention of PI rather than how to get to 100%. Anything extreme incurs high costs. We'll get back to this in Chapter 9, "Putting NHibernate into Action," when we discuss an infrastructure solution.

Note

What is an example of something completely binary in real life? Oh, one that I often remind my wife about is when she says "that woman was *very* pregnant."

Something we haven't touched on yet is that it also depends on at what point in "time" we evaluate whether we use PI or not.

Runtime Versus Compile Time PI

So far I have talked about PI in a timeless context, but it's probably most important at compile time and not as important at runtime. "What does that mean?" I hear you say? Well, assume that code is created for you, infrastructure-related code that you never have to deal with or even see yourself. This solution is probably better than if you have to maintain similar code by hand.

This whole subject is charged with feelings because it's controversial to execute something other than what you wrote yourself. The debugging experience might turn into a nightmare!

> ### Note
>
> Mark Burhop commented as follows:
>
> Hmmm... This was the original argument against C++ from C programmers in the early 90s. "C++ sticks in new code I didn't write." "C++ hides what is really going on." I don't know that this argument holds much water anymore.

It's also harder to inject code at the byte level for .NET classes compared to Java. It's not supported by the framework, so you're on your own, which makes it a showstopper in most cases.

What is most often done instead is to use some alternative techniques, such as those I mentioned with runtime-subclassing in combination with a provided factory, but it's not a big difference compared to injected code. Let's summarize with calling it emitting code.

The Cost for PI Entitites/Value Objects

I guess one possible reaction to all this is "PI seems great—why not use it all the time?" It's a law of nature (or at least software) that when everything seems neat and clean and great and without fault, then come the drawbacks. In this case, I think one such is overhead.

I did mention earlier in this chapter that speed is something you will sacrifice for a high level of PI-ness, at least for runtime PI, because you are then directed to use reflection, which is quite expensive. (If you think compile-time PI is good enough, you don't need to use reflection, but can go for an AOP solution instead and you can get a better performance story.)

You can easily prove with some operation in a tight loop that it is magnitudes slower for reading from/writing to fields/properties with reflection compared to calling them in the ordinary way. Yet, is the cost *too* high? It obviously depends on the situation. You'll have to run tests to see how it applies to your own case. Don't forget that a jump to the database is very expensive compared to a lot you're doing in your Domain Model, yet at the same time, you aren't comparing apples and apples here. For instance, the comparison might not be between an ordinary read and a reflection-based read.

POCO as a Lifestyle

A Typical Example Regarding Speed

Let's take an example to give you a better understanding of the whole thing. One common operation in a persistence framework is deciding whether or not an instance should be stored to the database at the end of a scenario. A common solution to this is to let the instance be responsible for signaling IsDirty if it is to be stored. Or better still, the instance could also signal itself to the Unit of Work when it gets dirty so that the Unit of Work will remember that when it's time to store changes.

But (you know there had to be a "but," right?) that requires some abuse of PI, unless you have paid with AOP.

> **Note**
>
> There are other drawbacks with this solution, such as it won't notice the change if it's done via reflection and therefore the instance changes won't get stored. This drawback was a bit twisted, though.

An alternative solution is not to signal anything at all, but let the infrastructure remember how the instances looked when fetched from the database. Then at store time compare how the instances look now to how they looked when read from the database.

Do you see that it's not just a comparison of one ordinary read to one reflection-based read, but they are totally different approaches, with totally different performance characteristics? To get a real feeling for it, you can set up a comparison yourself. Fetch one million instances from the database, modify one instance, and then measure the time difference for the store operation in both cases. I know, it was another twisted situation, but still something to think about.

Other Examples

That was something about the speed cost, but that's not all there is to it. Another cost I pointed out before was that you might get less functionality automatically if you try hard to use a high level of PI. I've already gone through many possible features you could get for free if you abandon some PI-ness, such as automatic bi-directional support and automatic implicit Lazy Load.

It's also the case that the dirty tracking isn't just about performance. The consumer might be very interested as well in using that information when painting the forms—for example, to know what buttons to enable.

POCO as a
Lifestyle

So as usual, there's a tradeoff. In the case of PI versus non-PI, the tradeoff is overhead and less functionality versus distracting code in the core of your application that couples you to a certain infrastructure and also makes it harder to do TDD. There are pros and cons. That's reasonable, isn't it?

The Cost Conclusion

So the conclusion to all this is to be aware of the tradeoffs and choose carefully. For instance, if you get something you need alongside a drawback you can live with, don't be too religious about it!

That said, I'm currently in the pro-PI camp, mostly because of how nice it is for TDD and how clean and clear I can get my Entities and Value Objects.

I also think there's a huge difference when it comes to your preferred approach. If you like starting from code, you'll probably like PI a great deal. If you work in an integrated tool where you start with detailed design in UML, for example, and from there generate your Domain Model, PI is probably not that important for you at all.

But there's more to the Domain Model than Entities and Value Objects. What I'm thinking about are the Repositories. Strangely enough, very little has been said as far as PI for the Repositories goes.

PI for Our Repositories

I admit it: saying you use PI for Repositories as well is pushing it. This is because the purpose of Repositories is pretty much to give the consumer the illusion that the complete set of Domain Model instances is around, as long as you adhere to the protocol to go to the Repository to get the instances. The illusion is achieved by the Repositories talking to infrastructure in specific situations, and talking to infrastructure is not a very PI-ish thing to do.

For example, the Repositories need something to pull in order to get the infrastructure to work. This means that the assembly with the Repositories needs a reference to an infrastructure DLL. And this in its turn means that you have to choose between whether you want the Repositories in a separate DLL, separate from the Domain Model, or whether you want the Domain Model to reference an infrastructure DLL (but we will discuss a solution soon that will give you flexibility regarding this).

Problems Testing Repositories

It's also the case that when you want to test your Repositories, they are connected to the O/R Mapper and the database.

Note

Let's for the moment assume that we will use an O/R Mapper. We'll get back to a more thorough discussion about different options within a few chapters.

Suddenly this provides you with a pretty tough testing experience compared to when you test the Entities and Value Objects in isolation.

Of course, what you could do is mock your O/R Mapper. I haven't done that myself, but it feels a bit bad on the "bang for the bucks" rating. It's probably quite a lot of work compared to the return.

Problems Doing Small Scale Integration Testing

In previous chapters I haven't really shown any test code that focused on the Repositories at all. Most of the interesting tests should use the Domain Model. If not, it might be a sign that your Domain Model isn't as rich as it should be if you are going to get the most out of it.

That said, I did use Repositories in some tests, but really more as small integration tests to see that the cooperation between the consumer, the Entities, and the Repositories worked out as planned. As a matter of fact, that's one of the advantages Repositories have compared to other approaches for giving persistence capabilities to Domain Models, because it was easy to write Fake versions of the Repositories. The problem was that I wrote quite a lot of dumb code that has to be tossed away later on, or at least rewritten in another assembly where the Repositories aren't just Fake versions.

What also happened was that the semantics I got from the Fake versions wasn't really "correct." For instance, don't you think the following seems strange?

```
[Test]
public void FakeRepositoryHaveIncorrectSemantics()
{
    OrderRepository r1 = new OrderRepository();
    OrderRepository r2 = new OrderRepository();

    Order o = new Order();

    r1.Add(o);
    x.PersistAll();

    //This is fine:
    Assert.IsNotNull(r1.GetOrder(o.Id));
```

```
//This is unexpected I think:
Assert.IsNull(r2.GetOrder(o.Id));
}
```

> ## Note
>
> As the hawk-eyed reader saw, I decided to change AddOrder() to Add() since the last chapter.

I'm getting a bit ahead of myself in the previous code because we are going to discuss save scenarios shortly. Anyway, what I wanted to show was that the Fake versions of Repositories used so far don't work as expected. Even though I thought I had made all changes so far persistent with PersistAll(), only the first Repository instance could find the order, not the second Repository instance. You might wonder why I would like to write code like that, and it's a good question, but it's a pretty big misbehavior in my opinion.

What we could do instead is mock each of the Repositories, to test out the cooperation with the Entities, Repositories, and consumer. This is pretty cheaply done, and it's also a good way of testing out the consumer and the Entities. However, the test value for the Repositories themselves isn't big, of course. We are kind of back to square one again, because what we want then is to mock out one step further, the O/R Mapper (if that's what is used for dealing with persistence), and we have already talked about that.

Earlier Approach

So it's good to have Repositories in the first place, especially when it comes to testability. Therefore I used to swallow the bitter pill and deal with this problem by creating an interface for each Repository and then creating two implementing classes, one for Fake and one for real infrastructure. It could look like this. First, an interface in the Domain Model assembly:

```
public interface ICustomerRepository
{
    Customer GetById(int id);
    IList GetByNamePattern(string namePattern);
    void Add(Customer c);
}
```

Then two classes (for example, FakeCustomerRepository and MyInfrastructureCustomerRepository) will be located in two different assemblies (but all in one namespace, that of the Domain Model, unless of course there are several partitions of the Domain Model). See Figure 6-1.

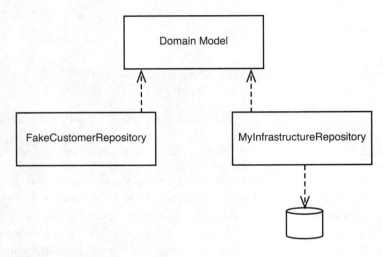

Figure 6-1   Two Repository assemblies

That means that the Domain Model itself won't be affected by the chosen infrastructure when it comes to the Repositories, which is nice if it doesn't cost anything.

But it does cost. It also means that I have to write two Repositories for each Aggregate root, and with totally different Repository code in each case.

Further on, it means that the production version of the Repositories lives in another assembly (and so do the Fake Repositories), even though I think Repositories are part of the Domain Model itself. "Two extra assemblies," you say, "That's no big deal." But for a large application where the Domain Model is partitioned into several different assemblies, you'll learn that typically it doesn't mean two extra assemblies for the Repositories, but rather the amount of Domain Model assemblies multiplied by three. That is because each Domain Model assembly will have its own Repository assemblies.

Even though I think it's a negative aspect, it's not nearly as bad as my having the silly code in the Fake versions of the Repositories. That feels just bad.

A Better Solution?

The solution I decided to try out was creating an abstraction layer that I call NWorkspace [Nilsson NWorkspace]. It's a set of adapter interfaces, which I have written implementations for in the form of a Fake. The Fake is just two levels of hashtables, one set of hashtables for the persistent Entities (simulating a database) and one set of hashtables for the Unit of Work and the Identity Map. (The Identity Map keeps track of what identities, typically primary keys, are currently loaded.)

POCO as a
Lifestyle

The other implementation I have written is for a specific O/R Mapper.

Note

When I use the name NWorkspace from now on, you should think about it as a "persistence abstraction layer." NWorkspace is just an example and not important in itself.

Thanks to that abstraction layer, I can move the Repositories back to the Domain Model, and I only need one Repository implementation per Aggregate root. The same Repository can work both against an O/R Mapper and against a Fake that won't persist to a database but only hold in memory hashtables of the instances, but with similar semantics as in the O/R Mapper-case. See Figure 6-2.

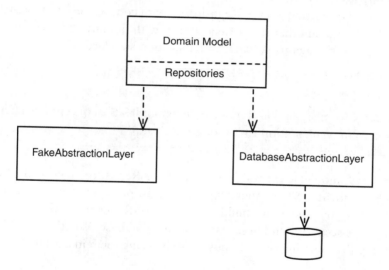

Figure 6-2   A single set of Repositories thanks to an abstraction layer

The Fake can also be serialized to/deserialized from files, which is great for creating very competent, realistic, and at the same time extremely refactoring-friendly early versions of your applications.

Another possibility that suddenly feels like it could be achieved easily (for a small abstraction layer API at least) could be to Mock the infrastructure instead of each of the Repositories. As a matter of fact, it won't be a matter of Mocking one infrastructure-product, but all infrastructure products that at one time will have adapter implementations for the abstraction layer (if that happens, that there will be other implementations than those two I wrote—it's probably not

POCO as a
Lifestyle

that likely). So more to the point, what is then being Mocked is the abstraction layer.

It's still a stretch to talk about PI Repositories, but with this solution I can avoid a reference to the infrastructure in the Domain Model. That said, in real-world applications I have kept the Repositories in a separate assembly anyway. I think it clarifies the coupling, and it also makes some hacks easier to achieve and then letting some Repository methods use raw SQL where that proves necessary (by using connection strings as markers for whether optimized code should be used or not).

However, instead of referring to the Persistence Framework, I have to refer to the NWorkspace DLL with the adapter interfaces, but that seems to be a big step in the right direction. It's also the case that there are little or no distractions in the Repositories; they are pretty "direct" (that is, if you find the NWorkspace API in any way decent).

So instead of writing a set of Repositories with code against an infrastructure vendor's API and another set of Repositories with dummy code, you write one set of Repositories against a (naïve) attempt for a standard API.

POCO as a
Lifestyle

> ### Note
>
> I'm sorry for nagging, but I must say it again: It's the concept I'm after! My own implementation isn't important at all.

Let's find another term for describing those Repositories instead of calling the PI Repositories. What about *single-set Repositories*? OK, we have a term for now for describing when we build a single set of Repositories that can be used both in Fake scenarios and in scenarios with a database. What's probably more interesting than naming those Repositories is seeing them in action.

Some Code in a Single-Set Repository

To remind you what the code in a Fake version of a Repository could look like, here's a method from Chapter 5:

```
//OrderRepository, a Fake version
public Order GetOrder(int orderNumber)
{
    foreach (Order o in _theOrders)
    {
        if (o.OrderNumber == orderNumber)
            return o;
    }
    return null;
}
```

OK, that's not especially complex, but rather silly, code.

If we assume that the OrderNumber is an Identity Field [Fowler PoEAA] (Identity Field means a field that binds the row in the database to the instance in the Domain Model) of the Order, the code could look like this when we use the abstraction layer (_ws in the following code is an instance of IWorkspace, which in its turn is the main interface of the abstraction layer):

```
//OrderRepository, a single-set version
public Order GetOrder(int orderNumber)
{
    return (Order)_ws.GetById(typeof(Order), orderNumber);
}
```

Pretty simple and direct I think. And—again—that method is done now, both for Fake and for when real infrastructure is used!

The Cost for Single-Set Repositories

So I have yet another abstraction. Phew, there's getting to be quite a lot of them, don't you think? On the other hand, I believe each of them adds value.

Still, there's a cost, of course. The most obvious cost for the added abstraction layer is probably the translation at runtime that has to be done for the O/R Mapper you're using. In theory, the O/R Mapper could have a native implementation of the abstraction layer, but for that to happen some really popular such abstraction layer must be created.

Then there's a cost for building the abstraction layer and the adapter for your specific O/R Mapper. That's the typical framework-related problem. It costs a lot for building the framework, but it can be used many times, if the framework *ever* becomes useful.

With some luck, there will be an adapter implementation for the infrastructure you are using and then the cost isn't yours, at least not the framework-building cost. There's more, though. You have to learn not only the infrastructure of your choice, but also the abstraction layer, and that can't be neglected.

POCO as a Lifestyle

Note

It was easier in the past as you only had to know a little about Cobol and files. Now you have to be an expert on C# or Java, Relational Databases, SQL, O/R Mappers, and so on, and so forth. If someone tries to make the whole thing simpler by adding yet another layer, that will tip the scales, especially for newcomers.

Yet another cost is, of course, that the abstraction layer will be kind of the least common denominator. You won't find all the power there that you can find in your infrastructure of choice. Sure, you can always bypass the abstraction layer, but that comes with a cost of complexity and external Repository code, and so on. So it's important to investigate whether your needs could be fulfilled with the abstraction layer to 30%, 60%, or 90%. If it's not a high percentage, it's questionable whether it's interesting at all.

Ok, let's return to the consumer for a while and focus on save functionality for a change.

Dealing with Save Scenarios

As I said at the end of the previous chapter, I will move faster from now on and not discuss all the steps in my thought process. Instead it will be more like going directly to the decided solution. Not decided as in "done," but decided as in "for now."

With that said, I'd still like to discuss tests, especially as a way of clarification.

Dealing
with Save
Scenarios

Now I'd like to discuss save scenarios from the consumer's point of view. So here's a test for showing how to save two new Customers:

```
[Test]
Public void CanSaveTwoCustomers()
{
    int noOfCustomersBefore =
        _GetNumberOfStoredCustomers();

    Customer c = new Customer();
    c.Name = "Volvo";
    _customerRepository.Add(c);

    Customer c2 = new Customer();
    c2.Name = "Saab";
    _customerRepository.Add(c2);

    Assert.AreEqual(noOfCustomersBefore,
        _GetNumberOfStoredCustomers());

    _ws.PersistAll();

    Assert.AreEqual(noOfCustomersBefore + 2,
        _GetNumberOfStoredCustomers());
}
```

At first glance, the code just shown is pretty simple, but it "hides" lots of things we haven't discussed before. First, it reveals what kind of consumer code I want to be able to write. I want to be able to do a lot of stuff to several different instances, and then persist all the work with a single call such as PersistAll(). (The call to _GetNumberOfStoredCustomers() goes to the persistence engine to check the number of persistent customers. It's not until after PersistAll() that the number of persistent customers has increased.)

A missing piece of the puzzle is that the Repository was fed with the _ws at instantiation time. In this way, I can control the Repositories that should participate in the same Unit of Work and those that should be isolated in another Unit of Work.

Yet another thing that might be interesting is that I ask the Repositories for help (the Add() call) in notifying the Unit of Work that there is a new instance for persisting at next PersistAll() call. I'm referring to the life cycle I want to have for a persistent instance (I touched on this in Chapter 5, so I won't repeat it here).

What I think is worth pointing out is that if I expect it to be enough to associate the Aggregate root with the Unit of Work, the instances that are part of the Aggregate and that the Aggregate root reaches will get persisted to the database as well when we say PersistAll().

Again, Aggregates assist us well; they provide a tool for knowing the size of graph that will be persisted because the Aggregate root is marked for being persisted. Again, Aggregates make for simplification.

Dealing with Save Scenarios

Note

O/R Mappers are often able to be configured for how far the reach of persist by reachability should go. But even when they are configured that way, the Aggregates are a very good guide in my opinion. What I mean is that I use the Aggregates for determining how far the reachability should reach, when I do the configuration.

Let's take a closer look at the reasoning behind the decisions discussed so far.

Reasons for the Decisions

Why did I choose as I did? First, I want to use the Unit of Work pattern. I want its characteristics: to create a logical Unit of Work.

So you can make lots of changes to the Domain Model, collect the information in the Unit of Work, and then ask the Unit of Work to save the collected changes to the database.

There are several styles of Unit of Work to use. The one I prefer is to make it as transparent as possible for the consumer and therefore the only message needed is to say Add() to the Repository (which in turn will talk to the Unit of Work).

If the reconstitution is done via the Repository, the Unit of Work-implementation can inject some object that can collect information about changes. Otherwise, there can be a snapshot taken at read time that will be used to control the changes by the Unit of Work at persist time.

I also chose to control save or not save (PersistAll()) outside of the Repositories. In this particular example, I could just as well have had PersistAll() directly on the CustomerRepository, but I chose not to. Why? Why not let Repositories hide Unit of Work completely? Well, I could, but I often find that I want to synchronize changes to several Aggregates (and therefore also to several different Repositories) in a single logical unit, and that's the reason. So code like this is not only possible to write, but also very typical:

```
Customer c = new Customer();
_customerRepository.Add(c);

Order o = new Order();
_orderRepository.Add(o);

_ws.PersistAll();
```

One alternative might be the following:

```
Customer c = new Customer();
_customerRepository.Add(c);
_customerRepository.PersistAll();

Order o = new Order();
_orderRepository.Add(o);
_orderRepository.PersistAll();
```

But then I have two different Unit of Work instances and two Identity Maps (it doesn't *have* to be that way, but let's assume it for the sake of the discussion), which can give pretty strange effects if we aren't very careful. After all, all five lines in the first example were one scenario, and because of that I find it most intuitive and appropriate to treat it like one scenario regarding how I deal with the Unit of Work and Identity Map as well. I mean, the scenario should just have one Unit of Work and one Identity Map.

Another thing that might be a problem is that when the Repository hid the Unit of Work it probably meant that there were two database transactions. That in turn means that you might have to prepare to add compensating operations when the outcome of a scenario isn't as expected. In the previous case, it's probably not too disastrous if the Customer is added to the database but not the Order. However, it can be a problem, depending upon your Aggregate design.

That said, Aggregates "should" be designed so that they are in a consistent state at PersistAll() time. But the loose relationship between Aggregates doesn't typically live under such strict requirements. That might make you like the second solution. On the other hand, the second solution would store two totally unrelated customers in the same PersistAll() if both of those customers were associated to the Repository. That is actually less important than grouping a customer and its orders together. Aggregates are about objects, not classes.

What speaks for the solution in the second example is if one Aggregate comes from one database and the other Aggregate is stored in another database at another database server. Then it's probably easiest to have two Unit of Work-instances anyway, one for each database. So, solution two is slightly less coupled.

Dealing
with Save
Scenarios

Note

I could even let Add() fulfill the transaction, but then I have different semantics from those I have discussed and expressed so far. It would be crucial to call Add() at the right point in time. This is less important with the solution I have chosen, as long as the call is done before PersistAll().

With Add() fulfilling the transaction, it would also mean that it's certainly not a matter of "gather all changes and persist them all at PersistAll()," which again is very different from my current solution.

While we're at it, why not then encapsulate the whole thing in the Entity instead so that you can write the following code?

```
Customer c = new Customer()
c.Name = "Saab";
c.Save();
```

I think it's moving away from the style I like. I think it breaks the *Single Responsibility Principle* (SRP) [Martin PPP], and it's low PI-level. I think I'm also moving into "matter of taste" territory.

I also have a problem with inconsistency if one save goes well and others do not. (You could argue that physical transaction and Unit of Work don't *have* to be the same, but that increases complexity in my opinion. The way I see it is if you don't have to do something, you shouldn't.)

However, by using my favorite technique, there's nothing to stop me from getting the same effects of storing one Aggregate at a time if I really want to by letting the Repositories hide the Unit of Work and Identity Map. It could then look like this:

```
Customer c = new Customer();
_customerRepository.Add(c);
_ws1.PersistAll();

Order o = new Order();
_orderRepository.Add(o);
_ws2.PersistAll();
```

Note

For the previous scenario, the end result would be the same with a single _ws, but that depended on the specific example.

**Dealing
with Save
Scenarios**

What I mean is that I *can* have one Unit of Work/Identity Map when I so wish, and several when I so wish. I think this is slightly more flexible, which I like a lot, and this is one more reason for my choice; namely that I currently prefer to see the Unit of Work as something belonging to the consumer of the Domain Model (that is the Application layer or the presentation layer) rather than the Domain Model itself.

If we assume that each Repository has its own Identity Map, it can get a bit messy if the same order is referenced from two different Repositories, at least if you make changes to the same logical order (but two different instances) in both Repositories.

As far as risks are concerned, what it boils down to is which risk you prefer. The risk of committing instances that you weren't done with because a PersistAll() call will deal with more instances than you expected? Or the risk of forgetting to commit a change because you'll have to remember what Repositories to ask to do PersistAll().

I'm not saying that it's a solution without problems, but again, I prefer the Identity Map *and* the Unit of Work to belong to the scenario.

> ### Note
>
> Deciding on what programming model you want is up to you, as usual. There are pros and cons to each.

I have mentioned Unit of Work and Identity Map together over and over again. It's such a common combination, not only in my text, but in products as well. For example, there is Persistence Manager in JDO [Jordan/Russell JDO] and Session in Hibernate [Bauer/King HiA].

I thought it might deserve a pattern, and I was thinking about writing it up, but when I discussed it with Martin Fowler he notified me that he discusses that in [Fowler PoEAA] when he talks about Identity Map and Unit of Work. That's more than enough, so I decided not to repeat more about that.

OK, now there's been a lot of talk and no action. Let's start building the Fake mechanism and see where we end up.

Let's Build the Fake Mechanism

Let's move on in an interface-based way for a while, or at least for a start. I have already touched on a couple of the methods, but let's start from the beginning. A reduced version of the interface of the abstraction layer (which I earlier in the chapter already called IWorkspace) could look like this:

```
public interface IWorkspace
{
    object GetById(Type typeToGet, object idValue);
    void MakePersistent(object o);
    void PersistAll();
}
```

So far the whole interface is pretty straightforward. The first method is called GetById() and is used for reconstituting an object from the database. You say what type you expect and the identity value of the object.

The second method, called MakePersistent(), is used for associating new instances with the IWorkspace instance so that they will be persisted at next PersistAll(). Finally, PersistAll() is for persisting what is found in the Unit of Work into the database.

MakePersistent() isn't needed if you have read the instance from the database with GetById(), because then the instance is already associated with the Unit of Work.

So far I think you'll agree that the API is extremely simple, and I think it is very important in order to keep complexity down in this abstraction layer. OK, it's not all that competent yet, so we need to add more.

More Features of the Fake Mechanism

The first thing that springs to mind is that we need to deal with transactions as a very important concept, at least from a correctness standpoint. On the other hand, it's not something that is important for most UI-programmers. (We could swap "UI-programmers" for "UI-code" just as well.) What I mean is that I don't want to put the responsibility for transaction management on the UI-programmer because it's too much of a distraction for him—and too important to be seen as a distraction. Still, I want adaptable transaction scope so that there isn't only a predefined set of possible transactions.

So my goals are pretty similar to those of declarative transactions in COM+, but I have chosen a pretty different API. Instead of setting attributes on the classes for describing whether they require transactions or not, I will just say that `PersistAll()` internally does all its work in an explicit transaction, even though you explicitly didn't ask for it

I know that on the face of it this feels overly simple to many old-timers. That goes for me as well, because I believe transaction handling is so important that I like to deal with it manually. If the goal is to be able to deal with something like 90% of the situations, however, I think `PersistAll()` could very well use an explicit transaction, and it's as simple as that.

Again, it sounds way too simplistic, and of course there are problems. One typical problem is logging. Assume that you log to the database server; you don't always want the logging operation to fail if the ordinary work fails. However, that's simple to deal with; you just use a separate workspace instance for the logging. If you want it to use the abstraction layer at all, the logging will probably just be implemented as a Service instead, which probably has nothing to do with the abstraction layer. As a matter of fact, there's a good chance that you will use a third-party product for logging, or perhaps something like log4net [Log4Net]. It's not something that will interfere with or be disturbed by the transaction API of the abstraction layer.

Another problem is that there might well be a need for the `GetById()` method to live in the same transaction as the upcoming `PersistAll()`. That won't happen by default, but if you want to force that, you can call the following method before `GetById()`:

```
void BeginReadTransaction(TransactionIsolationLevel til)
```

To emphasize this even more, there is also an overload to `GetById()` to ask for an exclusive lock, but this comes with a warning tag. Make sure you know what

Let's Build the Fake Mechanism

you're doing when you use this! For example, there should be no user interaction whatsoever after `BeginReadTransaction()` or read with exclusive lock and before `PersistAll()`.

But I digress—what is important for the Fake? Because the Fake only targets single-user scenarios, the transactional semantics aren't very important, and for reasons of simplicity those will probably not be dealt with at all. Still, the consumer code can be written with transaction-handling in mind when the Fake is used, of course, so you don't have to change the code when it comes to swapping the Fake for the real infrastructure.

I hear the now very frightened experienced developer exclaim, "Hey, what happened to `Rollback()`?"

Well, the way I see it, it's not important to have rollback in the API. If `PersistAll()` is responsible for commit or rollback internally, what will happen then is that when the consumer gets the control back from `PersistAll()`, all changes or none have been persisted. (The consumer is notified about a rollback by an exception.)

The exception to this is when you are after `BeginReadTransaction()` and you then want to cancel. Then you call the following method:

```
void Clean()
```

It will roll back the ongoing transaction and will also clean the Unit of Work and the Identity Map. It's a good idea to use `Clean()` after a failed transaction because there will be no attempt at all in NWorkspace to roll back the changes in Domain Model instances. Sure, it depends upon what the problem with the failed transaction was, but the simple answer is to restart.

Some problems can lead to a retry within `PersistAll()`. In the case of a deadlock, for example, `PersistAll()` can retry a couple of times before deciding it was a failure. This is yet another thing that simplifies life for the consumer programmer so that she can focus on what is important to her, namely to create a good user experience, not following lots and lots of protocols.

Now we have talked a lot about the functionality that is important for NWorkspace, but not for the Fake version of NWorkspace. Let's get back on track and focus for a while on the Fake and its implementation instead.

The Implementation of the Fake

I'm not going to drag you through the details of the Fake implementation—I'm just going to talk conceptually about how it's built, mostly in order to get a feeling for the basic idea and how it can be used.

The fake implementation uses two layers of Identity Maps. The first layer is pretty similar to ordinary Identity Maps in persistence frameworks, and it keeps track of all Entities that you have read within the current scenario. The second layer of Identity Maps is for simulating the persistent engine, so here the instances aren't kept on a scenario level, but on a global level (that is, the same set of Identity Maps for all scenarios).

So when you issue a call to GetById(), if the ID is found in the Identity Map for the requested type, there won't be a roundtrip to the database (or in case of the Fake, there won't be a jump to the second layer of Identity Maps). On the other hand, if the ID isn't found in the first layer of Identity Maps, it's fetched from the second layer, copied to the first layer, and then returned to the consumer.

The MakePersistent() is pretty simple; the instance is just associated with the first layer of Identity Maps. And when it's time for PersistAll(), all instances in the first layer are copied to the second layer. Simple and clean.

This describes the basic functionality. Still, it might be interesting to say a bit about what's troublesome, also. One example is that I don't want the Fake to influence the Domain Model in any way at all. If it does, we're back to square one, adding infrastructure-related distractions to the Domain Model, or even worse, Fake-related distractions.

One example of a problem is that I don't know which is the Identity field(s) of a class. In the case of the real infrastructure, it will probably know that by some metadata. I could read that same metadata in the Fake to find out, but then the Fake must know how to deal with (theoretically) several different metadata formats, and I definitely don't like that.

The simplistic solution I've adopted is to assume a property (or field) called Id. If the developer of the Domain Model has used another convention, it could be described to the Fake at instantiation of the FakeWorkspace.

Again, this was more information than you probably wanted now, but it leads us to the important fact that there are additional things that you can/ need to do in the instantiation phase of the Fake compared to the infrastructure implementations of NWorkspace.

To take another example, you can read from file/save to file like this:

```
//Some early consumer
IWorkspace ws = new
    NWorkspaceFake.FakeWorkspace("c:/temp/x.nworkspace");

//Do stuff...

((NWorkspaceFake.FakeWorkspace)ws).
    PersistToFile("c:/temp/x.nworkspace");
```

We talked quite a lot about PI and the Fake mechanism in a way that might lead you to believe that you must go for a PI-supporting infrastructure later on if you choose to use something like the Fake mechanism now. This is not

Let's Build the Fake Mechanism

the case at all. It's not even true that non-PI-supporting infrastructure makes it harder for you to use TDD. It's traditionally the case, but not a must.

Speaking of TDD, has the Fake affected our unit tests much yet?

Affecting the Unit Tests

Nope, certainly not all tests will be affected. Most tests should be written with classes in the Domain Model in as isolated a way as possible, without a single call to Repositories. For instance, they should be written during development of all the logic that should typically be around in the Domain Model classes. Those tests aren't affected at all.

The unit tests that should deal with Repositories are affected, and in a positive way. It might be argued that these are more about integration testing, but it doesn't have to be that way. Repositories are units, too, and therefore tests on them are unit tests.

And even when you do integration testing with Repositories involved, it's nice to be able to write the tests early and to write them (and the Repositories) in a way so that it is possible to use them when you have infrastructure in place as well.

I think a nice goal is to get all the tests in good shape so that they can run both with the Fake mechanism and the infrastructure. That way you can execute with the Fake mechanism in daily work (for reasons of execution time) and execute with the infrastructure a couple of times a day and at the automatic builds at check in.

You can also work quite a long way without infrastructure in place. You must, of course, also think a bit about persistence, and especially for your first DDD projects, it's important to work iteratively from the beginning. But when you get more experience, delaying the addition of the persistence will give you the shortest development time in total and the cleanest code.

This also gives you the possibility of another refactoring rhythm, with more instant feedback whether you like the result or not. First, you get everything to work with the Fake (which is easier and faster than getting the whole thing, including the database, to the right level), and if you're happy then you proceed to get it all to work with the infrastructure. I believe the big win is that this will encourage you to be keener to do refactorings that would normally just be a pain, especially when you are unsure about the outcome. Now you can give them a try pretty easily.

Of course, trying to avoid code duplication is as important for unit tests as it is for the "real" code. (Well, at least close to as important. There's also a competing strive to "show it all" inline.) Therefore I only want to write the tests once, but be able to execute them both for the Fake and the real infrastructure when in place. (Please note that this only goes for some of the tests of course. Most of the tests aren't about the Repositories at all so it's important that you partition your tests for this aspect.)

Structure of the Repository-Related Tests

One way of approaching this is to write a base class for each set of tests that are Repository-affecting. Then I use the Template Method pattern for setting up an IWorkspace the way I want. It could look like this, taking the base class first:

```
[TestFixture]
public abstract class CustomerRepositoryTestsBase
{
    private IWorkspace _ws;
    private CustomerRepository _repository;

    protected abstract IWorkspace _CreateWorkspace();

    [SetUp]
    public void SetUp()
    {
        _ws = _CreateWorkspace();
        _repository = new CustomerRepository(_ws);
    }

    [TearDown]
    public void TearDown()
    {
        _ws.Clean();
    }
}
```

Let's Build
the Fake
Mechanism

Then the subclass, which looks like this:

```
public class CustomerRepositoryTestsFake :
        CustomerRepositoryTestsBase
{
    protected override IWorkspace _CreateWorkspace()
    {
        return new FakeWorkspace("");
    }
}
```

OK, that was the plumbing for the tests related to Repositories, but what about the tests themselves? Well, there are several different styles from which to choose, but the one I prefer is to define as much as possible in the base class, while at the same time making it possible to decide in the subclass if a certain test should be implemented or not at the moment. I also want it to be impossible to forget to implement a test in the subclass. With those requirements in place, my favorite style looks like this (first, how a simplified test looks in the base class):

```
[Test]
public virtual void CanAddCustomer()
{
    Customer c = new Customer();
    c.Name = "Volvo";
    c.Id = 42;
    _repository.Add(c);
    _ws.PersistAll();
    _ws.Clean();

    //Check
    Customer c2 = _repository.GetById(c.Id);
    Assert.AreEqual(c.Name, c2.Name);

    //Clean up
    _repository.Delete(c2);
    _ws.PersistAll();
}
```

Note that the second level of Identity Maps isn't cleared when new FakeWorkspace("") is done because the second level Identity Maps of the Fake are static and therefore not affected when the Fake *instance* is recreated. That's just how it is with a database, of course. Just because you open a new connection doesn't mean the Customers table is cleared.

So it's a good thing that the Fake works in this way, because then I will need to clean up after the tests with the Fake just as I will when I'm using the tests with a real database, *if* that's the approach I'm choosing for my database testing.

Of course, IWorkspace must have Delete() functionality, which I haven't discussed yet, otherwise it won't be possible to do the cleaning up. As a matter of fact, in all its simplicity the Delete() is quite interesting because it requires an Identity Map of its own for the Fake in the Unit of Work. Instances that have been registered for deletion will be held there until PersistAll(), when the deletion is done permanently.

To support this, IWorkspace will get a method like this:

```
void Delete(object o);
```

Unfortunately, it also introduces a new problem. What should happen to the relationships for the deleted object? That's not simple. Again, more metadata is needed to determine how far the delete should cascade—metadata that is around for the real infrastructure, but not useful here. (The convention currently used for the Fake is to not cascade.)

OK, back to the tests. In the subclass, I typically have one of three choices when it comes to the CanAddCustomer() test. The first alternative is to do nothing, in which case I'm going to run the test as it's defined in the base class. This is hopefully what I want.

The second option should be used if you aren't supporting a specific test for the specific subclass for the time being. Then it looks like this in the subclass:

```
[Test, Ignore("Not supported yet...")]
public override void CanAddCustomer() {}
```

This way, during test execution it will be clearly signaled that it's just a temporary ignore.

Finally, if you "never" plan to support the test in the subclass, you can write it like this in the subclass:

```
[Test]
public override void CanAddCustomer()
{
    Console.WriteLine
        ("CanAddCustomer() isn't supported by Fake.");
}
```

OK, you still *can* forget a test if you do your best. You'd have to write code like this, skipping the Test-attribute:

```
public override void CanAddCustomer() {}
```

There's a solution to this, but I find the style I have shown you to be a good balance of amount of code and the risk of "forgetting" tests.

I know, this wasn't YAGNI, because right now we don't have any implementation other than the Fake implementation, but see this just as a quick indicator for what will happen later on.

Let's Build the Fake Mechanism

Note

This style could just as well be used in the case of multiple implementations for each Repository.

For many applications, it might be close to impossible to deal with the whole system in this way, especially later on in the life cycle. For many applications, it's perhaps only useful for early development testing and early demos, but even so, if it helps with this, it's very nice. If it works all the way, it's even nicer.

In real life, the basics (there are always exceptions) are that I'm focusing on writing the core of the tests against the Fake implementation. I also write CRUD tests against the Fake implementation, but in those cases I also inherit to tests for using the database. That way, I test out the mapping details.

That said, no matter if you use something like the ideas of the abstraction layer or not, you will sooner or later run into the problems of database testing. I asked my friend Philip Nelson to write a section about it. Here goes.

Database Testing

By Philip Nelson

At some point when you are working with DDD and all the various flavors of automated testing, you will probably run into a desire to run a test that includes access to a database. When you first encounter this, it seems like no problem at all. Create a test database, point your application at the test database, and start testing.

Let's focus more on automated testing, so let's assume you wrote your first test with JUnit or NUnit. This test just loaded a User domain object from the database and verified that all the properties were set correctly. You can run this test over and over again and it works every time. Now you write a test to verify that you can update the fields, and because you know you have a particular object in the database, you update that.

The test works, but you have introduced a problem. The read test no longer works because you have just changed the underlying data, and it no longer matches the expectations of your first test. OK, that's no problem; these tests shouldn't share the same data, so you create a different User for the update test. Now both tests are independent of each other, and this is important: at all times you need to ensure that there are no residual effects between tests. Database-backed tests always have preconditions that you must meet. Somewhere in the process of writing your tests, you must account for the fact that you have to reset the database to meet the preconditions the test expects. More details on that to come.

At some point, you will have written tests for all the basic User object life cycle states, let's say *create, read, update,* and *delete* (CRUD). In your application, there may very well be other database-backed operations. For example, the User object may help enforce a policy of maximum failed login attempts. As you test the updating of the failed login attempts and last login time fields, you realize that your update actually isn't working. The update test didn't catch the problem because the database already had the field set to the expected value. As the smart person you are, you figured this out very quickly. However, young Joe down the hall has just spent four hours working on the problem. His coding skills aren't so much the problem as much as his understanding of how the code connects to the database and how to isolate the data in this test from all the other test data he now has. He just doesn't notice that the LastUpdateDate field is not reset between tests. After all, the code is designed to hide the database as an implementation detail, right?

Database
Testing

At this point, you start to realize that just having separate test data for each test is going to be more complicated than you want it to be. You may or may not have understood as clearly as necessary just how important it was to reset the data between tests, but now you do. Fortunately, your xUnit test framework has just the thing for you. There is a setup and teardown code block that is just made for this sort of thing. But like most things in programming, there is more than one way to do it, and each has its strengths and weaknesses. You must understand the tradeoffs and determine the balance that suits you best.

I would categorize the techniques available to you in four ways:

- Reset the database before each test.

- Maintain the state of the database during the run.

- Reset the data for just the test or set of tests you are running before the run.

- Separate the testing of the unit from the testing of the call to the database.

Reset the Database Before Each Test

At first glance, this might seem the most desirable, but possibly the most time-consuming, option. The plus to this approach is that the whole system is in a known state at the start of the test. You don't have to worry about strange interactions during test runs because they all start at the same place. The downside is time. After you have gotten past the initial parts of your project, you will find yourself waiting while your test suite runs. If you are doing unit testing and running your tests after each change, this can very quickly become a significant part of your time. There are some options that can help. How they apply to you will depend on many things, from the type of architecture you use to the type of database system you use.

One simple but slow approach is to restore the database from backup before each test. With many database systems, this is not practical because of the amount of time it takes. However, there are some systems where it is possible. If you are programming against a file-based database, for example, you may only need to close your connections and copy a file to get back to the original state. Another possibility is an in-memory database, such as HSQL for Java, that can be restored very quickly. Even if you are using a more standard system like Oracle or SQL Server, if your design for data access is flexible enough, you may be able to switch to an in-memory or file-based database for your tests. This is especially true if you are using an O/R Mapper that takes the responsibility of building the actual SQL calls for you and knows multiple dialects.

The project DbUnit offers another way to reset a database before the test runs. Essentially, it's a framework for JUnit that allows you to define "data sets" that are loaded on clean tables before each test run. Ruby on Rails has a similar system that allows you to describe your test class data in the open YAML (YAML Ain't Markup Language) format and apply it during test setup. These tools can work well, but you may start running into problems as these database inserts may be logged operations that can be too slow. Another approach that could work for you is to use bulk load utilities that may not be as extensively logged. Here is how this might work for SQL Server. First, use a database recovery option on your test database of Simple Recovery. This eliminates most logging and improves performance. Then, during test design, do the following:

- Insert data into a test database that will only act as a source of clean data for your tests

- Call transact sql commands that export the test data to files

- Write transact sql commands to do bulk insert of the data in these files

Then during the test setup method, do the following:

- Truncate all your tables. This is not a logged operation and can be very fast.

- Issue the bulk copy commands created earlier to load the test data into the test database.

A variation of this technique is to set up your test database and load the initial test data using normal data management techniques. Then, provided your database supports such an operation, detach the underlying data files from the server. Make a copy of these files as these will be the source of your clean test data. Then, write code that allows you to

- Detach the server from its data files

- Copy the clean test data over the actual server files

- Attach the database to the copy

In many cases, this operation is very fast and can be run in the test fixture setup or, if the amount of data isn't too large, in the test setup itself.

Yet another variation supported by some of the O/R Mapping tools is to build the database schema from mapping information. Then you can use your Domain Model in test setup to populate data as needed for each test suite or possibly for each test fixture.

Maintain the State of the Database During the Run

You are probably thinking "But that is a data management exercise!", and you are correct. There is another technique that is even simpler to execute. Essentially, what you do is to run each test in a transaction and then roll back the transaction at the end of the test. This could be a little challenging because transactions are not often exposed on public interfaces, but again, this all depends on your architecture. For MS .NET environments, Roy Osherove came up with a very simple solution that draws on ADO.NET's support for COM+ transaction enlistment. What this tool does is allow you to put a [Rollback] attribute on specific test methods, allowing those methods to be run in their own COM+ transaction. When the test method finishes, the transaction is then rolled back automatically for you with no code on your part and independent of the teardown functionality of the class.

What's really great about this technique is that your tests can be blissfully unaware of what's happening underneath them. This functionality has been packaged up in a project called XtUnit [XtUnit] and is an extension to the NUnit testing framework. This is by far the simplest approach to keeping your database in pristine shape. It does come with a price, though. Transactions are by their nature logged, which increases the execution time. COM+ transactions use the Distributed Transaction Coordinator, and distributed transactions are slower than local transactions. The combination can be brutal to the execution speed of your test suite.

Naturally, if you are testing transaction semantics themselves, you may have some additional problems with this technique. So depending on the specifics of your project, this can be a really great solution or a solution in need of a replacement as the number of tests grows. Fortunately, you would not necessarily have to rewrite much code should test speed become a problem because the solution is transparent to the test. You will either be able to live with it, or you will have to adopt other techniques as your project grows.

Reset the Data Used by a Test Before the Test

This approach relieves you and your system of having to reset the entire database before the test call. Instead, you issue a set of commands to the database before or after the test, again typically in the setup and/or teardown methods. The good news is that you have much less to do for a single class of tests. The previous techniques can still be used, but now you have the additional option of issuing simple insert, update, or delete statements as well. This is now less painful, even if logged, because the impact is less. Again, reducing the logging effort with database setup options is still a good idea if your system supports it.

Database
Testing

There is a downside, though. As soon as you make the leap to assuming you know exactly what data will be affected by your test, you have tied yourself into understanding what not just the code under test is doing with data, but also what additional code the code under test calls out to. It may get changed without you noticing it. Tests may break that are not an indication of broken code. A bug will get filed that may not be a bug at all but is maintenance work just the same.

It is possible to use this technique successfully, but after many years of test writing, I have found this approach to be the most likely to break without good reason. You can minimize this, though. If you mock out the classes your code under test calls out to, that code won't affect the database. This is in spirit much closer to what is meant by a unit test. Mocking is not useful if you are automating system tests where the interactions between real classes are exactly what you want to test. At any rate, doing this requires an architecture decision to allow for easy substitution of external classes by the testing framework. If you are going to do that, you have naturally found yourself working toward the final option I am covering here.

Don't Forget Your Evolving Schema!

You will no doubt find yourself making changes to the database over time. While in the initial stages you may want to just modify the database directly and adjust your code as needed, after you have a released system, it's time to think about how these changes should become part of your process. Working with a test system actually makes this easier.

I prefer the approach of creating and running alter scripts against your database. You could run these scripts immediately after your database reset, but because all that database state is contained in your source controlled development environment, it probably makes sense to develop the scripts and use them to modify your test environment. When your tests pass, you check it all in and then have the scripts automatically set up to run against your QA environment as needed.

It's even better if this happens on your build server because the running of the alter scripts is then tested often before it's applied to your live systems. Of course, that assumes you regularly reset your QA environment to match your live environment. I'm sure there are many variations of this process, but the most important thing is to plan ahead to ensure a reliable release of both code and database changes.

Separate the Testing of the Unit from the Testing of the Call to the Database

Few things in the Agile community's mailing lists and forums generate more discussion than the testing of code that interacts with databases. Among those who are practicing (and still defining) the techniques of TDD, it is a highly held value that all code can be tested independently as units as they are written. In the spirit of TDD, it wouldn't make sense to write a test for a class and start out your implementation with a direct call to a database. Instead, the call is delegated out to a different object that abstracts the database, which is replaced with a stub or a mock as you write the test. Then you write the code that actually implements the database abstraction, and test that *it* calls the underlying data access objects correctly. Finally, you would write a few tests that test that your infrastructure that connects real database calls to your code works correctly. As the old saying goes, most problems in coding can be solved with another layer of indirection. As always, the devil's in the details.

First, let's clarify a few definitions. A stub is a replacement piece of code that does just enough to not cause problems for the caller and no more. A stub for a database call, such as a call to a JDBC Statement, would be accomplished by having a bare-bones class that implements the Statement's interface and simply returns a ResultSet when called, possibly ignoring the parameters passed and certainly not executing a database call.

A mock Statement would do all that and also allow the setting of expectations. I'll say more on that in a moment. Like a stub, the test would use the mock command instead of the real command, but when the test was complete, it would "ask" the mock command to "verify" that it was called correctly. The *expectations* for a mock Statement would be values for any parameters the call needed, the number of times that executeQuery was called, the correct SQL to be passed to the statement and so on. In other words, you tell the mock what to expect. Then you ask it to *verify* that it did receive these expectations after the test is complete.

When you think about it, I think you have to agree that a unit test for a User class should not have to concern itself with what the database does. So long as the class interacts with the database abstraction correctly, we can assume the database will do its part correctly or at least that tests to your data access code will verify that fact for you. You just have to verify that the code correctly passes all the fields to the database access code, and you have done all you need to do. If only it could always be that simple!

To take this to its logical conclusion, you might end up writing mock implementations of many of the classes in your code. You will have to populate the members and properties of those mocks with at least enough data to satisfy

Database
Testing

the requirements of your tests. That's a lot of code, and an argument could be made that just having to support that much code will make your code harder to maintain. Consider this alternative. There are some new frameworks available in a variety of languages that allow you to create mock objects from the definitions of real classes or interfaces. These dynamically created mocks allow you to set expectations, set expected return values and do verification without writing much code to mock the class itself. Known collectively as Dynamic Mocks, the technique allows you to simply pass in the class to mock to a framework and get back an object that will implement its interface.

There are many other sources of information on how to mock code, but much less on how to effectively mock database access code. Data access code tends to have all these moving parts to deal with: connections, command objects, transactions, results, and parameters. The data access libraries themselves have driven the creation of a wide variety of data access helpers whose aim it is to simplify this code. It seems that none of these tools, the helpers, or the underlying data access libraries like JDBC or ADO.NET were written with testing in mind. While many of these tools offer abstractions on the data access, it turns out to be fairly tricky work to mock all those moving parts. There is also that issue of having to test the mapping of all those fields between the data access code and rest of your classes. So here are some pieces of advice to help you through it.

Test everything you can without actually hitting your database access code. The data access code should do as little as you can get away with. In most cases, this should be CRUD. If you are able to test all the functionality of your classes without hitting the database, you can write database tests that only exercise these simpler CRUD calls. With the aid of helper methods you may be able to verify that the before and after set of fields match your expectations by using reflection to compare the objects rather than hand coding all the property tests. This can be especially helpful if you use an O/R Mapper, such as Hibernate, where the data access is very nicely hidden, but the mapping file itself needs to be tested. If all the other functionality of the class is verified without the database hit, you often only need to verify that the class's CRUD methods and the mapping are working correctly.

Test that you have called the data access code correctly separately from testing the database code itself. For example, if you have a User class that saves via a UserRepository, or perhaps a Data Access Layer in nTier terminology, all you need to test is that the UserRepository is called correctly by your upper-level classes. Tests for the UserRepository would test the CRUD functionality with the database.

To test certain types of data access, these simple CRUD tests may not be adequate. For example, calls to stored procedures that aren't directly related to class persistence fall in this category. At some point, you may need to test that these procedures are called correctly, or in your test you may need data back from one of these calls for the rest of your test. Here are some general techniques to consider in those cases where you really are going to mock JDBC, ADO.NET, or some other data access library directly.

You must use factories to create the data access objects and program against interfaces rather than concrete types. Frameworks may provide factories for you, as the Microsoft Data Access Application Block does in its more recent versions. However, you also need to be able to use these factories to create mock implementations of the data access classes, something not supported out of the box by many factory frameworks. If you have a factory that can be configured by your test code to provide mocks, you can substitute a mock version of these data access classes. Then you can verify virtually any type of database call. You still may need mock implementations of these classes, though. For ADO.NET, these can be obtained from a project called .NET Mock Objects [MockObjects]. Versions for other environments may also be available. The only combination of a factory-based framework that can work with mocks directly that I am aware of is the SnapDAL framework [SnapDAL] that builds on .NET Mock Objects to supply mock implementations of the ADO.NET generic classes and was built to fully support mock objects for the ADO.NET generic interfaces.

Whether you can use these frameworks or not depends on many factors, but one way or another, you will need your application to support a factory that can return a real or a mock of your data access classes. When you get to a position where you can create mock instances of your data access classes, you can now use some or all of the following techniques to test:

- The mock returns result sets, acting as a stub for your code. The result set gets its data from the test code in standard mock object style.

- The mock can return test data from files, such as XML files or spreadsheets of acceptance test data provided by your business units.

- The mock can return test data from an alternate database or a more refined query than the real query under test.

- If you can substitute a data access command, you can "record" the data access and later "play it back" from a mock object in your tests because you would have access to all the parameters and the returned results.

- Mocks can have expectations verified of important things like the connection being opened and closed, transactions committed or rolled back, exceptions generated and caught, and data readers read, and so on.

Database Testing

I hope these ideas can get you started with an appreciation for the many possibilities there are for testing database-connected code. The text was written basically in order of complexity, with database resetting or the rollback techniques being the easiest to implement. Fully separating out the data access code from the rest of your code will always be a good move and will improve your testing success and test speed. At the most fine-grained level, allowing for mock versions of your actual database calls offers great flexibility in how you gather, provide, and organize test data. If you are working with legacy code that uses the lower-level data access libraries of your language, you would probably move toward this sort of approach. If you are starting a new application, you can probably start with the idea of simply resetting your database between tests and enhance your test structure as test speed begins to affect your productivity.

◆

Thanks, Phil! Now we are armed to deal with the problem of database testing no matter what approach we choose.

Note

Neeraj Gupta commented on this by saying, "You can use the Flashback feature of Oracle database to bring the database back to the previous state for the testing."

We have come quite a long way, but there is one very big piece of the preparing for infrastructure puzzle that we haven't dealt with at all. How did I solve _GetNumberOfStoredCustomers?

What I'm missing is obviously querying!

Querying

Querying is extremely different in different infrastructure solutions. It's also something that greatly risks affecting the consumer. It might not be apparent at first when you start out simply, but after a while you'll often find quite a lot of querying requirements, and while you are fulfilling those, you're normally tying yourself to the chosen infrastructure.

Let's take a step back and take another solution that is not query-based. Earlier, I showed you how to fetch by identity in a Repository with the following code:

```
//OrderRepository
public Order GetOrder(int orderNumber)
```

```
{
    return (Order)_ws.GetById(typeof(Order), orderNumber);
}
```

However, if `OrderNumber` isn't an identity, the interface of the Repository method must clearly change to return a list instead, because several orders can have ordernumber 0 before they have reached a certain state. But then what? `GetById()` is useless now, because `OrderNumber` isn't an Identity (and let's assume it's not unique because I said the answer could be a list). I need a way to get to the second layer of Identity Maps of the Fake for the `Orders`. Let's assume I could do that with a `GetAll(Type typeOfResult)` like this:

```
//OrderRepository
public IList GetOrders(int orderNumber)
{
    IList result = new ArrayList();
    IList allOrders = _ws.GetAll(typeof(Order));

    foreach (Order o in allOrders)
    {
        if (o.OrderNumber == orderNumber)
            result.Add(o);
    }

    return result;
}
```

It's still pretty silly code, and it's definitely not what you want to write when you have infrastructure in place, at least not for real-world applications.

Single-Set of Query Objects

Just as with the Repositories, it would be nice to write the queries "correctly" from day one in a single implementation which could be used both with the Fake and with the real infrastructure. How can we deal with that?

Let's assume that we want to work with Query Objects [Fowler PoEAA] (encapsulate queries as objects, providing object-oriented syntax for working with the queries) and we also change the signature from `GetAll()` to call it `GetByQuery()` and to let it take an `IQuery` (as defined in NWorkspace) instead. The code could now look like this:

```
//OrderRepository
public IList GetOrders(int orderNumber)
{
    IQuery q = new Query(typeof(Order));
    q.AddCriterion("OrderNumber", orderNumber);
    return _ws.GetByQuery(q);
}
```

OK, that was pretty straightforward. You just create an IQuery instance by saying which type you expect in the result. Then you set the criteria you want for holding down the size of the result set as much as possible, typically by processing the query in the database (or in the Fake code, in the case of when you're using the Fake implementation).

Note

We could pretty easily make the query interface more fluent, but let's stay with the most basic we can come up with for now.

That was what to do when you want to instantiate part of the Domain Model. Let's get back to the _GetNumberOfStoredCustomers() that we talked about earlier. How could that code look with our newly added querying tool? Let's assume it calls the Repository and a method like the following:

```
//CustomerRepository
public int GetNumberOfStoredCustomers()
{
    return _ws.GetByQuery(new Query(typeof(Customer))).Count;
}
```

It works, but for production scenarios that solution would reduce every DBA to tears. At least it will if the result is a SELECT that fetches all rows just so you can count how many rows there are. It's just not acceptable for most situations.

We need to add some more capabilities in the querying API. Here's an example where we have the possibility of returning simple types, such as an int, combined with an aggregate query (and this time aggregate isn't referring to the DDD pattern Aggregate, but, for example, to a SUM or AVG query in SQL):

```
//CustomerRepository
public int GetNumberOfStoredCustomers()
{
    IQuery q = new Query(typeof(Customer),
        new ResultField("CustomerNumber", Aggregate.Count));
    return (int)_ws.GetByQuery(q)[0];
}
```

A bit raw and immature, but I think that this should give you an idea of how the basic querying API in NWorkspace is designed.

It would be nice to have a standard querying language, wouldn't it? Perhaps the absence of one was what made Object Databases not really take off. Sure, there was Object Query Language (OQL), but I think it came in pretty late, and it was also a pretty complex standard to implement. It's competent, but complex. (Well, it was probably a combination of things that hindered Object Databases from becoming mainstream; isn't it always?) I'll talk more about Object Databases in Chapter 8, "Infrastructure for Persistence."

What I now want, though, is a querying standard for persistence frameworks—something as widespread as SQL, but for Domain Models. Until we have such a standard, the NWorkspace version could bridge the gap, for me at least. Is there a cost for that? Is there such a thing as a free lunch?

The Cost for Single-Set of Query Objects

Of course there's a cost for a transformation, and that goes for this case, too. First, there's a cost in performance for going from an IWorkspace implementation to the infrastructure solution. However, the performance cost will probably be pretty low in the context of end-to-end scenarios.

Then there's the cost of loss of power because the NWorkspace-API is simplified, and competent infrastructure solutions have more to offer and that is probably much worse. Yet another cost is that the API of NWorkspace itself is pretty raw and perhaps not as nice as the querying API of your infrastructure solution. OK, all those costs sound fair, and if there's a lot to be gained, I can live with them.

I left out one very important detail before about querying and the Identity Map: bypassing the cache when querying or not.

Querying and the Cache

I mentioned earlier that when you do a GetById(), if that operation must be fulfilled by going to persistence, the fetched instance will be added to the Identity Map before being returned to the consumer. That goes for GetByQuery() as well; that is, the instances will be added to the Identity Map.

However, there's a big difference in that the GetByQuery() won't investigate the Identity Map before hitting persistence. The reason is partly that we want to use the power of the backend, but above all that we don't know if we have all the necessary information in the Identity Map (or cache if you will) for fulfilling the query. To find out if we have that, we need to hit the database. This brings us to another problem. GetById() starts with the Identity Map; GetByQuery() does not. This is totally different behavior, and it actually means that GetByQuery() bypasses the cache, which is problematic. If you ask for the new Customer Volvo that has been added to the Identity Map/Unit of Work, but has not been persisted, it will be found if you ask by ID but not when you ask by name with a query. Weird.

To tell you the truth, it was a painful decision, but I decided to let GetByQuery()
do an implicit PersistAll() by *default* before going to the database. (There's an
override to GetByQuery() to avoid this, but again, it's the default to implicitly call
PersistAll().) I came to the conclusion that this default style is probably most in
line with the rest of NWorkspace and its goal of simplicity and the lessened risk
of errors. This is why I made some sacrifices with transactional semantics. Some
might argue that this violates the principle of least amount of surprise. But I
think it depends on your background, what is surprising in this case.

The biggest drawback is definitely that when doing GetByQuery(), you might get
save-related exceptions. What a painful decision—but I need to decide something for now to move on.

Do you remember the simple and unoptimized version of the _GetNumberOf-
StoredCustomers()? It's not just slow—it might not work as expected when it looks
like this (which goes for the optimized version as well):

```
public int GetNumberOfStoredCustomers()
{
    return _ws.GetByQuery(new Query(typeof(Customer))).Count;
}
```

The reason it won't work for my purpose is that GetByQuery() will do that
implicit PersistAll(). Instead, an overload must be used like this, where false is for
the implicitPersistAll parameter:

```
public int GetNumberOfStoredCustomers()
{
    return _ws.GetByQuery(new Query(typeof(Customer)
        , false)).Count;
}
```

Querying

Note

And of course we could (and should) use the aggregate version instead.
The focus here was how to deal with implicit PersistAll().

All this affects the programming model to a certain degree. First of all, you
should definitely try to adopt a style of working in blocks when it comes to querying and changing for the same workspace instance. So when you have made
changes, you should be happy about them before querying because querying
will make the changes persistent.

> ### Note
>
> You might be right. I might be responsible for fostering a sloppy style of consumer programmers. They just code and it works, even though they forget about saving explicitly and so on.

An unexpected and unwanted side effect is that you can get totally different exceptions from GetByQuery() from what you expect because the exception might really come from PersistAll(). Therefore, it's *definitely* a good idea to do the PersistAll() explicitly in the consumer code anyway.

And again, if you hate this behavior, there's nothing to stop you from using the overload. (Actually, with GetById() you could do it the other way around, so that an overload goes to the database regardless, without checking the Identity Map.) *"I don't care about my own transient work; I want to know what's in the database."*

That was a bit about how querying works in relation to the Identity Map. Next up is where to host the queries.

Where to Locate Queries

As I see it, we have at least the following three places in which to host query instances:

- In Repositories

- In consumers of Repositories

- In the Domain Model

Let's discuss them one by one.

In Repositories

Probably the most common place to set up queries is in the Repositories. Then the queries become the tool for fulfilling method requests, such as GetCustomersByName() and GetUndeliveredOrders(). That is, the consumer might send parameters to the methods, but those are just ordinary types and not Query Objects. The Query Objects are then set up in accordance with the method and possible parameter values.

In Consumers of Repositories

In the second case, the queries are set up in the consumers of the Repositories and sent to the Repositories as parameters. This is typically used in cases of highly flexible queries, such as when the user can choose to fill in any fields in a large filtering form. One such typical method on a Repository could be named `GetCustomersByFilter()`, and it takes an `IQuery` as parameter.

In the Domain Model

Finally, it might be interesting to set up typed Query Objects in the Domain Model (still queries that implement `IQuery` of NWorkspace). The consumer still gets the power of queries to be used for sending to Repositories, for example, but with a highly intuitive and typesafe API. How the API looks is, of course, totally up to the Domain Model developer.

Instead of the following simple typeless query:

```
//Consumer code
IQuery q = new Query(typeof(Customer));
q.AddCriterion("Name",
"Volvo");
```

the consumer could set up the same query with the following code:

```
//Consumer code
CustomerQuery q = new CustomerQuery();
q.Name.Eq("Volvo");
```

In addition to getting simpler consumer code, this also further encapsulates the Domain Model.

It's also about lessening the flexibility, and that is very good. Don't make everything possible.

Assuming you like the idea of Domain Model-hosted queries, which queries do we need and how many?

Aggregates as a Tool Again

That last question may have sounded quite open, but I actually have an opinion on that. Guess what? Yes, I think we should use Aggregates.

Each of your Aggregates is a typical candidate for having Query Object in the Domain Model. Of course, you could also go the XP route of creating them when needed for the first time, which is probably better.

Speaking of Aggregates, I'd like to point out again that I see Aggregates as the *default* mechanism for determining how big the loadgraphs should be.

Note

With loadgraph, I mean how far from the target instance we should load instances. For example, when we ask for a certain order, should we also load its customer or not? What about its orderLines?

And when the default isn't good enough performance-wise, we have lots of room for performance optimizations. A typical example is to not load complete graphs when you need to list instances, such as Orders. Instead, you create a cut down type, perhaps called OrderSnapshot, with just the fields you need in your typical list situations. It's also the case that those lists won't be integrated with the Unit of Work and Identity Map, which probably is exactly what you want, again because of performance reasons (or it might create problems—as always, it depends).

An abstraction layer could support creating such lists so that your code will be agnostic about the implementation of the abstraction layer at work. It could look like this:

```
//For example OrderRepository.GetSnapshots()
IQuery q = new Query(typeof(Order), typeof(OrderSnapshot)
    , new string[]{"Id", "OrderNumber", "Customer.Id"
    , "Customer.Name"});
q.AddCriterion("Year",
year);
result _ws.GetByQuery(q);
```

For this to work, OrderSnapshot must have suitable constructor, like this (assuming here that the Ids are implemented as Guids):

Querying

```
//OrderSnapshot
public OrderSnapshot(Guid id, int orderNumber
    , Guid customerId, string customerName)
```

Note

Getting type explosion is commonly referred to as the Achilles heel of O/R Mappers, which I provided an example of earlier. In my experience, the problem is there, but not anything we can't deal with. First, you do this only when you really have to, so not all Aggregate roots in your model will have a snapshot class. Second, you can often get away with a single snapshot class for several different list scenarios. The optimization effect of doing it at all is often significant enough that you don't need to go further.

Another common approach is to use Lazy Load for tuning by loading some of the data just in time. (We'll talk more about this in a later chapter.)

And if that isn't powerful enough, you can write manual SQL code and instantiate the snapshot type on your own. Just be very clear that you are starting to actively use the database model as well at that point in time.

One or Two Repository Assemblies?

With all this in place, you understand that you have many different possibilities for how to structure the Repositories, but you might wonder how it's done in real-world projects.

In the most recent large project of mine (which is in production—it's not a toy project), I use a single set of Repositories, both for Fake execution and execution against the database. There are a few optimizations that use native SQL, but I used a little hack there so that if the optimized method finds an injected connection string, it calls out to another method where I'm totally on my own.

Otherwise, the un-optimized code will be used instead. That way, the Fake will use the un-optimized version, and the database-related code will typically use the optimized version.

Again, this is only used in a handful of cases. Not extremely nice and clean, but it works fine for now.

Specifications as Queries

Yet another approach for querying is to use the Specification pattern [Evans DDD] (encapsulate conceptual specifications for describing something, such as what a customer that isn't allowed to buy more "looks like"). The concept gets a describing name and can be used again and again.

Using this approach is similar to creating type safe Domain Model-specific queries, but it goes a step further because it's not generic querying that we are after, but very specific querying, based on domain-specific concepts. This is one level higher than the query definitions that live in the Domain Model, such as CustomerQuery. Instead of exposing generic properties to filter by, a specification is a concept with a very specific domain meaning. A common example is the concept of a gold customer. The specification describes what is needed for a customer to be a gold customer.

The code gets very clear and purposeful because the concepts are caught and described as Specification classes.

Even those Specification classes could very well spit out IQuery so that you can use them with GetByQuery() of IWorkspace (or equivalent) if you like the idea of an abstraction layer.

Other Querying Alternatives

So far we have just talked about Query Objects as being the query language we need (sometimes embedded in other constructs, though). As a matter of fact, when the queries get complex, it's often more powerful to be able to write the queries in, for example, a string-based language similar to SQL.

I haven't thought about any more query languages for NWorkspace. But perhaps I can someday talk some people into adding support for NWorkspace queries as output from their queries. That way, their queries (such as something like SQL, but for Domain Model) would be useful against the infrastructure solutions that have adapter implementations for NWorkspace.

I can't let go of the idea that what querying language you want to use is as much of a lifestyle choice as is the choice of programming language. Of course, it might depend even more on the situation as to which query language we want to use, if we can choose. That's a nice way to end this subject for now, I think (more to come in Chapter 8 and 9). It's time to move on.

Summary

So we have discussed what Persistence Ignorance is and some ideas of how to keep the infrastructure out of the Domain Model classes, while at the same time prepare for infrastructure. We also discussed database testing, and a lot of attention was spent on an idea of introducing an abstraction layer.

In the next chapter, we will change focus to the core of the Domain Model again, this time focusing on rules. You will find that lots of the requirements in the list we set up in Chapter 4 are about rules, so this is a near and dear topic when Domain Models are discussed.

Chapter 7

Let the Rules Rule

In the last chapter, we took a nice break and looked at some infrastructure preparations. Now we'll return to the core model for a chapter. This chapter is about rules.

The topic of rules is a huge one. We will deal with part of it, focusing mainly on validation rules. We will do it by addressing the requirements defined in Chapter 4, "A New Default Architecture," and add some comments where appropriate.

Looking back at the requirements list in Chapter 4 (the list will be repeated shortly), we can clearly see that the majority of the requirements have something to do with rules. As I see it, this is one area where Domain Models really shine. We can go quite a long way without needing a rules engine. As Evans says [Evans DDD], using several paradigms at the same time is problematic, so we are doing ourselves a favor if we can avoid mixing Domain Models with rules engines. (To give you a sense of how complex it can be to mix paradigms, that is why mixing OO and Relational models is so tricky.)

Categorization of Rules

In my last book [Nilsson NED], there was a chapter called "Business Rules" in which I provided a bunch of example problems related to where to locate the rule evaluation. For some reason, almost all the examples ended up being checked in the database. Yet that was from my database era, and now I'm a Domain Model guy, so you will find that this chapter is totally different. Is that for the better? I definitely think so, and I hope you will agree.

OK, where shall we start? How about some categorization of rules?

Categorization of Rules

If we try to categorize rules, we quickly find out that there are many dimensions to consider. For example, there are attributes such as the following:

- Where to execute (in which tier/layer)
- When to execute

229

- Degree of complexity (simple constraints, spanning several fields, spanning several instances, and so on)

- Starting actions or not

- And so on, and so forth

I'm sorry, but I won't be dealing with this much other than directing you to some other books on the subject, such as von Halle's book [von Halle BRA], the one by Ross [Ross BRB], and Halpin's [Halpin IMRD]. You will find that these books are pretty data-focused, but they are nevertheless highly interesting.

Let's try to get started from another angle. Let's define some principles and then get our hands dirty.

Principles for Rules and Their Usage

I think the word principle is very good because it's not strict. It's much easier to come up with principles than categories, probably because of the built-in vagueness. Still, principles are descriptive regarding intention. That's exactly what I need here and now.

Two-Way Rules Checking: Optional (Possible) to Check Proactively, Mandatory (and Automatic) to Check Reactively

Principles for Rules and Their Usage

You should be able to check in advance (proactively) whether there will be a problem (for example, trying to persist the current changes) so that you can take corrective measures. That way, the programming model will be easier.

And if you fail to check in advance, there is no mercy, but you will learn (reactively) that there were problems via an exception.

All States, Even When in Error, Should be Savable

Users hate to learn from applications that they can't save the current changes because of errors. A friend of mine has compared it to not being allowed to save a word processing document if you have spelling errors.

All is a "big" word, but we will try to at least come close. We should try to avoid reaching those states that won't be persistable.

It's also important to think about what error means here. An order might be considered to be in error if it's too large. But until the user tries to submit the order it's not really an error, just a situation he needs to deal with before submitting. And he should be able to save that order before he submits it so he can continue working on it later on, to solve the problem and submit it then.

Rules Should Be Productive to Use

It should be productive to work with rules, both when consuming the rules and when defining the rules themselves.

The productivity for consuming rules will be addressed by making it possible to fetch metadata to be used for setting up the UI. That will cut the times you find problems when you check because the UI has helped so that some problems just won't happen. (Just watch out so you don't trust the UI to be all that is needed regarding rules checking.)

The productivity goal for defining rules might be reached with a small framework that lets you focus on the interesting parts of the rules, and the boilerplate code will be dealt with for you.

Rules Should Optionally be Configurable so that You Can Add Custom Rules

Some rules are scenario dependent while others are not, so it might be important not only to be able to declare all rules directly in the class definitions. Instead, you need to be able to add custom rules dynamically for certain use cases, but also during deployment as configuration information.

I think that the configuration aspect is particularly useful when you build products that will be used by many different customers. If you are building a system for a single customer, it's probably of less value.

Rules Should Be Located with State

Rules should at least be *defined* as closely as possible to the relevant Domain Model classes. By this I don't mean the implementation of the rules themselves but the declarations. We want encapsulation of the usage so that we easily get the "complete" picture of a Domain Model class by inspecting its class.

I think this principle helps another principle that could be called "Rules should be consistent." When the codebase reaches a certain size, there is a risk that the rules may interfere or even contradict each other. Having the rules together and together with the state should help to some degree with managing the rulebase.

Rules Should be Extremely Testable

We will spend a lot of time working with and testing the rules. For this reason, it's important to have a test-friendly design for the rules.

In reality, adding rules also *creates* problems with testing. You need to set up instances to correct states. You can write test helpers (such as private methods in the test fixture) for dealing with that, but it's still a hindrance.

The System Should Stop You from Getting into a Bad State

A good way of simplifying how to work with rules is to avoid the need for them when possible. One way of doing that is, for example, to work with creation methods that will set up the Domain Model objects in a valid state that can never be made invalid.

Starting to Create an API

Starting to
Create an
API

We'll come back to these principles and evaluate how we fulfilled them later in the chapter, but now it's time to come back down to Earth and take up some of the problems outlined in Chapter 4. I'm going to start with the external API and see where we end up. I believe that will give a good, pragmatic feeling about the whole thing.

So to remind you, the problems or requests outlined in Chapter 4 were the following:

1. List customers by applying a flexible and complex filter.

2. List the orders when looking at a specific customer.

3. An order can have many different lines.

4. Concurrency conflict detection is important.

5. A customer may not owe us more than a certain amount of money.

6. An order may not have a total value of more than one million SEK.

7. Each order and customer should have a unique and user-friendly number.

8. Before a new customer is considered OK, his or her credit will be checked with a credit institute.

9. An order must have a customer; an order line must have an order.

10. Saving an order and its lines should be automatic.

11. Orders have an acceptance status that is changed by the user.

Let's take one of the problems; say, problem 6, "An order may not have a total value of more than one million SEK."

How shall we approach this problem? There are several options to choose from.

You could create something like a simple rule-checking engine where you can send your instances to be validated, or you could let the instances take responsibility for that themselves. I like the idea of letting the instances take responsibility for themselves as much as possible (or at least as far as is appropriate) and therefore prefer the latter. Perhaps this is a bit naïve, but also very simple in a positive way.

If I write a test to get started, it could look like this:

```
[Test]
public void CantExceedMaxAmountForOrder()
{
    Order o = new Order(new Customer());

    OrderLine ol = new OrderLine(new Product());
    ol.NumberOfUnits = 2000000;
    ol.Price = 1;
    o.AddOrderLine(ol);

    Assert.IsFalse(o.IsValid);
}
```

What we did was to add a property to the Order called IsValid. A pretty common approach I think. There are also some obvious problems, such as the following:

- *What* was the problem? We only know that there was one, not what it was.

- We *allowed* an incorrect transition.

- What if we *forgot* to check?

All we did was to check if everything was OK or not. We will come back to the mentioned problems, but we have something more basic to deal with first. A more important problem is this question:

What is it the order is valid for (or not valid for)?

Context, Context, Context!

Context is, as always, very important but pretty much forgotten in the approach we started out with. We need to address this before moving on because it's *crucial* to the rest of the discussion.

I think the reason for the common approach of IsValid as some kind of general, catch-all test might be because of too much focus on persistence. If we decouple persistence from rules a bit and try to adhere to the principle of letting all states be savable, we might end up with another approach.

Then I think the *transitions* will be the interesting thing regarding rules. For example, when an order is in the state of NewOrder, more or less everything might be allowed. But when the order should transition to the Ordered state, that will only be allowed if certain rules are fulfilled.

So *saving* an order that is in the state of NewOrder should be possible even if the order isn't valid for enter Ordered state. Approaching rules this way will focus rules on the model meaning and not let a technicality, such as persisted or not, affect the model.

That said, there is a reality full of practical problems, and we need to deal with that well. So even if we have the intention of focusing on the model, we have to be good citizens regarding the infrastructure also. Let's see if thinking about persisted or not as a special state helps, but first I think it's important to discuss what could give us problems regarding rules if we don't think enough about the infrastructure.

Starting to Create an API

Database Constraints

Even though you might choose to focus on putting all your rules in the Domain Model, you will still probably end up with some rules in the database. A typical reason for this is efficiency. Some rules are most efficiently checked in the database; that's just how it is. You can probably design around most of them, but there will probably still be a couple of situations where this is a fact of life.

Another reason is that you might not be able to design a new database, or you might not be able to design the database exactly as you would like it, but you have to adjust to a current database design. Yet another reason is that it's often considered a good thing that the database can take care of itself, especially if several different systems are using the same database.

The impedance mismatch between object-orientation and Relational databases that we discussed in Chapter 1, "Values to Value," will also show up here. For example, the strings in the database will most likely have static max lengths, such as VARCHAR(50). That a certain string isn't allowed to be longer than that is kind of a generic rule, but it's mostly related to persistence. The transition to Persisted state won't be allowed if the string is too long.

So it's probable that you will have to deal with rules whose invalidity won't be detected until the state is persisted to the database. That in its turn represents a couple of problems.

First, parsing error information is troublesome, especially when you consider that a typical O/R Mapping solution often tries to be portable between different databases. Or rather, the heart of the problem is that the O/R Mapper probably won't be able to do the mapping for you when it comes to errors and tell you what field(s) caused the problem in the Domain Model; for example, when there's a duplicate key error.

Furthermore, the error will come at an inconvenient point in time. Your Domain Model has already been changed, and it will probably be very hard for you to recover from the problem without starting all over again. In fact, the general rule is often that you should start over instead of trying to do something smart.

Still, we do like the idea of making it possible to save our instances at any time. (In any case, we have set up some *preferences* even if we can't follow them to 100%. The extreme is often extremely costly.)

As I see it, try to design for as much proactivity as possible (or as appropriate) so that the number of exceptions from the database will be extremely few. For those that are still possible, be prepared to deal with them one by one in code, or be prepared to roll back the transaction, toss out the Domain Model changes, and start all over again. A bit drastic, but that's the way I see it. The key to all this is design, so you make the problem as small as possible.

OK, that was the purely technical side of it (that the database might show its discomfort with us). But it's not just a matter of that the rules are infrastructure-related *only* or domain-related *only*. There are connections.

Bind Rules to Transitions Related to the Domain *or* the Infrastructure?

What we have said so far is that we should try hard to not enter an invalid state. If we follow that, we can always persist (if we don't think about the infrastructure-related constraints for the moment).

That principle is the ideal. In reality, it will be hard not to break certain rules during a multiple step action. For example, should you disallow the change of the name of a customer to a name that the rule thinks is too short? Well, perhaps, but it might just prevent the user from doing what he wants to do: namely deleting the old name and inserting a new one instead.

It's possible to deal with this by having a method called `Rename(string newName)` that takes care of the work. During the execution of the method, the state of the object isn't correct, but we only consider it a problem before and after the method execution.

> ### Note
>
> This is in line with invariants according to *Design by Contract* [Meyer OOSC]. Such invariants are like assertions that the instance should abide by at all times, both before the method execution and after. The only exception is *during* the method execution.

Another approach is to simply not set the property until you've finished with the change. Let's see if I can come up with another example. Assume that there are two fields, and either both field have to be set or neither of them. Again, a method would solve the problem, but if you scale up this problem or consider that the UI would prefer to have the properties exposed with setters, it's clear that it's hard not to get into an inconsistent state there from time to time.

Another question might be if we should trust that we *didn't* reach an invalid state? And *if* we against all odds did reach an invalid state (a *really* invalid one, such as an erroneous change when the state of the order is Ordered), should we allow that to be stored?

Starting to Create an API

It might be that the database won't allow us to have that protection for some error situations. But even if you try hard to let the database take care of itself regarding rules, you will probably let some things slip through, and if you have moved to Domain Model-focused way of building applications, your database is probably not as rigid when it comes to self-protection. After all, domain-focused rules that are somewhat advanced are most often *much* easier to express in the Domain Model than in a Relational database, and you also *want* to have them in the Domain Model.

The question is: can we trust the "environment"? I mean, can we trust that we won't persist a state that shouldn't be possible to reach? For example, can we expect that we don't have any bugs? Can we expect that the consumer isn't creative and won't use reflection for setting some fields to exciting values?

Refining the Principle: "All States, Even when in Error, Should Be Savable"

Let's see if we can form an example of how I think about the principle I called "All states, even when in error, should be savable."

Assume again an order that can be in two states, NewOrder and Ordered. We have only one domain-related transition rule: the order may not be too large to enter Ordered. That gives us the valid combinations in Table 7-1.

Table 7-1 *Valid Combinations of Order States and Rule Outcomes*

Order States	Rule Outcomes
NewOrder	Not too large
NewOrder	Too large
Ordered	Not too large

So far, it feels both simple and exactly what we want. Let's add the dimension of persisted or not, as shown in Table 7-2.

Table 7-2 *Valid Combinations of Order States and Rule Outcomes*

Order States	Rule Outcomes	Persisted or Not
NewOrder	Not too large	Not persisted
NewOrder	Not too large	Persisted
NewOrder	Too large	Not persisted
NewOrder	Too large	Persisted
Ordered	Not too large	Not persisted
Ordered	Not too large	Persisted

First, I'd like to point out that we expect that the transitions to Ordered combined with Too large will not be possible.

Even more important, if for some reason it does happen, it's an example of a state that is in real exceptional error and that should *not* be savable.

Note

Your mileage might vary regarding if you will check the domain-related transition rules at persist time as well or not. It might be considered a bit extreme in many cases.

Please note that by adhering to the refined principle of "all states should be savable," we are not back to the IsValid idea I started the chapter with. It's now IsValidRegardingPersistence, and lots of "errors" are now OK to persist.

Requirements for a Basic Rules API Related to Persistence

Now that we have decided on a specific context for now, that of the transition to the state of persisted, let's start the discussion about an API regarding that. We will get back to other (and from the model's point of view, more interesting) state transition problems, both general and specific, afterward.

> ### Note
>
> As usual, the discussion here is really more about some *generic* ideas than the API itself. I'm not trying to tell you how you should create your interfaces/APIs, I'm just trying to give my thoughts on the subject and hope that you may be prompted to find your own solutions.

Requirements for a Basic Rules API Related to Persistence

I'd like to take a new code example where we apply the idea about being proactive regarding not persisting exceptional state errors and/or problems that will throw exceptions from the persistence engine.

I'm going for the latter: showing a situation when the persistence engine would throw an exception. (Again, the former problem should be hard to get to. If everything works as expected, that state shouldn't be possible to reach.)

Assume that Order has Note, and Note is defined as VARCHAR(30) in the database. Depending on your solution for persistence, you might get an exception when trying to save a long string, or you will lose information silently. The important thing here is that I will proactively catch the problem. It could look like this:

```
[Test]
public void CantExceedStringLengthWhenPersisting()
{
    Order o = new Order(new Customer());
    o.Note = "012345678901234567890123456789012345567890";


    Assert.IsFalse(o.IsValidRegardingPersistence);
}
```

So instead of asking if the order is IsValid, I changed the name of the property to IsValidRegardingPersistence to make it very clear that the order isn't valid in the context of being persisted.

Let's set up a simple interface for the purpose of letting the consumer ask an Aggregate root if it's in a valid state or not for being persisted. It could look like this:

```
public interface IValidatableRegardingPersistence
{
    bool IsValidRegardingPersistence {get;}
}
```

So you let your classes that have persistence-related rules implement that interface. Normally the consumer only has to ask the Aggregate [Evans DDD] root if it's valid or not to be persisted and the Aggregate root will check its children.

Externalize Rules á la Persistence?

As you saw in the code snippet, I chose to let the Domain Model classes themselves be responsible for checking rules; considering how we like to deal with persistence (from the "outside"), that might feel strange.

This might be something to think about, but for now I'll stick to my first idea here, partly because I think the rules are at the heart of the Domain Model. The rules are not "just" an infrastructural aspect, as persistence is.

Good, we are back on track.

Back to the Found API Problems

Several pages back I found out a couple of problems with the API I started to sketch. I delayed the discussion because I wanted to first deal with the problem of lack of context. With that out of the way, let's get back to those problems to see if they still apply to the previous code snippet (CantExceedStringLengthWhen-Persisting()). The problems were

- *What* was the problem? We only know that there was one, not what it was.

- We allowed an incorrect transition.

- What if we forgot to check?

Let's discuss those three problems in the context of the persistence-related rules.

What Was the Problem?

The first problem still applies. If the instance isn't valid, it might well be interesting to find out which rules have been broken. The Aggregate root will aggregate the broken rules from all its children as well as from itself and return the broken rules as an IList.

Let's add to the interface for dealing with this. It could look like this:

```
public interface IValidatableRegardingPersistence
{
    bool IsValidRegardingPersistence {get;}
    IList BrokenRulesRegardingPersistence {get;}
}
```

Note

As I see it, the list of broken rules is an implementation of the Notification pattern [Fowler PoEAA2].

One important thing mentioned with that pattern is that it's not only errors that we need to be informed about, but warnings/information as well. Another thought that springs to mind is that the broken rules list I have talked about is pretty focused on Aggregates, but we can, of course, aggregate (pun not intended) several such lists into a single one in an Application layer [Evans DDD], such as from several Aggregate root instances.

Requirements for a Basic Rules API Related to Persistence

We Allowed an Incorrect Transition

Sure, the Note became too long, and that could be considered to be a transition to an invalid state. But I can't say I think of that thing as very interesting most often. I would probably let the order be around with a too-long Note for some time to make it possible for the user to delete a few letters of the Note.

Unfortunately, in this case, the too-long Note won't be possible to save. *That* transition between not persisted and persisted, on the other hand, is interesting here. But it *won't* be allowed. (As I said, I will get an exception or the string will be truncated silently.)

The transition to persisted is a bit "special." We will get back to the problem of allowing incorrect transitions in the context of domain-related rules shortly.

What If We Forgot to Check?

If the consumer doesn't follow the protocol of first checking the possibility of a transition before trying to make the transition, we have an exceptional situation, and exceptional situations throw exceptions. The same applies here, too. So if we tried to transition to persisted, we would like to throw an exception that is subclassing ApplicationException and will hold an IList of broken rules.

Again, the consumer isn't following the protocol, and that's an exceptional situation.

We got caught up in a specific transition problem: transition to persisted. It's time to change focus from infrastructure-related transitions to domain-related for a while, but we will try to move some of the ideas with us, such as that it's an exception if the consumer does not follow the protocol.

Focus on Domain-Related Rules

Let's work with the remaining feature requirements from Chapter 4, one by one. We started out with the feature requirement number 6, which was called "An order may not have a total value of more than one million SEK," but we got interrupted when we realized that the context was missing from the sketched API. Let's see if we can transform the test a bit. It looked like this before:

```
[Test]
public void CantExceedMaxAmountForOrder()
{
    Order o = new Order(new Customer());

    OrderLine ol;

    ol = new OrderLine(new Product());
    ol.NumberOfUnits = 2000000;
    ol.Price = 1;
    o.AddOrderLine(ol);

    Assert.IsFalse(o.IsValid);
}
```

Focus on Domain-Related Rules

As you know by now, I think there are several problems with this snippet. To follow the ideas discussed so far, we could add a transition method to Ordered state; for example, the method could be called OrderNow(). But I would still not be happy with that, because OrderNow() would most probably throw an exception before we get a chance to check.

Again, I'd like to leave the focus of what is persisted and what is not for now. The interesting part here is that when we try to transition to Ordered, we can't do that. Let's reflect that with some changes to the test.

```
[Test]
public void CantGoToOrderedStateWithExceededMaxAmount()
{
    Order o = new Order(new Customer());

    OrderLine ol = new OrderLine(new Product());
    ol.NumberOfUnits = 2000000;
    ol.Price = 1;
    o.AddOrderLine(ol);

    try
    {
        o.OrderNow();
        Assert.Fail();
    }
    catch (ApplicationException ex) {}
}
```

It's important to consider whether when we are in the Ordered state if we will then check in AddOrderLine() so that we aren't going to break the rule. I could let AddOrderLine() transition the order back to NewOrder, if AddOrderLine() would be allowed at all. That avoids the problem.

Another problem is that if one of the OrderLines is changed when we are in Ordered, that might break the rule. A typical solution in this case would be to work with immutable OrderLines instead so that they can't be changed. Let's change the test to reflect that.

Focus on
Domain-
Related
Rules

```
[Test]
public void CantGoToOrderedStateWithExceededMaxAmount()
{
    Order o = new Order(new Customer());

    o.AddOrderLine(new OrderLine(new Product(), 2000000, 1));

    try
    {
        o.OrderNow();
        Assert.Fail();
    }
    catch (ApplicationException ex) {}
}
```

Note

I could use the `ExpectedException` attribute of NUnit instead of the `try catch` and `Assert.Fail()` construction. That would make the test shorter. The only advantage of the used construction is that I will check that the expected exception happens at the `OrderNow()` call, and that is actually most often a small advantage.

When an `OrderLine` has been added, it can't be changed any longer, and for this simple example, the rule only has to be checked in the `OrderNow()` and `AddOrderLine()` methods now.

Let's move on with the list.

Rules that Require Cooperation

Feature number 5 was: "A customer may not owe us more than a certain amount of money." This rule sounds extremely simple at first, but the devil is in the details. Let's start and see where we end up. An initial test could go like this:

```
[Test]
public void CanHaveCustomerDependentMaxDebt()
{
    Customer c = new Customer();
    c.MaxAmountOfDebt = 10;

    Order o = new Order(c);
    o.AddOrderLine(new OrderLine(new Product(), 11, 1));

    try
    {
        o.OrderNow();
        Assert.Fail();
    }
    catch (ApplicationException ex) {}
}
```

Focus on
Domain-
Related
Rules

However, that will probably not work at all. Why not? Well, the order needs to be able to find the other orders of a certain state for the customer at hand and what typically solves that is the `OrderRepository`.

Note

As you might recall, I chose to go for a unidirectional relationship between `Order` and `Customer` classes. That's why I ask the `OrderRepository` for help (as one of several possible strategies for simulating bidirectionality) for going from `Customer` to its `Orders`.

We could deal with that by injecting _orderRepository to the order in the constructor like this:

```
Order o = new Order(c, _orderRepository);
```

But was this a good solution? As usual, that depends on the particular application. Letting the Order check the current debt for the Customer when it's time for OrderNow() might be a bit late regarding the usability aspect for the user. Perhaps a better solution would be to ask what the maximum amount of a new order can be before creating the order. Then the user creates the new order, and the user can get feedback in the UI when the limit is reached. This doesn't change the API we just saw, but it is more of a convenience.

A variation to the location of responsibility would be to ask the Customer about IsOrderOK(orderToBeChecked). In a way, it feels natural to let the Customer be responsible for deciding that because the Customer has the data that is needed to make the judgment. If we think about the domain and try to code in the spirit of the domain, is it likely that we give (or should give) the customer the responsibility of checking the orders? Perhaps it is if we state the question a bit differently, saying that we should ask the customer to *accept* the order. As a matter of fact, that's pretty similar to what we coded previously except that OrderNow() was located on the Order. That might be an indication of something.

Another problem with the solution shown in the code snippet is that the _orderRepository is injected in the order instance. If you reconstitute an order from persistence and you do that by using an O/R Mapper, you're not in charge of the creation of the order instance. You could inject the _orderRepository in the Repository during reconstitution, though, but it feels a little bit like a hack (consider, for example, when you read a list of orders and then you have to inject the Repository into each instance of the list). After having thought about it, let's try to keep the responsibility in the order for checking itself, but provide the Repository via a setter instead or at the time of the check as a parameter to the OrderNow() method (but that strategy has a tendency of not scaling well).

Focus on
Domain-
Related
Rules

Note

I think this discussion points out a weakness in at least some OR Mappers: that you don't control the instance creation during reconstitution as much as you would like, especially considering the growing popularity of Dependency Injection frameworks, as we will discuss in Chapter 10, "Design Techniques to Embrace."

Locating Set-Based Processing Methods

No matter which of the styles previously discussed you prefer, you might think a minute or two about how to check the current debt. Of course, you *could* write code like this (assuming that we use orders and not invoices for determining the current debt, which is probably a bit twisted):

```
//Order, code for checking current debt for OrderNow()
decimal orderSum = 0;
IList orders = _orderRepository.GetOrders(c);

foreach (Order o in orders)
{
    if (_HasInterestingStateRegardingDebt(o))
        orderSum += o.TotalValue;
}
```

I think that code is a no-no! A better solution would be to expose a method on the OrderRepository with a method called something like CurrentDebtForCustomer(), taking a Customer instance as parameter.

Note

With Repository interface design, it's often a good idea to provide overloads, such as X(Customer) and X(Guid). It is annoying having to instantiate a Customer just to be able to call the method if you hold on to the ID of the Customer.

I know what the database guys are thinking right now. "What about real-time consistency? Will the Repository method execute with the transaction isolation level of serializable in an explicit transaction during save at least?" Well, it is possible, but there are problems.

One problem is that the O/R Mapper you are using (if we assume for the moment that an O/R Mapper is being used—more about that in later chapters) might not allow you to take detailed control of the persist process regarding validation, locking, and so on. Another problem is that the nature of the persist process means it might take some time if you have lots of dirty instances to be persisted, so the lock time for all orders for the customer might be pretty long.

I think that in this case it's usually OK not to expect real-time consistency here, only something pretty close to real-time consistency. I mean, check the sum of the other orders just before saving this order, but do not span the read with a high isolation level or not even do the check within the same transaction.

I think that goes pretty much hand in hand with what Evans says regarding Aggregates [Evans DDD]. He says something like strive for real-time consistency within an Aggregate, but not between Aggregates. Consistency problems between Aggregates can be dealt with a little later.

So if you find the approach acceptable (again, we are talking about a pretty low risk here, for a typical system at least), but you would like to detect the problem, you could create some batch program that kicks in every now and then and checks for problems like this and reports back. Or why not put a request on a queue at persist time that checks for problems like this regarding the particular customer? It's such an unlikely problem, so why should any user have to wait synchronously for it to be checked?

The fact that I think the method is atomic signals that we should use a Service [Evans DDD] instead to make the whole thing more explicit. The Service could check the current debt and therefore be used proactively by the Order at good places in time. It could also be used pretty much reactively at save time, and some sort of request could be put on a queue and be used reactively after save. The Service would probably use the same Repository method as was just discussed, but that's not anything the caller needs to know, of course.

What should it do reactively after the save? Perhaps move the order to one of two states so that when the user stores an order, it goes into state NewOrder. Then the Service kicks in and moves the order to state Accepted or Denied, as shown in Figure 7-1.

Focus on
Domain-
Related
Rules

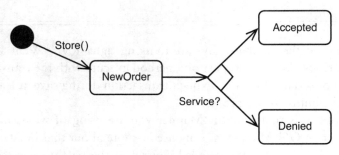

Figure 7-1   State graph

After all this rambling I think we have three decent solutions to the problem: one with pretty tight coupling (everything being done in real time, possibly with high transaction isolation level), one with less coupling (but that is perhaps a bit more complex because there are more "moving parts"), and finally one where we don't do anything extra beyond what was shown in the test (but with a small risk of inconsistency that we will have to track delayed). Would one of these suit you?

OK, we touched upon using a Service for helping us out with a costly processing problem. Services in the Domain Model often arise from another necessity as well.

Service-Serviced Validation

Completely by coincidence, we do need such a rule that is by its very nature service-based. I'm thinking about feature 8, "Before a new customer is considered OK, his or her credit will be checked with a credit institute."

We could very well call that credit institute service in the Grant() method, or we could use a solution similar to the one I just sketched, letting our Service kick in after persist, taking care of both calling the external service and moving the customer to one of two states. One problem with this approach is that I'm binding domain rules a bit too much to persistence.

Another big problem with this approach of moving some functionality out of the sandbox of the current Unit of Work/Identity Map is that what you might have in your local cache will be out of sync with the database because processing takes place in the autonomous Service. Of course, that's the risk you *always* have with caching, if the cache could be bypassed.

If you know that the cache will be invalidated because of an explicit Service call in real time, it's pretty easy. Just kill the cache. It might be expensive to recreate it, though, or perhaps you even know exactly what needs to be refreshed. On the other hand, if you don't know when the operation that invalidates the cache will happen, you have to take extra care and refresh the cache as often as possible. As I see it, all this hints at being aggressive with your cache management and not letting the cache get too big and live for a long time, at least not for the data that changes quite frequently.

> ### Note
>
> When I talk about cache here, I'm mostly thinking about the Identity Map [Fowler PoEAA].

Let's focus some more on transitions.

Trying to Transition when We Shouldn't

I used different states for increasing the fulfillment of the "always savable" principle before. But a "critical" passage is when the user wants to make a transition in the state graph. Sure, we could deal with this in a similar way to what we discussed before so that we move to a temporary state and then a Service takes responsibility for moving to the real state or to a failure state. I guess there are situations where this makes sense, but for feature 11, "Orders have an acceptance status that is changed by the user," it might just feel ridiculous, depending on what the context is.

Note

Did you notice how it all came together? I talked about OrderNow() before, and that might have seemed to be kind of a technical solution to the problem of "always savable," but it was core to the requirements. And according to the requirements, Accept() might make more sense.

OK, "ridiculous" is too strong a word, but if we assume that the rules for checking are just a couple of simple constraints without the cross Aggregate border problems, I would prefer to apply the principle discussed earlier: that is, letting the user make a proactive check, and if the result is positive, the state-changing method will execute successfully. A picture, I mean code, says more than a thousand words:

Focus on Domain-Related Rules

```
[Test]
public void CanMakeStateTransitionSafely()
{
    Order o = new Order(new Customer());

    Assert.IsTrue(o.IsOKToAccept);

    //We can now safely do this without getting an exception...
    o.Accept();
}
```

Checking the IsOKToAccept property is optional, but not doing it and then calling Accept() at a time when we shouldn't is exceptional, and we will get an exception. Exceptions are for exceptional problems; for "expected problems" bool is fine.

We often don't just wonder if it will be OK or not, but we also want to get a list of reasons why it's not OK. In these cases, the proactive method could return a list of broken rules instead, something like this:

```
[Test]
public void CanMakeStateTransitionSafely()
{
    Order o = new Order(new Customer());

    Assert.AreEqual(0, o.BrokenRulesIfAccept.Count);
```

```
//We can now safely do this without getting an exception...
o.Accept();
}
```

I prefer to do this on a case-by-case basis. There is no standard interface or anything to implement, just a principle for interface design. So this is actually just a protocol for making it possible to be proactive regarding broken rules detection.

The Transaction Abstraction

The transaction abstraction is a powerful one, and one that is underutilized. An alternative solution to the transition problem would be to use the transaction abstraction for the Domain Model and validations as well. Then during the transaction, it wouldn't matter if the state wasn't correct; only before and after would matter. For example, the API could then look like this:

```
//Some consumer...
DMTransaction dMTx = Something.StartTransaction();
c.Name = string.Empty;
c.Name = "Volvo";
dMTx.Commit();
```

In the code snippet, the rules weren't checked until Commit(). As you understand, this opens up a can of worms that needs to be dealt with, but it might be an interesting solution for the future.

The solution becomes even more interesting if you consider the new System.Transaction namespace of .NET 2.0. In the future, we might get transactional list classes, hash tables, and so on. It gets even more interesting considering transactions spanning both the Domain Model and the database. Again, loads of problems, but interesting.

Obviously there are lots of variations to the problem of state transitions. One such problem is deciding when an action should be taken as well. Stay tuned.

Business ID

The example of a state transition that is paired with an action is feature 7 on the feature list, "Each order and customer should have a unique and user-friendly number."

A spontaneous solution to the problem is letting the database take care of the problem with a built-in mechanism, such as IDENTITY does for MS SQL

Server. But there are problems with this approach. First of all, you will have processing outside of your Domain Model, which comes at a cost. You will need to force a refresh of the affected instance, which is not too hard but is something to keep track of and might get a bit complex.

Another problem is that the value might come too early, long before the user has decided to move on with the Order, when he still just considers it to be in "perhaps" state. (Obviously, there are solutions to that as well.)

Yet another problem is that O/R Mappers will often cause you problems if you also use the IDENTITY as a primary key. The semantics for using a Guid as the primary key, which requires less coupling to the database, are often a bit different.

Note

In no way am I saying that you must use the IDENTITY (as the auto increasing property is called in SQL Server) column as a primary key just because you have such a column. You can let it be an alternate key only, but you might get tempted from time to time.

Focus on Domain-Related Rules

So what are the alternatives? There are several of them. Probably the easiest and most direct one is to let the Repository have a method for grabbing the next free Id in some way. It could look something like this (assuming that an Order shouldn't get an OrderNumber until it's accepted):

```
//Order
public void Accept()
{
    if (_status != OrderStatus.NewOrder)
        throw new ApplicationException
            ("You can only call Accept() for NewOrder orders.");

    _status = OrderStatus.Accepted;
    _orderNumber = _orderRepository.GetNextOrderNumber();
}
```

Note

Instead of ApplicationException (or a subclass), it might be a good idea to use InvalidOperationException or a derivative.

Yet this opens up a whole can of worms, at least in systems that are some-what stressed from time to time or if the OrderNumber series is not allowed to have holes in it. It means that the GetNextOrderNumber() won't write changes to the data-base, or at least it will not commit them. This means that you need an expensive lock wrapping the Accept() call and the following persist method.

Yet another approach is to use what will *probably* be the next value and then be prepared for duplicates if someone else already has used it.

If you are prepared to catch exceptions during the persist method because of duplicate key, what do you do then? Well, you could call Accept() again, but then Accept() will throw an exception the way it is currently written.

Perhaps it's better to just ask for a new OrderNumber in the code trying to recover from the duplicate key exception. That in its turn creates another set of prob-lems, such as talking to the database during the persist method or detecting which instance has the problem in the first place (and for which column if there are several candidate keys for the instance).

All these problems can be avoided if you accept holes in the number series and if the method for grabbing the next number also commits the current max in a way similar to how IDENTITY works in SQL Server. I mean, IDENTITY allows holes, and it will waste a value if you do a ROLLBACK.

To make it even clearer that the GetNextOrderNumber() actually makes instant changes to the database and doesn't wait for the next call to the persist method, I think we should use a Service instead. My Repositories don't make decisions for themselves when doing a commit and such, but Services do because Services should be autonomous and atomic.

So with these changes in place, the Accept() method could now look like this (assuming that an IOrderNumberService has been injected to _orderNumberService in the order before the call):

```
//Order
public void Accept()
{
    if (_status != OrderStatus.NewOrder)
        throw new ApplicationException
            ("You can only call Accept() for NewOrder orders");

    _status = OrderStatus.Accepted;
    _orderNumber = _orderNumberService.GetNextOrderNumber();
}
```

Now the risk of problems during the persist method is reduced so much that it's exceptional if one arises.

Focus on Domain-Related Rules

You'd be right if you think I avoided the problem by accepting holes in series (which was actually even stated as OK with the defined requirements), but sometimes that just isn't possible. I strongly dislike such series, but there are still situations where you can't avoid them. Then what? Well, I guess I would go back to square one. If that wasn't enough, I would probably turn the whole transition method into a Service instead, moving the order to Accepted status and setting an ordernumber. This is not as pure or clean as doing the work in the Domain Model, but when reality calls, we should respond.

OK, so far we have discussed quite a lot of different problems that we have to deal with when it comes to rules in the Domain Model. There is one more to look at before we move on.

Avoiding Problems

Feature 9, "An order must have a customer; an order line must have an order," is a great example of a rule that I'd like to not have as a rule at all if possible, but I'd rather force it in the constructor instead. Then there's no need to check for it.

Clean, simple, efficient. Just good. I know, I know, this sets your alarm bells ringing. Of course there are problems, too.

For example, it's possible that you'd like to have an instance of an order without first having to decide on the customer because of the UI design.

Focus on Domain-Related Rules

Note
This can be dealt with in the UI, of course, in several different ways. Still, it might not feel good to create a "problem" if we don't have to.

Another problem is that the creation code might get so complex that it can throw exceptions itself, and then we are back into the problems again with how to expose broken rules, and so on. We also said that exceptions should be exceptional, so it just doesn't feel right to toss exceptions in the creation code for saying that there was a broken rule.

There is one thing that eases the burden somewhat. We could let the feature request talk about persistent instances and not transient instances. I'm thinking about OrderLine, for example. In my current design, OrderLine isn't an Aggregate on its own, but is one part of the Order Aggregate instead. Therefore, the only way to make an OrderLine persistent is to associate it to an Order with AddOrderLine(). Until then, I probably don't care that the OrderLine doesn't have an Order. The OrderLine can't be stored, and the persist method won't throw an exception either because of an orphan OrderLine (because the persist method won't know about it at all).

Sure, it might be the case that some processing in the OrderLine requires knowledge of the Order, but if not, I think this is a fine solution.

> ### Note
>
> And right now I think it's arguable whether the OrderLine needs the knowledge of its Order at all. We can probably most often avoid that bidirectionality that we will have otherwise.

I don't know if you've noticed it, but I come back to one of the DDD-patterns, the Aggregate, over and over again. I'd like to take a break and talk about that before moving on.

Aggregates as the Tool Again

The unit for checking rules is... Aggregates! I have found Aggregate design to be extremely important, and it is something I spend quite a lot of time on in my current design work.

I briefly talked about rules aggregation earlier in this chapter, but let's reiterate and delve a little bit deeper.

Aggregate Roots Aggregate Rules

When the consumer of an Aggregate root asks for broken rules regarding persistable or not, he should receive broken rules from the complete Aggregate and not only the root instance.

The aggregation doesn't necessarily have to use the same IValidatableRegardingPersistence interface for the children classes; I actually prefer it not to because that will disturb my strategy for reactively checking for validity at persist. (I don't mean disturb as in creating severe problems, but more as in duplicating execution cycles for no reason.)

Also, this way the Aggregate root has to decide if the ordinary rules of the children should be used or not. Context is king.

An Obvious Aggregate-Level Rule: Versioning

I'd like to end this short section about Aggregates with just a few words about feature 4. Concurrency conflict detection is important. That feature could be thought about as a kind of business rule, but I'd like to think about it as a technical problem more than a business problem. It's also the case that most O/R

Mappers have at least some support for concurrency conflict detection, but I'll leave talking about that here and postpone it until Chapter 8, "Infrastructure for Persistence," and Chapter 9, "Putting NHibernate into Action."

Let's change focus a little bit. Before we get into discussing the implementation of the API, let's first see if we should add anything more.

Extending the API

We have talked about the rule API regarding persistence-related rules and how to get information about problems with those. What more do we need of the API?

Well, depending on the application we are building, we might really need loads of other rules-related things. Inspired by the principles I started the chapter with, one thing that springs to mind is how nice it would be to be able to check for rules very proactively, especially when in the UI. Another important thing is to be able to add customized rules, not only at compile time but also at deployment time. Let's start with a look at consuming the rules in the UI.

Ask for Rules to Be Used to Set Up UI

Extending
the API

I mentioned [Nilsson NED] that I wanted to reuse my rules from the logic layers in the user interface. Not duplicate, but reuse. Now is the time.

The approach I'm going to use here is to let the classes expose metadata that can be used by the UI if it wants to.

A similar approach is the one taken with Web Services that expose an XSD Schema, providing requirements on the data. I'm going for a slightly different approach to start off, providing lists of instances with similar information.

Note

Martin Fowler describes the problem in some detail [Fowler Fixed-LengthString]. He proposes a slightly different approach where an object for a string knows the maximum length on its own, for example.

Make It Possible to Inject Rules

It would be nice to be able to define rules on a case-by-case basis because some rules will obviously be very dependent on context.

Frequently, you want the customer to be able to add his own specific rules, and letting him do that isn't too hard if you create and expose a simple language for the customer to use to add rules.

Refining the Implementation

So far we have been focusing on the rules API from a consumer viewpoint. I think it would be interesting to write about some ideas on how to implement the rules as well. So let's get under the hood of the Order class and try out some ideas.

Before we actually start "refining" we need to come up with a very simple solution to the problem so that we have something to start with.

A Naïve Implementation

Let's see...first of all, we need a test. We can reuse something from before and change it a bit. The CantExceedStringLengthWhenPersisting() test will do. It looked like this:

```
[Test]
public void CantExceedStringLengthWhenPersisting()
{
    Order o = new Order(new Customer());
    o.Note = "012345678901234567890123456789012345678 90";


    Assert.IsFalse(o.IsValidRegardingPersistence);
}
```

We need to write an IsValidRegardingPersistence property on the Order class for the test even to compile. Something like this should work:

```
//Order
public bool IsValidRegardingPersistence
{
    get
    {
        if (Note.Length > 30)
            return false;

        return true;
    }
}
```

Note

Of course, I haven't forgotten the TDD mantra of red, green, refactor, red, green, refactor. I just didn't want to slow down your reading rhythm here.

OK, that works. Let's take a copy of the test (clipboard inheritance), change the name, and expand it a bit:

```
[Test]
public void TryingIdeasWithTheRulesAPI()
{
    Order o = new Order(new Customer());
    o.Note = "01234567890123456789012345678909";
    Assert.IsTrue(o.IsValidRegardingPersistence);

    o.OrderDate = DateTime.Today.AddDays(1);
    Assert.IsFalse(o.IsValidRegardingPersistence);

    o.OrderDate = DateTime.Today;
    Assert.IsTrue(o.IsValidRegardingPersistence);

    o.Note += "012345";
    Assert.IsFalse(o.IsValidRegardingPersistence);
}
```

Refining the Implementation

As you saw, I added one more rule stating that the `OrderDate` can't be a future date, and for some reason (not too much of a stretch) that rule was mandatory regarding persistence.

Note

To make the `OrderDate` rule obviously and mandatory connected to infrastructure, it shouldn't be allowed to be smaller/larger than what your database can store in a `DATETIME` (if there is such a difference for your database).

In order to get a green test, we need to change `IsValidRegardingPersistence` a little bit, as follows:

```
//Order
public bool IsValidRegardingPersistence
{
    get
    {
```

```
            if (Note.Length > 30)
                return false;

            if (OrderDate > DateTime.Today)
                return false;

            return true;
    }
}
```

I think that will do for now as far as rules complexity goes. Not too much, eh?

The next step is to report back to the user, so we need to write a BrokenRulesRegardingPersistence property. Again, let's do something extremely basic, but first we need to make a few changes to the test:

```
[Test]
public void TryingIdeasWithTheRulesAPI()
{
    Order o = new Order(new Customer());
    o.Note = "012345678901234567890123456789";
    Assert.IsTrue(o.IsValidRegardingPersistence);
    Assert.AreEqual(0, o.BrokenRulesRegardingPersistence.Count);

    o.OrderDate = DateTime.Today.AddDays(1);
    Assert.IsFalse(o.IsValidRegardingPersistence);
    Assert.AreEqual(1, o.BrokenRulesRegardingPersistence.Count);

    o.OrderDate = DateTime.Today;
    Assert.IsTrue(o.IsValidRegardingPersistence);
    Assert.AreEqual(0, o.BrokenRulesRegardingPersistence.Count);

    o.Note += "012345";
    Assert.IsFalse(o.IsValidRegardingPersistence);
    Assert.AreEqual(1, o.BrokenRulesRegardingPersistence.Count);
}
```

And then a first implementation:

```
//Order
public IList BrokenRulesRegardingPersistence
{
    get
    {
        IList brokenRules = new ArrayList();

        if (Note.Length > 30)
            brokenRules.Add("Note is too long.");

        if (OrderDate > DateTime.Today)
            brokenRules.Add("OrderDate is in the future.");
```

```
        return brokenRules;
    }
}
```

This is often not detailed enough information about broken rules, but at least we have started. What feels worse right now is that I don't want to express the same rules in both the `IsValidRegardingPersistence` and the `BrokenRulesRegardingPersistence` properties, so for now let's change `IsValidRegardingPersistence` to an execution inefficient solution instead, which cuts down on duplication.

> ### Note
>
> This inefficiency regarding execution is often not much to worry about if you put it in relationship to some database calls, for example.

```
//Order
public bool IsValidRegardingPersistence
{
    get {return BrokenRulesRegardingPersistence.Count == 0;}
}
```

OK, we have dealt with the possibility of asking whether the instance is in a valid state for being persisted at any time and what the current problems are ("dealt with" is an overstatement, but still).

There is another protocol, though, and that relates to transitions. Let's deal with a transition and make it possible to get information about the problems. We will also deal with the situations reactively (that is, we'll react if the transition is attempted when there are known problems).

Let's say that a rule for being able to `Accept()` an order is that the `Customer` for the order must be in `Accepted` state. It could go like this:

```
[Test]
public void TryingTheAcceptTransitionWithTheRulesAPI()
{
    Order o = new Order(new Customer());

    Assert.IsFalse(o.IsOKToAccept);
    o.Customer.Accept();
    Assert.IsTrue(o.IsOKToAccept);
}
```

You should note especially that for a new `Order` (`NewOrder` state), it's okay to have a `Customer` that isn't accepted.

Then if we make the `Customer` `Accepted`, it's okay to `Accept()` the `Order` as well.

Refining the Implementation

One more thing I'd like to show, though, is that the general rules for the Order will be applied at the transitions as well, so let's add that to the test:

```
[Test]
public void TryingTheAcceptTransitionWithTheRulesAPI()
{
    Order o = new Order(new Customer());

    Assert.IsFalse(o.IsOKToAccept);
    o.Customer.Accept();
    Assert.IsTrue(o.IsOKToAccept);

    o.OrderDate = DateTime.Today.AddDays(1);
    Assert.IsFalse(o.IsOKToAccept);

    try
    {
        o.Accept();
        Assert.Fail();
    }
    catch (ApplicationException ex) {}
}
```

<table>
<tr><td>Note</td></tr>
<tr><td>What also happens is that the new Order as default for OrderDate is set to DateTime.Today in the constructor. That's why it is IsOKToAccept directly.</td></tr>
</table>

Refining the Implementation

And while I was at it, I also showed what will happen if the transition is tried even though it shouldn't work.

We need to do something in the Order for this. First, let's do something in IsOKToAccept.

```
//Order
public bool IsOKToAccept
{
    get
    {
        if (Customer.Status != CustomerStatus.Accepted)
            return false;

        return IsValidRegardingPersistence;
    }
}
```

As you saw, I first checked the specific rules (or rule in this case) and then the persistence related rules, because I don't want to move on with something that won't be savable; therefore, I want to point out problems (persistence related ones as well) as early as possible.

Again, I need to change this a bit if I also want a method for telling what broken rules there will be if I call the Accept(), but that's simple and not important to show right now.

The same goes for the Accept() method. It's pretty simple and just needs to check IsOKToAccept before doing the transition.

What might be a bit "tricky," or at least not obvious, is that now the rules for the IsValidRegardingPersistence just got a bit more complex, because after we enter the Accepted status of the Order, we will have to check the same rules even in the IsValidRegardingPersistence property. We moved the real processing to the BrokenRulesRegardingPersistence property as you saw before, so that is where you will see the change:

```
//Order
public IList BrokenRulesRegardingPersistence
{
    get
    {
        IList brokenRules = new ArrayList();

        if (Note.Length > 30)
            brokenRules.Add("Note is too long.");

        if (_orderDate > DateTime.Today)
            brokenRules.Add("OrderDate is in the future.");

        if (_OrderIsInThisStateOrBeyond(OrderStatus.Accepted))
            _CollectBrokenRulesRegardingAccepted(brokenRules);

        return brokenRules;
    }
}
```

Refining the Implementation

So in _CollectBrokenRulesRegardingAccepted(), there will be a specific rule evaluation for entering (or rather, in this case, being in) the Accepted state.

Note

You may have noticed that I used the Collecting Parameter pattern [Beck SBPP] for _CollectBrokenRulesRegardingAccepted(). I sent in the list of broken rules and asked the method to add more broken rules to the list if appropriate.

To summarize all this, I think you recognize plenty of smells and lack of functionality. For example:

- Code explosion in `BrokenRulesRegardingPersistence` because rule evaluation is manually coded

- Returned information about broken rules is just `strings`, which isn't enough

- We haven't addressed customization

- We haven't addressed providing information about the rules themselves to be used by the UI

It's time to refine this naïve implementation a little bit, without showing the iterations for getting there. Let's reuse the tests and generalize the implementation a bit.

Creating Rule Classes—Leaving the Most Naïve Stage

I think creating rule classes for the basic needs so that they can be used declaratively will cut down on code explosion, manual rule evaluation, and deal with customization and providing information about the rules to the outside.

The complex rules always have to be coded by hand for each situation and are hard to customize by adding information in a config file. Furthermore, it's not important to provide information about the complex rules to generic forms. Those rules aren't my target here. They aren't uninteresting; on the contrary, I *want* to code them by hand. If they fit into the big picture, that's fine, but what I'm trying to say is it's not important that they are declared.

My target for what should be declared is the simple rules: those that are uninteresting to write by hand over and over again. Let's give it a try.

> **Note**
>
> As always, watch out so you don't fall into the trap of building frameworks up front. It's generally better to let them show themselves in your code and then you go from there. [Fowler Harvested Framework]

My rule classes should implement an interface; let's call it `IRule`:

```
public interface IRule
{
    bool IsValid {get;}
```

Refining the Implementation

```
    int RuleId {get;}
    string[] ParticipatingLogicalFields {get;}
}
```

IsValid is used to check if the rule is valid or not. The RuleId is used for making it possible to translate rules information and such. It requires some extra information, typically in the form of long constant lists, but I'll leave that to the reader.

The idea regarding ParticipatingLogicalFields is that the consumer should be able to mark out the fields that are affecting a certain broken rule.

And a rule class could look like the following example. This one is for checking that a date is within a certain range:

```
public class DateIsInRangeRule : RuleBase
{
    public readonly DateTime MinDate;
    public readonly DateTime MaxDate;

    //Note: Only the "largest" constructor is shown here.
    public DateIsInRangeRule(DateTime minDate, DateTime maxDate,
        int ruleId, string[] participatingLogicalFields,
        string fieldName, object holder)
        : base(ruleId, participatingLogicalFields, fieldname
        , holder)
    {
        MinDate = minDate;
        MaxDate = maxDate;
    }

    public override bool IsValid
    {
        get
        {
            DateTime value = (DateTime)base.GetValue();

            return (value >= MinDate && value <= MaxDate);
        }
    }
}
```

Refining the
Implementation

I also needed a base class (RuleBase) for generic functionality, such as reading values by reflection, and for taking away the infrastructure part of the game from the subclasses. All that is left for the subclasses is the "interesting" code (and some constructors—I only showed one in the previous snippet).

> ### Note
>
> By the way, `fieldName` can be either a field or a property.
>
> If you wonder what `holder` is, it's the Domain Model instance, such as an order instance, that is using the rule object.

I think a figure would help here to explain the different pieces. See Figure 7-2.

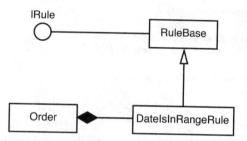

Figure 7-2   Overview of `IRule`, `RuleBase`, `DateIsInRangeRule`, and a Domain Model class

Then we "only" have to write classes, such as `DateIsInRangeRule`, for the different needs that crop up. It's a piece of highly reusable code that is being written, but it will take some effort.

You might be wondering why I wanted to use reflection. "Want" isn't exactly correct, but I want the positive *effect* of reflection. I mean, I like to be able to define the rule once, and then let it execute without providing the *value* to check against explicitly. Instead, I'd provide the field/property that *has* the value. Let's look at how it could be done.

Refining the Implementation

> ### Note
>
> A possible optimization is to only use reflection when really needed. For example, when you use reference types, you don't have to go via reflection to get the same effect. On the other hand, that does increase the complexity a little bit, so watch out carefully.
>
> Gregory Young added the following: "Another answer here might be to use code generation to amortize the reflections overhead."

Setting Up a List of Rules

We have one rule class so far. Let's assume a similar one for MaxStringLengthRule as well. It's time to put them to use. When using them in an Order class, it could look like this:

```
//Order
private IList _persistenceRelatedRules = new ArrayList();
private DateTime _orderDate;
public string Note = string.Empty;

private void _SetUpPersistenceRelatedRules()
{
    _persistenceRelatedRules.Add(new DateIsInRangeRule
        (MyDateTime.MinValue, DateTime.Today, "OrderDate", this));

    _persistenceRelatedRules.Add(new MaxStringLengthRule
        (30, "Note", this));

}
```

Then in the constructors of the Order, I just call the _SetUpPersistenceRelatedRules().

Note

I'm not putting any effort into giving the rules instances good identifiers. Therefore, I used a constructor here where I'm not providing the values at all.

Using the List of Rules

I have the persistence related rules in place. Let's see how this could affect the BrokenRulesRegardingPersistence implementation.

```
//Order
public IList BrokenRulesRegardingPersistence
{
    get
    {
        IList brokenRules = new ArrayList();

        RuleBase.CollectBrokenRules(brokenRules
            , _persistenceRelatedRules);

        if (_OrderIsInThisStateOrBeyond(OrderStatus.Accepted)
            _CollectBrokenRulesRegardingAccepted(brokenRules);

        return brokenRules;
    }
}
```

Note

Do you remember I said that the list of broken rules is an implementation of the Notification pattern [Fowler PoEAA2]? I still think it is, but I have moved away slightly.

Gregory Young described the difference like this: "The key difference is that the actual rule (IRule) is exposed as opposed to a surrogate object which simply says it has been broken as is the case with the Notification pattern."

A good bonus, thanks to the solution, is that we can easily write a Rule-Base.IsValid() that we provide with the list of _persistenceRelatedRules as a parameter. That way we can increase the execution efficiency for the IsValid property without increasing the amount of code duplication. I mean, that implementation should just see if it finds any rule that is invalid. There is no need to collect a list of broken rules, no need to go through all the rules even though the first one is broken, and so on.

Back to the basic flow. Let's have a look at how CollectBrokenRules() in RuleBase could look:

```
//RuleBase
public static void CollectBrokenRules
    (IList brokenRules, IList rulesToCheck)
{
    foreach (IRule r in rulesToCheck)
        if (! r.IsValid)
            brokenRules.Add(r);

}
```

That was about the persistence related rules; very straightforward. But what about the rules per transition?

Dealing with Sublists

One solution to this problem could be to set up transition-specific lists as well, such as _acceptedSpecificRules. When that is in place, the BrokenRulesRegardingPersistence method can be written like this:

```
//Order
public IList BrokenRulesRegardingPersistence
{
```

```
get
{
    IList brokenRules = new ArrayList();

    RuleBase.CollectBrokenRules(brokenRules
        , _persistenceRelatedRules);

    if (_OrderIsInThisStateOrBeyond(OrderStatus.Accepted)
        RuleBase.CollectBrokenRules(brokenRules,
            _acceptedSpecificRules);

    return brokenRules;
}
}
```

That way, most of the work has moved to defining the list of rules (again, we can only go so far with this approach, but it is actually quite a long way).

I now put all the rules in one bucket (or actually several if there are transition-based lists as well): an instance-based one. With some work, both of the rules examples shown so far (DateIsInRangeRule and MaxStringLengthRule) could be changed to a list of static rules instead. I need to change the date rule so that it will evaluate what DateTime.Today is on its own instead of getting it in the constructor. I could also provide relative dates to the constructor as -1 and 1 to mean one day before and one day after today. I could also create some functionality that will only let the static list live until it's a new day. Of course, you should strive to move the rules to static lists instead, if possible. That will potentially reduce the overhead a lot. With that said, it's not affecting the principle much, if at all.

Refining the Implementation

Let's move on instead of looking more into those details regarding scope.

An API Improvement

My friend Ingemar Lundberg pointed out that it felt a bit strange to use a property for BrokenRulesRegardingPersistence, and Christian Crowhurst suggested that it would be better to let a method use a collecting parameter and return a bool. Something like this:

```
public bool CheckX(IList brokenRules)
```

Do you remember IsOKToAccept and BrokenRulesIfAccept? This idea will reduce the size of the API and not split the check and the detailed error information into two separate pieces. Those two pieces could very well be rewritten into one method like this:

```
public bool CheckOKToAccept(IList brokenRules)
```

The consumer code will be slightly affected. Instead of this:

```
//Some consumer...
if (! o.IsOKToAccept)
    _Show(o.BrokenRulesIfAccept);
```

You would typically write something like this:

```
//Some consumer...
IList brokenRules = new ArrayList();
if (! o.CheckOKToAccept(brokenRules))
    _Show(brokenRules);
```

Regarding the collecting parameter brokenRules, if it's not initialized (null) when CheckOKToAccept() starts, CheckOKToAccept() can ignore it and only return the bool. That's at least one approach, but an overload to CheckOKToAccept() without a parameter feels more intention revealing. (It's not really a split into two methods, but just a chaining from one of the overloads to the other. It's also the case that even if the bool is true, the returned list *can* have warnings for example.)

An additional consequence is that it steers a consumer away from executing rule checking code twice, once for the IsOKToAccept and again for the BrokenRulesIfAccept. For example, it is unlikely that the client will write the following code:

```
//Some consumer...
if (! o.CheckOKToAccept())
{
    IList brokenRules = new ArrayList();
    o.CheckOKToAccept(brokenRules);
    _Show(brokenRules);
}
```

I like this.

Customization

There are loads of ways to achieve customization of a Domain Model; for example, you could let different customers who are using your application add some behavior of their own. One appealing solution is to use the Decorator pattern [GoF Design Patterns], while another is to provide inheritance hooks and configurable creation code.

Yet another, and pretty simplistic, technique is to make it possible to define the rules, or at least add specific rule instances, by describing them in the form of configuration files.

With the current solution draft, we have most of it in place. What we need is a way of adding rules, so let's sketch a new interface called ICustomRules:

```
interface ICustomRules
{
    void AddCustomRule(IRule r);
}
```

In this first draft, I just assume that we can add persistence related rules and that they go to the instance-based list of rules. That can (and should) be refined if you need to.

Note

Talking about needing to add rule instances to static lists reminds me of an old wish of mine. I'd like to be able to define static interfaces as well. Why not?

Now you can add more rules during instantiation of Domain Model classes, but—as I said—instantiation gets a bit messy, and you should probably use a Factory of some sort.

The good news is that the customization we just talked about works seamlessly with the possibility of dragging out information about the rules, which comes in very handy for creating the forms.

Providing the Consumer with Metadata

Refining the Implementation

The persistence related rules should be treated as something that can be dragged out of the Domain Model instance proactively. This is because they could be easily used by the consumer. I add another method to the IValidatableRegardingPersistence interface:

```
interface IValidatableRegardingPersistence
{
    bool IsValidRegardingPersistence {get;}
    IList BrokenRulesRegardingPersistence {get;}
    IList PersistenceRelatedRules {get;}
}
```

Then it's up to the consumer to do something interesting with the rules she finds. There will probably be some rules that are easily used by the UI when new forms are shown, such as fields that are required, certain value ranges, lengths of strings and so on.

Conceptually, I like the solution. Something like this should be useful for a great number of projects. But I can't help feeling that it is still a bit smelly, especially regarding the transition-specific rules, at least if the scale of the problem increases.

A Problem Suitable for a Pattern?

What do you think about using the State pattern [GoF Design Patterns] here? We discussed it quite a lot in Chapter 2, "A Head Start on Patterns." It's quite appealing if you ask me, and it means I can delegate the responsibility of the transition-specific lists out into the certain state classes. It's actually a problem that the State pattern is pretty much made for.

You can also work with several levels in the inheritance hierarchy regarding the different states; for example, if an instance-based rule definition is the same for several of the states.

What About the Complex Rules?

As I said, I don't mind writing the complex rules by hand. I *want* to spend my time there.

I think applying the Specification pattern [Evans DDD] is often a good idea for complex rules.

What we try to achieve when using Specifications is to express important domain concepts in code. The common theme with DDD is to be concept-focused. (The focus is on domain concepts instead of just technical concepts. For example, numeric intervals and string lengths are more of technical concepts most often.)

For example, there might be a Specification class called ReadyToInvoiceSpecification with a method like this:

```
public bool Test(Order o);
```

Refining the Implementation

Let's take a quick and simple example. Assume that you'd like to create a single invoice for a customer, even if the customer currently has several orders that can be invoiced. Perhaps you then would like to ask the customer if he has something to invoice. A method on the Customer class could look like this (assuming that an IOrderRepository has already been injected):

```
//Customer
public IList OrdersToInvoice(ReadyToInvoiceSpecification
    specification)
{
    IList orders = _orderRepository.GetOrders(this);
    IList result = new ArrayList();
    foreach (Order o in orders)
    {
        if (specification.Test(o))
            result.Add(o);
    }

    return result;
}
```

As always, it's context-dependent whether a certain design is recommended or is even possible, but my focus here was just to provide you with a simple example that shows how the concept could be applied and that the code is very clear and yet highly flexible. (Remember, the Specification parameter had been configured before being sent in.)

Again, the rules for what makes an order invoicable are encapsulated in the Specification, not spread out in several methods.

> ### Note
>
> A very nice feature of a Specification implementation is if you can let it be evaluated in the database as well, so that it can be used for concept-focused querying.

The problem with the Specification approach as I see it is how to make it easy for the UI to automatically do smart things beforehand instead of letting the rule break. On the other hand, I can often live with that problem, especially if Specifications are used for somewhat more advanced problems that are hard to be proactive about anyway. On the other hand, if a Specification is using a concept similar to IRule, the parts of the Specification could be used as usual regarding proactivity for automatically setting up the UI.

I also must point out how nice complex rules that are encapsulated as Specifications are when it comes to unit testing. It's very easy to test the Specifications separately.

Binding to the Persistence Abstraction

In the previous chapter, I talked about how to prepare for the persistence infrastructure by working with an abstraction layer that I called NWorkspace (which is just an example of such an abstraction of course). As you might have guessed, it has some support for validation as well, because the reactive nature needs to be dealt with when we make calls to PersistAll().

Of course, I don't want the persistence abstraction to expect a certain interface to be implemented on the Aggregate roots.

Make the Validation Interface Pluggable

Therefore, I made it possible to inject an IValidator to the IWorkspace. The IValidator interface looks like this:

```
public interface IValidator
{
    bool IsValidatable(object entity);
    bool IsValid(object entity);
    IList BrokenRules(object entity);
}
```

The IWorkspace implementation talks to the IValidator implementation, and the IValidator implementation then decides what interfaces to look for on the entities. In my case, the IValidator implementation looks for IValidatableRegardingPersistence implementations and knows what to do with the IValidatableRegardingPersistence implementation in order to throw an exception during PersistAll(), if necessary. To make this a bit more concrete, see Figure 7-3.

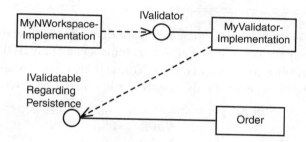

Figure 7-3   Overview of the collaborating pieces

Just as with the database itself, the IValidator is reactive, but it reacts at a step earlier than the database and it often reacts on slightly more complex and domain focused rules.

To make testing easier, I also have an implementation of IValidator that is called ValidatorThatDoesNothing. I mean for it to be used for unit tests when you don't want to have the validation to interfere. Then you inject ValidatorThatDoesNothing to the IWorkspace implementation instead of the one looking for IValidatableRegarding-Persistence instances. It took 30 seconds to write, and I think that's a decent investment compared to how useful it is.

Alternative Solution for Approaching the Reactive Validation on Save

As I have touched on earlier, there are problems for certain O/R Mappers regarding what you can do at the validation spot in the persist pipeline. Therefore, it might be interesting to think about what you can do to deal with that.

In my implementation, I prefer to check the rules in real-time; that is, when someone wants to know. As I've mentioned, I like the idea of using Services for dealing with problems related to what can't be done at the validation spot.

One alternative solution is to update the list of broken rules after each change to a property so that it is pre-calculated when it is needed. Depending on your call patterns, it could either be more or less efficient than my way of doing it.

Note

Gregory Young pointed out that with the metadata on the rules mentioned earlier (what fields affect what rules), one can be very efficient about rechecking rules and always having current validation.

A problem is that it requires some help with dirty tracking, or you will have to write loads of code yourself in your setters (unless you apply AOP for dealing with the crosscutting concern of course). You will also have to use properties instead of public fields, even if public fields would otherwise do very well.

Note

This style is used in the CSLA.NET-framework [Lhotka BO], which also has support for something I haven't touched upon: multi-step undo.

Another solution is to hold on to a flag called `IsValidated` that is set to true each time you reproduce the list of broken rules and set to false after each change. At the validation spot for the persist-pipeline, you expect the `IsValidated` to be true, or you throw an exception. That affects the programming model slightly because it makes the `IsValidRegardingPersistence` call or `BrokenRulesRegardingPersistence` call mandatory. The other drawback (if you consider the mandatory call a drawback, and I think I do) is that you have similar problems with the dirty tracking as I just mentioned.

Anyway, it's good to have a couple of different approaches prepared in case you find problems with your first choice.

Reuse Mapping Metadata

There's one more idea I need to get out of my system before moving on. I have already said that I like the principle of defining once but executing where most appropriate (such as in the UI, the Domain Model, or the database). This idea is very much in line with that.

If you find that you put a lot of energy into defining loads of simple rules by hand, such as maximum string lengths, you should consider setting up those rules dynamically instead by reading metadata somewhere. For example, you have the information in the database, but using that might be a bit troublesome depending on your mapping solution. An alternative might be the metadata mapping data itself. Perhaps you'll find the source for several rules there.

Anyway, the important part of the idea is to read the data from somewhere when you start up the application, set up the rules dynamically, and then you are done.

Of course, as with all the other ideas in this chapter, this isn't the answer to every problem. It is just one more tool for solving the big puzzle.

Generics and Anonymous Methods to the Rescue

If you are using an environment that supports generics (such as .NET 2.0), you can of course apply generics to the solution proposals discussed previously and gain slightly in explicitness, type safety, and performance. That goes, by the way, for most of the chapters discussed so far.

To take a small example, instead of this:

```
IList BrokenRulesRegardingPersistence {get;}
```

You could with generics use:

```
IList<IRule> BrokenRulesRegardingPersistence {get;}
```

Not a dramatic improvement or something we can't live without (as is shown throughout the book), but an improvement that will affect (again positively) many places in your code.

Another technique I have not had in the environments I've been working in most of the time is anonymous methods (similar to blocks or closures as it's called in other languages).

The idea is to be able to send a block of code as a parameter to a method, but the block of code can use variables that are in scope of the method that received the block.

Some people have discussed it as a way of implementing Specifications without creating new classes, although I think that means that you will lose some of the explicitness and clarity with the Specifications *naming*, which is a powerful feature of Specifications. Instead, I currently think of anonymous methods more as a good technique for providing variations to reusable assets. For example, you can inject part of the implementation of a method at will. It's a different way of thinking about customizability.

Just to give you a taste of the whole thing if you are new to the technique, let's combine generics and anonymous methods to a snippet we discussed previously and see if it can be improved. Do you remember the loop for seeing if a Customer needs to be invoiced? It looked like this:

```
//Customer
public IList OrdersToInvoice(ReadyToInvoiceSpecification
    specification)
{
    IList orders = _orderRepository.GetOrders(this);
    IList result = new ArrayList();
    foreach (Order o in orders)
    {
        if (specification.Test(o))
            result.Add(o);
    }

    return result;
}
```

Here it is again in a slightly modified version:

```
//Customer
public List<Order>OrdersToInvoice(Predicate<Order>
    readyToInvoicePredicate)
{
    List<Order> orders = _orderRepository.GetOrders(this);
    return orders.FindAll(readyToInvoicePredicate);
}
```

Generics
and
Anonymous
Methods to
the Rescue

This time, the parameter is a predicate for if an Order can be invoiced or not. The call provides an anonymous method as the parameter. The call could be like this, assuming a very simple algorithm at this point in time:

```
c.OrdersToInvoice(delegate(Order o) {return o.Status == OrderStatus.ToBeInvoiced;});
```

That "Specification" or predicate is sent to the FindAll() method of the generic List for filtering out orders that can be invoiced.

At the time of this writing, it's still early for me regarding both generics and anonymous methods, but I'm sure they will make a huge difference regarding how I design in the foreseeable future. I'm not just talking about tiny things as in the examples above, but more like a mind shift.

But at the same time, they are just some more tools for the toolbox; they won't change *everything*, of course.

What Others Have Done

I have occasionally touched on what others have done and written about in this respect, and before we end I'd like to touch on two more sources.

The first is *Streamlined Object Modeling* [Nicola et al. SOM], which has a thorough discussion both about different rules and strategies for design and implementation of the same, all in object-oriented context.

The second is *Enterprise Patterns and MDA* [Arlow/Neustadt Archetype Patterns], which discusses archetype patterns for how to organize rules. I think you will find that many of the ideas there are useful for moving on from here.

Summary

All these years and this topic still feels a bit immature and with no obvious solutions. That said, we have touched on several ideas for how to deal with rules, some typical and some a little more atypical.

We discussed quite a lot about rule objects as an implementation technique, but we have also touched on other variants. As always, no solution is the best for all situations. For example, the rule objects I sketched were probably most appropriate for pretty simple rules and if you have many rules.

The major takeaways in this chapter were probably that you should try to decouple persistence and the domain-related rules as much as possible. (Still, there are connections for some of the rules.) Working with different states is a very powerful solution for getting close to the "all states should be savable" goal. Finally, remember that the rules are very context-connected, and try to focus on the model meaning of the rules.

In this chapter, we have dealt with many of the feature requests defined in Chapter 4, but now we will move on to the needed infrastructure, with a focus on persistence support.

Summary

PART III

Applying PoEAA

In this part, we put several of the patterns in Fowler's *Patterns of Enterprise Application Architecture* [Fowler PoEAA] into context by discussing what we need from the infrastructure for providing persistence support to our domain model. We will look at how those requirements are fulfilled by an example tool.

This part is about a distraction—the infrastructure. Yet the infrastructure is very valuable.

Chapter 8

Infrastructure for Persistence

Where are we? We have built a Domain Model from the ground up, and it's in DDD [Evans DDD] style. So far, I've been pushing like crazy for delaying the decisions about infrastructure as long as possible. Sure, we did talk quite a lot about how we could prepare for simplifying the infrastructure addition in Chapter 6, "Preparing for Infrastructure," but now is the time to add the mechanics for supporting the Domain Model: the infrastructure. We will also make some modifications to the Domain Model we have been discussing as the answer to the feature list first mentioned in Chapter 4, "A New Default Architecture."

Important to note is that we will do this because we *have* to, not because we *want* to. That's not the same thing as saying it's not important. It's just that we want to put as much of our efforts as possible on the domain problems.

But before we start discussing the infrastructure, the obvious question is *what* infrastructure is needed? As a matter of fact, a great deal of infrastructure is needed, such as infrastructure for

- Authorization

- Integration (service requests and responses)

- Data management and access (persistence)

- Presentation (which might be a stretch to call that infrastructure)

- Logging

And so on, and so forth. I guess it might be my background as a database guy that makes me see it this way, but I think persistence is the most obvious and interesting infrastructure. At least this is what we will be focusing on in the upcoming chapters.

As we define the needed infrastructure for persistence, we will also make small changes to the current Domain Model design here and there in order to make it fit the typical choice of persistence infrastructure better.

Note

A design approach that does *not* use iterations is very dangerous. Let's assume that you are responsible for nothing but the Domain Model and the persistence. Even so, you should work a little on the Domain Model, choose and try the persistence infrastructure, work on the Domain Model, check the persistence infrastructure, and so on. This is *especially* how you should proceed with your first couple of DDD projects, but is always a good idea to some extent.

Let me also clarify that I totally understand that the UI, for example, is extremely important and that it might be considered an insult to talk about it just as "mechanics." Of course I (and the users) extremely value a usable UI. It's also frequently the case that much of the total project time is spent on the UI. With that said, our focus here is the Domain Model. Discussing good UI design is not the purpose of this book (although there is some coverage in Chapter 11, "Focus on the UI").

We have decided to focus on persistence infrastructure. The next question then is what requirements do we have on the persistence infrastructure for being a persistence infrastructure that *enables* us to focus on the domain?

Requirements on the Persistence Infrastructure

Requirements
on the
Persistence
Infrastructure

Let's repeat again that I want the infrastructure to stay out of the way of the Domain Model as much as possible so that I can focus on creating a powerful Domain Model for solving the business problem without having more distractions than are necessary. For example, I believe that I should be able to work with as high a level of *Persistence Ignorance* (PI) as possible, so that's a requirement of the infrastructure.

At the same time, it's also important not to put too much responsibility on the consumer of the Domain Model. I want to provide the consumer with a very simple API so that the consumer programmer can focus on what is important to him: creating a good experience for consumer users.

I have already defined certain desirable features for the life cycle of the persistent entities in Chapter 5, "Moving Further with Domain-Driven Design," but let's repeat it again here in Table 8-1.

Table 8-1 *Summary of the Semantics for the Life Cycle of the Domain Model Instances*

Operation		Result Regarding Transient/Persistent
Call to new	→	Transient
Repository.Add(instance) or persistentInstance.Add(instance)	→	Persistent in Domain Model
x.PersistAll()	→	Persistent in Database
Repository.Get()	→	Persistent in Domain Model (and Database)
Repository.Delete(instance)	→	Transient (and instance will get deleted from database at x.PersistAll)

Another way of thinking about the requirements of the persistence infrastructure is to look at the non-functional requirements I have. Typical examples are scalability, security, and maintainability.

Of course, this varies widely, not only concerning the requirements, but also because a certain persistence framework can sometimes fail and sometimes succeed for the same mix of non-functional requirements. The reason for this is that the success or failure depends on the type of application, the usage patterns, and so on. I have to leave it up to the reader to define her own mix of non-functional requirements and to check whether a certain persistence framework can fulfill the requirements by carrying out careful tests. Just remember that if your appetite for non-functional requirements becomes too big, it will cost you a lot somewhere else.

Requirements
on the
Persistence
Infrastructure

Note

Most often it's very hard to get the customer to express any non-functional requirements at all. If you succeed, the risk is that he will want everything to 100%, and that's when it's good to remember the cost side of it.

For further discussion of non-functional requirements, see [POSA 1], [Fowler PoEAA] or [Nilsson NED].

As you may have noticed, I didn't mention it as a requirement on the persistence framework to be able to have a network between the consumer and the Domain Model. Building it is very possible, as we did in Valhalla [Valhalla]. However, it's probably better to think along the lines of explicit boundary where networks are involved and design the crossing borders in a service-oriented way. This is why I seldom see the need for the shortcut that remoting represents.

So, we have defined requirements to fulfill for the Domain Model's sake, and we have defined how to use the API for the persistence framework.

With the requirements now in place, let's get going and make some choices about the infrastructure. First is the location for the persistent data.

Where to Store Data

Assume we start with a clean sheet of paper; how would we like to store the data? We have at least four choices:

- RAM

- File system

- Object database

- Relational database

Note

I realize that this may be a case of apples and oranges because it is a two-part problem: what to store (Objects, Hierarchies, such as XML, or Tables) and where to store it: (RAM, File system, Object database, or Relational database). But that's not without problems, either. After thinking through it a couple of times, I think my original way of describing it is good enough, so let's move on.

I'll start with RAM.

RAM

Storing the data in RAM isn't necessarily as silly as it might first sound. What I'm thinking about is seeing the Domain Model as the database itself while at the same time keeping persistent storage of all changes as a log on disk so that the Domain Model can be re-created in case of a system crash.

The beauty is that you avoid mapping from the Domain Model onto something else. The Domain Model is persistent by itself.

You could also store hierarchies in memory, with XML documents as a typical example. Then you do get some impedance mismatch because you are using two models and need to transform between them. On the other hand, you do get some functionality for free, such as querying if you find XPath and XQuery to be good languages for that.

No matter what you "store" in RAM, one problem is the size of RAM. If you have 2 GB of RAM in your machine leftover when the system and other applications have taken their part, your database shouldn't be larger than 2 GB or performance will suffer.

On the other hand, 64-bit servers are becoming more and more common, and RAM prices are dropping all the time. For a majority of applications, the current as well as the next generation of hardware is often enough, at least when considering the possible maximum size of the database.

Another problem is that it takes time to recreate the Domain Model after a system crash, because working through a huge log will take time. The problem is minimized if the RAM-based solution takes snapshots to disk every now and then of the current Domain Model. But the problem is still there, and taking snapshots might be a problem in itself because it will bring the system on its knees and might cause periods of waitstate for other requests when the snapshot is taken.

Note

Gregory Young pointed out that to make the issue of snapshots smaller, context boundaries can be used within the domain and they can be snapshotted separately.

One of the worst problems with this approach comes in making changes to the schema. What you'll have to do is serialize the objects to disk, and then deserialize them into the Domain Model again with the new schema, which is a tedious task. Working with XML instead of pure classes helps with this problem.

Another big problem is that of transactions. Fulfilling *Atomicity, Consistency, Isolation and Durability* (ACID) is not easily done without hurting scalability a lot. First, instead of using the "try and see" approach in this case it's better to prepare for a transaction as much as possible in order to investigate whether the task is likely to succeed. ("I need to do this; will that get me into trouble?") Of course, this won't solve the whole problem, but at least it will reduce it. It's good to be proactive here, especially considering that you have very good efficiency because there are probably no process boundaries or network involved.

> ### Note
>
> This depends on the topology. If you consume the Domain Model (and therefore the "database" in this case) from another machine, there *are* process boundaries and networks to cross.

Again, being proactive didn't provide any transactional semantics, it just made a rollback less likely. One approach I've heard about requires a RAM twice the size of the Domain Model if transactions are needed so that the changes can be done in the copy of the Domain Model. If all changes are successful, they are redone in the ordinary Domain Model. Meanwhile, the Domain Model is inherently single-user. Keep in mind that operations are usually extremely fast, and yet this does not seem scalable to me. I also consider it to be a sign of immaturity, so expect better solutions to this later on. At the time of this writing, there are lightweight transaction managers in the works or being introduced, which might be a good solution to the problem.

One more problem is that there is no obvious choice for a query language. There are some open source alternatives, but again, this feels a bit immature at the moment. This problem gets bigger when you consider reporting and the need for ad-hoc querying done by end users and not just querying from within the application. For example, typical report writer tools for end users are pretty useless in this case.

Where to Store Data

> ### Note
>
> If possible, reporting should be done on a dedicated server and dedicated database anyway, so this might be less of a problem than what was first anticipated. On the other hand, in reality there is often at least a grey zone of what are reports and what are lists for supporting the daily transactional work, so to speak. And voilá, the problem is back.

Yet another problem is that navigation in the Domain Model is typically based on traversing lists. There might not be built-in support for indexing. Sure, you can use hash tables here and there, but they only solve part of the problem. You can, of course, add an in-memory indexing solution if you need it. On the other hand, you should note that this certainly won't be a problem as early on as it is for disk-based solutions.

Finally, as I've already said a couple of times, I consider this approach to be a bit immature, but very interesting and promising for the future, at least in certain situations.

File System

Another solution is to use the file system instead of RAM. What to persist is the same as with RAM, namely the Domain Model objects or XML. As a matter of fact, this solution could be very close to the RAM solution. It could be the same if the database is small, and it might "only" spill out to disk when the RAM is filled to a certain level.

This approach has similar problems to the previous one, except that the size of RAM isn't as much of a limiting factor in this case. On the other hand, the performance characteristics will probably be less impressive.

I believe that it might be pretty appealing to write your own solution for persisting the Domain Model (or XML documents also), but as always when you decide to roll your own infrastructure, you have to be prepared for a lot of work. I know that nothing is more inspiring to a developer than hearing that "it's too hard" or "too complex," so if they haven't already done so, now just about everybody will be writing their own file system-based solution, right? Just be prepared for it to be deceptively simple at first, but the devil is in the details, and the complexity increases as you move forward.

If you do decide to build a Domain Model that could spill out to disk when persisting, what you actually create is quite like an object database. (Perhaps that gives a better sense of the amount of work and complexity.)

Object Database

Historically, there have been many different styles of object databases, but the common denominator was that they tried to avoid the transformation between objects and some other storage format. This was done for more or less the same reasons as I have been talking about when wanting to delay adding infrastructure to the Domain Model, as well as for performance reasons.

Note

The number of styles increases even more if we also consider the hybrids, such as object-relational databases, but I think those hybrids have most often come from a relational background and style rather than from the object-oriented side.

As it turned out, the number of distractions was not zero. In fact, you could say that the impedance mismatch was still there, but compared to bridging the gap between objects and a relational database, using object databases was pretty clean.

So far, the problems with object databases have been as follows:

- Lack of standards

- No critical mass

- Maturity

- More of a niche product

- Integration with other systems

- Reporting

Note

Where to
Store Data

My evil friend Martin Rosén-Lidholm pointed out that many of the same arguments actually could be used against DDD and O/R Mapping compared to data-oriented solutions in a .NET-world, considering Microsoft's application blocks, papers, guidelines, and so on.

I'll pretend I didn't hear that. And a focus on the domain will probably become more and more popular for Microsoft's guidance as well, which Martin totally agrees with.

I'm certainly no expert on object databases. I've played with a couple of them over the years, and that's about the extent of it. For more information, my favorite books on the subject are [Cattell ODM] and [Connolly/Begg DB Systems].

There was a time, around 1994, when I thought object databases were taking over as the de facto standard. But I based that idea on purely technical characteristics, and life isn't as simple as that. Object databases were promising a decade ago. They are used very much in certain situations today, but above all, they are still just promising. As I see it today, the de facto standard is still relational databases.

Relational Database

As I said, the de facto solution for storing data in applications is to use a relational database, and this is the case even if you work with a Domain Model.

Storing the data in a relational database means that the data is stored in tabular format, where everything is data, including the relationships. This has proved to be a simple and yet effective (enough) solution in many applications. But no solution is without problems, and in this case when we want to persist a Domain Model in a relational database, the problem is the impedance mismatch. However, I talked about that at length in Chapter 1, "Values to Value," so I won't repeat it here.

If we go this route, the most common solution is to use an implementation of the Data Mapper pattern [Fowler PoEAA]. The purpose of the Data Mapper pattern is to bridge the gap between the Domain Model and the persistent representation, to shuffle the data both ways. We'll come back to that pattern in a few minutes.

Choosing what storage solution to use isn't obvious. Still, we have to make a choice.

Before choosing and moving forward, I'd like to think about a couple of other questions.

Where to Store Data

One or Several Resource Managers?

Another, completely different, question to ask is whether one resource manager should be used or several. It might turn out that you don't have a choice.

The Domain Model excels in a situation where there are several resource managers because it can completely hide this complexity from the consumers if desired. But we should also be clear that the presence of multiple resource managers adds to the complexity of mapping the Domain Model to its persistence. In order to make things simpler in the discussion, I'll only assume one resource manager here.

Other Factors

In reality, we rarely start with a clean sheet of paper. There are factors that color our decision, such as what we know ourselves. A good way of becoming efficient is to work with technology that you know.

Other typical factors that come into play, apart from the raw technology factors that we talked about earlier and that didn't prove a clear winner, are what systems the customer has invested in (bought and trained the staff in).

Maturity in solutions is also a very influential factor when it comes to the data. Losing data vital to the business processes just isn't an option, so customers are often picky if you choose what they think is an unproven solution.

Choose and Move On

Taking the technological reasons, as well as the other factors I have mentioned, into consideration, it's no wonder the relational database is a common choice. Therefore, let's assume this and move on. It feels like a decent choice, and will probably be the default choice for a long time to come.

It actually makes me want to add some requirements to the list of our requirements on the persistence infrastructure:

- Dealing carefully with the relational database. (Sticking as closely as possible to how we would program it manually.)

- Strong querying support. (Which is, to a large degree, what the previous bullet was about.)

- Support for concurrency collision detection.

- Support for advanced mapping, such as different inheritance strategies (even if I will probably be careful using "inheritance" in the database) and fine-grained types in the Domain Model.

As I said, what is then needed is an implementation of the Data Mapper pattern. The question is *how* to implement that pattern.

Approach

There are certainly many different ways of dealing with the Data Mapper pattern, but I think the most typical are the following:

- Custom manual code

- Code generation of custom code

- Metadata mapping (O/R Mapping)

Let's start discussing custom manual code.

Custom Manual Code

Here you will typically write persistence code on your own. The code will reside in the repositories. Of course, helper classes should be used, but that won't solve all the problems. Some typical technical problems are then the following:

- How to save changes in a complete graph

- How to express and translate queries

- Is Unit of Work needed?

- Is Identity Map needed?

- Is Lazy Load needed?

Note

I think a sentence about each of the patterns mentioned previously is in order. The Unit of Work pattern [Fowler PoEAA] is about capturing information about changes that are done to the Domain Model during a logical unit of work. That information can then be used to affect the persistent representation.

The Identity Map pattern [Fowler PoEAA] is about keeping no more than one instance for each entity in the session. It's like an identity-based cache. This is vital for bridging the impedance mismatch. When you work with objects, you want to be able to use the built-in object identity, the address to the object.

Finally, the Lazy Load pattern [Fowler PoEAA] is about loading subgraphs just in time.

Approach

Unit of Work and Identity Map are needed, according to the requirements we set up. That also goes for querying. Lazy Load *might* not be needed though. It can be solved pretty easily on your own if you need it occasionally. With that said, it's nice if we get support for in case we do need it.

So it seems as if there is some work to do. And those were just a couple of examples. There is more, much more to it.

If you decide to stick to the requirements I defined, you will find that you are about to build a specific and (hopefully) simplified O/R Mapper if you go for custom manual code. That means that we have kind of left this categorization and moved to the third one. Let's ignore that for now and just assume that we will be trying really hard to live without Unit of Work, Identity Map, Lazy Load, dynamic and flexible querying, and so on.

First, you have to decide how everything should work in detail. And when all that work has been done, you have to apply it to your complete Domain Model. This is very tedious, time-consuming, and prone to errors. Even worse, the problem will hit you again each time you make changes to the Domain Model from now on.

Code Generation of Custom Code

Another approach is to use code generation (such as custom built, a generic tool with your custom written templates, or a purchased complete solution if you find something appropriate) for dealing with the Data Mapper pattern. What I mean here is to use a solution similar to the one with custom manual code, but when the design is settled, it's used over and over again with the help of code generation.

This approach has the same problems as custom manual code, plus complexities with the code generation itself, of course. The up side is that the productivity will be much better when the design itself is mature.

Approach

Another common problem with code generation-based solutions is that of source code control. A small change to the Domain Model will usually force you to check out (if you use a tool for source code control that requires a checkout before making changes) all the classes that deal with the Data Mapping and regenerate them all. It could be worse, but it's still inconvenient.

There are more problems, such as adding loads of uninteresting code to the code base, code that isn't to be read by any humans, only the compiler.

A common problem is that the generated code is often tightly coupled to a specific database product. Even if that's solvable with an abstraction layer, the problem is still there if you need to support different database *schemas*. Then you need to keep one generated code base per schema. This is also a viable option for different database products, even though it's not a very smooth solution.

Another problem is that you will probably have fewer possibilities for run-time tuning. Take how the optimizer of a relational database works as a comparison. Only "what" is decided statically, "how" is decided at runtime, and therefore "how" can change depending upon the situation. I don't see this as a big problem for most applications at the moment, though. Moreover, if you compare a specific scenario with the same approaches for generated code and reflective code, it is often possible to squeeze out better performance from generated static code than from reflective code.

Perhaps a worse problem is that of new generator versions. I have the gut feeling that it's hard to get a new version of a generator into production because it will have to re-generate all the code.

Also, if the database schema changes, it's not possible to make changes at runtime without a recompile. But this is something that's rarely recommended anyway. These sorts of changes should involve the developers.

The code generation being of roundtrip style or forward only is a pretty big difference. If it is roundtrip style, your changes to the generated code will be preserved, while in the case of forward only style, you should never change the generated code because changes will be lost at next generation.

Let's end on an up note. Debugging might be easier with a solution based on code generation than based on metadata mapping. All the code is "there," but the code might be hard to understand, and there is a lot of it.

Often the catalyst for wanting to look further is the lack of dynamics, such as when it comes to querying. And I also said that if we decide to implement dynamic querying, Unit of Work, Identity Map, and so on, I think we should take a good look at the next category: the O/R Mapper.

Metadata Mapping (Object Relational (O/R) Mapper)

Approach

A specific style of the Data Mapper pattern is what is called the Metadata Mapping pattern. You define the relationship between the Domain Model and the Relational database in metadata. The rest of the work is done for you automatically.

The most typical implementation is probably that of O/R Mappers. I will use the term O/R Mapper as a product family that takes care of Metadata mapping.

> ### Note
>
> My friend Mats Helander describes O/R Mapping as Tai Chi.
>
> Tai Chi is composed of two halves. The first half is about learning to elevate and lower the arms slowly, in harmony with the breathing. The second half is everything else. This isn't a joke. No matter how good you get at Tai Chi, you are "expected" or recommended to continue to spend as much time on the first move as on all the other moves together.
>
> O/R Mapping is also composed of two halves. The first is about shuffling data between objects in memory and rows in the database and back. The other half is everything else.

As you can probably guess by now, most O/R Mappers have built-in support for Unit of Work, Identity Map, Lazy Load, and Querying.

But there's no solution without problems. A common complaint against O/R Mappers is that they are incapable of creating really good SQL code. Let's have a look at some examples that are often brought up. First is UPDATE with the WHERE clause. Look at the following example:

```
UPDATE Inventory
SET Balance = Balance - 1
WHERE Id = 42 AND Balance >= 1
```

This means that I only want to change the balance if there are products in stock. Otherwise, I do not want to change the balance. This is usually not supported directly by O/R Mappers. Instead, the approach that O/R Mappers would take here is to read the Inventory row with an optimistic lock, make the change, and write it back (hoping for the best that there was no concurrency exception).

To clarify, here's an example of the optimistic approach (in this case as a SQL batch, but note that we aren't holding on to any locks because there is no explicit transaction, so this exemplifies the scenario):

```
--Remember the old Balance.
SET @oldBalance =
    (SELECT Balance
    FROM Inventory
    WHERE Id = 42)

--Calculate what the new Balance should be...

UPDATE Inventory
SET Balance = @newBalance
```

```
WHERE Id = 42 AND Balance = @oldBalance
--If @@ROWCOUNT now is 0, then the update failed!
```

Alternatively, it would read the Inventory row with a pessimistic lock, make the change, and write it back. Both approaches would cause scalability to suffer.

Another complaint about O/R Mappers is that they are often ineffective for updating large numbers of rows. The approach for updating all products via an O/R Mapper will probably be to read all products into a list, loop the list, and update the products one by one. If that could have been done with a single UPDATE statement instead, the throughput would have been tremendously better.

Yet another complaint is that it's hard to balance the amount to read. Either too little is read and there will therefore be lots of roundtrips when lazy loading, or more is read than is necessary. Type explosion is a common result from this, defining several variations of the type definitions.

But we can look at it the other way around as well. Can a person write all code extremely well and be consistent? And are all the developers on the team as good as the best one? Even *if* that's the case, should we use person hours for this if we get good enough performance with an automatic approach?

Note

To be fair, the point just made is also valid for code generation.

We found some pros and some cons. I like that, because it makes me feel that I understand (to some degree) the technology that is being discussed.

Choosing Again

Is this an easy choice? Of course not, but in my experience the approach that best fulfills the requirements we decided on together is the O/R Mapper. Intellectually, it feels like a decent approach for many situations, but it's not without problems.

If we are in YAGNI-mood, I think O/R Mappers make sense because we can solve the problem in a simple way (hopefully without adding distractions to the Domain Model) and stand strong for the future. And when the performance isn't good enough, these (hopefully rare) cases can be dealt with by custom code. This is probably a very efficient way of dealing with the problem, at least as long as not all the problems are performance problems, but that's hardly the case.

So let's assume we've chosen the O/R Mapper.

Approach

Classification

Let's have a closer look at what an O/R Mapper is. We'll discuss this from two different angles. First, we'll discuss it from one dimension: different characteristics. Next, we'll discuss it from some of the PoEAA patterns that are implemented. We'll reuse those classifications when giving examples of how it all works in a specific O/R Mapper in the next chapter.

To be clear, everything I'm about to discuss is applicable even in the case of custom code (except for mapping style). That also goes for the patterns description. But in order to become more concrete, we will be thinking about O/R Mappers from now on.

The first classification is about the style of Domain Model that is supported.

Domain Model Style

How much, and in what way, do we have to adapt the Domain Model to work with the O/R Mapper? The three most typical and general aspects are

- Persistent Ignorant
- Inheritance
- Interface implementation

Persistent Ignorant

Persistent Ignorant means that you make no changes at all to the Domain Model in order to make it persistable. Of course, there's a scale here, and it's not a matter of being completely black or white. For example, reflection-based approaches set some requirements. AOP-based approaches set other requirements.

Inheritance

A common approach historically is to require the Domain Model classes to inherit from a super class provided by the Persistence Framework.

Interface Implementation

Finally, another common approach historically is to require the Domain Model classes to implement one or more interfaces provided from the Persistence Framework.

This was just one aspect showing how you might have to adapt your Domain Model to fit the persistence framework. Loads of other things might have to be done regarding Versioning and Lazy Load, for example, but we'll come back to that later in the chapter.

Mapper Style

Metadata-based mappings are often implemented in two different ways:

- Code generation

- Framework/reflective

As the sharp-eyed reader will have noticed, I just mentioned code generation again, this time in the context of O/R Mappers. However, there's one important difference. Now the code generation is done, typically just before compilation, by reading metadata and spitting out the mapping code. Of course, code generation of custom code could be done in a similar way, but the *main* difference is that the appetite regarding what to support varies. This definition is not extremely distinct, but it's a start.

Framework/reflective means that there is no source code generated before compilation time for the mapping work. Instead, the mapping is dealt with by reading metadata at runtime.

Note

As you probably suspect, things are even fuzzier. For example, how should we categorize static AOP? I try to keep the description and categorization simple and clean.

It's also important to note that code generation and framework don't have to be mutually exclusive.

Classification

Starting Point

When you are working with a certain O/R Mapper, you can often choose one or more starting points from the following list:

- Database schema

- Domain Model

- Mapping information

By starting point I mean what you focus on when you start building your application. Of course, it's beneficial if the O/R Mapper supports several starting points because there's then a greater chance you can use it for the different situations in which you will find yourself.

As you know by now, I prefer to start working from the Domain Model; however, you can't always have that and may have to start from the database schema instead or at least keep a close eye on the database schema. You may also have to start working from the mapping information instead, describing the classes' relationships to tables in a UML-like diagramming tool, for example.

If you prefer starting from the Domain Model, but the persistence framework that you want to try out doesn't support that, you can work around the problem by seeing the UML Editor or Database Design as a way of *writing* your Domain Model. It's a bit awkward, though. And TDD, for example, won't be as natural to apply.

Mapping Legacy Databases

Even though the starting point might be the database, this doesn't have to imply that it is forced by the persistent framework or that the designer prefers to work in this way. It can also be that you have a legacy database that must be used.

Be prepared for it to be much harder to go that route with an O/R Mapper (unless it's specialized for that), especially if you aren't allowed to change the design of the database at all. Often it's at least allowed to add views, columns, and tables to the database even if you aren't allowed to change existing columns. That can help! (Changes that existing apps aren't affected by are pretty likely to be allowed, but watch out because the existing apps might not be the most robust around.)

It's especially troublesome if the legacy database design isn't in great shape, which can happen if the application has been in production for a couple of years.

Something else about this point is how do you move further when you are "done" with the first one (such as the Domain Model)? Does the chosen O/R Mapper provide any help with creating the other two parts to any extent? For example, you have the Domain Model, and now you need the database and metadata. Can you get that automatically? It's not as though this is a show-stopper if it's not supported; you can often create such basic tools on your own pretty easily. But it's an advantage if that has been taken care of for you.

Classification

So let's now assume that we have the Domain Model, database, and mapping information in place. Let's discuss what the API will look like.

API Focus

The API focus comes in two alternatives:

- Relational Tables

- Domain Model

This is stretching things, because from the start the whole purpose of O/R Mappers was to let developers work with objects instead of tables. Therefore, for typical O/R Mappers, the API focus is always Domain Model. (An example of an API that is more focused on relational tables is that of the Recordset pattern, implemented with DataTable in .NET.)

Another very important aspect of the API, and one that isn't the same for every O/R Mapper, is querying.

Query Language Style

I find it quite hard to categorize this one, but let's give it a try. From the developer's perspective, the querying with the O/R Mapper is generally done in one or more of the following ways:

- String-based, SQL-ish

- Query Object-based

I believe it's fitting to explain each of these a little bit more.

String-Based, SQL-ish

By this I mean query languages that look quite similar to SQL, but work with classes in the Domain Model instead of the tables in the database. Some queries, especially advanced ones, are very well expressed in a language like this. On the other hand, the typical drawback is the lack of type safety.

It's important to note, though, that this way of stating queries isn't necessarily string-based at the implementation level, only at the API level.

Query Object-Based

The second typical query language is to use objects to represent queries, following the Query Object pattern [Fowler PoEAA]. Simple queries are often better expressed in this approach, it's possible to have type safety, and the developer doesn't have to know much about querying semantics in order to be efficient. The problem, though, is that complex queries might require lots of code to express, and the code quickly gets hard to read.

Raw SQL

Yet another nice solution to have for rare cases is to be able to express the query in SQL, but to receive the result as Domain Model instances. Of course, that has the problem of making your code database-coupled, but if you can't find another solution, it's great to at least have the option. This is very handy when you need to optimize. And if you need to get entities as the result and the SQL-integration can take care of that for you, it will cut down on the code amount you have to write.

Of course we should be allowed to jump out to SQL without receiving the result as Domain Model instances as well.

Which Approach?

As I see it, ideally the tool should support several approaches. This is because sometimes string-based expressions are best, while for other situations query object-based expressions are most suitable.

The querying *style* in itself is only part of the story. Another important aspect is how *competent* the querying solution is. That is part of the next topic.

Advanced Database Support

Or "How much will the DBA respect you?"

Classification

To be flexible enough for you not to have to jump out of the sandbox all the time, the O/R Mapper needs to support some database close operations that aren't obvious from the Domain Model perspective. However, they are great when the time comes for optimizations.

Some examples are

- **Aggregates**

  A very basic feature of SQL is the capability to do things like SELECT SUM(x), MIN(y), MAX(z). When you work with a Domain Model focus, it might be slightly less common that you need those aggregates, but they are still very useful and sometimes necessary.

- **Ordering**

  It might prove most efficient to order the result set in the database without having to do the ordering in the Domain Model.

- **Group By**

  Something else you can do when you work with SQL is to use GROUP BY. It's especially common for ad-hoc queries and reporting, but is still occasionally useful in Domain Model-focused applications.

- **Scalar queries**

  It's not necessarily the case that you always want to fetch complete instances back. Sometimes it's just field values, perhaps some from one class and some from another.

It's also very nice if there are other ways to move functionality to the database, functionality that fits best in the database, typically data-intensive operations. What I'm thinking about here is usually the capability to call stored procedures, but it could also include other custom ways of moving functionality, such as user-defined functions.

The main problem with this is that we might lose portability of the application and the database design. But if we use this as an optimization technique, used only when really necessary, the problem is minimized.

The other big problem is that if we jump out of the sandbox, we are on our own, but that's not all. We must also take care to do what it takes for the integration with the sandbox. It might be that we have to purge the Identity Map after we have called a stored procedure. Nobody can decide that for us; we have to judge it on our own.

Note

I think this is a good example of what Joel Spolsky talks about in his article "The Law of Leaky Abstractions" [Spolsky Leaky Abstractions]. Abstractions are great, but you have to know a lot about what's happening behind the scenes as well.

I think that's the way to think about and use O/R Mappers. You shouldn't expect them to hide everything. You have to know what's going on behind the abstraction. See the O/R Mapper as a tool that helps you with a tedious task that you *could* do manually, but practically don't want to.

Classification

Other Functionality

That was a whole range of features, but there's more; for example,

- **What back ends are supported?**

  It might be a nice feature for you if the particular O/R Mapper supports several different backends so that you aren't just tied to one, such as Oracle or SQL Server.

- **Not just an O/R Mapper**

  Many products that are O/R Mappers are also much more than that. For instance, they might help you out with data binding (to bind controls in your UI to your objects without any custom code), with business rules, or with bi-directionality management.

- **Advanced caching**

  Advanced caching isn't necessarily important to you, but if you do need it, it's nice if it is supported by the chosen product. With advanced caching, I'm not just thinking about the cache in the form of the Identity Map, but also a cache that is used for querying. I mean that when you query for certain customers, for example, that query might execute against the second-level cache instead of touching the database.

- **Advanced support for controlling transactions**

  Examples of this feature include how well you can control transactions regarding isolation levels, lessen the deadlock risk by avoiding escalations from read locks to write locks, and whether distributed transactions are supported. Pretty disparate things, but they might be pretty important, no question about that.

  Also interesting in this context is what technique is used for transaction control. Typical options are manual control, interception-based, and hiding the whole thing with a persistence manager.

- **Open source**

  Pros and cons when it comes to open source versus commercial products are not in the scope of this book. Still, it's a factor to take into consideration when you're about to choose O/R Mapper.

- **Version (generation)**

  And last on the list, it's important to consider what generation the O/R Mapper is. That might say something about what maturity to expect.

Classification

Keep stored in your head somewhere that "less is sometimes more." It might be that the bigger the product's focus, the less the product is focused on details. It doesn't have to be that way, of course; I just want to point out that it's not as easy to judge what product is best just by counting features.

Let's have a look at the classification from a totally different angle.

Another Classification: Infrastructure Patterns

In this second part of the classification, I will use some of the PoEAA patterns [Fowler PoEAA], some of which are focused on infrastructure.

Again, this description can be used even if you decide to go the custom route. Who knows, perhaps this description will help one or two readers avoid creating their own custom solutions and instead choose one of the existing solutions. I think this is usually a good idea because it's *so* much work building your own full-fledged solution. Been there, tried that.

Metadata Mapping: Type of Metadata

We need to describe the relationship between the Domain Model and the database schema in metadata; that's what Metadata Mapping [Fowler PoEAA] is all about. O/R Mappers are implementations of the Metadata Mapping pattern, but different mappers use different types of metadata. Typical examples are

- XML document(s) or other document formats

- Attributes (annotations might be a clearer term; for example, [MyAttribute] in C#)

- Source code

As usual, each one comes with its own catch. For instance, XML documents suffer from XML hell. For most developers, XML isn't a very productive format to work with. It's often said that XML isn't for people but for parsers, but it's still the case that tools aren't up to par here, so we often find ourselves sitting there editing huge XML documents.

Another problem with the XML documents is that they are external to the Domain Model source code, so it's easy for them to get out of synch with each other. And many IDEs lack an understanding of the semantics of the XML documents, and therefore refactoring won't work seamlessly.

Attributes are used for decorating the Domain Model, so the risk of getting out of synch with the Domain Model is somewhat smaller. A bigger problem in this case is that the Domain Model is slightly more coupled to the database. If you want to use your Domain Model with two different databases, there is a greater risk that you'll have to have two different versions of the source code for the Domain Model if you use attributes than if you use some external type of metadata. This might not be a huge problem, but it can be. It's also harder to get an overview of the mapping in this case, but tooling can help.

It is debatable whether providing the mapping information in source code is a category of its own. It's actually just another document format. Anyway, I thought having just two categories was a bit cheap. The distinction I'm after here is that the source code describes the mapping information in a procedural way rather than a declarative way. I also see this option as something coming between XML documents and Attributes. The metadata is in the source code and compiled, but it's written in a way that you get it as an overview. To some this means "nice C# code instead of ugly XML." I can't say that I totally disagree. Still, this is an esoteric option, not commonly used.

And as usual, it doesn't have to be "one and only one." For example, perhaps the information is provided as attributes but can be overridden by XML information.

Are you wondering what to describe in metadata? It's the relationship between the Domain Model and the database, but to become concrete, we need an example. We could take Identity Fields as an example.

Identity Field

An Identity Field [Fowler PoEAA] of an entity holds on to the value of the Primary Key of the underlying table in the database. That's how the relationship between the entity instance and the table row is handled.

Another
Classification:
Infrastructure
Patterns

When it comes to new entities, the values for Identity Fields can be generated in at least four different layers:

- Consumer

- Domain Model

- Database

- O/R Mapper

The first two are very similar from the O/R Mapper's perspective. As the O/R Mapper sees it, the value is provided and out of the control of the O/R Mapper. The O/R Mapper just has to hope that the Consumer or Domain Model follows the protocol. If I may choose, I prefer the Domain Model to the Consumer.

A problem here is for O/R Mappers that use the Identity Field value to judge if an instance is new and should be inserted or updated.

> **Note**
>
> This is a good example of letting one thing have two responsibilities. It's simple and it looks good at first, but problems are waiting around the corner.

The third option is pretty common, but it comes with some semantic problems. It means that the database uses something like IDENTITY (SQL Server) or Sequence (Oracle) for setting the value of the primary key when the entity is persisted. The problem is that this is pretty late in the life cycle, and there can be problems with the sets where you have added the Entity when the identity value changes.

Finally, the O/R Mapper itself can take care of the generation of the values of the Identity Fields, and that's the most convenient solution, at least for the O/R Mapper.

So what all this comes down to is that it might be a good idea to keep two identities around for entities. One is a natural identity, let's call it Business Identity, that can get its value at different times in the life cycle, not necessarily from the very start (not all entities have such an identity, though). It's also common to have more than one such identification per class.

The second is the Identity Field, which is more of a Persistence ID or Database ID. If we compare this with Relational database terms, we get Table 8-2.

Table 8-2 *Domain Model Terms by Relational Database Terms*

Domain Model	Relational Database
Business ID	Alternate Key
Identity Field	Primary Key

You'll find a good discussion of this in [Bauer/King HiA].

This is actually something I need to apply as an implementation detail in my current Domain Model. For example, the OrderNumber of Order is a Business ID rather than an Identity Field. That's very apparent in the Equals()/HashCode() implementations, which creates problems for sets, for example. Therefore, I also add Id fields whose values are generated by the O/R Mapper when the newly created entity instance is associated with its repository. After that, the value won't change ever again. I use Guid for those Id fields, as shown in the diagram in Figure 8-1.

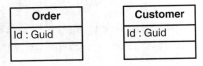

Figure 8-1 Added Identity Fields to the entities that had Business IDs

---

Note

The OrderNumber and CustomerNumber are still around. Also note that the repositories will change slightly because of this. There will be new overloads for GetOrder() and GetCustomer().

This was a change that was very much needed for the infrastructure and is therefore a typical example of a distraction. It was not anything I did for the sole purpose of just one specific O/R Mapper, but rather as a simplification for more or less all O/R Mappers.

Note

It's ironic. When we built Valhalla, we decided that using Guids should be compulsory. We weren't altogether happy with that decision because it put a "must" on the developer, and it was on our list for future changes. Now when I'm using other persistence frameworks, I'm free to choose. Nevertheless, I still think it's often a good idea to use a Guid as the Identity Field.

Another
Classification:
Infrastructure
Patterns

Let's get back to the metadata with another example of what it contains.

Foreign Key Mapping

Another thing that typically appears in metadata is the Foreign Key Mapping pattern [Fowler PoEAA]. It's a description of the foreign keys and the related associations in the Domain Model.

Unlike the Identity Fields, this isn't about copied values in the Domain Model. Instead, it's just a metadata thing.

There are a variety of relationships that can be used, and the ones that are supported by the O/R Mappers can differ quite a lot. To my experience, most of the time you will only use relatively few types of relationships, but when you need something more esoteric, you are glad if you find support for it.

Embedded Value

One very important way of bridging the Impedance Mismatch is the possibility of having coarse-grained tables and fine-grained classes in the Domain Model. That's where the Embedded Value pattern [Fowler PoEAA] comes in.

It means that you should be able to store a customer in a single Customers table in the database, but work with the customer as a Customer object and an Address object in the Domain Model. (This example was very simplistic; in reality, the difference is often very large.)

In the simplest form (let's call it level one), you are able to just describe the relationship between the Embedded Value and the columns in the database table. Level two is where you might have to write assisting code that helps out with the translation for advanced cases.

Inheritance Solutions

Inheritance hierarchies in the Domain Model don't have a perfect match in the relational database because inheritance isn't a relational database concept (at least not before SQL:1999, which few database products support at the time of this writing). Furthermore, inheritance in the Domain Model is probably less commonly used than many would expect. That said, when you need to use it, you should be able to support it with the O/R Mapper.

There are three different type solutions to the problem. They are Single Table Inheritance, Class Table Inheritance, and Concrete Table Inheritance [Fowler PoEAA]. I have chosen to group them together because they are just different solutions to the same problem.

The main difference is regarding how many tables are used for storing an inheritance hierarchy. Assume Person as base class and Student and Teacher as subclasses. Then the different patterns will lead to the following typical tables, as shown in Table 8-3. From there you can probably easily deduce what columns will go where.

Table 8-3 *Patterns for Persistence of Inheritance Hierarchies and What Tables Are Needed*

Pattern	Tables in the Database
Single Table Inheritance	People
Class Table Inheritance	People, Students, Teachers
Concrete Table Inheritance	Student, Teachers

If the O/R Mapper only supports one of those, your flexibility in the database design has decreased compared to if you had all three from which to choose. You have to decide whether that's important or not.

Identity Map

In my early attempts to create an O/R Mapper, I first thought I could skip the Identity Map, but I came to the conclusion that it gets too complex and there is too much responsibility for the consumer programmer.

On the other hand, a lot also depends on your Domain Model design. If you never have relationships between entities in different Aggregates, the need for the Identity Map decreases. So DDD ideas, such as simplification and decoupling within the Domain Model, make it easier to live life without an Identity Map. That said, I still think it's useful to have an active Identity Map.

Another
Classification:
Infrastructure
Patterns

Note

If you think about O/R Mapping as a work horse that goes between database and object, the Identity Map might not be important. But that's not what we are talking about here, because then we would need to do more work. Here we'd like to just support the Domain Model with as simple (or rather as good) a solution as possible.

The Identity Map can be used for other things as well and not only for controlling the object graph the consumer knows about. For instance, it can be used for dealing with building M:N relationships of objects in the Domain Model when reading from the database.

Note

M:N describes the relationship regarding cardinality/multiplicity between objects by saying it is many-to-many. For example, a house has many people staying there, and at the same time every person can own several houses.

It's also often considered a cache for performance reasons, but as you know, I'm not overly cache-friendly, so I see the Identity Map as a convenience for the programming model rather than as a means to improve performance.

Different O/R Mappers differ regarding what "session" level you can/must have the Identity Map for. It can be machine, a process, and/or a session.

Another pattern often goes hand in hand with the Identity Map. I'm thinking about Unit of Work.

Unit of Work

Most O/R Mappers use, or at least have support for, the Unit of Work pattern. The main difference is really how transparent the Unit of Work is for the consumer. Where the O/R Mapper is of "runtime-Persistence Ignorant" style, the consumer might have to talk to the Unit of Work explicitly for registering a new instance to be inserted at next persist. Other O/R Mappers are more transparent, but then you probably will have to instantiate with a factory supplied by the O/R Mapper. There are pros and cons to these approaches.

The "session" level might also differ for the Unit of Work, at least in theory, just as I said for the Identity Map.

Lazy Load/Eager Load

I've said before that my Domain Model style isn't using Lazy Load [Fowler PoEAA] a lot within my Aggregates [Evans DDD]. Even so, it's a piece of the puzzle that we need to have in the persistence infrastructure, and we need to be able to use it as an optimization.

Instead, as the default strategy for my Aggregates, I use load eagerly. Or aggressively, or greedily, or span loading, or pre-load, or whatever you like to call it. I will from now on call it Eager Load.

Eager Load is pretty much the opposite of Lazy Load; you load the complete graph immediately instead of delaying loading parts of the graph until later.

As I see it, Eager Load goes hand in hand with Aggregates [Evans DDD], at least as the default solution.

> ### *Note*
>
> To some I might have put too much emphasis on Aggregates when it comes to reading scenarios. I have been using Aggregates as the *default* load scheme and optimized when I have found the need for it.
>
> After all, Aggregates are most important for *write* scenarios. When seeing it that way, adding a need for something like a `GetForWrite()` to the protocol before making changes to an Aggregate instance might make sense. The `GetForWrite()` would load everything from the Aggregate, possibly with read consistency.
>
> If you do have a concept that is spanning many instances and you want to treat it as a unit, Aggregates is the thing, and it has implications.
>
> I also think the read-only/writable distinction is often something nice for users, who have to actively choose to move into write mode. Another good thing about it is that the user won't start making changes to an already stale object when optimistic concurrency control is used, which means that the risk of collisions becomes smaller. This approach also translates nicely to pessimistic concurrency control schemes.

There are many different implementation variants for Eager Load. It's often solved with OUTER JOINs in SQL, and the resultset is then broken down to the graph. The other most common solution is to batch several SELECT statements after each other.

Another Classification: Infrastructure Patterns

A competent O/R Mapper should support both Lazy Load and different Eager Load strategies, which goes both for lists and single instances. It may even apply for Lazy Loading groups of fields of a single instance, even if I don't consider that crucial. Such a group of attributes could always be factored out into a Value Object instead, which would make a lot of sense in most situations. And then we are back to Lazy Load/Eager Load of instances again.

Controlling Concurrency

As I've said several times already, the Aggregate pattern is a good tool for controlling concurrency. Thanks to it, I get the unit I want to use and work with as a single whole. Yet that's not the complete solution. I also need to avoid collisions or detect whether collisions have occurred so that we don't get inconsistent data (and *especially* not without being notified).

From [Fowler PoEAA], we find the following solutions to the problem:

- **Coarse-Grained Lock**

  Instead of locking on the instance level, this pattern suggests locking a more coarse-grained unit. We can, for example, use it on the Aggregate root level, thereby implicitly locking all the parts of the Aggregate.

- **Optimistic Offline Lock**

  Expect no conflict, but *check* before commit.

- **Pessimistic Offline Lock**

  Prevent conflicts by an exclusive check-out mechanism.

This reminds me that I now want to add some versioning information to the Domain Model as a way of stating where we need to deal with controlling concurrency, for dealing with feature 4, "Concurrency conflict detection is important." I think my Aggregate roots should get a Version field to support Optimistic Offline Lock. It's *not* an automatic action. Instead, you add it where you need it. You'll find the change in Figure 8-2.

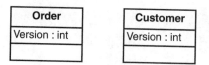

Figure 8-2   Added Version fields to some of the Aggregate roots

It's not too much of a problem if your O/R Mapper doesn't support Pessimistic Offline Lock. First of all, you should be careful when using it at all because it's pretty costly when it comes to overhead. Second, if you need it, you can build a decent solution on your own pretty easily. (I discussed a solution based on a custom Locks-table in my previous book [Nilsson NED].)

Summary

Summary

Now we have discussed the need for persistent infrastructure to some extent. After having introduced the subject and defined some requirements on the needed persistent infrastructure, we discussed the subject from different angles such as classifications and some of the PoEAA patterns.

But the whole discussion was pretty abstract. Some examples would help make it more concrete. That's the intention of the next chapter. There we will use NHibernate for the examples.

Chapter 9

Putting NHibernate into Action

This chapter is different from most of the other chapters in the book. Instead of being somewhat abstract, this one will be pretty much hands-on. What we will do here is apply what was discussed in Chapter 8, "Infrastructure for Persistence," by using NHibernate [NHibernate] as an example of a Persistence framework.

This chapter starts with an introduction to NHibernate, including how to get started, how to deal with the mapping, and what the API looks like.

Then we will position NHibernate regarding the classifications discussed in Chapter 8, and we'll also take a look at how NHibernate implements the infrastructure patterns discussed in the previous chapter.

This chapter ends with a discussion of how NHibernate fits in the big picture of DDD.

Why NHibernate?

You might wonder why I chose NHibernate. Well, it's not because NHibernate is necessarily the best solution available. What is the best car? That's a silly question, right? It's always the standard answer: "It depends."

These are my motivations for choosing NHibernate for this chapter:

- **Java heritage**

    NHibernate is a port of the popular Hibernate [Hibernate]; therefore, many people know it, and there are a great deal of books and lots of other resources available for it. Furthermore, Object Relational Mapping is pretty mature in Java-land, contrary to .NET-land.

- **Open source**

  NHibernate is open source, and that makes it very approachable and easy to try.

In no way is this chapter intended to be an exhaustive guide to NHibernate. The purpose is just to make the discussions in Chapter 8 less abstract. I will also avoid getting into enumerating feature after feature; that's not very interesting, and that aspect of this book wouldn't be current for more than a few weeks after writing this chapter.

A possible effect, although not one of my main intentions, might be that the chapter could easily be written for any other Persistence Framework as well, therefore making it a little easier to compare different solutions. Let's see if that happens. (Hopefully there will then be a separate section entitled "What else *should* have been included in the comparison?".)

I will also not be discussing NHibernate in the context of an abstraction layer, such as NWorkspace [Nilsson Workspace]. The focus here will be on NHibernate itself and its API.

Let's start with an introduction to NHibernate.

A Short Introduction to NHibernate

What we are about to discuss here is a product that deals with Metadata Mapping [Fowler PoEAA], an O/R Mapper, which is called NHibernate.

As I said, NHibernate is a port from the very popular O/R Mapper in Java-land called Hibernate, originally created by Gavin King [Bauer/King HiA]. The port is based on version 2.1 of Hibernate, which is considered a pretty old version, but the port doesn't strictly just move the code base for that particular Hibernate version. Instead, features from later versions of Hibernate as well as other features have been added here and there.

NHibernate (and Hibernate) is open source. As I write, NHibernate is released as version 1.0. You can download it from here: [NHibernate].

The proof of the pudding is in the eating, so let's see how NHibernate is used.

Preparations

Let's assume you have a Domain Model and you now want to write some consumer code against the Domain Model.

Note

One more requirement is that you want to make the Domain Model persistent. Therefore, you also have a database product, but don't think about the database *schema* for the moment.

First, you need to set a reference in the consumer to the NHibernate framework (namely nhibernate.dll). That wasn't too hard.

Then you need to configure the usage of NHibernate in the consumer of the Domain Model. You can either do that in code or in a .config file. Typically a .config file is used, so let's assume that. Some things that are configured can be what the database product in question is, the connection string to the database, and logging. You will find lots of examples of .config files to copy and paste from at the NHibernate site, so I won't go into detail here, but I'll just take it for granted that you have a suitable .config file in place.

What you then try to do just once per application execution is to set up a SessionFactory. The reason for not creating several is that the cost is fairly high. The SessionFactory will analyze all metadata and build up memory-based structures for that. As you might guess from its name, the SessionFactory is then used for instantiating new instances that implement ISession.

ISession is the string to pull in order to get work done against the database and is also the interface that you will interact with all the time from the consumer perspective.

Next, it's nice if you can use a helper for the ISession management. This can be done with different levels of sophistication, but here a simple attempt would be good enough for our purpose. If we assume that our Domain Model is called ADDDP.Ordering.DomainModel, a simplified helper called NHConfig could look like this:

```
public class NHConfig
{
    private static ISessionFactory _sessionFactory;

    static NHConfig()
    {
        Configuration config = new Configuration();
        config.AddAssembly("ADDDP.Ordering.DomainModel");
        _sessionFactory = config.BuildSessionFactory();
    }

    public static ISessionFactory GetSessionFactory()
    {
        return _sessionFactory;
    }
}
```

Making more assumptions, we are now working with a rich client application; therefore, we think it's enough to have a single ISession instance. At least, let's start that way. Then the following code might be suitable for the start of the application, or perhaps for a single form:

```
_session = NHConfig.GetSessionFactory().OpenSession();
_session.Disconnect();
```

So when you want to get an ISession to act on, you can use the following little snippet over and over again:

```
_session.Reconnect();

//Do stuff...

_session.Disconnect();
```

And finally, when the application terminates (or the form is closed, depending upon your chosen strategy), you close the ISession like this:

```
_session.Close();
```

Note

One ISession per form or one per application are just two of several possible strategies.

OK, that was all good fun, but it was completely useless considering what we accomplished in the database. Opening and closing ISessions is not enough, and we need to persist changes to the database as well. For that to be possible, we need to make some more preparations.

Some Mapping Metadata

In the preparations so far, the Domain Model itself hasn't been affected at all. However, we do need to do something—not to affect it, but rather to complement it. We need to add mapping information to show the relationship between the Domain Model and the database. Typically, this mapping information is created in a separate XML file per Entity [Evans DDD], and those files are stored in the project directory for the Domain Model.

So far, we haven't created a schema in the database, so we are pretty free to work as we like. The only thing we have is the Domain Model. We can use tools for creating the mapping information and/or the database schema, but the only thing that is important for this introduction is showing what a mapping file could look like, given a certain Domain Model Entity and database table. Let's pick a simple Entity from our Domain Model. I think Customer fits the requirements pretty well. You find the Entity and its Value Objects [Evans DDD] in Figure 9-1.

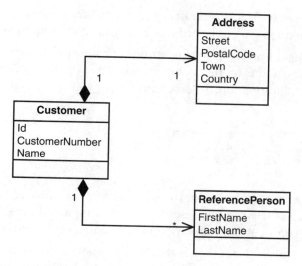

Figure 9-1 Customer Entity and Address and ReferencePerson Value Objects

In the database, both the Customer and the Address are probably stored in a single table. The DDL for those two classes could look like this:

```
create table Customers (
  Id UNIQUEIDENTIFIER not null,
  CustomerNumber INT not null,
  Name VARCHAR(100) not null,
  Street VARCHAR(50) not null,
  PostalCode VARCHAR(10) not null,
  Town VARCHAR(50) not null,
  Country VARCHAR(50) not null,
  primary key (Id)
)
```

A Short Introduction to NHibernate

Note

It felt strange writing that piece regarding the Town and Country at least. I would probably factor them out in a real situation, but that's not important for this discussion.

The Reference Persons table is missing from the DDL above, but you can probably deduce it from Figure 9-1.

Then the missing piece, which is the interesting piece here, is the mapping file.

Note

Again, please note that I never said you had to create the database table before the mapping file. The order of how you work is up to you.

If I can choose, I prefer to start with the Domain Model, then write the mapping files, and from that automatically generate the database from the mapping information. To accomplish that, you can use the following snippet:

```
Configuration config = new Configuration();
config.AddAssembly("ADDDP.Ordering.DomainModel");
SchemaExport se = new SchemaExport(config);
se.Execute(true, true, false, true);
```

In my experience, I often want to add some more constraints to the database, on top of what can be described in the mapping file, and I do that by writing some custom code. A bit raw, but it solves the problem.

With that in place, I can regenerate the development database as often as I like, even before every test execution (if it's not becoming too slow).

Let's take it piece by piece. First, you need to describe the document, something like this for `Customer.hbm.xml`:

```
<?xml version="1.0" encoding="utf-8" ?>
<hibernate-mapping xmlns="urn:nhibernate-mapping-2.0"
    namespace="ADDDP.Ordering.DomainModel"
    assembly="ADDDP.Ordering.DomainModel">
```

I provided the `namespace` and `assembly` tags here, so the rest of the mapping information can be expressed less verbosely because that information won't have to be repeated.

A Short
Introduction
to
NHibernate

Note

If you want the metadata to be within the assembly, don't forget to set the property of the XML file to be an Embedded Resource.

Then you describe the name of the class for the Entity and the name of the table. For example, like this:

```
<class name="Customer" table="Customers">
```

Then you describe the Identity Field [Fowler PoEAA], not only the name in the class and the table (in the upcoming example the property name and the column name are the same, so the column tag isn't needed), but also the strategy that is used for creating a new value. It could look like this:

```
<id name="Id" access="field.camelcase-underscore"
    unsaved-value="00000000-0000-0000-0000-000000000000" >
    <generator class="guid" />
</id>
```

In this specific example, a guid is generated by NHibernate when a new instance is associated with the ISession.

Then the simple properties are mapped, such as Name, like this:

```
<property name="Name" type="AnsiString" length="100"
    not-null="true" />
```

Normally NHibernate can understand what type to use for the properties by investigating the class by reflection, but in the case of strings, I provide a specific type to get VARCHAR instead of NVARCHAR if I automatically generate the schema from the mapping information. The length is also used for generating DDL from the mapping information, but because I like moving along that route, I take the extra work of adding that information.

Note

Information like this is also very useful for your custom validation.

NHibernate also makes it possible to map not only properties, but fields as well. As a matter of fact, Customer.Name isn't a property (which NHibernate considers the default and therefore doesn't have to be expressed) but a public field, so I need to add an access-tag like this to get it all correctly:

```
<property name="Name" access="field" type="AnsiString"
    length="100" not-null="true" />
```

And it works for all accessor types, even private, so you are pretty free to choose a strategy. For example, you often expose something slightly different in your property get to what is stored, or you do some interception on get/set. In these cases, you need to map, for example, the private field instead.

Mapping a private field could look like this:

```
<property name="_customerNumber"
    access="field" not-null="true" />
```

Assuming that you do map private fields, it's a good idea to use naming rules. This is so your query code doesn't have to be written to use the name of the private fields (for example, _customerNumber), but rather ordinary, nice property names (like CustomerNumber). It could look like this:

```
<property name="CustomerNumber"
    access="field.camelcase-underscore" not-null="true" />
```

> ### Note
>
> Sure, there are pitfalls here (as always), but I usually find it good enough to map private fields instead of introducing separate private properties purely for the aspect of persistence. If it works, fine. If not, I can always change it when/if the need arises.
>
> This is the topic of a heated debate, though. Many prefer to map to persistency-specific private properties instead.

Finally, (well, it could be done *before* the simple properties just as well—it just happened to be like this here) we need to describe how the used Value Object is mapped to the single Customers table. It could look like this in the mapping file for Customer (the Address class won't have any mapping information of its own because it's a Value Object and not an Entity):

```
<component name="Address" access="field">
    <property name="Street" access="field.camelcase-underscore"
        type="AnsiString" length="50" not-null="true" />

    <property name="PostalCode"
        access="field.camelcase-underscore"
        type="AnsiString" length="10" not-null="true" />

    <property name="Town" access="field.camelcase-underscore"
        type="AnsiString" length="50" not-null="true" />

    <property name="Country" access="field.camelcase-underscore"
        type="AnsiString" length="50" not-null="true" />
</component>
```

And a list of Value Objects such as ReferencePerson could look like this:

```
<bag name="ReferencePersons" access="field.camelcase-underscore"
    cascade="all">
    <key column="OrderId" />
    <composite-element class="ReferencePerson">
```

```
        <property name="FirstName"
            access="field.camelcase-underscore" not-null="true"/>

        <property name="LastName"
            access="field.camelcase-underscore" not-null="true"/>
    </composite-element>
</bag>
```

Let's take another example. In earlier chapters I sketched that OrderLine should be a Value Object. If so, the mapping in the Order regarding OrderLine might look similar to what was just shown.

But it's not too much of a twist to later on find out that the OrderLine might have a list of its own, such as a list of notes. If so, that's a good reason for transforming OrderLine into an Entity instead. That is, it's transformed to an Entity for technical and infrastructural reasons rather than conceptual. We have to be pragmatic. If so, the mapping information in Order changes to this instead (and OrderLine will have mapping information of its own):

```
<bag name="OrderLines" access="field.camelcase_underscore"
    cascade="all">
    <key column="OrderId" />
    <one-to-many class="OrderLine" />
</bag>
```

For the sake of the example, let's also assume that we want the OrderLine to have a field pointing back to the Order (despite what I have said earlier about trying to use bidirectionality sparingly). So in the OrderLine XML file that was added when OrderLine was transformed to an Entity, there is now a many-to-one section like this:

```
<many-to-one
    name="Order"
    access="field.camelcase-underscore"
    class="Order"
    column="OrderId" />
```

An important point here is that you are on your own regarding the bidirectionality. So in the AddOrderLine() method of Order, it could now look like this:

```
//Order
public void AddOrderLine(OrderLine ol)
{
    _orderLines.Add(ol);
    ol.Order = this;
}
```

Finally, this also means that OrderLine will have an Identity Field of its own, whether it's used or not in the Domain Model.

If you fill in the open sections in the files, we are ready to make the consumer code much more interesting.

A Tiny API Example

Let's now take a look at some small code snippets showing how consumer code could look when NHibernate is put to work carrying out some *Create, Read, Update, and Delete* (CRUD) operations. CRUD is often a large part of the persistence-related work of an application. The first of the snippets to look at is the C in CRUD.

CRUD-C: Create

To create a new instance (or row) in the database, you just instantiate a new Customer, set its properties, and call the methods you want. When you're ready to save it, you use the snippet we talked about before for reconnecting an ISession. Then you associate the instance with the ISession, and you then call Flush() on the ISession to store all changes.

All together, it could look like this:

```
//A consumer
Customer c = new Customer();
c.Name = "Volvo";

_session.Reconnect();
_session.Save(c);
_session.Flush();
_session.Disconnect();
```

In this case, I was specific and told the ISession that it should lead to an INSERT (because I called Save()). I could have called SaveOrUpdate() instead, and then NHibernate would have decided on its own whether it should be an INSERT or an UPDATE. The information used in that case is the value of the Identity Field, and it's compared to what you indicated for unsaved-value in the mapping file ("00000000-0000-0000-0000-000000000000" in the case of Guids). If the Identity Field matches the unsaved-value, it's time for an INSERT; otherwise, it would be an UPDATE.

It is also important pointing out that the INSERT is delayed and won't happen when you say Save(), but rather when you say Flush(). The reason for this is that you should be able to make many changes in the consumer and then get them all persisted together and as late as possible.

Did we succeed in writing to the database? The easiest way to check that is to read the instance back, so let's do that.

A Short
Introduction
to
NHibernate

CRUD-R (One): Read One

The second example is to read one instance (row in the database) by its Identity Field. From now on, let's assume that we use the ordinary reconnect/disconnect snippet and just focus on the specific code instead.

As usual, you talk to the ISession instance. You call Load()/Get() and say what type you are looking for and its Identity Field value. It could go like this:

```
Customer c = (Customer)_session.Load(typeof(Customer), theId);
```

But beware. This didn't necessarily prove anything if you didn't close the ISession since the last Flush(), because the ISession will provide you with the instance from the Identity Map [Fowler PoEAA] when you call Load()/Get() instead of going to the database. What you can do to force a database jump (instead of opening a new ISession) is to call Evict() on the instance by saying that you don't want the Identity Map to keep track of the instance any longer. It could look like this:

```
_session.Evict(customer);
```

That was good, but what if you don't know the identity value? Perhaps you only know part of the name of the customer and want to fetch all instances that match that name pattern. This takes us over to the next example, that of read many.

CRUD-R (Many): Read Many

There are two specific languages for querying in NHibernate. But we are going to use Hibernate Query Language (HQL) for this example. It's pretty similar to SQL, yet different. In order to fetch all customers with a name that starts with "Vol", the code could look like this:

```
//A consumer
string hql = "select from Customer where Name like 'Vol%'";
IList result = _session.CreateQuery(hql).List();
```

So in the result, you will get a list of customers with names that start with "Vol", just as you expected.

Normally, you wouldn't write code as static as this and would use parameterization instead. But again, I just want to show very simple code here in order to give you a quick feeling of how it *could* be done.

CRUD-U: Update

We found lots of instances with names starting with "Vol". We saw that we needed to make some changes to one of them. We made the changes to the properties of that instance, and we are now ready to persist the changes. Again,

A Short Introduction to NHibernate

we can use SaveOrUpdate(), but here we know that it's a question of an UPDATE, so we use Update() like this instead (continuing from the previous snippet):

```
Customer c2 = (Customer) result[0];
c2.Name = "Ford";
_session.Update(c2);   //Can be skipped
_session.Flush();
```

As a matter of fact, because we found the instance via a read, we didn't have to make the Update() call at all. The instance was already associated with the ISession and so it would have been taken care of anyway at Flush() time.

CRUD-D: Delete

One of the found instances was wrong, so it should be deleted. That could be done like this:

```
//A consumer
Customer c3 = (Customer) result[1];
_session.Delete(c3);
_session.Flush();
```

As you probably guessed, Delete() is delayed until Flush().

That was pretty straightforward, wasn't it?

Transactions

Before we leave the API example, I think it's important to have a look at how transactions can be controlled when NHibernate is used, because transactions are used a great deal.

If you are used to other ways of manual transaction control, it's easy to understand how it's done with NHibernate as well. What you do is grab an ITransaction instance, which you can then use to make either a Commit() or Rollback() (Commit() will by default automatically do a Flush()). The complete snippet could look like this:

```
//A consumer
ITransaction tx = _session.BeginTransaction();
try
{
    tx.Commit();
}
catch (Exception ex)
{
    tx.Rollback();
    ...
```

> ### Note
>
> Suddenly I used exception handling in the code snippet. The reason is that Rollback() makes most sense then. Of course, exception handling should be used for the other snippets as well, but here in the book it would mostly be a distraction.

I think that finishes an extremely short introduction. See the NHibernate site [NHibernate] for much more information on how to get started.

We now move on to positioning the chosen example of a Persistence Framework with the structure that was presented in Chapter 8. First, let's take a look at the overall requirements.

Requirements of the Persistence Infrastructure

As I said, before we go into the details, I think it's fitting to discuss the overview requirements that were defined in Chapter 8. I'm thinking about Persistent Ignorant (PI) level, supported life cycle, and database treatment.

High Level of Persistent Ignorant

The programming model of NHibernate isn't far from being runtime-PI, especially regarding the Domain Model itself. But that also comes with a price. For example, NHibernate doesn't help you at all with the inverse property management where you want to have bidirectional relationships. Instead, you are totally on your own.

Another example of such a price is that NHibernate won't help by telling you whether or not your instances are dirty by using an IsDirty property or something similar. (NHibernate will decide which instances should be persisted at persist time, but that's not what I'm referring to here.)

These are just two examples of the high level of PI coming at a price. Another such cost is performance, which might become problematic because of the high PI.

There are also some things that you have to do with your Domain Model classes in order to make it possible for them to become persisted by NHibernate at all. Here are some typical examples:

- It's not possible to use readonly for fields.

  The most intention revealing construction if you need a read-only property in a class is to use the readonly keyword, but then NHibernate can't set the field by reflection. Therefore, it has to be converted to private field + a public get property.

- All classes must have default constructors.

  So even if you don't need one in your Domain Model, you have to have a constructor without any parameters. The constructor can be internal and even private, but you still need to add it.

- You should avoid strongly typed collections.

  I often don't see that as a very bad thing anyway. I mean, I like to use IList, for example, instead of a CustomerList class. Generics, of course, is also very good.

  (Unfortunately, at the time of writing, generics isn't well supported by NHibernate, so you have to go through some jumps here and there.)

- You shouldn't set Identity Fields.

  Normally, you would give Identity Fields default values, such as Guid.NewGuid(), but that's not a good idea if it's possible to avoid it when you use NHibernate because NHibernate uses the Identity Field values to determine if it should be an UPDATE or INSERT. If you provide a default value (unless you set it to unsaved-value, of course), NHibernate will always expect UPDATE if you don't explicitly provide guidance. (You can also use the version tag for signaling INSERT/UPDATE.)

This isn't too bad, but there are still some things that lower the PI level. To be honest, I don't know how to avoid the problem when using the readonly statement, so I guess it won't be any better in other solutions unless they manipulate your code.

Requirements of the Persistence Infrastructure

Certain Desirable Features for the Life Cycle of the Persistent Entities

In Chapter 5, "Moving Further with Domain-Driven Design," (and it's repeated in Chapter 8) I talked about the simple life cycle I needed to support for my Domain Model instances. The summary is repeated here again in Table 9-1.

Table 9-1 *Summary of the Semantics for the Life Cycle of the Domain Model Instances*

Operation		Result Regarding Transient/Persistent
Call to new	→	Transient
Repository.Add(instance) or persistentInstance.Add(instance)	→	Persistent in Domain Model
x.PersistAll()	→	Persistent in Database
Repository.Get()	→	Persistent in Domain Model (and Database)
Repository.Delete(instance)	→	Transient (and instance will get deleted from database at x.PersistAll)

This is easily mapped to NHibernate and is therefore easily supported. Let's add one more column for mapping Table 9-1 to NHibernate. Then it looks as in Table 9-2:

Table 9-2 *Summary of the Semantics for the Life Cycle of the Domain Model Instances, with NHibernate*

Operation	NHibernate		Result Regarding Transient/Persistent
Call to new	Call to new	→	Transient
Repository. Add(instance) or persistentInstance. Add(instance)	ISession. Save(), Update(), SaveOrUpdate(), or associate with persistent instance	→	Persistent in Domain Model
x.PersistAll()	ISession.Flush()	→	Persistent in Database
Repository.Get()	ISession.Load(), Get() or List()	→	Persistent in Domain Model (and Database)
	ISession.Evict(), Clear() or Close()	→	Transient (but not deleted); not in control of the Identity Map/Unit of Work
Repository. Delete(instance)	ISession.Delete()	→	Transient (and instance will get deleted from database at x.PersistAll)

Requirements of the Persistence Infrastructure

As you saw in Table 9-2, I added one more row about how to free the Identity Map/Unit of Work of an instance (or all instances). That wasn't something I envisioned before that I would need, but in reality I run into situations when this is needed, such as when "moving" instances between sessions.

Let's conclude by stating that there's not much more to say about this right now.

Note

There are loads of details, of course, but we are staying at a bird's eye view here.

I know, you think I was thinking too much about NHibernate when I wrote that section in Chapter 5, don't you? That may be so, but you will find that most other O/R Mappers support this as well.

Deal Carefully with the Relational Database

Finally, I want the O/R Mapper to deal carefully with the Relational database. That is, I want it to treat the database in the same way or at least similar to how we would when we are programming it manually and being extra careful.

If the previous requirement (the life cycle) was "easy," this one is much harder and will vary quite a lot between different O/R Mappers.

It's easy to be critical about how NHibernate deals with the database in certain situations and think that you could do better manually. I have said over and over again that I think it makes sense not to optimize every call to the database because it most often doesn't matter much anyway. Instead, you can always go to the code and optimize the places where it really is needed. Still, the requirement is set because I don't want to optimize at all more than is necessary, and when I optimize I don't want to have to go to ordinary SQL more than is absolutely necessary.

Note

I hope this didn't sound like "avoid SQL at any price" or "use only O/R Mappers that are extremely function-rich."

SQL is great, and I like using it when that's the best solution.

So what are the problem areas to look out for regarding NHibernate? An obvious one I think is that when we move processing out from the database, for example, we avoid having logic in stored procedures (and actually avoid stored procedures altogether). This is intentional because we want to achieve a better maintenance story by having all the logic in the Domain Model and its nearby surroundings. (And again, when we really have to, we can optimize the rare places with stored procedures.)

Another typical example of a problem area is when we do processing that is normally set-based, such as increasing a column value of all instances of a certain class (for example, setting the Price of all products to Price = Price * 1.1). Doing that in SQL is perfectly normal and recommended. With NHibernate, the sets will be single row sets regarding how it's processed against the database. This can also be a good thing, because the validation rules are most often instance-based, and we want them to be processed for large updates, too. However, the cost might be too high.

A third problem is that the consumer of the Domain Model probably doesn't care about the database at all. He or she might create a huge load on the backend without realizing it or actually be almost incapable of realizing it. That's one drawback to the nice isolation and abstraction the Domain Model provides.

A fourth problem is that of selective updates if a certain criterion is met, such as

```
UPDATE x SET y = 42 WHERE y >= 1
```

That has to be dealt with by a pre-read instead.

A fifth is the "reading way too much" problem when too many complex types are read even though just a tiny amount of information is really needed. This is especially common if you haven't used a somewhat careful Aggregate design and haven't used Lazy Load.

Yet another classic problem is that of n+1 selects. Assume you fetch all Orders in the database and that OrderLines are Lazy Loaded. Then you touch each Order and its OrderLines. Then there will be a new SELECT issued for each Order's OrderLines. If you don't use Lazy Load, the problem will be smaller, but then you run the risk of getting into the problem just mentioned of fetching too much in some scenarios.

Neither of these examples is specific to NHibernate, but they are pretty normal for O/R Mappers. An example of a problem that I think is more related to NHibernate is that of IDENTITY or sequences. Using such an Identity Field leads to earlier INSERTs to the database than what you probably expect.

All in all, it's my opinion that NHibernate does a good job of fulfilling those overview requirements, especially if you are happy with the nature of how O/R Mappers typically work and the tradeoffs that are involved!

Classification

OK, I have introduced NHibernate, and we have had a general look at how it deals with the requirements. We are now ready to investigate NHibernate further, and this time with the help of the disposition used in Chapter 8. But instead of discussing the alternatives in an abstract way, I will now position NHibernate as being an example of the alternatives to each category and also discuss how the solution looks in a little bit more detail.

First up is the Domain Model style that NHibernate expects us to use. We have already touched upon this topic, but let's say a few more words about it.

Domain Model Style

I said in Chapter 8 that the three most usual aspects for Domain Model styles that O/R Mappers use include the following:

- PI

- Inheritance

- Interface implementation

Life isn't black and white, but in this case I think the choice is easy. The way I see it, NHibernate gives us a high level of PI. You don't have to inherit from certain base classes, and you don't have to implement certain interfaces. You don't even have to reference any NHibernate assemblies in your Domain Model.

Mapper Style

When it comes to Mapper style, I said that Metadata-based mappings are often exemplified in two different ways:

- Code generation

- Framework/reflective

Again, it's pretty easy to position NHibernate because it's a typical example of a Framework/reflective solution. Sure, there is some code generation support in NHibernate, but that is typically used when generating one of the three parts of the Domain Model, Metadata or database schema by looking at one (or two) of the other parts. For example, assume you have the metadata—from that you can create database schema. That's not what I meant by code generation as the mapper style. The mapper style is defined by how the mapping is done at run-time, and for that, NHibernate *doesn't* use code generation.

One exception to the rule is when we look at what is done to support Lazy Load [Fowler PoEAA]. Then at runtime NHibernate will swap, for example, your used list class for some proxy instead. In order for this to work, you have to expose the list as an interface and not as a concrete class.

Note

Note that I didn't mention the usage of interfaces as a means of lowering PI level earlier in the chapter. The reason for this decision was that Lazy Loading is a feature and not something you have to use.

The opinion on that varies, but as I see it, Lazy Loading is an optimization technique and not something you have to use all the time.

Is it good or bad that NHibernate is using the Framework/reflective approach? I really believe that it is mostly a good thing when it comes to O/R Mappers.

Starting Point

When you are working with a certain O/R Mapper, you can often choose one or more starting points from the following list:

- Database schema

- Domain Model

- Mapping information

NHibernate allows you to start with any of these, and it's not just a hack, but it's supported by design. With that said, if you have to start from a legacy database schema that you aren't allowed to change, having a look at something like iBATIS [iBATIS] might be a good idea.

Classification

API Focus

The API focus comes in one of two alternatives:

- Tables

- Domain Model

But I said that this doesn't really apply when it comes to the most common O/R Mappers because their main purpose is to provide a Domain Model view of the world while using a Relational database for the persistence. So the answer here is easy. NHibernate uses the Domain Model as the API focus.

Query Language Style

Now it gets interesting. The querying capabilities category is a category where the various solutions differ quite a lot. The subcategories I defined in Chapter 8 included the following:

- String-based, SQL-ish

- Query Object-based

NHibernate has implementations for both of these styles, called HQL and Criteria objects in NHibernate. I have already given an example of what an HQL query could look like when searching for all Customers whose names start with "Vol". If I want to express the same thing with Criteria objects, it could look like this:

```
//A consumer
IList result = _session.CreateCriteria(typeof(Customer))
    .Add(Expression.Like("Name", "Vol%"))
    .List();
```

In the previous snippet, you also saw an example of chaining of several method calls. It works because Add() returns an ICriteria just as CreateCriteria(). This helps to make the usage of criteria queries slightly more readable.

Classification

> ### Note
>
> In this chapter, I'm just touching briefly on how different things are accomplished with NHibernate, but in no other case is my briefness so apparent as when it comes to the huge topic of querying. Please refer to [Bauer/King HiA] for more information.

In Chapter 8, I also mentioned that it's good to have the possibility to go over to raw SQL as a last resort, typically to solve performance problems, and you can do that with NHibernate. Both variants are supported so that you can get Entities back and you can get to the raw connection and do whatever you want to.

NHibernate also provides something in between the ordinary query mechanisms and raw SQL that they call report queries (also sometimes called flattening queries). It can look like this in action:

```
//A consumer
string hql = "select new CustomerSnapshot(c.Id, c.Name) " +
    "from Customer c";
IList result = _session.CreateQuery(hql).List();
```

So here the result won't have Customer instances, but CustomerSnapshot instances. For it to work, you need to provide a matching constructor on the Value Object (CustomerSnapshot in the previous case) and to mention CustomerSnapshot in a mapping file via an import directive like this:

```
<import class="CustomerSnapshot" />
```

Note that CustomerSnapshot just holds on to flat data (typically read-only) according to NHibernate. Identities won't be tracked in the Identity Map, and no changes will be tracked in the Unit of Work.

Talking about querying, that's actually exactly what the next category is about as well.

Advanced Database Support

The examples I provided in Chapter 8 for "advanced database support" (not advanced for a database guy, but perhaps for an object guy) follow:

- Aggregates

- Ordering

- Group by

- Scalar queries

All four of these are supported by both HQL and Criteria objects in NHibernate. Let's take an example of each, beginning with an aggregate query finding the number of instances of Customer. In HQL, it could look like this:

```
//A consumer
string hql = "select count(*) from Customer";
```

Classification

```
int numberOfCustomers =
    (int)_session.CreateQuery(hql).UniqueResult();
```

> **Note**
>
> Again, note that it's not table names but classes that are used in HQL.

The second example, to order the result set in the database so that it doesn't have to be done in the Domain Model (which might often be a good thing), could look like this in HQL. In this case we are ordering the fetch operation of all customers by Name.

```
select from Customer order by Name
```

Group by is mostly used for reporting purposes, but you could still use it in your application. Here I'm grouping on Name and counting how many instances for each name (a bit twisted, but it shows the syntax):

```
//A consumer
string hql =
    "select c.Name, count(*) from Customer c group by c.Name";
IList result = _session.CreateQuery(hql).List();
```

Finally, an example of a scalar query could be to only fetch the Name of the Customers whose names start with "Vol" (which by now you'll recognize as my favorite criterion), but as a matter of fact you just saw another example when I executed the group by query earlier. To get to the values in the result, the IList called result contains a list of object arrays. Here's a snippet for continuing from the previous example, listing the names and the number of instances for each name:

```
//A consumer, continuing from previous snippet
foreach (object[] o in result)
{
    Console.WriteLine("{0}   {1}", (string)o[0], (int)o[1]);
}
```

Classification

Scalar queries are especially useful in situations where you find it too expensive to fetch complete Customer instances but want a more lightweight result, and you don't want to define a class.

Of course, the result won't be typesafe in this case, but you could use a variation, namely the one I talked about earlier in this chapter called report query (or a flattening query).

An alternative is to provide mapping variations, but then I think it's an even bigger thing you have done. That is obviously violating the Aggregates because you are making it possible to update the instances without making it mandatory to load the complete Aggregates. Warning bells should go off.

Let's end this section with something that might be "obvious" to you if you come from an object background, but might look like magic if you come from an SQL background.

```
select o.Customer.Name, count(*) from Order o group by o.Customer.Name
```

The query itself was very simple, but note that data is fetched from two tables, and there is no mention about that in the from clause (that is, there is no join). Of course, the mapping information is used to determine what needs to be done at execution time with the HQL query.

Other Functionality

Finally, we have a mix of other functionality to check for NHibernate.

- **What backends are supported?**

    This is a typical example of something that could become a long and tedious feature enumeration, so I won't go into detail here. Let's just say that NHibernate supports several different databases (most of the major commercial and open source databases). Check the site [NHibernate] for current information. You can also write your own plugin if you miss the database you need to work with.

- **Not just an O/R Mapper**

    NHibernate is pretty focused on being an O/R Mapper and nothing else. The philosophy is to do one thing and do it well.

Note

Of course, NHibernate does other things as well, but those other things are just not the focus. And they are not too many or too big either.

- **Advanced caching**

    Advanced caching is one area where NHibernate isn't really up to par when compared to Hibernate, but I think it's rapidly becoming better. On the other hand, to me that's not usually a big deal. There are many problems with second-level caching, so that option is often ruled out.

- **Advanced support for controlling transactions**

Support for manual transaction control is pretty good in NHibernate. There are situations where you might be taken by surprise if you don't watch out (for instance, when you execute a query in the middle of a transaction, NHibernate will then Flush() changes to the database before executing the query). That's a tradeoff between querying not going "through" the cache or ordinary transaction control. The good news is that it's controllable by your code.

To bind this to Chapter 8, the typical way of dealing with transactions in NHibernate is "manual control."

Note

On top of that, you can also build something that uses any of the more automatic approaches mentioned in Chapter 8.

- **Open source**

As I've said already, NHibernate is an open source project, so you can investigate the source code and even build your own branch.

- **Version (generation)**

It's hard to decide what version NHibernate is in. At the time of writing, it's called version 1 by the team building it, but at the same time, I would say that the quality is higher than with typical first versions. NHibernate is also a port from Hibernate, which is second generation or actually third now, but that's not reflected in NHibernate. Anyway, let's call it generation 1.

Classification

Let's have a look at how NHibernate positions itself in the classifications from a totally different angle: the infrastructure patterns angle.

Another Classification: Infrastructure Patterns

Without further ado, let's get started with type of metadata.

Metadata Mapping: Type of Metadata

In Chapter 8, I defined three different types of metadata for the Metadata Mapping pattern [Fowler PoEAA]:

- XML document(s) or other document formats

- Attributes

- Source code

This category was simple regarding NHibernate because its metadata is typically XML documents. You *can* describe the metadata in source code as well in the works, but that's not the mainstream thing to do at all.

There are attribute-based approaches as well, but they generate metadata as XML documents.

Identity Field

I have already touched on the matter of how you deal with Identity Fields in NHibernate, but I'd like to go a little deeper. Earlier I showed how to map an Identity Field that is of the Guid type. Let's take a look at the Product Entity, which has an int for the Identity Field, and the value is generated with an IDENTITY (auto incrementing column) in the database. It could then look like this:

```
<id name="Id" access="field.camelcase-underscore"
    unsaved-value="0" >
    <generator class="identity" />
</id>
```

As I said in Chapter 8, when it comes to new entities, the values for Identity Fields can be generated in at least four different layers:

- Consumer

- Domain Model

- Database

- O/R Mapper

Another
Classification:
Infrastructure
Patterns

In the case of the guid, you can generate it in all the layers, but it's recommended that you do it in the O/R Mapper. In the example with IDENTITY just shown, the value is generated in the database, and that actually affects the programming model a lot. First, there will be a database jump earlier than you expect. Second, there might be an INSERT just to grab the IDENTITY value. Both examples are something I consider to be problems, and therefore I don't like to use IDENTITYs more than is necessary.

NHibernate Supports COMBs

As a matter of fact, Guids are often a very nice solution. But perhaps some of you have read my article about a possible cost of INSERTs when you use Guids as primary keys [Nilsson COMB]. The problem is that the INSERT throughput might be *many* times lower for tables with Guids for primary keys than if you use ints. That's not a problem you will typically get, but it might come and bite you if you have very large tables and a high INSERT load. I suggested a solution to the problem in the article I called "COMB." It's basically a Guid, but kind of a sequential one. I was very surprised to see that NHibernate added support for COMB in a specific alpha version. To use the COMB generator, the metadata could look like this (the only difference is that generator is guid.comb and not just guid):

```
<id name="Id" access="field.camelcase-underscore"
    unsaved-value="00000000-0000-0000-0000-000000000000" >

    <generator class="guid.comb" />
</id>
```

It is easiest for you if you let NHibernate generate the Guids for you, but that's not always possible, of course. Sometimes you must use assigned Identity Fields instead, which makes it quite a bit harder. For example, you can't let NHibernate determine using UPDATE or INSERT by looking at unsaved-value. Instead, you will typically tell NHibernate what to do with explicit calls to Save() or Update() instead of SaveOrUpdate().

Another Classification: Infrastructure Patterns

Note

As I said earlier in this chapter, you can use the version tag+unsaved-value tag for helping you out when you prefer to set the Identity Field values on your own.

These were just a few examples of strategies for Identity Fields. NHibernate supports many more. You can also plug in your own strategies quite easily.

Foreign Key Mapping

A foreign key mapping could look like this in a mapping file; here (in the Order. hbm.xml file) it is describing that an Order has a Customer:

```
<many-to-one name="Customer" access="field.camelcase-underscore"
    class="Customer" column="CustomerId" not-null="true" />
```

Without going into details, I would say that NHibernate has strong support for many relationship styles that will solve most of your needs in that area. It's not very easy, though, to learn to use all variations effectively, but you can go a long way with a few basic ones.

On the other hand, what is pretty easy is using the Embedded Value pattern [Fowler PoEAA] with NHibernate.

Embedded Value

NHibernate uses the word component (as if that word didn't have enough different meanings) for describing an Embedded Value. Let's repeat again what it could look like in the mapping file to describe that a Customer has an Address:

```
<component name="Address" access="field">
    <property name="Street" access="field.camelcase-underscore"
        type="AnsiString" length="50" not-null="true" />

    <property name="PostalCode"
        access="field.camelcase-underscore"
        type="AnsiString" length="10" not-null="true" />

    <property name="Town" access="field.camelcase-underscore"
        type="AnsiString" length="50" not-null="true" />

    <property name="Country" access="field.camelcase-underscore"
        type="AnsiString" length="50" not-null="true" />
</component>
```

Note that the Customers table contains all columns, but the Customer class has just an Address field.

When that is in place, using the Embedded Value from the consumer is very easy to understand. It could look like this, for example:

```
Console.WriteLine(aCustomer.Address.Street);
```

Something to think about, however, is whether the Value Object Address should be immutable or not. I would probably choose immutable in this particular example, but it's not always an easy choice.

If you decide to use mutable, you could write the code like this instead of instantiating a new Address:

```
aCustomer.Address.Street = "Large Street 42";
```

> ### Note
>
> If you have an Embedded Value that should be used in many other classes, it could be a good idea to implement IUserType so that you don't have to describe the mapping over and over again. That's also the case if the storage is different from the type to expose. The translation is then done by the IUserType implementation.
>
> Consequently, one downside is that the Domain Model will have to refer to nhibernate.dll, or you will have to have the specific code in a separate assembly and inherit the basic Domain Model class instead.
>
> I try to avoid this if possible. When the ordinary approach for Embedded Value can be used, everything is just fine. For tricky cases, it's often possible to do the translation manually instead in property get/set from/to private fields and then map those private fields to the database.
>
> A typical example of when I avoid a certain construct or deal with it with custom get/set code is when it comes to applying the typesafe enum pattern [Bloch Effective Java] (for example, for adding behavior to enums). First, I think twice if I can't just live with an ordinary C# enum. Second choice is custom get/set code so I don't have to deal with IUserType. It feels like a quite big solution for a tiny thing.
>
> To end this note, just one more thing: Don't exaggerate your tries to avoid a reference to nhibernate.dll in your Domain Model. If the benefit is bigger than the cost...

Another Classification: Infrastructure Patterns

Inheritance Solutions

NHibernate supports all three different inheritance solutions, namely Single Table Inheritance, Class Table Inheritance, and Concrete Table Inheritance [Fowler PoEAA]. If we assume that Customer and Vendor inherits from Company, the mapping information could look like this:

```
<discriminator column="Type" type="AnsiString" length="8"
    not-null="true" />
```

Then, something like the following is needed for each subclass, where the specifics are described (that is, the mapping information that isn't for the Company class):

```
<subclass discriminator-value="Customer" name="Customer">
    <property name="CustomerNumber"
        access="field.camelcase-underscore"/>
</subclass>

<subclass discriminator-value="Vendor" name="Vendor">
    <property name="VendorNumber"
        access="field.camelcase-underscore"/>
</subclass>
```

From that you understand that the only variation in each case is a single specific field, CustomerNumber and VendorNumber. In this case, we will have just a single Companies table, and it would look like this (meaning that we used Single Table Inheritance here):

```
create table Companies (
  Id UNIQUEIDENTIFIER not null,
  Type VARCHAR(8) not null,
  Version INT not null,
  Name VARCHAR(100) not null,
  Street VARCHAR(50) not null,
  PostalCode VARCHAR(10) not null,
  Town VARCHAR(50) not null,
  Country VARCHAR(50) not null,
  CustomerNumber INT null,
  VendorNumber INT null,
  primary key (Id)
)
```

That means that for Vendors, CustomerNumber will be NULL, and vice versa. The Type column will have the value "Customer" or "Vendor" (or normally some smaller symbols).

Another
Classification:
Infrastructure
Patterns

Note

I know, some of you are feeling so uncomfortable regarding this example because you prefer to use something like the Party archetype instead [Arlow/Neustadt Archetype Patterns]. Or at least you prefer not such an overuse of inheritance, if the only variation was a single field and nothing else.

My intention was just to show an obvious and clear example.

And as you would probably expect, when the inheritance mapping is in place, the consumer code can forget about how the inheritance hierarchy is actually stored and focus on how to use the inheritance hierarchy instead.

Identity Map

NHibernate uses an Identity Map on an ISession level. You can easily see this if you read an instance by Id with Load(), make a change to the row directly in the database, and then read the instance again with Load() (with the same ISession instance). You won't see the change because NHibernate didn't roundtrip to the database after the first Load(), but instead the instance was grabbed from the Identity Map.

NHibernate also uses the Identity Map when it comes to querying; not for finding instances, but for placing the Identities in the Map to support future Load() calls from the Identity Map.

If you'd like to force an instance away from the Identity Map, you can call Evict() on the ISession, or Clear() to clear the Identity Map from all instances, or of course Close() the ISession.

Unit of Work

It probably won't come as a surprise to learn that NHibernate uses the Unit of Work pattern [Fowler PoEAA] as well, and again it's dealt with in the ISession. That said, the implementation is pretty different from the most typical one. Instead of registering what has happened with the Unit of Work, NHibernate takes a snapshot of the instances when they are read from the database. At flush time, the instances known by ISession are compared to the snapshots to create a Unit of Work at that point in time.

To be clear, in a way deletes *are* registered and so are notifications of new instances with, for example, SaveOrUpdate().

As always, there are pros and cons to this solution, and one obvious drawback is when there are many instances to investigate, only to find that just one should be flushed. That's one reason for why Hibernate (that's right, Hibernate, not NHibernate, at least not at the time of this writing) 3 has been changed regarding this.

Another Classification: Infrastructure Patterns

Lazy Load/Eager Load

If you do want to use (automatic) Lazy Load [Fowler PoEAA] with NHibernate, that's easily done. You just declare it in the metadata like this, for example:

```
<bag name="OrderLines" access="field.camelcase-underscore" cascade="all" lazy="true">
    <key column="OrderId" />
    <one-to-many class="OrderLine />
</bag>
```

Now the OrderLines of an Order are lazily loaded when the OrderLines are needed for the first time. In order for this to work, however, you must have a connected ISession.

If you don't use the lazy="true" declaration in the metadata, you will effectively get Eager Load instead. NHibernate supports several different approaches for Eager Load, such as OUTER JOIN and several SELECT statements batched after each other.

What might be important is that when you do Eager Load with several SELECT statements, you might get read inconsistency (which might be a bigger problem in the case of Lazy Load) in this case, too. This can be avoided with explicit transaction control and by increasing the Transaction Isolation Level to serializable [Nilsson NED], but it's rarely a serious problem, so I won't go into details here.

You can also control in code whether you want Eager/Lazy Load. That's something you can do when you use querying, but we are satisfied with the discussion about querying we've had already in this chapter.

Controlling Concurrency

Finally, we need support for controlling concurrency. Fowler [Fowler PoEAA] describes the following solutions to the problem:

- Coarse-Grained Lock

- Implicit Lock

- Optimistic Offline Lock

- Pessimistic Offline Lock

NHibernate deals with Optimistic Offline Lock if you add a <version> tag to the entities, like this:

```
<version name="Version" access="field.camelcase-underscore" />
```

Then, if the row in the database has another value of the version column compared to what you expect it to be at persist time, someone else has updated the row, and there's a conflict in concurrency (and you'll get a StaleObjectStateException).

You'll have to deal with the other three mechanisms yourself. NHibernate doesn't support them out of the box.

Bonus: Validation Hooks

Something that wasn't discussed in Chapter 8 but that I added here as a small bonus is validation hooks. NHibernate has an IValidatable interface that will get calls by NHibernate at Flush().

But then I need to reference the nhibernate.dll in the Domain Model, so I prefer a solution like the one I used in Chapter 7, "Let the Rules Rule." I mean, I can use an IInterceptor (yet another NHibernate interface, but in this case not used by the Domain Model) implementation for checking the rules implicitly and thereby use whatever interface of my Domain Model classes I want to. (And using an interface for the Domain Model classes isn't necessary at all, of course.)

To use a custom IInterceptor implementation, you provide it as a parameter when instantiating ISession like this:

```
//A consumer
_session = NHConfig.GetSessionFactory()
    .OpenSession(new MyCustomInterceptorImpl());
```

Just watch out that you can't do everything in the validation code when using this approach; for example, you can't call out by using the same ISession instance, which might create a problem here and there, but we have touched on some strategies that can be used for dealing with this problem in Chapter 7, so I won't repeat those here.

NHibernate and DDD

I bet some of you are screaming for some examples that put all this about NHibernate into the context of DDD. I'd like to end the chapter with exactly that.

Again, I'm not going to use an abstraction layer like NWorkspace here; still, what I describe here could be used for other O/R Mappers as well (and it would be simplified if you *do* use an abstraction layer).

First, a few words about how to structure the assemblies.

Overview of the Assemblies

Conceptually, I like to think about the repositories as part of the Domain Model, but when no abstraction layer is used on top of the O/R Mapper, I let the repositories live in a separate assembly. That way, I will get the dependencies shown in Figure 9-2.

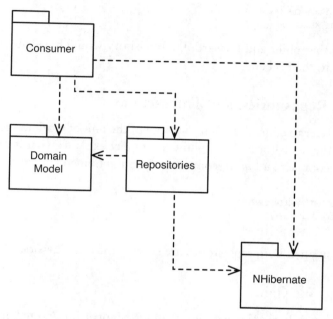

Figure 9-2 Typical assembly dependencies

Note that the Domain Model doesn't have a dependency to NHibernate now. Still, the Domain Model can use the Repositories if needed. One approach is that the Repositories are implementing interfaces that are in the Domain Model. Then those interface implementations (repositories) are injected in the Domain Model instances at suitable spots.

ISession and Repositories

For all this to work, it assumes that the consumer injects ISession instances to the repositories. That means that the following snippet:

```
Customer c = (Customer)_session.Load(typeof(Customer), theId);
```

can be transformed into the following code if a repository takes care of some of the work (not much in this simple case, but some):

```
Customer c = customerRepository.GetCustomer(theId);
```

That snippet assumed that the customerRepository was instantiated this way:

```
//A consumer
ICustomerRepository customerRepository =
    new CustomerRepository(_session);
```

So from that point and forward, the repository would have an ISession to use for talking to the backend.

ISession, Repositories, and Transactions

Finally, I prefer to control the start and end of the unit of work in the consumer, outside of the repositories. The following snippet explains what it can look like (with very compact and *not* recommended transaction code):

```
//A consumer
customerRepository.Add(customer);
orderRepository.Add(order);
_session.BeginTransaction().Commit();
```

In that snippet, both repositories are sharing the same ISession.

What Did We Gain?

Let's take a step back. We just took the O/R Mapper for granted and discussed how it could fit in with the concept of repositories.

Think about it the other way around. I mean, we have a repository and now we want to fill it with real code. Assume that you decide to write manual code there. The API for the repository consumer can be the same thing with other implementations, of course, but instead of the following line:

NHibernate and DDD

```
Customer c = (Customer)_session.Load(typeof(Customer), theId);
```

you would probably have to write quite a lot of code. For example, you need to define the SELECT statement so you get all the columns you need for the customer instance you are about to reconstitute.

Then you need to instantiate the customer instance and shuffle all the values from the resultset row to the instance.

Sure, we can all do that. It's not the complexity that is the problem; it's that this most often is an uninteresting piece of work. And there is a *lot* more to it. For example, the customer also had a list of ReferencePersons that should be reconstituted at the same time and a whole bunch of other things as well.

When we are done with that code, every single change to the schema or Domain Model will lead to more tedious work for us. Remember, this was a single get operation of a single object.

If we instead use an O/R Mapper, changes are often dealt with by making a few changes to the mapping information and that's it. I believe I'm *much* more efficient dealing with changes when I don't hand code the uninteresting persistence code.

That thought can be seen in a larger perspective also, because if I know that changes won't be too expensive, I'm much more inclined to do refactorings than in the opposite case!

Let's end this section with a short story from a recent project. I think changes in that project that only affect the pieces (the Domain Model and the database schema) that are dealt with by the O/R Mapper are probably done a magnitude cheaper compared to the changes that affect the persistence code that we have hand tuned! (That said, don't forget that O/R Mappers are *of course not* the silver bullet either. There are pros and cons.)

Summary

By applying an O/R Mapper such as NHibernate, the design and code we started sketching out in Chapter 4, "A New Default Architecture," and forward can be followed pretty closely and non-intrusively. NHibernate lets us build our Domain Model in a PI manner.

I see this family of tools (the O/R Mappers) as enablers for making it possible to focus on DDD, but at the same time they need to provide openings for us to handcraft pieces of the persistence code when needed.

Of course, it's not just gold and green forests. For example, I would really like to see awareness of DDD from O/R Mappers like NHibernate, which would simplify the whole thing and lead to even better end results. Still, applying NHibernate as part of your infrastructure, I think, is a big step in the right direction.

So, what's next? The last part of the book, Part IV, "What's Next?" is what's next.

The first chapter of that part starts with a discussion about larger contexts, having several models at play. After that there is a focus on interesting design techniques for now and the future. Those are *Service-Oriented Architecture* (SOA), *Inversion of Control/Dependency Injection* (IoC/DI) and *Aspect Oriented Programming* (AOP).

Summary

PART IV

What's Next?

In this part, there is a focus on other design techniques to keep an eye on and start using. The other focus is on how to deal with the presentation layer when it comes to bridging that gap to the Domain Model and how to deal with developer testing of the UI. This part is almost exclusively written by guest authors.

This part is about other techniques. I'm not implying that a movie is better than theatre, only different.

Chapter 10

Design Techniques to Embrace

Where are we?

We have now spent quite a lot of time discussing and applying the basics of DDD. We have written many unit tests, designed our Domain Model carefully, and made the Domain Model persistent with an O/R Mapper. What's left?

A story about a well-known industry leader in a multinational company goes like this. He held a meeting after the company's profits, quality, and so on were better than ever before and said something like: "Now I want all of us to spend one minute thinking how good we are..." A minute later he recommenced, taking up problems, criticizing, and so on. It was business as usual.

After we have thought nice thoughts about ourselves for a minute, what do we need to focus on now?

Of course, there are dozens of things to consider. First of all, we are by no means done with even the basics of the Domain Model, let alone the details. But we have started out nicely, and we are also in good shape for taking on problems such as performance characteristics, concurrency issues, security, and so on. I will actually leave all this as an exercise for you, the reader, because I hope your appetite has been whetted so you are forced to give it a try on your own if you haven't before.

Instead, in this Chapter I will start with a short discussion about how you can scale up the DDD principles used so far, mostly by focusing on the Bounded Context pattern [Evans DDD]. After that we will discuss three different design techniques that I think are worth looking at today. They are Service Orientation, Inversion of Control/Dependency Injection, and Aspect Orientation.

Design Techniques to Embrace

I asked a couple of my friends to write about those design techniques, and we have their contributions here, but I penned the first section in this chapter myself. Over to "Context is King."

Context Is King

I think it's pretty common not to give enough thought to how important the context is. For example, when the GoF patterns [GoF Design Patterns] are discussed and used by developers without prior experience of these patterns, it is typical to forget that there is a context for when the patterns are suitable.

A good idea/solution/anything, but in the wrong context it isn't necessarily any better than a bad counterpart. That's just the way it is.

Let's take a step back before we focus more on the specific context-related concept of this section. First, here's a word on layers and partitions.

Layers and Partitions

Back in 1994, Grady Booch's book, *Object-Oriented Analysis and Design* [Booch OOAD], was published. It gave me a better understanding of what Jim Rumbaugh's book, *Object Modeling Technique* [Rumbaugh OMT], had introduced to me a few years before. One such example was layers and partitions. The concept of layers was quite familiar to me, but not partitions the way Booch described them. He saw partitions as slices in the other dimension compared to the layers.

To make this more concrete with an example, two typical layers are the UI and the Domain Model. Two possible partitions might be the subsystem for registering orders and the subsystem for administering user complaints. Both partitions might have a UI and a Domain Model.

Today, just as it was back then, I think layering has received much more focus than partitions. Layering has been a very important way of providing "separation of concerns." You probably have a firm grasp of what the idea is: to live by the principle of *Single Responsibility* (SRP) [Martin PPP].

In a way, this almost total focus on layering is changing. I think layering has relaxed a bit with DDD, at least compared to the rigorous layering I used in the past [Nilsson NED]. (Well, we are still *very* focused on factoring out the infrastructure from the Domain Model.)

Context Is
King

> ### Note
>
> We discussed layering according to DDD in Chapter 4, "A New Default Architecture."

At the same time, there is an increasing understanding of how you can't create one single huge Domain Model, or at least that it's often too complex, costly, or inefficient to go that route in large-scale situations. I also think *Service Orientation* (SO) is a driving force when it comes to the increased interest in partitioning. The whole problem simply becomes more evident.

Because of the increased interest in partitioning, the interest in layering might lessen. It's just not as important or beneficial with a rigorous layering design for a tiny partition.

Let's have a closer look at the reasons for partitioning.

Reasons for Partitioning

While layering is often based on technical reasoning, partitioning is often based on organizational reasons. Sure, partitioning could also be done for a technical reason; for instance, a certain partition might become stale faster and might be one we'd like to swap for another implementation later on. The idea then might be to make it obvious and easy to achieve when the day comes.

But again, organizational reasons are important for partitioning, such as because one team takes care of this and another team takes care of that. This is totally in line with a discussion I had with some colleagues about motivations for layering. None of them thought that layering was good to use for organizing a team. That's something I've done from time to time, and (to my mind) with success. What I think they all really meant was that it's a *better* idea to organize the team around partitions instead. And then the layering is less stressed inside each partition. We will, of course, still see that different people have different main interests and expertise, and we shouldn't fight that. We should just not create a large department of UI developers that builds the UI for all applications, another department of Domain Model developers, and yet one more department of database developers. Out of those two dimensions (if you have to choose), the most important is the domain problems that should be solved, not what technologies to use. Remember that when organizing the team also.

What also matters regarding whether you need partitioning or not is the size of the development effort. For a tiny system, one partition might be all that is needed; for a large system, a good partition design might be extremely important to succeed.

To summarize this, I think that first it's a matter of partitions, and then inside those partitions it's a question of layers, not the opposite.

Let's see if we can couple this to DDD, which brings me to talking a little about the Bounded Context pattern [Evans DDD].

Context Is
King

Bounded Context

A common question is "How should we deal with complexity?" And just as common an answer is "divide and conquer." Use of hierarchies is one way of dividing and conquering.

DDD is pretty much about hierarchies. One extremely useful tool that I've been emphasizing a lot is the Aggregate pattern, which is a pretty coarse-grained unit. Entities is another unit, and Value Objects is yet another (all found and discussed at length in [Evans DDD]).

If we go in the opposite direction, "up" from Aggregates, we will find that Bounded Contexts isn't the same as aggregates, but rather the same as subsystems or sub-models.

The basic idea with Bounded Context is to be very explicit about in what context the model applies. You should also be very strict about the model and its concepts *within* the Bounded Context; what is outside doesn't really matter that much.

From a narrow perspective, a good reason for the division into several Bounded Contexts is to be able to think about all the details within one model and to be able to keep it pure. At the same time, from a wider perspective we can think about "large" abstractions that are easy to grasp and think about in overview terms.

A strong advantage of the Aggregate is its boundary. It simplifies life, decreases coupling, and makes connections more explicit. Again we find advantages of a boundary, this time on a higher level with the Bounded Context.

Note

Although I see great value in boundaries, there are also costs. You might introduce a lot of overhead when it comes to communication and performance. As usual, keep it simple and add complexity when you gain more than the cost.

Context Is King

If we bind this to the example I used in the previous chapters, that of the sales order, there might be one bounded context for ordering and another for shipping. This is not how I started to talk about it in my little example, but in a real-world, large scale situation it *might* make sense from a technological standpoint, and different parts of the organization might very well be dealing with each of those business processes, which might be a good reason for the split.

How Do Bounded Contexts and Partitions Relate?

I've been talking about partitions and Bounded Contexts, but that doesn't mean that I see them as the same thing. It's *possible* that the Bounded Context is the same as a typical partition. It might also be that a Bounded Context is built up of several partitions instead, but probably not the opposite.

Scaling up DDD Projects

A typical reason for applying Bounded Contexts is that they provide a way of making it possible to scale up DDD to larger contexts. Instead of having one huge Domain Model that a huge team touches, it might make the effort of understanding the model much easier if you split the model into several smaller ones, letting the development groups focus on their own models.

Bounded Contexts might also help preserve the Ubiquitous Language from becoming un-crisp and having loose definitions. Instead what you will get are several Ubiquitous Languages, one per Bounded Context, which is partly a bad buy. But on the other hand, each of these will be more powerful and exact. Rather two good, than one bad.

When you find out that what you thought was a single model has started to have concepts with different meanings and that the Ubiquitous Language isn't as clear and crisp as before, that can very well be a sign that it has actually become two models. Instead of fighting it, it can often be wise to promote this evolution and define two different Bounded Contexts.

It's time to shift focus and talk about another reason for partitioning of Domain Models.

Why Partition a Domain Model—SO?

Assuming that we already have a large Domain Model, why would we need to partition it? This is not a new problem, but I think SO has made the problem more apparent than when compared to other solutions for distributed systems, such as EJB and COM+. In those systems, the partitioning was helpful but most often not so strictly enforced, as is the norm for SO systems.

> ### Note
>
> I'm aware that many SO people don't think from the Domain Model and out, but start with the interfaces instead. As I see it, it's always a bit of each.

This book is *not* about integration or messaging, but merely about architecture and design for *one* service or *one* application. But we relax the focus of the book for a section and have a look at an introduction to Service Oriented Architecture (SOA) that Udi Dahan has written.

An Introduction to SOA
By Udi Dahan

Both DDD and SOA are relatively new concepts, the first being quite well-defined, and the second less so. While there are those who claim that SOA has been around since the early CORBA days, never has there been such broad vendor and industry buy-in for "just an architecture."

So What Is SOA Anyway?

Although a number of definitions of SOA have been proposed, no one definition has been declared the victor. Most definitions are based around the idea that systems are composed of independent services. However, what exactly constitutes a service is unclear. One definition of SOA that cannot be refuted is that SOA is a way to develop software. Specifically, SOA deals with systems or applications that are, or can be, distributed. The acknowledgement that distribution is a primary architectural issue is one of the underlying currents of SOA.

Why Do We Need SOA?

Software that is meant to run in a distributed environment needs to be designed differently. This is a fundamental shift from distributed object thinking where applications would use non-local resources "transparently," with no knowledge of the location of these resources. The problems that arose with distributed object architectures were primarily found in performance. The semantics of working with local and remote resources need to be different, a hard-learned lesson that has become a litany in distributed systems development: "Chunky over chatty."

Chunky interfaces, also known as coarse-grained interfaces, cause more work to be performed in a single call than fine-grained interfaces, which require multiple calls to perform the same amount of work. The explicit coordination and resource-locking that needs to take place over fine-grained interfaces is totally encapsulated in a single chunky call. This results in client code that is less coupled to the server code implementation.

In fact, the evolution of distributed systems architecture has been punctuated by the introduction of new ideas and the sobering effects of reality—performance. Despite the fact that Moore's law has held over the years, and apparently will continue to hold, the world of large-scale systems development continues to be preoccupied with performance. However, it is not so much performance as a static measure that is interesting, but rather scalability, the dynamic measure of performance over varying loads, that architects strive to maximize.

SOA is the next step on the ladder of architectural evolution that will enable new systems to be built, and older systems to be utilized, in scalable solutions.

How Is SOA Different?

While current distributed systems development practices design layers and deploy them in physical tiers, SOA unifies these two concepts into "services," which are both the unit of design and deployment. The other aspect that differentiates SOA from current practice is the codification of communication between services; while there are no restrictions on how layers or tiers should communicate, services must communicate according to message-exchange-patterns defined by a schema. There is also both theoretical and practical support for using only one-way asynchronous messaging for inter-service communication; however, this has not yet won industry-wide support.

> ### Note
>
> Note that "schema" doesn't necessarily dictate XML, but rather the set of messages that flow between services.
>
> While XML, and SOAP by extension, are not prerequisites of SOA, the extensibility of XML makes the versioning of schema much easier.

What Is a Service?

Besides being both the unit of design and the unit of deployment, services are surprisingly ill-defined for the size of the buzz surrounding SOA. Instead of defining what a service is, most of the literature describes properties of services. One such example is the four tenets of Service Orientation:

- Services are autonomous

- Services have explicit boundaries

- Services expose schema and contract, not class or type

- Service compatibility is determined based on policy

While these properties do indeed drive the design of scalable services (and will be discussed in more detail later), they apparently provide little guidance on the design of distributed systems. Architects just beginning to employ service-oriented techniques to their designs have no information about which elements should be grouped together into services, how to recognize and define service boundaries, and how these services are to be implemented using classic OO patterns. On top of that, the technologies surrounding the "pure" architectural aspects of SOA continue to be in a state of flux, and the various vendor offerings appear to be little more than repackaging of current products. Is it any wonder that SOA is already being dismissed as hype?

What Goes in a Service?

The question previously raised as to what elements of design are grouped together into a single service is not new to most developers and architects. This question has already been asked at the introduction of components and objects. While composing several objects/classes into a component is just fine, the same cannot be said of components and services. A service is *not* just a collection of components but rather a fundamental shift in how we structure our software.

By taking into account that communication with a service is based on message exchanges, we find that services are composed of different types of elements and not just "components" or "objects." In order to expose functionality, services use a message schema. This schema is composed of several elements: the most basic include the "data types" (like Customer) that define entities, the messages that define what operations can be performed (not necessarily on a per-entity basis), and the service contract that defines interactions with the defined messages (a CustomerChangeRequest will result in a CustomerChangeReply, for instance). It is quite clear that a message schema is neither an object nor a component, yet it is a necessary part of a service.

Another part of services that is often overlooked is the service host. A service would not be able to provide functionality without having some kind of executing environment in which to run. Web services using HTTP will likely have either IIS, Apache, WebSphere or some other Web server as their host. Other services may be hosted by COM+, a Windows Service, or even something as simple as a console application. Although the industry has been moving toward transport-independent services, certain host implementation details (like protocol) do affect services in significant ways. HTTP and other TCP-based protocols are all connection-oriented. In distributed systems where elements may fail, reboot, or simply respond slowly, connection-oriented protocols can cause performance to suffer until time-outs occur. Connectionless protocols (like UDP) cause other problems—there are no built-in mechanisms to recognize that a message did not arrive at its destination. If anything, *the* necessary part of any service is its host.

Beyond these atypical elements, services will indeed be composed of components and/or objects. Yet, not just any composition will meet the guidance prescribed by the 4 SOA tenets. A thorough discussion of their meaning is in order.

Where Do the Four Tenets Lead Me?

The first two tenets (autonomy and explicit boundaries) go hand in hand; each service is independent of other services, and it is clear where one service ends and another begins. Some ramifications of this include the fact that should one service crash, other services wouldn't crash as a result. Therefore, at the most basic level, different services should run in different processes, so a thread could not enter a different service as a result of a method call. At more profound levels, there should be no way one service could lock resources in another service—transactions (of the ACID type) should be limited in scope to a single service.

Note

The term "transaction" was originally used to describe a way of working with relational databases and the four properties of transactions were given the acronym ACID: Atomic, Consistent, Isolated, Durable. A common implementation for databases to fulfill these requirements, the relevant rows, pages, and tables were locked within the scope of a transaction.

The third tenet (schema, not class) seems to be talking about interoperability, that to communicate between services, we use XML on the wire—the so-called lowest common denominator. However, at its most basic level, this tenet is talking about separation of concerns. The class that implements the desired behavior is decoupled from the external clients that "call it." This is quite different from Java RMI, COM, or .NET remoting, where client-code must reference server types. When using schema, an explicit mapping needs to be performed between external message formats and internal class invocations. This enables us to change the internal implementation of a service, going so far as to change which class or interface is invoked without affecting external clients.

There is an even deeper meaning to the third tenet, and it is versioning. While types can form hierarchies such that one type is a kind of another type, history has proven versioning types to be horrendously difficult—DLL hell comes to mind. One of the goals of versioning a service is to avoid having to update client-code already deployed. This goes so far as to say that the deployed clients will continue communicating with the same endpoints as before. The benefit inherent in schemas that is absent in types is that schemas can be compatible, even though they are different. This is where the extensibility of XML is important.

For example, after deploying version 1 of our service and client, we would like to roll out version 2 of the service so that we can deploy several new clients (version 2) that require more advanced functionality from the service. Obviously, we wouldn't want to break existing clients by such a change, nor would we want to have to upgrade them. In order for this to be possible, version 2 of the service's schema needs to be compatible with version 1, a task more difficult and less developer-friendly when communicating without schema. Imagine having to tack on to the end of each method signature something like "`params object[] extraData`".

The fourth property of services in SOA (compatibility is based on policy) further reinforces the first two points—the service decides whether or not it will respond to a given request and adds another dimension; metadata is transferred as a part of the request. This metadata is called policy. In most presentations given, policy is described using examples such as encryption or authentication capabilities. The idea is based on a separation of concerns; the schema that defines the logical communication is independent of the encryption policy. If you have information you'd like to pass between services without expressing it in your schema, policy is one way to do it.

What Is a Service? Take 2

Now that we've discussed these properties of services, let's summarize with what a service *is*. Once upon a time, we all wrote applications, applications that the user interacted with. Today, we're going to call applications "services," and they'll be able to interact not only with users but with other "services." Note that distributed applications aren't going to be called "distributed services," but will rather be modeled as a bunch of services that work together. The rule-of-thumb for the confused is "one .exe per service," or when it comes to web applications, "one root Web directory per service." The flip-side of the coin relates to databases; while there won't necessarily be one database per service, there should not be shared databases between services. Shared databases are really back doors into the service, bypassing validity checks and logic—in essence, violating its autonomy and increasing coupling between the services.

The Place of OO in SOA

Now that it is clear that an application is really a service, a part of a larger whole, how then does object-orientation, the accepted practice for application development, fit into SOA? Although some have proclaimed SOA to be the next generation of application development, effectively replacing OO, nothing of the kind has happened yet. It has taken over two decades for mainstream development to move from procedural-oriented to OO programming. It is unlikely that were a shift from OO to SOA possible, it would happen in any less time.

In fact, SOA and OO operate on different levels. OO deals with the design and code of a single deployment unit while SOA deals with a solution comprised of multiple deployment units. SOA does not suggest new or alternate ways of designing or coding the internal logic of a given application or service. There is no reason SOA and OO should not be cooperative technologies. The question that SOA does bring to the table when developing OO applications is how these applications will accept and respond to messages coming from sources other than the user, and even in parallel to user activity. The fact that a given application can receive requests and, at the same time, issue its own requests to other services brings us to the conclusion that interactions no longer follow the classic "client-server" pattern.

Client-Server and SOA

Not so long ago, most application development was described as client-server. For example, client software would "send requests" (SQL) to a database server and receive responses from it. Later, client-server fell out of favor and was replaced with 3-Tier (or N-Tier) where the rise of the application server began. Again, requests went one way and responses the other.

However, as systems grew and became more interconnected, the N-Tier concept blurred as application servers began to make requests from other application servers acting as their clients. The inherent ordering found in the tiered architectures wasn't being seen in practice. Finally, client-side software was beginning to receive events asynchronously from its servers, in essence responding to requests—something that it wasn't explicitly designed for.

An
Introduction
to SOA

Beyond the SOA theory that states that client software should also be designed as a service, there is a real need for client code to be able to receive messages. Consider the case where an action on the server takes a very long time to complete, longer than the time-out duration for HTTP, possibly even days. This is not at all unusual for operations that require human intervention. While the client may poll the server for completion, this places undue load on the server, requiring a background task on the client. If we were to use that same background task to listen for messages notifying about work completion, we could relieve the server of this load. This solution is both feasible with today's technology and simple to implement.

In this manner, the client may receive any number of types of messages, effectively becoming a service. In fact, these message exchanges could better be described as conversations between an initiator and a target than requests/response pairs between client and server. There are no inherent constraints as to which services can initiate a conversation and which can respond.

One-Way Asynchronous Messaging

We have seen that in cases of long response times we must disconnect the response message from the flow of the request message. Yet, can an initiating service ever know how long it may take the target to respond to a request? Even if the previous result arrived quickly, that is no guarantee of future responsiveness. In essence, if all interactions with a service were based on this idea, that service's clients would be insulated from the impacts of load on the service. This paradigm has other benefits as well.

Because the initiator no longer requires a synchronous response, the target service is now free to perform the processing at the time most beneficial to it. Should the target service be under heavy load, it could schedule the processing of new messages for a later time. In other words, we are able to perform programmatic load balancing over time. For instance, we can write code that takes into account the nature of the request when scheduling it for future processing.

In the previous synchronous request-response paradigm, the initiator was only capable of receiving the response from the target. Now that the initiator is listening for a response, the constraint that only the target service can return the response is lifted. The target service can now offload returning responses to other services.

The advantages of using one-way asynchronous message-exchange patterns are numerous. Both the flexibility of the solution and its scalability are increased. These benefits obviously have a cost attached to them, but we will later see that the cost is not that great.

How SOA Improves Scalability

By using one-way asynchronous messaging, a service is able to moderate load by queuing requests. This results in services that do not degrade in performance under increasing load because no performance-draining resources (like threads) are acquired. By keeping resource utilization near constant at any load above that giving maximum performance, services developed using one-way asynchronous messaging achieve better performance characteristics, as shown in Figure 10-1.

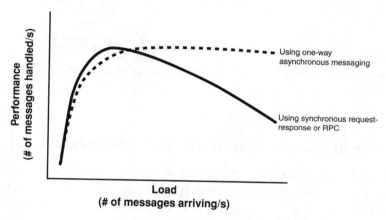

Figure 10-1 Performance under load for one-way asynchronous and synchronous request-response/RPC messaging

Note that while under small loads, the time to process a single message this way may well be greater than when using classic RPC. This is secondary to the greater throughput achieved under heavy load.

The Design of a SOA Service

The high-level design of a service which employs one-way asynchronous messaging may look similar to that shown in Figure 10-2.

In this design, when a message is received, no processing is done on it beyond placing it in a queue (this minimizes the number of threads held open by the application server, regardless of the load or processing time). Next, a processing thread will, at some future time, take the message from the queue and process it. If this processing requires sending messages to other services, the responses will be received exactly the same way as any request. Furthermore, the processing thread will not need to wait for these responses, but can continue handling new messages; the state of the processing of previous messages is held in some store that can be retrieved when responses have arrived. Note that processes may be used instead of threads when using an out-of-process queue like MSMQ to better enable scale-out growth by running those processes on separate machines.

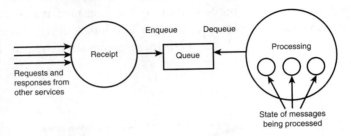

Figure 10-2   Hypothetical high-level design of a service which employs one-way asynchronous messaging

How Would a Service Interact with Other Services?

Let's consider an example of how a service would process a request that involves retrieving information from other services and focus on how the actual processing works. (Note that in the figures that follow, when one horizontal arrow appears below another arrow, this means that the lower arrow represents an event which occurred at a later point in time than that of the higher arrow.)

First, a request arrives at our service, is placed into a queue, and then handled. In order to handle the request, information needs to be retrieved from three other services. After requests are dispatched to the other services, the state of processing the original request (pending responses 1, 2, and 3) is saved (see Figure 10-3).

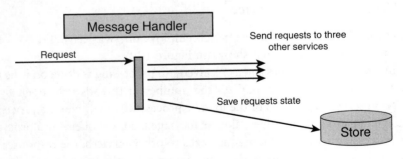

Figure 10-3   Request is dispatched to other services and state is stored

An
Introduction
to SOA

When a response from service #2 arrives, it waits in the queue until it reaches a message handler. The message handler retrieves the state of the original request from the store and updates it (pending responses 1 and 3). Because the processing of the original request has not been completed, the handling of response #2 is now finished (see Figure 10-4).

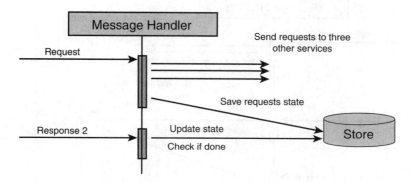

Figure 10-4 One response is processed

Should another request arrive before processing of the previous request is complete, it would have no impact on the processing of the original request. It could begin its own processing and send requests to any number of other services in the same manner. We can interleave the processing of multiple requests with the same resources (see Figure 10-5).

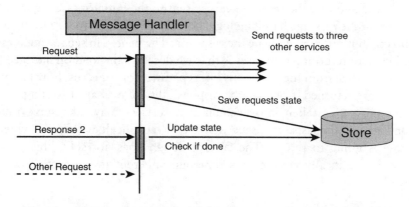

Figure 10-5 Another incoming request won't affect the first request that is still being processed

When the response from service #3 arrives, it is handled in the same way as the response from service #2. Because not all necessary responses have been received, again no response will be sent to the initiator of the original request (see Figure 10-6).

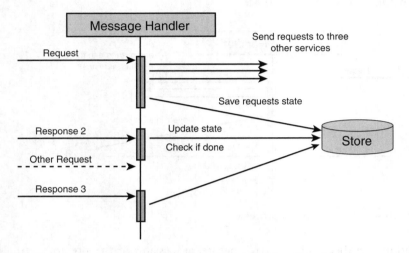

Figure 10-6 Another response comes, but one response is still lacking

Finally, only when the response from service #1 arrives for message handling can the processing of the original request be completed. After updating the state of the original request in the store, the service now knows that all responses have arrived and that the response can be sent to the initiator (see Figure 10-7).

Note that the message handling logic need not send the response to the initiator directly but rather can queue the response. The benefit in separating message handling from returning responses is that we decrease the load on message handling logic. Also, from the perspective of separation of concerns, how and when responses are returned is outside the responsibility of message handling.

Although we've taken into account that services may take some time to respond to our requests, the issue that we haven't dealt with yet is when no response is going to return. The current design does not solve this problem because it specifically circumvents time-outs inherent in connection-oriented protocols.

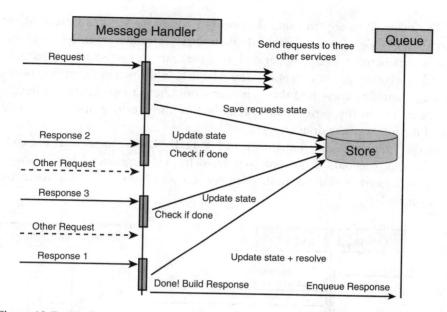

Figure 10-7 Final response for first request arrives, and the result can be enqueued

SOA and Unavailable Services

While in the classic RPC style of distributed systems we would receive an exception when trying to connect to a remote server that was down, in this design we may not receive any exception or response at all. What is required then is some way to know that the handling of a certain request has timed out. This can easily be taken care of by assigning a timer to each request sent. However, this is not the interesting part of the problem.

When the time waiting for a response expires, what should be done? This is another area in the design where domain logic is required. The questions that need to be answered by the domain logic are varied and include the following:

- Should an error be returned?

- Should a partial result be returned?

- Should we attempt to retry sending the request?

- Should a combination of these be used?

- Should the same behavior be used regardless of the message?

The other advantage in using the previous design for services instead of the classic RPC-style design is that the domain logic performed when a remote service is unavailable is cleanly separated from the main message-handling path. In the RPC-style design, an exception would have been thrown in the middle of the message-handling code, and the code that would have to be written to handle the exception in the various ways described by the previous questions would cloud the intent of the domain logic.

In the interaction diagram shown in Figure 10-8, we can see that the code that handles timeouts is not only separated from the message-handling code, but is separated in time as well. Both request and failure handling logic are encapsulated.

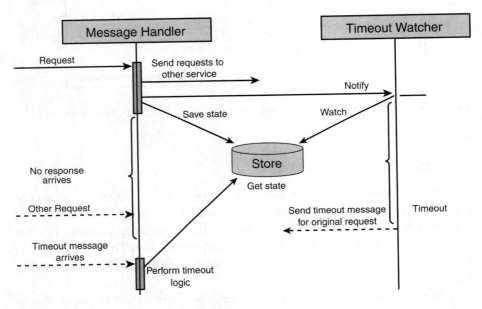

Figure 10-8   Applying a timeout watcher

Complex Messaging Processes

When developing services using the previous design, we are also able to construct complex and robust inter-service workflows. For instance, when Request A is received, send requests to services Alpha and Beta. When a response is received from either Alpha or Beta, if the response value is greater than some threshold, send a request with the threshold value to service Gamma; otherwise, send a request with the response value to service Delta. If service Delta is unavailable, partial results are to be returned. If service Alpha is unavailable or returns an error, the error should be returned to the initiator of the request, and so on. During this entire process, other messages can be processed as well, and many other complex processes can unfold concurrently. Not only is concurrent execution possible, but it is resource-efficient, even under load.

Scaling Services

We've already seen the increased scalability SOA provides by utilizing one-way asynchronous messaging. However, can services designed this way efficiently make use of increasing numbers of processors on the same box? What about increasing numbers of servers?

Let's first look at the message handling. The message handling thread/process is stateless—for each request, it finds the appropriate state in the store and processes the result accordingly. Therefore, we can increase the number of concurrent message handlers without harming correctness. Because each of the message handlers is independent of others, there will be no need for in-memory locking or for a given message handler to wait (unless it has no messages to process).

For a single box with multiple processors, this means that we can increase the number of message handlers and increase throughput. For multiple servers, we could place the message receipt, queue, and store on a single server while placing more message handlers on each additional server.

The ultimate advantage of the scale-out scenario described is that it enables addition of more servers at runtime. By monitoring the number of items in the queue, we can know when the system has reached peak capacity, and then add more resources without taking the system down or hindering performance in any way.

Summary

The main point to remember about SOA is that it is "merely" an evolution of best practices of distributed systems development. The core OO principles of separation of concerns and independence of interface from implementation continue to be reflected in service-oriented practices. Although many topics have been touched upon, each topic has depth that cannot be explored in such an introduction. Hopefully you have understood what SOA is *not* and what tools shouldn't be used between services. How the logic of a service is internally structured is a question that I assume will never be decisively answered, but I'm sure Jimmy will get you on track.

An
Introduction
to SOA

◆

Thanks, Udi!

And for readers who would like to get more into depth with SOA, or more specifically messaging, a good book to start with is [Hohpe/Woolf EIP].

One of the driving forces behind SOA is to reduce coupling. Another technique for reducing coupling is the subject of the next section.

I have pretty often written in this book about Dependency Injection, but I applied it only manually. To many people, injecting what the instance will need in the constructor is the most natural thing in the world. That's easy looking at it on a small scale and something we want to be able to do during test, but on a large scale during runtime it becomes tricky, cumbersome, and something that makes reuse much harder than it has to be.

In the next section, Erik Dörnenburg will discuss inversion of control as the principle and Dependency Injection as the pattern. Erik, the readers are yours.

 ## Inversion of Control and Dependency Injection
By Erik Dörnenburg

Previous chapters discussed how domain objects and the corresponding infrastructure can be designed and developed. In this section, I want to present a particular design technique, or pattern, that can be used to assemble objects at runtime. The general principle is known as *Inversion of Control* and the particular pattern has been named *Dependency Injection*.

No Object Is an Island

Almost any object in our applications that provides business functionality depends on other objects. These can be objects that provide data or a service of some form. When we design and develop our objects using TDD, we usually explicitly provide the objects required, and often we use stubs or mocks in place of them to isolate the object under test. At runtime, however, our objects require a real implementation, and in one way or another all objects in our application must be instantiated and wired up.

The most common approach to resolving a dependency between one object and another is to place the responsibility for creating or acquiring the dependent object with the object that has the dependency. The simplest way to do this is to have the object that has the dependency instantiate the object it requires.

As an example, let us assume we are creating a pricer, an object that calculates the price for a financial instrument such as a bond. Of course, the pricer needs the bond that should be priced, but we decide that this is not part of the state of the pricer object and is to be passed in with each pricing request. Therefore, our class could look as follows:

```
public class BondPricer {
    public double GetPrice(Bond bond) {
        /* do something really complicated here */
    }
}
```

The price of the bond depends on other factors, though, and one example is something called a discount curve. (It does not matter whether you are familiar with the domain or not; for this example, the pricer could also depend on a wombat and nothing would be different.) A curve can be used to price many different bonds and remains relatively constant. We therefore decide that the curve should be part of the state of the pricer and keep it in a member variable which is initialized in the constructor.

```
//BondPricer
private readonly DiscountCurve curve;

public BondPricer() {
    curve = new DiscountCurve();
}
```

Note that we could have created the curve on demand, but the discussion on when lazy instantiation is useful is a different one. In any case, the pricer now has a direct dependency on the curve. It is also likely that the discount curve object itself depends on other objects that it instantiates at an appropriate time. This looks like a viable approach, but upon closer inspection problems become visible: We have a functioning set of objects to price our bonds, but how flexible and maintainable is our solution?

Let us assume that the discount curve object reads the individual points of the curve from a database. This is what the users wanted. In a later iteration, we are asked to build a feature that allows the users to analyze what-if scenarios. For this the users want to specify the points for the curve in the UI. Nothing easier than that: We create an interface from the DiscountCurve class and provide two separate implementations, DatabaseDiscountCurve and InMemoryDiscountCurve. We change BondPricer class so that it only uses the methods on the interface and is thus no longer coupled to the database-based implementation.

Unfortunately, even though the calculation code in the bond pricer only depends on the discount curve interface, we must instantiate a concrete implementation of the IDiscountCurve interface at some point, the constructor of BondPricer in this example. At this point, we have to decide which of our two

Inversion of Control and Dependency Injection

implementations we want to instantiate, but whichever one we choose, our class is coupled to the interface as well as to that implementation. The following diagram (Figure 10-9) shows the class design and clearly illustrates the problem: the *creates* link between the BondPricer and the DatabaseDiscountCurve.

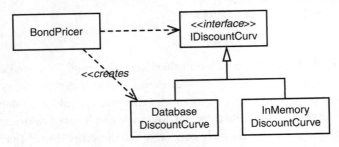

Figure 10-9   Dependencies when direct instantiation is used

Another issue with direct instantiation is that there is no single place in the application to control the creation of discount curves, which makes it impossible to reuse the same instance for different purposes. This can be quite problematic, and if we consider that the original version of the curve loads information from a database, it becomes obvious that recreating new instances can have a severe impact on the performance of our application.

Before we discuss Inversion of Control and Dependency Injection, let us first look at another common approach to solving these issues.

Factories, Registries, and Service Locators

One way to address the coupling issue is through the use of the *Factory* pattern. We create a factory class that provides the required objects; in our case, an object that implements the discount curve interface.

```
public class DiscountCurveFactory {
    public static IDiscountCurve GetCurve() {
        return new DatabaseDiscountCurve();
    }
}
```

Inversion of
Control and
Dependency
Injection

```
public class BondPricer {
    private readonly IDiscountCurve curve;

    public BondPricer() {
        curve = DiscountCurveFactory.GetCurve();
    }
}
```

With this factory, the pricer is no longer tightly coupled to a curve implementation, which is what we wanted to achieve. Unfortunately, in its place, the factory class itself is now tightly coupled to a specific IDiscountCurve implementation, so it remains difficult to use different curve implementations in different applications of the pricer. To overcome this problem we could create a factory interface and pass in different factory implementations, but this means that we would have to solve the problem of getting the right factory, which is similar to getting the right objects. In other words, we would add a level of indirection that provides additional flexibility but would just move the key problem we have.

What we have not shown in the code is that the Factory pattern also addresses the issue of instance management. Because we have a central place in our code that is responsible for providing curve instances, namely the GetCurve() method, we can choose to implement alternative policies that apply to the entire application. For example, rather than always creating a new curve, we could maintain a single instance or, if our application is multi-threaded, we could choose to manage a pool of instances.

In a further step toward complete decoupling, we can replace the factory with an implementation of the *Registry* pattern [Fowler PoEAA]. Much like a factory, a registry provides objects of a given type but rather than hard-coding the type of object, it externalizes this decision and instantiates the objects using reflection. This approach represents an improvement on the Factory pattern for our purposes because we have now separated two concerns: We have one class that is responsible for the provisioning of objects, the registry, and we can move the code that decides which concrete class to use in each case to other more suitable places in our code base.

The implementation of such a registry is simple but effective and finally achieves our goal of decoupling BondPricer from a concrete implementation of IDiscountCurve.

```
public class DiscountCurveRegistry {
    private Type curveType;

    public static void RegisterCurveType(Type aType) {
        curveType = aType;
    }
    public static IDiscountCurve GetCurve() {
        return (IDiscountCurve)Activator.CreateInstance(curveType);
    }
}
```

Figure 10-10 shows the resulting class design. It highlights that the pricer only depends on the interface, but it also draws our attention to two important implications of using a registry: The pricer depends on the registry class, and we need some other code, an assembler, that provides the concrete implementations to the registry.

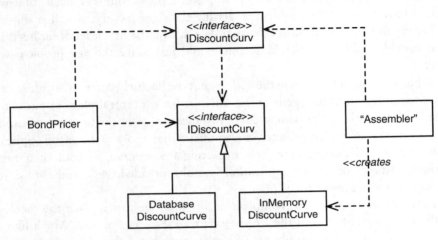

Figure 10-10   Dependencies when a Registry is used

The curve objects we are using in this example are data sources, but it is easy to see that we can use the same patterns to locate services providing objects (for example, an audit service that writes the calculated price to a log). Used in this way, the pattern is often referred to as *Service Locator* [Alur/Crupi/Malks Core J2EE Patterns].

In implementation, most locators go one step further and do not provide individual sets of register and get methods for each service, but instead provide a single set of generic methods and a dynamic naming scheme.

```
public class Locator {
    public static void RegisterType(String name, Type aType) { ... }
    public static Object GetInstance(String name) { ... }
}
```

Using a Service Locator, we register a concrete curve implementation with the locator under a name, most likely the name of the interface. With this setup, our bond pricer can now get hold of the discount curve by asking the locator for one.

```
public class BondPricer {
    private readonly IDiscountCurve curve;

    public BondPricer() {
        curve = (IDiscountCurve)Locator.GetInstance("MyBank.IDiscountCurve");
    }
}
```

We have chosen to use strings in our naming scheme, which is a common practice, but object types would serve equally well. Using object types has the advantage of maintaining full support for automatic refactorings provided by our IDE and also helps with better error checking, though these benefits come at the expense of some flexibility. Whichever approach we choose, the pattern remains the same and provides the same degree of decoupling.

Constructor Dependency Injection

With registries and service locators, we have managed to decouple an object from the objects on which it depends by using an indirection, in this case a somewhat glorified lookup table. Setup code is responsible for deciding which concrete implementations to use, and the responsibility for finding the dependent objects lies with the object that has the dependencies. It uses the passive locator object and actively pulls the objects it requires from the locator whenever it deems necessary.

In contrast to that, Dependency Injection turns this process around and makes the object that has the dependencies passive. The object declares its dependencies but is otherwise completely oblivious as to where the dependencies come from. The process for resolving the dependencies and finding the dependent objects is left to an external mechanism, which may be implemented in a variety of ways. Usually, applications contain generic infrastructure code that loads a configuration file or uses an internal registry to keep a list of all objects and their dependencies. However, the Dependency Injection pattern is not concerned with this aspect. The infrastucture code is strictly complimentary, and it is even possible to satisfy the dependencies by passing in the objects from application code.

There are several flavors of dependency injection. Let us have a look at *Constructor Dependency Injection* first. Following this pattern, an object declares its dependencies in its constructor, and the code that creates the object ensures that valid instances are supplied at runtime.

Inversion of Control and Dependency Injection

```
public class BondPricer {
    private readonly IDiscountCurve curve;

    public BondPricer(IDiscountCurve aCurve) {
        curve = aCurve;
    }
}
```

An important observation is that this code does not depend on anything but concepts related to the problem domain. It does not require a reference to a factory or registry, and it is not concerned with finding or creating the instances. As such, dependency injection promotes the design of elegant software, which usually exhibits a good separation between domain and infrastructure concerns.

Figure 10-11 shows the design using dependency injection. We have also included an assembler object that is responsible for creating the pricer and the curve on which the pricer depends. The diagram highlights the fact that with this design there is no dependency from any domain specific object to generic infrastructure code such as the assembler.

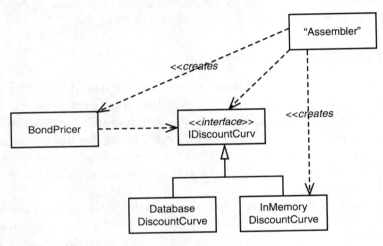

Figure 10-11　Dependencies when Dependency Injection is used

The fact that the bond pricer is not coupled to any infrastructure code also improves testability. Consider the first implementation of the pricer, which used the initial implementation of the discount curve that loads its points from the database. Tests of this class would always hit the database, and we know from previous chapters that this is a bad idea. With constructor injection, we can easily supply a stub or a mock implementation of each dependency, and so it is very straightforward to make the tests of the pricer independent of the database.

Inversion of Control and Dependency Injection

```
[Test]
public void testPriceIncludesValuesForOutstandingCoupons () {
    IMock curveMock = new DynamicMock(typeof(IDiscountCurve));
    IDiscountCurve curve = curveMock.MockInstance as IDiscountCurve;
    BondPricer pricer = new BondPricer(curve);
    /* do actual test */
}
```

This approach is simpler than any solution that can be achieved with the other patterns we have discussed before. If we had opted for a design with a registry, for example, it would have been necessary for the test to create a registry and register the mock with it. With dependency injection, we simply pass in the required object. The underlying reason for this simplicity is the high level of decoupling provided by the Dependency Injection pattern, which makes it easy to use an object in multiple environments, at a minimum in the normal runtime environment and the testing environment.

We have not managed to replace all the functionality of the Registry pattern by introducing the Dependency Injection pattern. In the previous design, the registry did also provide another important service, namely a mapping between abstract types, the IDiscountCurve interface, and a concrete implementation to be used in a given application or context.

Surprisingly often, it is sufficient to hard-code the mapping in the code that creates the object. In our example, we may have two different methods that are invoked from different points in the user interface, one that prices the selected bond based on information from the database and another one that first asks the user for a few points, then constructs an in-memory curve from the points and finally creates a pricer based on that curve. In both cases, we can simply configure the pricer in the corresponding methods. As a matter of fact, using a registry in this example would feel awkward.

```
public class BondInfoForm : Form {
    private TextBox priceTextBox;

    private Bond SelectedBond { get { … } }

    public void CalculateActualPrice() {
        DatabaseDiscountCurve curve = new DatabaseDiscountCurve();
        BondPricer pricer = new BondPricer(curve);
        priceTextBox.Text = pricer.GetPrice(this.SelectedBond);
    }
    public void CalculateScenarioPrice() {
        InMemoryDiscountCurve curve = new InMemoryDiscountCurve();
        this.GetCurvePointsFromUser(curve);
        BondPricer pricer = new BondPricer(curve);
        priceTextBox.Text = pricer.GetPrice(this.SelectedBond);
    }
}
```

In many cases, simplicity is a trade off, and simple designs often fail to address more complex requirements. Fortunately, the simplicity in creating components designed according to the Dependency Injection pattern does not make it hard to create complex mapping and configuration schemes, and there are several

Inversion of Control and Dependency Injection

lightweight IoC containers that can fulfill the same role as a registry. (I will discuss two of them later.) This means that we can choose between a simple hard-coded solution as shown previously and a more flexible mapping provided by some infrastructure code.

Another interesting consideration is an object that has optional dependencies. In the case of the bond pricer, the accuracy of certain calculations can be increased by taking local holidays into account, which means that a holiday calendar is an optional dependency. With constructor dependency injection, we express this by providing two constructors, one for each valid set of dependencies.

```
public class BondPricer {
    private readonly IDiscountCurve curve;
    private readonly IHolidayCalendar calendar;

    public BondPricer(IDiscountCurve aCurve) {
        curve = aCurve;
    }
    public BondPricer(IDiscountCurve aCurve
        , IHolidayCalendar aCalendar) : this(aCurve) {
        calendar = aCalendar;
    }
}
```

It would also be possible to use a constructor with all arguments and pass in null for the optional ones, but this makes the contract less explicit, especially when the number of dependencies increases. It is therefore advisable to always provide one constructor for each valid set of dependencies and, if possible, to chain the constructors. If this seems impossible, it is probable that the class in question has too many dependencies and should be broken up.

Setter Dependency Injection

As the aptly chosen name suggests, *Setter Dependency Injection* uses setters rather than the constructor to inject the dependencies. Consequently, the pricer has a default constructor but requires an additional property with a setter.

```
public class BondPricer {
    private IDiscountCurve curve;

    public BondPricer() {
    }
    public IDiscountCurve DiscountCurve {
        set { curve = value; }
    }
}
```

Inversion of
Control and
Dependency
Injection

Setter injection provides the same degree of decoupling as constructor injection, and it is easy to see that creating pricer objects in unit tests is as straightforward as with constructor injection. An important difference is that the pricer is in an invalid state until the setter method has been called, something that is not possible with constructor injection. Additionally, we cannot declare the curve variable as `readonly` because it is not initialized in the constructor and, finally, with setter injection it is a little more tricky and error-prone to implement final initialization functionality that needs to be run after all the dependencies have been injected.

Setter injection has its uses despite these shortcomings because it scales better to components with many dependencies. In a component with three optional dependencies and a strict view on constructor injection, we would need eight constructors. One could argue that the component needs refactoring, but this is not always practical, and it is good to have a pattern at hand for situations like this. In a similar vein, many existing objects have a default constructor and properties, and therefore we can only use them with IoC containers that support Setter Dependency Injection.

There are further styles of Setter Dependency Injection, such as Interface Driven Setter Dependency Injection, that use marker interfaces to distinguish setter methods that describe dependencies from other public setter methods. These styles are either not widely used or do not significantly change the key characteristics of setter injection, so I will not discuss them here.

Inversion of Control

Having discussed the Dependency Injection pattern and concrete implementations of it, let us now turn to *Inversion of Control*, also known as the *Hollywood Principle* ("Don't call us, we'll call you!"). Strictly speaking, IoC is not a pattern but a general principle that simply states that objects should rely on their environment to provide other objects rather than actively obtaining them.

Historically, the term IoC was frequently used to describe the approach certain containers took to create components at runtime. Looking at these containers, Martin Fowler raised an important question, namely "What aspect of control are they inverting?" He suggested that we recognize the setter- and constructor-based approaches implemented by these containers as a concrete pattern and use the more specific name Dependency Injection for it [Fowler InversionOfControl]. This also allowed people to distinguish between the Dependency Injection pattern and other types of IoC.

Inversion of
Control and
Dependency
Injection

A widely used pattern that adheres to the IoC principle but is not a Dependency Injection variant is *Contextualized Dependency Lookup.* For our bond pricer, using this pattern would mean that we continue to use a registry-like class, which is often called *context* in this pattern, but let the container provide this context to our object, which is the inversion of control aspect. In code this can look as follows:

```
public interface IServiceContext {
    public Object GetInstance(String name);
}

public interface IComponent {
    public void Initialize(IServiceContext context);
}

public class BondPricer : IComponent {
    private IDiscountCurve curve;

    public void Initialize(IServiceContext context) {
        curve = (IDiscountCurve)context
            .GetInstance("MyBank.IDiscountCurve");
    }
}
```

On closer inspection, this pattern looks like a hybrid between the Service Locator and the Setter Dependency Injection patterns. This is no accident because historically this pattern is one of the first IoC patterns and proved to be an important stepping stone to the more elegant Dependency Injection patterns.

Dependency Injection with the Spring.NET Framework

The Spring.NET application framework [Spring.NET], which is a port of the widely used Java Spring framework [Spring], provides a very flexible IoC container that supports various flavors of Dependency Injection. This container is simply a component, actually an interface with several implementations, that is responsible for loading the configuration and setting up the objects accordingly. Historically, the term container was used to illustrate that an IoC container can be an alternative to a standard J2EE container on the Java platform.

Returning to the constructor injection example described earlier, let us examine how we would use the container provided by Spring.NET to get a configured instance of a pricer.

The preferred way to describe components and their dependencies with Spring.NET is with an XML configuration file. We declare our objects by type, including the assembly they are loaded from, and then resolve the dependency of the pricer on the discount curve by a nested constructor-arg element in the declaration of the pricer.

```
<objects>
    <object name="DbCurve" type="MyBank.DatabaseDiscountCurve, MyBank"/>
    <object name="DbPricer" type="MyBank.BondPricer, MyBank">
      <constructor-arg><ref local="DbCurve"/></constructor-arg>
    </object>
</objects>
```

To access the objects in our code, we can create an instance of IApplicationContext, tell it to load the configuration from the config file, and then ask it for an object by name. The context ensures that all dependent objects are created and injected where required.

```
IApplicationContext context = new XmlApplicationContext("spring.xml");
BondPricer pricer = (BondPricer)context.GetObject("DbPricer");
```

In real applications, it is uncommon to use the application context so directly because it makes the code that creates the pricer dependent on the context. This is very similar to the dependency between our classes and the registry in the Registry pattern that we wanted to avoid. If we assume that the class that requires the pricer is a Windows form, we can use dependency injection for the form itself and add the form to the XML configuration. Now, when the form is created, the pricer is injected by the container and the form does not have to deal with the application context.

In this case, however, there must be some other piece of code that creates the form, and this code would look up the form from the context and would therefore be coupled to the context. Clearly, it cannot be turtles all the way down. To solve this issue most containers provide integration with the application frameworks, Spring.Web for example, such that the initial application-specific components, the Windows forms and Web pages, can simply use dependency injection while the application framework is responsible for creating them using the context. If there is no integration for a particular container/framework combination it is best to use dependency injection as much as possible and limit the dependency on the context to one class.

If we prefer to use setter injection, we can use the setter-based pricer implementation discussed before and change the Spring.NET configuration element for the pricer. The code that obtains the pricer remains unchanged because the container deals with creating the objects.

Inversion of Control and Dependency Injection

```
<objects>
  <object name="DbCurve" type="MyBank.DatabaseDiscountCurve, MyBank" />
  <object name="DbPricer" type="MyBank.BondPricer, MyBank" >
    <property name="DiscountCurve">
      <ref local="DbCurve"/>
    </property>
  </object>
</objects>
```

The authors of Spring.NET generally advocate setter injection, but the container supports both styles equally well. As a matter of fact, nothing stops us from combining constructor and setter injection. If we design our pricer so that it declares it as required, or non-optional, dependency on the discount curve in the constructor and provides a settable property for the optional dependency on the holiday calendar, we can configure a pricer with a calendar as follows:

```
<objects>
  <object name="DbCurve" type="MyBank.DatabaseDiscountCurve, MyBank" />
  <object name="Calendar" type="MyBank.DefaultHolidayCalendar, MyBank" />
  <object name="DbPricer" type="MyBank.BondPricer, MyBank" >
    <constructor-arg><ref local="DbCurve"/></constructor-arg>
    <property name="HolidayCalendar">
      <ref local="Calendar"/>
    </property>
  </object>
</objects>
```

This only scratches the surface of the possibilities that Spring.NET offers, but even these simple features can help enormously with configuring components that are designed according to the Dependency Injection pattern. One can even argue that placing too much and too complex logic into the configuration file provides flexibility that is rarely needed at the expense of maintainability.

Auto-Wiring with PicoContainer.NET

The configuration files used in the previous section were easy to understand and their purpose, namely to declare a few classes and the dependencies between them, was very explicit. However, they are relatively verbose, and they duplicate information that is also available via the .NET type system. For example, the fact that the pricer depends on a curve is expressed in the declaration of the constructor on the pricer class. In fact, all the information required in our example is available from the type system.

Most IoC containers support the resolution of dependencies based on run-time information. This feature is known as *auto-wiring* because the setting of dependent components, the wiring, occurs automatically, without any additional

Inversion of Control and Dependency Injection

configuration. Spring.NET supports auto-wiring as an alternative to XML files, but I will use PicoContainer.NET [PicoContainer] in this section to add variety and because for this container, auto-wiring is the preferred option.

Using PicoContainer.NET, the only step that is required to enable the container to resolve dependencies and create objects is to register the concrete implementation classes with the container.

```
IMutablePicoContainer pc = new DefaultPicoContainer();
pc.RegisterComponentImplementation (typeof(DatabaseDiscountCurve));
pc.RegisterComponentImplementation ("pricer", typeof(BondPricer));
```

By placing the declarations into code, we remove redundancy and we get better support from the IDE because it is now able to detect misspelled type names, and it can also safely rename types in automated refactorings.

The objects are obtained from the container in almost the same way as they are obtained from the application context in Spring.NET, and for that reason the same considerations regarding a dependency on the container apply: Almost all classes should make use of dependency injection, leaving only one central class that interacts with the container to obtain the initial components.

```
BondPricer pricer = (BondPricer)container.GetComponentInstance("pricer");
```

The previous example also shows that, in addition to using the type system, PicoContainer.NET supports named components: the pricer in this example. This makes it possible to look up objects without having to specify their type, which introduces another degree of decoupling.

Optional dependencies are handled automatically because PicoContainer. NET uses the most complex constructor for which it can satisfy the dependencies. In the previous example, PicoContainer.NET uses the one argument constructor for BondPricer, which only takes a curve, but if we add the registration of the holiday calendar, PicoContainer uses the two argument constructor when we get the pricer object.

```
IMutablePicoContainer pc = new DefaultPicoContainer();
  pc.RegisterComponentImplementation (typeof(DatabaseDiscountCurve));
pc.RegisterComponentImplementation(typeof(HolidayCalendar));
pc.RegisterComponentImplementation ("pricer", typeof(BondPricer));
```

As far as object dependencies are concerned, we are not losing any flexibility by using type-based auto-wiring instead of a configuration file-based approach, and at the same time we benefit from an improved development experience. Auto-wiring does not work equally well if a class expects parameters, such as hostnames, port numbers and timeouts, in their constructor because primitive types do not convey much information about their intended purpose. If we register two integers with the container, one that specifies a port number and the

Inversion of Control and Dependency Injection

other one a timeout, the container sees both of them as integers and has no way of determining which one to use in a constructor that takes one integer.

The underlying question is whether the container should support the injection of required components in the same way as it handles the setting of configuration parameters or whether both requirements are seen as different concerns that should be handled with the most suitable approach for each concern. Using type-based auto-wiring arguably provides benefits over configuration files when managing dependencies, so one could use auto-wiring for this purpose. In the same scenario, configuration parameters can be set with setters for named properties, which is arguably more intuitive for that purpose.

A third IoC container that is available for the .NET platform is Windsor, which is part of the Castle project [Castle]. The core container implementation of the Castle project, which the developers call micro-kernel, uses type-based auto-wiring but it also allows plug-ins to add additional dependency resolution strategies. The Windsor container [Windsor], which is based on the micro-kernel, adds support for configuration files, thus allowing developers to choose the most appropriate mechanism. This is an approach that was successfully pioneered by NanoContainer [NanoContainer], a Java container that is layered on top of the Java version of PicoContainer.

Nested Containers

The fact that the container in Spring.NET is named ApplicationContext hints at the fact that the container defines a context for the objects that retrieve components from the container. These objects interact with the returned objects, and their behavior depends on the concrete implementations provided by the container; hence, the container can be seen as the provider of a context in which objects act. The name further suggests that the context created from the configuration file is application-wide, and all lookups in an application share the same context.

Web applications use multiple contexts, and most Web frameworks make them explicit in the form of application, session, and request objects. Request-handling code, such as the code behind a Web page, usually depends on several components. Some of the components are part of the application context because they can be shared by all request handlers while others are part of the individual request context because they should only be used by a single request.

Some IoC container implementations support this model and allow containers to be nested, which means that a container can have a parent container and, as a direct consequence, child containers. When a container cannot satisfy all dependencies required to create a component, it tries to obtain the missing components from its parent container, which in turn can request components from its own parent container. This set-up broadly resembles the Chain of Responsibility design pattern [GoF Design Patterns].

As an example, consider the creation of a request handler or page that has a dependency on a database connection and a logger. The database connection should only be used by one request at a time while the logger can be shared by all requests. This, however, is of no concern to the request handler.

```
public ResultPage : Page {
    private Logger logger;
    private IDbConnection connection;

    public ResultPage(Logger aLogger, IDbConnection aConnection) : base() {
        logger = aLogger;
        connection = aConnection;
    }
}
```

In our application, a container is associated with the application. Additionally, each session has a child container, and for each request in a session, a child container of the corresponding session container is created. Our application maps a request URL to a page type, and it contains the following generic code that creates new request handlers for a given page type:

```
public RequestHandlerFactory {
    IPicoContainer sessionContainer;

    public Page CreatePage(Type pageType) {
        IMutablePicoContainer reqContainer = CreateRequestContainer();
        reqContainer.RegisterComponentImplementation(pageType);
        return (Page)reqContainer.GetComponentInstance(pageType);
    }
    private IMutablePicoContainer CreateRequestContainer() {
        IMutablePicoContainer pc = new DefaultPicoContainer(sessionContainer);
        pc.RegisterComponentImplementation (typeof(SqlDbConnection));
        /* register all other components here that should be available
           to requests on a per request basis. */
        return pc;
    }
}
```

After the request container is created in the CreatePage() method, the code registers the page type with the request container so that the page itself can use dependency injection. When it retrieves the actual page instance in the third line, the request container tries to create the page but, assuming a ResultPage is required, it cannot resolve the dependency on the Logger class because this has not been registered with the request container. In this situation, it will try to obtain

Inversion of Control and Dependency Injection

the missing component from its parent, the session container, which also does not contain a logger and thus requests the logger from its parent, the application container. Provided that a logger is registered with that container, all dependencies for the page can be satisfied and it is created by the request container.

The advantage of this approach is that on the one hand components can be registered and shared at the appropriate level, while on the other hand objects that retrieve components from a container only have to deal with one container and can rely on it to find the required components in the chain of containers.

Service Locator Versus Dependency Injection

At this point we have discussed two different patterns that solve the coupling and instance management issues described at the beginning of this chapter. The question remaining is when to use which pattern.

It is safe to say that the Service Locator pattern is more commonly used today, but this is not necessarily because it is a better match for most applications. Instead, the most likely reason is that the Service Locator pattern has been around for a long time while Dependency Injection is a comparatively new pattern that is not as well known yet. In fact, developers arrived at the Dependency Injection pattern when they tried to improve the Service Locator pattern.

The complete decoupling of the components from the dependency resolution mechanism that is achieved by the Dependency Injection pattern improves testability because the tests do not have to set up specialized versions of a locator to provide stubs or mocked objects. It also helps with reuse in large systems as it avoids the problematic situation where different components to be used in a system are tied to different locator implementations.

Another advantage of the Dependency Injection pattern, especially with Constructor Dependency Injection, is that all dependencies of an object are easily visible in code. Modern IDEs are capable of highlighting all usages of a service locator in a given class (by pressing Ctrl-Shift-F7), but even with a sophisticated IDE this is not as easy as looking at a constructor.

It is often stated that Dependency Injection couples the life cycle of the object *A* that has the dependencies with the life cycles of the objects *B* and *C* it depends on, because *B* and *C* must be created before *A* so that they can be injected. This is not a problem with the Service Locator pattern because the creation of *B* and *C* can be postponed until they are requested from the locator by *A*. Fortunately, the same can be achieved, if not as naturally, with the Dependency Injection pattern, as one usage of the *Component Adaptors* in PicoContainer shows. Instead of injecting an instance of the actual class, the container injects a proxy that only creates the real instance when it is first used and from then on forwards all method calls to it. This is completely transparent to the object that has the dependencies, but it effectively decouples their lifecycles.

Summary

In this section, we looked at two issues that arise in the construction of any software system: the coupling of objects that depend on other objects and the managing of component instances. We first described how these issues can be addressed with the commonly used Factory, Registry, and Service Locator patterns. Realizing that these patterns have certain shortcomings, we discussed the Dependency Injection pattern, which addresses these issues in a novel way. This pattern, which is based on the Inversion of Control principle, provides better decoupling and scales well, from simple problems to very complex dependencies. It also improves testability, which is important for TDD, and allows domain models to be completely separated from infrastructure code, which makes it a useful tool for DDD.

As with almost any pattern, Dependency Injection is not a silver bullet and one cannot make the general recommendation to always replace the use of the Service Locator pattern with Dependency Injection. It is important to understand the differences and benefits of each pattern and use them appropriately. We have also seen that the Dependency Injection pattern has several flavors that provide trade-offs. Fortunately, choosing a certain flavor does not affect testability, which is important for development, and the containers that are used at runtime generally support all main variants. We can therefore choose, or even mix, different flavors as required.

The most important consideration when designing systems is to separate concerns, in this case configuration and usage of components, and then choose the most suitable design pattern from a rich catalogue.

◆

Thanks, Erik!

I just want to stress once more what Erik ended with. You can think about Dependency Injection as what Martin Fowler talks about in his DSL article [Fowler LW] when he says that development can be thought of as creating good abstractions and then configuring them. Dependency Injection is one approach to taking care of part of the configuration.

I had to bite my tongue not to say "configuration aspect" in the previous sentence. You wouldn't have forgiven me for providing such a weak thread to

Inversion of Control and Dependency Injection

the next subject, right? As a matter of fact, Dependency Injection and *Aspect-Oriented Programming* (AOP) actually often live in symbiosis, as you soon will find out.

Do you remember the discussions about Repository design? We can choose among several principles, such as

1. Specific Repositories

2. A base class

3. A base class with generics

The problem with approaches 2 (on top of the lack of type safety, if you see that as a problem) and 3 is that they kind of create an automatic, unnatural abstraction that all Repositories will have. For example, not all Repositories should have delete possibilities.

The answer might be to create a smaller base class and write specific code for the variations. If you go that route, you might find that your base class will only have perhaps two or three methods (GetById(), MakePersistent(), and so on) and you get pretty close to approach 1 again.

You can try to lessen the code duplication by factoring out general code into helper classes that your specific Repositories delegate to. Then you'll have to write that boring and tedious delegation code, which won't make anyone happy.

Instead of starting with a base class that "never" has the right granularity, another approach is to build up the right Repository out of several tiny aspects, mixing in the right aspects to the right Repository. This is another way of thinking about the problem. It may not necessarily always be the right way (there is never one right way), but it is definitely worth more thought. I asked my friend Aleksandar Seović to write a short introduction to *Aspect Orientation* (AO).

◆ Aspect-Oriented Programming (AOP)

By Aleksandar Seović

In the last couple of years, AOP has been generating a lot of buzz in the software development community. AOP was invented in the late 1990s by Gregor Kiczales [Gregor Kiczales] and his team at Xerox PARC labs in an attempt to solve a problem of code duplication in object-oriented systems by encapsulating *crosscutting concerns* of the system into reusable *aspects*.

AspectJ [AspectJ], which could be considered a reference AOP implementation, was released in 2001 and has spurred a lot of activity in the Java community, including a number of alternative AOP implementations.

While most of the AOP-related activity is still happening in the Java community, there are several .NET AOP implementations that you can use today to reap the benefits of AOP, such as Spring.NET AOP [Spring.NET], Loom.NET [Loom.NET] and AspectSharp [AspectSharp].

What Is the Buzz About?

The basic premise behind AOP is that even though OOP helps reduce the amount of code duplication when compared to procedural languages, it still leaves a lot to be desired. Core OOP features, such as inheritance and polymorphism, as well as documented design patterns, such as Template Method [GoF Design Patterns], help to minimize duplication in the core application logic. However, code that implements crosscutting concerns, such as logging or security, is still very difficult if not impossible to modularize using OOP by itself.

Even though every article ever written on AOP that you run across will probably have the same boring example, we will use method invocation logging to show you what types of problems AOP tries to address.

Let's assume that we've implemented a simple calculator service that supports four basic arithmetic operations—addition, subtraction, division and multiplication—as the following code shows. Note how simple and readable the methods are because they only contain the core logic.

```
public class Calculator : ICalculator
{
    public int Add(int n1, int n2)
    {
        return n1 + n2;
    }

    public int Subtract(int n1, int n2)
    {
        return n1 - n2;
    }

    public int Divide(int n1, int n2)
    {
        return n1 / n2;
    }

    public int Multiply(int n1, int n2)
    {
        return n1 * n2;
    }
}
```

Aspect-
Oriented
Programming
(AOP)

For the sake of argument, let's say that a new user request comes up that requires you to log every call to your service methods. Class name, method name, parameter values passed to it, and its return value should be logged.

Using only OOP, this seemingly simple request would force you to modify all four methods and add logging code to them. The end result would look similar to this:

```
using System;

namespace LoggingAspectDemo
{
    public class LoggingCalculator : ICalculator
    {
        public int Add(int n1, int n2)
        {
            Console.Out.WriteLine("-> LoggingCalculator.Add
                (" + n1 + ", " + n2 + ")");
            int result = n1 + n2;
            Console.Out.WriteLine("<- LoggingCalculator.Add
                (" + n1 + ", " + n2+ ") returned " + result);

            return result;
        }

        public int Subtract(int n1, int n2)
        {
            Console.Out.WriteLine("-> LoggingCalculator.Subtract
                (" + n1 + ", " + n2 + ")");
            int result = n1 - n2;
            Console.Out.WriteLine("<- LoggingCalculator.Subtract
                (" + n1 + ", " + n2 + ") returned " + result);

            return result;
        }

        public int Divide(int n1, int n2)
        {
            Console.Out.WriteLine("-> LoggingCalculator.Divide
                (" + n1 + ", " + n2 + ")");
            int result = n1 / n2;
            Console.Out.WriteLine("<- LoggingCalculator.Divide
                (" + n1 + ", " + n2 + ") returned " + result);

            return result;
        }

        public int Multiply(int n1, int n2)
        {
            Console.Out.WriteLine("-> LoggingCalculator.Multiply
                (" + n1 + ", " + n2 + ")");
            int result = n1 * n2;
```

Aspect-
Oriented
Programming
(AOP)

```
        Console.Out.WriteLine("<- LoggingCalculator.Multiply
            (" + n1 + ", " + n2 + ") returned " + result);

        return result;
    }
  }
}
```

As you can see, similar logging code exists in each of the methods.

Note

As you understand, the previous example could have been done a bit better even without AOP, such as by using the Decorator pattern [GoF Design Patterns], but we are trying to make a pedagogic point here, so please be patient.

It's also the case that the Decorator pattern would affect the consumer because it has to instantiate the decorator instead of the decorated class, and if you need to add multiple services you need to implement and chain multiple decorators.

There are many problems with this approach:

- There is a lot of code duplication, which is never a good sign. In this case, duplicate code could possibly be simplified by creating static utility methods for logging that would take class and method name and parameter or return values as arguments, but duplication itself cannot be removed using OOP.

- Logging code distracts a reader from the core logic of the method, thus making the method less readable and more difficult to maintain in the long run.

- Code that implements core logic is longer than necessary. Methods that could've been simple one-liners had to be broken into result assignment and its return, just so the result could be printed in the logging code.

- If you had to remove logging code at some point, you would be faced with a daunting task of manually removing or commenting out all the logging code from your classes.

- If you decided that you want to log the full class name, including namespace, you would have to find all the methods that contain logging code and add missing namespace information by hand.

Aspect-Oriented Programming (AOP)

- The same applies if you decide that you want to log exceptions such as overflow and division by zero when they occur—you'd have to add a try/catch block and a statement that would log exceptions in many, many places throughout your code base.

Of course, one could argue that if you used a sophisticated logging solution, such as Log4Net [Log4Net] or Enterprise Library Logging Application Block [Enterprise Library Logging], instead of plain `Console.Out.WriteLine` statements, you could turn logging off by simply changing the configuration setting, without the need to touch any of your classes.

While that is entirely true, it really misses the point in this case. Your core logic would still be intermingled with ancillary logging code, and you would still have to edit many methods by hand if you wanted to make any changes to the logging logic. Moreover, if we change our example from logging to security policy enforcement or transactions, you won't be able to turn it on or off so easily either.

What AOP promises to do for you is to allow you to separate crosscutting code, such as logging or security, into aspects and to apply those aspects easily to all the classes and methods that need them. Of course, there is a lot more to AOP than this. It also allows you to separate business rules from the core logic and to change your existing objects by adding both state and behavior to them. We'll see examples of this in the following sections.

What is important to understand is that AOP is not a replacement for OOP—it is simply an extension to it that allows you to go to places that are difficult to reach with OOP alone. Good object-oriented principles and practices still apply. Actually, it is probably even more important than ever before to have a solid OO design in place, as it will make application of aspects much easier.

AOP Terminology Defined

Before we dig deeper and show you examples of AOP in action, it is important to understand basic AOP terminology, which is not as difficult as it first seems. So I offer some definitions for the following terms:

- An **advice** is a piece of code that you want to encapsulate and reuse. For example, logging code would be implemented as an advice and applied wherever you need it. There are several types of advice, such as *before*, *after*, and *around* advice.

Aspect-
Oriented
Programming
(AOP)

- An **introduction** is a somewhat special type of advice that only applies to classes. Introductions allow you to introduce new members into existing classes, both state and behavior, and could be used to achieve the benefits of multiple inheritance in languages that do not support it, without its tradeoffs. (Introduction is called mixin in some languages.)

- A **joinpoint** is any place in the code where an advice *could* be applied. In theory, a joinpoint could be almost anything—instance variable, for loop, if statement, and so on. In practice, however, most commonly used joinpoints are classes, methods, and properties.

- A **pointcut** identifies a set of joinpoints where advice *should* be applied. For example, if you want to apply transaction advice to all the methods that are marked with Transaction attribute, you would have to declare a pointcut that identifies those methods.

- An **aspect** groups advices and the pointcuts they apply to, which is in a way similar to how a class groups data and associated behavior together.

AOP in .NET

Enough theory—let's see how AOP can help us solve real-world problems that we face almost every day during development.

Examples in this section are built using the Spring.NET AOP implementation, so you will need to download and install the latest Spring.NET release in order to try them.

Note

Please note that, as of this book's writing, the examples in this section are based on the planned implementation of the AOP support in Spring. NET. Visit this book's Web site (www.jnsk.se/adddp) for information about changes, or check the official Spring.NET documentation, which can be found at www.springframework.net.

Modularizing Logging Code Using an Aspect

So let's see how we can leverage AOP to solve the problems associated with the previous logging code.

Creating a Logging Advice   The first thing we need to do is create an advice
that will encapsulate logging code:

```
using System;
using System.Text;
using AopAlliance.Intercept;

namespace LoggingAspectDemo
{
    public class MethodInvocationLoggingAdvice
        : IMethodInterceptor
    {
        public object Invoke(IMethodInvocation invocation)
        {
            Console.Out.WriteLine("-> " +
                GetMethodSignature(invocation));
            object result = invocation.Proceed();
            Console.Out.WriteLine("<- " +
                GetMethodSignature(invocation)
                + " returned " + result);
            return result;
        }

        private string GetMethodSignature
            (IMethodInvocation invocation)
        {
            StringBuilder sb = new StringBuilder();
            sb.Append(invocation.Method.DeclaringType.Name)
                .Append('.')
                .Append(invocation.Method.Name)
                .Append('(');

            string separator = ", ";
            for (int i = 0; i < invocation.Arguments.Length;
                i++)
            {
                if (i == invocation.Arguments.Length - 1)
                {
                    separator = "";
                }
                sb.Append(invocation.Arguments[i])
                    .Append(separator);
            }
            sb.Append(')');

            return sb.ToString();
        }
    }
}
```

Aspect-
Oriented
Programming
(AOP)

This advice will log the class name, method name, and parameter values and return values for each call to the method to which it is applied.

It uses the ToString() method to print parameter and return values. That might not be sufficient in all cases, but it should work for the vast majority of methods, especially if you take care to implement ToString() for your application classes. In the case of an exception, this advice will simply propagate it, so any error handling code you might have in place should work fine.

It's in the Invoke() method where most of the magic happens. What we are basically saying here is that we want to log the start of the method call, capture the result by assigning the value of the invocation.Proceed() call to a result variable, and log the result before returning it. The call to invocation.Proceed() is critical—that is what causes our calculator method to be executed.

The GetMethodSignature() helper method is used to build a method signature in a generic fashion by inspecting the invocation object. You'll probably notice that we called GetMethodSignature() twice, even though it seems that we could've optimized the advice a bit by assigning its result to a local variable and using that variable instead. The reason for that is so that we can also see any changes in the parameters that were used, in case they are modified by our advised method. This is especially helpful when logging calls to methods that have "out" parameters.

Now that we have our advice defined, what happens if we find out that we need to log any exceptions that the advised methods throw? As you can probably guess by now, this change is trivial—all we need to do is add necessary logic to our advice's Invoke() method:

```
public Object Invoke(IMethodInvocation invocation)
{
    Console.Out.WriteLine("-> "
        + GetMethodSignature(invocation));
    try
    {
        object result = invocation.Proceed();
        Console.Out.WriteLine("<- "
            + GetMethodSignature(invocation)
            + " returned " + result);
        return result;
    }
    catch (Exception e)
    {
        Console.Out.WriteLine("!! "
            + GetMethodSignature(invocation)
            + " failed: " + e.Message);
        Console.Out.WriteLine(e.StackTrace);
        throw e;
    }
}
```

Aspect-
Oriented
Programming
(AOP)

Changing GetMethodSignature() to include the class namespace is even simpler, so we'll leave it as an exercise to the reader.

Applying a Logging Advice   Creating an advice is only half of the story. After all, what good is an advice if it's never used? We need to apply the logging advice to our Calculator class from the first code listing, which in Spring.NET can be accomplished in two ways.

The first approach is to apply it using code. While this is very simple in this particular case, it is not ideal because you are manually applying an advice to a particular object instead of relying on the container to apply it automatically for you wherever necessary based on aspect configuration. Nevertheless, let's see how we can apply our logging advice in the code.

```
using Spring.Aop.Framework;

...

ProxyFactory pf = new ProxyFactory(new Calculator());
pf.AddAdvice(new MethodInvocationLoggingAdvice());
ICalculator calculator = (ICalculator) pf.GetProxy();
```

That's it—with only three lines of code you have applied the logging advice to all the methods of the Calculator instance and obtained a reference to it. You can now call any method on it, and you will see that the calls are properly logged.

The Spring.NET declarative approach to AOP is much more powerful and doesn't require you to write any code. However, it does require you to use Spring.NET to manage your objects, which is out of the scope of this section. For the sake of completeness, I will show you what a declarative aspect definition would look like in this case, but you will have to refer to the Spring.NET Reference Manual for more details:

```
<aop:aspect name="MethodInvocationLoggingAspect">
  <aop:advice
    type="LoggingAspectDemo.MethodInvocationLoggingAdvice"
    pointcut=
      "class(LoggingAspectDemo.Calculator) and method(*)"/>
</aop:aspect>
```

This will cause the Spring.NET container to apply the advice we created to all the methods of all instances of a Calculator class.

Just to give you a feel for the power of the declarative approach and AOP in general, this is all you would have to change in the previous declaration to apply our logging advice to all the methods of all the classes in the LoggingAspect-Demo namespace:

Aspect-
Oriented
Programming
(AOP)

```
<aop:aspect name="MethodInvocationLoggingAspect">
  <aop:advice
    type="LoggingAspectDemo.MethodInvocationLoggingAdvice"
    pointcut="class(LoggingAspectDemo.*) and method(*)"/>
</aop:aspect>
```

Adding State and Behavior to an Existing Class

The second example we are going to cover uses a combination of *introduction* and *before advice* to implement and enforce object locking.

Let's say that you have domain objects in your application that you need to be able to lock within a session. When the object is locked, every attempt by other sessions to modify its state should result in a LockViolationException being thrown.

Using the OOP-only approach, you would add necessary state and methods to classes that need this behavior either directly or by making them inherit from some base class that implements core locking and unlocking functionality.

The former solution is bad because it results in a lot of duplicate code. The second solution is OK as long as the classes that need locking behavior belong to the same class hierarchy and all of them need to support locking. If they belong to different hierarchies, or if you don't want to introduce locking behavior into them all, you are back to square one.

A much better approach is to leverage AOP features and declaratively add locking support only to the classes that need it. This can be easily accomplished using a combination of introduction and before advice.

Implementing Locking Introduction   The first step in this case is to create an introduction that will be used to add state and behavior to advised classes. In order to do that, we need to define an interface that we want to introduce.

```
namespace LockableAspectDemo
{
    public interface ILockable
    {
        void Lock();
        void Unlock();
        bool IsLocked { get; }
    }
}
```

The next step is to create an introduction class that implements this interface. In this example, we will assume that we are writing an ASP.NET Web application and will use HttpContext.Current.Session.SessionID as a session ID for locking purposes.

```
using AopAlliance.Aop;

namespace LockableAspectDemo
{
    public class LockableIntroduction : ILockable, IAdvice
    {
        private bool isLocked;
        private string sessionId;

        public void Lock()
        {
            isLocked = true;
            sessionId = HttpContext.Current.Session.SessionID;
        }

        public void Unlock()
        {
            isLocked = false;
            sessionId = null;
        }

        public bool IsLocked
        {
            get
            {
                return isLocked && sessionId
                    != HttpContext.Current.Session.SessionID;
            }
        }
    }
}
```

So far we've created an introduction that we want to use. Now we need to create an advice that will enforce the lock implemented by this introduction.

Implementing a Lock Enforcement Advice In this particular case, we don't need a full-blown *around advice*, such as the one we used in the logging example. All that our advice needs to do is to check whether the target object is locked and throw an exception if it is.

For that purpose, we can use a somewhat simpler *before advice*, which doesn't require us to make a call to IMethodInvocation.Proceed():

```
using System;
using System.Reflection;
using Spring.Aop;

namespace LockableAspectDemo
{
    public class LockEnforcerAdvice : IMethodBeforeAdvice
    {
```

```
        public void Before(MethodBase method, object[] args,
        object target)
        {
            ILockable lockable = target as ILockable;
            if (lockable != null && lockable.IsLocked)
            {
                throw new LockViolationException
                 ("Attempted to modify locked object.", target);
            }
        }
    }
}
```

Applying Locking Aspect to Domain Objects   The last step is to apply the introduction and advice we defined earlier to domain objects that we want to make lockable. For the purpose of this example, let's say that we want to make the Account class and all its descendants lockable.

First, let's create a sample Account class.

```
namespace LockableAspectDemo.Domain
{
    public class Account
    {
        private string name;
        private double balance;

        public Account() {}

        public Account(string name, double balance)
        {
            Name = name;
            Balance = balance;
        }

        public virtual string Name
        {
            get { return name; }
            set { name = value; }
        }

        public virtual double Balance
        {
            get { return balance; }
            set { balance = value; }
        }

        [StateModifier]
        public virtual void Withdraw(double amount)
        {
            balance -= amount;
        }
```

```
[StateModifier]
public virtual void Deposit(double amount)
{
    balance += amount;
}
    }
}
```

We'll omit descendants for brevity, but we can assume that locking also needs to be applied to the CheckingAccount, SavingsAccount, and MoneyMarketAccount classes that inherit from our base Account class.

There are several things that make this class suitable for proxy-based AOP. First of all, properties are implemented using a combination of private fields and property getters and setters. If you used public fields instead, it would be impossible for an AOP proxy to intercept property access.

Second, all properties and methods are declared as virtual. This allows Spring. NET to create a dynamic proxy by inheriting the Account class and injecting interception code. If methods were final, the Account class would have to implement an interface in order to be proxied using the composition proxy. If neither interface nor virtual methods were present, it would've been impossible to create a proxy for the Account class and apply AOP advices to it.

The final thing to notice is the usage of the StateModifier attribute. We defined this attribute primarily to show how advices can be applied based on attributes, but this is also a case where using an attribute makes a lot of sense. It provides additional metadata that makes it very obvious which methods modify object's state.

We could've used the StateModifier attribute in front of property setters as well, but in my opinion that is somewhat redundant. In addition to that, omitting StateModifier in the case of properties gives us an opportunity to show you how to define a composite pointcut.

While it is possible to configure the locking aspect using a code-only approach, it is somewhat cumbersome, so we'll show you only the declarative approach in this case.

```
<aop:aspect name="LockEnforcementAspect">
  <aop:pointcut name="StateModifiers"
    expression="class(Account+)
      and (setter(*) or attribute(StateModifier))"/>
  <aop:advice type="LockableAspectDemo.LockableIntroduction"
    pointcut="class(Account+)"/>
  <aop:advice type="LockableAspectDemo.LockEnforcerAdvice"
    pointcut-ref="StateModifiers"/>
</aop:aspect>
```

Aspect-
Oriented
Programming
(AOP)

Most of the declaration should be self-explanatory. Things that deserve attention are

- The plus sign behind the class name in the pointcut definition specifies that the pointcut should match the specified class and classes derived from it.

- The expression "setter(*)" is used to match all property setters, regardless of their type and name.

- The expression "attribute(StateModifier)" is used to match all the members that are marked with the StateModifier attribute.

Finally, we need to create a client that will leverage the introduced ILockable interface the same way as if it was implemented directly by the Account class.

```
using LockableAspectDemo.Domain;

namespace LockableAspectDemo.Services
{
    public class AccountManager
    {
        public void TransferFunds(Account from, Account to
            , double amount)
        {
            ILockable acctFrom = from as ILockable;
            ILockable acctTo = to as ILockable;

            try
            {
                acctFrom.Lock();
                acctTo.Lock();

                from.Withdraw(amount);
                to.Deposit(amount);
            }
            finally
            {
                acctFrom.Unlock();
                acctTo.Unlock();
            }
        }
    }
}
```

As you can see, by using AOP we can truly modularize the object locking feature and apply it wherever appropriate without the shortcomings of the pure OOP approaches.

Aspect-Oriented Programming (AOP)

> ### Note
>
> While the previous example is technically no different than if we used `lock` statements to synchronize access to `acctFrom` and `acctTo` from the multiple threads, there is a big difference in the semantics between the two. With `ILockable` we could keep the lock for the duration of the multiple HTTP requests, not just for the single request.

Moving Business Rules into Aspects

The final example we are going to show in this section demonstrates a somewhat advanced AOP usage. We do not recommend that you start experimenting with AOP by moving all your business rules into aspects. It is probably the best idea to introduce AOP into your projects slowly by making them handle obvious crosscutting concerns, such as logging, security, and transactions. However, we feel it is important that you understand its full potential so you can apply it effectively when you become more familiar with it.

Every business application has various business rules that are typically embedded into the application logic. While this works just fine for most rules and most applications, it makes them less flexible than they need to be and usually requires code modification when business rules change. By moving some of the business rules into aspects, you can make the application much easier to customize. Unlike in previous examples, removing code duplication is usually not the main reason you would move business rules into aspects—the primary driver in this case is increased application flexibility.

The best candidates are rules that cause secondary logic to be implemented along with the core logic. For example, the core logic of the `Account.Withdraw()` method from the previous example is to reduce the account balance. Secondary logic would be to enforce minimum balance requirements or to send an email alert to the account holder when balance falls below a certain amount.

Let's see what our `Account` class would look like if we added both minimum balance enforcement and a balance alert to it.

Aspect-Oriented Programming (AOP)

```
using System;

namespace BusinessRulesDemo.Domain
{
    public class Account
    {
        private AccountHolder accountHolder;
        private string name;
```

```csharp
    private double balance;
    private double minimumBalance;
    private double alertBalance;

    // Spring.NET IoC injected collaborators
    private INotificationSender notificationSender;

    public Account() {}

    public Account(string name, double balance)
    {
        Name = name;
        Balance = balance;
    }

    public virtual Person AccountHolder
    {
        get { return accountHolder; }
        set { accountHolder = value; }
    }

    public virtual string Name
    {
        get { return name; }
        set { name = value; }
    }

    public virtual double Balance
    {
        get { return balance; }
        set { balance = value; }
    }

    public virtual double MinimumBalance
    {
        get { return minimumBalance; }
        set { minimumBalance = value; }
    }

    public virtual double AlertBalance
    {
        get { return alertBalance; }
        set { alertBalance = value; }
    }

    // injected by Spring.NET IoC container
    public virtual INotificationSender NotificationSender
    {
        set { notificationSender = value; }
    }
```

```
[StateModifier]
public virtual void Withdraw(double amount)
{
    if (balance - amount < minimumBalance)
    {
        throw new MinimumBalanceException();
    }

    balance -= amount;

    if (balance < alertBalance)
    {
        notificationSender.SendNotification
        (accountHolder.Email,
        "Low balance",
        "LowBalance.vm", this);
    }
}

[StateModifier]
public virtual void Deposit(double amount)
{
    balance += amount;
}
    }
}
```

While you could argue that the minimum balance check should remain in the Account class, it is obvious that the notification sending code is not the primary functionality of the Withdraw() method, which makes it a great candidate for an aspect. Let's refactor it.

Creating a Notification Advice   First, we'll create a generic advice that will be used to send notifications.

```
using System.Reflection;
using BusinessRulesDemo.Domain;
using Spring.Aop;

namespace BusinessRulesDemo
{
    public class AccountBalanceNotificationAdvice :
        IAfterReturningAdvice
    {
        private INotificationSender sender;
        private string subject;
        private string templateName;

        public INotificationSender Sender
        {
```

Aspect-Oriented Programming (AOP)

```
            get { return sender; }
            set { sender = value; }
        }

        public string Subject
        {
            get { return subject; }
            set { subject = value; }
        }

        public string TemplateName
        {
            get { return templateName; }
            set { templateName = value; }
        }

        public void AfterReturning(object returnValue,
            MethodBase method, object[] args, object target)
        {
            Account account = (Account) target;
            if (account.Balance < account.AlertBalance)
            {
                sender.SendNotification(
                        account.AccountHolder.Email,
                        subject, templateName,
                        target);
            }
        }
    }
}
```

In this example we are using an *after advice* that checks if the new balance is below the alert balance level and sends a notification if it is. We also defined several properties on the advice class in order to show how you can configure advices using the Spring.NET IoC container.

Tight coupling between the advice and our Account class is not a problem in this case because we know that our advice will only apply to instances of the Account class anyway—we are simply using the advice to move the notification sending rule outside the core logic of the Account class.

What this really buys us is flexibility. If we sell the application to another client who wants us to remove the notification we can easily do it by removing the advice application from the configuration file. Similarly, if a client asked us to implement the logic in such a way that automatic transfer from a Line of Credit account happens whenever the balance falls below a minimum amount allowed, we could easily implement another advice and apply it to our Account class instead, or even in addition to the notification advice.

Aspect-
Oriented
Programming
(AOP)

Applying the Advice Just like in the previous example, we will only show the declarative aspect configuration to complete this example.

```
<aop:aspect name="BalanceNotificationAspect">
  <aop:advice
    type="BusinessRulesDemo.AccountBalanceNotificationAdvice"
    pointcut="class(Account+) and method(Withdraw)">
    <aop:property name="Sender" ref="NotificationSender"/>
    <aop:property name="Subject" value="Low Balance"/>
    <aop:property name="Template"
      value="~/Templates/LowBalance.vm"/>
  </aop:advice>
</aop:aspect>
```

The only thing worth pointing out here is that you can use Spring IoC features to configure your advices, just like you would use it to configure any other object. In this example, we are using that to specify the notification subject and the filename of the NVelocity message template, as well as the instance of the notification sender to use.

Summary

AOP can help you solve some of the problems you are facing every day. While it would be great to have support for AOP in .NET on the language and CLR level, there are tools in the .NET open source community that can give you a decent set of AOP features today.

Probably the best way to start learning more about AOP is to download some of these tools and experiment with them, and maybe even start introducing them into real-world projects to help with the basic usage scenarios, such as logging or profiling. As you become more knowledgeable about AOP and more familiar with the tool of your choice, you will likely find many other areas of your application where aspects can help you.

◆

Thanks, Aleksandar!

So by applying AOP to the problem of Repository design as I talked about before Aleksandar's section, some interfaces to introduce for CustomerRepository could be GetByIdable, Deletable, and so on.

Pretty neat, don't you think? And of course there are more obvious things to use AOP for, such as the ordinary example of logging. It's a bit boring, as Aleks pointed out, but after all a very useful technique for solving a common problem.

Aspect-
Oriented
Programming
(AOP)

Summary

In this chapter we have covered three very different and potentially very important design techniques that you need to keep an eye on or start investigating. In the last chapter, we will discuss presentation services, which are often pretty important as well: important in the past, present, and the future.

Chapter 11

Focus on the UI

Testing the database and the User Interface (UI) is hard. We discussed testing of the database in Chapter 6, "Preparing for Infrastructure," but I owe it to you to have some material about testing of the UI as well. You'll find quite a lot of that in this chapter.

We will also discuss UI design that is more in line with DDD than usual, at least when compared to *Rapid Application Development* (RAD) in .NET. We will do that by investigating the *Model-View-Controller* (MVC) and *Model-View-Presenter* (MVP) patterns.

We will also look at other types of mapping: not object relational mapping this time, but object-to-object mapping and UI mapping.

But first of all, to get us into the right mood, here is a "prepilogue" by my old friend Dan Byström. What's a "prepilogue" you may ask? It's an early or "pre" epilogue. I asked Dan to write a short epilogue for my book. What he came up with was good and fitting, but on reflection, it was more like an introduction to the last chapter rather than an ending to the book. So here is Dan's prepilogue.

 ## A Prepilogue
By Dan Byström

Now you're sitting here, admiring your work: the most perfect Domain Model ever to see the light of day. You have managed to do what at first seemed like an impossible mission: you have mapped a large part of your customer's business to your Domain Model. Not only that—you have gotten rid of quite a bunch of special cases and shown your customer a more general view of their business than they could ever imagine.

A
Prepilogue

And if this wasn't enough, the interface is clean and the code is even cleaner. Whoever it is who uses this Domain Model will gasp in amazement at your achievement and secretly envy you. What more could you ask for? Now you can surely die happy!

"Did you say *whoever*? Who is *whoever* in this case, anyway?"

"Well," you say, "it is any programmer who uses a .NET-enabled language." (Or you may say that it is all Java developers, or some other group, depending upon your implementation.)

"So hundreds of thousands of programmers may use your Domain Model? That's quite something!"

"Yeah, isn't it just great?" you answer. "I have encapsulated a big chunk of the business model as well as the whole issue of data storage into this model so it can easily be used without having to mess with these gory details."

"Are you sure nobody but programmers will be interested in using your Domain Model?"

"What do you mean?"

"Well, I'm just curious... don't you think that there are a lot of *users* out there who would like to benefit from your work? In fact, isn't it the *users* who ordered your Domain Model in the first place?"

"Yes that's true. What are you getting at?"

"Don't you think that you need a *user interface* in order to let these *users* come in contact with your brand new Domain Model then?"

"Oh..."

I currently have the good fortune to be working with Jimmy on a project where he focuses on the Domain Model and does the O/R Mapping, while I focus on the UI. As a lucky twist of fate, it so happens that we both feel like winners and think that the other one has pulled the shortest straw.

When I develop an application I consider the UI to be the central part, because without the UI the application won't be, well, usable. This is equally true for data representation and data storage part as well, in most business applications. What it really comes down to is just a matter of *perspective*, personal *taste*, and *interest*.

Some programmers don't seem to have a problem with mixing direct DB access right into the UI. One extreme example of this is obviously classic data-binding, in which you bind your user controls directly to database fields. Every time I've tried that I've promised myself never to try it again! (On the other hand, I'm really looking forward to finding an easy way to bind directly to the Domain Model.)

As the application grows and has to be maintained, logical layers come as a blessing.

Having the data of the UI logically bridged away in a separate view, a Presentation Model [Fowler PoEAA2], is yet another great enhancement.

I really can't say I live up to this myself when it comes to simple UIs, but for the tricky parts I definitely do it this way, even if it's not totally pure all the time. I'm sad to say I don't work with projects with unlimited budgets. (On the other hand, if the problem is simple, only a simple solution should be used.)

In fact, the very first time I faced a SQL Database (before that I had always coded my own storage mechanisms, which I still prefer when possible) I immediately realized that I needed some kind of layer between the database and my UI, although it took more than ten years before I encountered the phrase *Domain Model*.

So a Domain Model is *great* for UI programmers. But it is really just the beginning. The fun starts here!

◆

Good! Thanks, Dan!

So let's think some more about the presentation services in the context of a rich Domain Model, first from the perspective of a rich client and with a focus on testing.

As Martin Fowler said [Fowler PoEAA], the MVC pattern is one of the most misunderstood patterns around. Still, it's very powerful and widely popular. The purpose and basic idea of the pattern isn't so hard to grasp, but as usual, the devil's in the details. Christoffer Skjoldborg will clarify how MVC can be applied, and he will discuss it in the context of a detailed example.

The Model-View-Controller Pattern
By Christoffer Skjoldborg

The intent of the Model-View-Controller pattern (MVC) is to break UI behavior up into separate pieces in order to increase reuse possibilities and testability. The three pieces are the View, the Model, and the Controller.

The **Model** is some representation of entity state. It can range from simple data structures (XML documents, DataSets, and Data Transfer Objects) to a full-blown Domain Model if you have one.

The **View** should consist *only* of logic directly related to "painting the pixels on the screen." Keeping the View as "dumb as possible" is often the major design objective when applying MVC. The rationale is that Views/Screens in practice require a human eye to be tested. This is an error prone and costly process compared to automated unit tests. If we minimize the logic we put in the

Views in the first place, we minimize the risk of introducing bugs that can only be detected by manual testing, or, in other words, we minimize the manual testing efforts we have to apply.

Finally, the **Controller**, which is really the heart of the MVC, is the glue that ties the Model and the View together. The Controller receives messages when the user interacts with the View, translates those messages into actions that are performed on the underlying Model, and then updates the View accordingly.

The MVC Pattern has its roots in the Smalltalk community back in the 70s and 80s [MVC History].

As mentioned, one of the main reasons for introducing MVC is to increase testability. Other benefits are as follows:

- The very process of explicitly extracting the code from the Views does tend to force more structure upon the UI code than would otherwise have been the case. Many modern tools make it very easy to just click your way around and quickly add code behind various events without thinking too hard. By deploying the MVC pattern, one must exercise a bit more effort and be very explicit about what goes on in the UI.

- It makes it easier to change the look and feel or even support entire new UIs or even Platforms. The reuse value in MVC is sometimes exaggerated a bit, especially when it comes to cross platform (rich client/Web/handheld device) portability. Often the Controller will have to be modified significantly in order to make full use of the target platform's capabilities.

- Different team members can work simultaneously on the View and the controller, even if you use a file-locking source control system, because they can now easily be separated.

Example: Joe's Shoe Shop

The MVC pattern is a very loosely formulated design pattern, which means that you are faced with numerous implementation detail decisions to be made when using it. This can indeed be a staggering experience, so before we dig into the various variations of MVC I'll show you a sample implementation that will get you started. As with most other book examples, I have to keep it fairly simplistic in order to preserve the overview. However, it is not very far from what I would do in a real-world application of the same complexity, and when I'm done with the example I will elaborate on some of the key areas where you might want to improve on the foundation laid in the sample and offer a few suggestions on how to do that.

I'm using C# and Windows Forms here, but the code should be simple enough to be understood even if you are not familiar with C# and Windows Forms.

Consider a product catalog for a shoe shop, Joe's Shoe Shop. Joe only sells two types of shoes: dancing shoes and safety shoes. Dancing shoes have a hardness property and safety shoes a maximum pressure. All shoes have an ID, name, and price. The screen that Joe uses to maintain his catalog could look something like this:

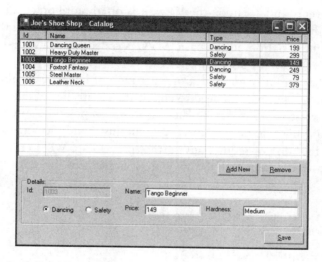

Figure 11-1   Joe's Shoe Shop—Catalog screen

Shoes can be viewed, added, removed, and updated. When a new shoe has been saved, the ID cannot change anymore. When Joe selects a dancing shoe, he expects to see the hardness of the shoe, and when he selects a safety shoe, he expects to see the maximum pressure that the shoe can withstand. While this View is probably not the most complex you have ever seen, it does have a few important and common concepts such as a grid and parts of the screen that dynamically need to change based upon actions in other parts in the screen.

In order to detach logic from the View, we first determine roughly which events/user interactions we think we need to handle. In this case, it would be events such as the following:

- LoadView to load data and instantiate the entire View when first brought up.

- SelectedShoeChanged would occur when the user changes the active shoe.

- AddNewShoe when the user clicks the Add New button.

- RemoveShoe when the user clicks the Remove button.

- ChangeType needs to change the description of the variant label (Hardness or Max Pressure) as well as clear the value.

- Save saves the changes made by the user.

All these events would be prime candidates for methods on the Controller class. Even though the MVC pattern formally states that the Controller should receive the events and act upon the View, it is often more practical to have the View subscribe to the events and then delegate the handling onto the Controller. (This slight variation on the basic MVC is called Model-View-Presenter by Martin Fowler [Fowler PoEAA2].)

Now we have a fairly good idea of what kind of logic we would like to put in the Controller, but we still need to enable the Controller to talk to the View. Remember, we strive to make the View as dumb as possible, so we'd prefer to make the Controller do all the hard work and just hand the View some simple instructions that do not require any further processing. We do this by defining an interface, ICatalogView, which the View must implement.

```
public interface ICatalogView
{
    void SetController(CatalogController controller);
    void ClearGrid();
    void AddShoeToGrid(Shoe shoe);
    void UpdateGridWithChangedShoe(Shoe shoe);
    void RemoveShoeFromGrid(Shoe shoe);
    string GetIdOfSelectedShoeInGrid();
    void SetSelectedShoeInGrid(Shoe shoe);
    string Id{get;set;}
    bool CanModifyId{set;}
    string Name{get;set;}
    ShoeType Type{get;set;}
    string Price{get;set;}
    string VariantName{get;set;}
    string VariantValue{get;set;}
}
```

At first glance, some of the method names in the ICatalogView interface may look like they expose some fairly complex functionality, but in reality the functionality is strictly related to painting pixels on the screen, interacting with various UI widgets, enabling/disabling buttons, and so on. A subset of the implementation is shown in the following code listing.

Note

This section will focus on the scenario of loading the View with the list of shoes, and that goes for all the shown code regarding the View, the Controller, and the test.

If you'd like to see the complete codebase, you can download that from this book's Web site at www.jnsk.se/adddp.

```
public void SetController(CatalogController controller)
{
    _controller=controller;
}

public void ClearGrid()
{
    // Define columns in grid
    this.grdShoes.Columns.Clear();
    this.grdShoes.Columns.Add("Id", 50
        , HorizontalAlignment.Left);
    this.grdShoes.Columns.Add("Name", 300
        , HorizontalAlignment.Left);
    this.grdShoes.Columns.Add("Type", 100
        , HorizontalAlignment.Left);
    this.grdShoes.Columns.Add("Price", 80
        , HorizontalAlignment.Right);

    this.grdShoes.Items.Clear();
}


public void AddShoeToGrid(Shoe shoe)
{
    ListViewItem parent;
    parent=this.grdShoes.Items.Add(shoe.Id);
    parent.SubItems.Add(shoe.Name);

    parent.SubItems.Add(Enum.GetName(typeof(Shoe.ShoeType),
    shoe.Type));

    parent.SubItems.Add(shoe.Price.ToString());
}

public void SetSelectedShoeInGrid(Shoe shoe)
{
    foreach(ListViewItem row in this.grdShoes.Items)
    {
        if(row.Text==shoe.Id)
        {
```

```
            row.Selected=true;
            break;
        }
    }
}
```

The SetController() enables us to tell the View which Controller instance it must forward events to, and all event handlers simply call the corresponding "event" method on the Controller.

You might notice that several methods on the ICatalogView interface make use of a Shoe object. This Shoe class is a Model class. It is thus perfectly fine to have the View know about the Model. In this example, the Shoe is an extremely simple domain class with no behavior, whereas in a real-world Domain Model you would probably have much more functionality in the domain classes.

```
public class Shoe
{
    public enum ShoeType
    {
        Dancing=1,
        Safety=2
    }
    public string Id;
    public string Name;
    public ShoeType Type;
    public decimal Price;
    public string VariantValue;

    public Shoe(string id, string name, ShoeType type,
        decimal price, string variantValue)
    {
        Id=id;
        Name=name;
        Type=type;
        Price=price;
        VariantValue=variantValue;
    }
}
```

Note

You might wonder why I use the singular "Shoe" and not "Pair of Shoes" or something similar as a class name. I'm simply staying with the lingo used by shoe professionals here. I've noticed that they always say "this shoe" and "that shoe" where others would say "this pair of shoes" or "these shoes." This, plus the word Shoe is more straightforward as a class name than PairOfShoes.

At this point we have two pieces of the puzzle: the View and the Model. Both are mainly concerned with state; the Model holds the in-memory state in a structured format, and the View holds the visual representation as well as means to modify the state. Let's hook up the two through the Controller. We already have a rough idea of the types of events we need to handle, but in order to get the specifics pinned down, I'll start out by writing tests for each of the events. In the tests I will be using NMock [NMock].

You'll find the code in the next listing, but let me first comment on the pieces. The getTestData() is a private helper method that builds up a list of shoes in memory. This is used as the Model in the remainder of the test suite.

There is one test for each identified method on the Controller, as I said, we will focus here on the scenario of loading the View with data, and therefore the test that is shown is the LoadView_test().

First I create the viewMock that represents the View in the test, and then I create the shoes list (the Model), and finally the Controller (what I want to test). Notice how the Controller is fed the mock implementation of the View in its constructor. It will operate on this mock just as it would a real View because all the Controller knows about the View is the ICatalogView interface.

Next I tell the viewMock which calls to expect and with what parameters. These represent the "orders" I expect our dumb View to receive from the Controller. I then call the event handler I want to test in the Controller, and finally I ask the viewMock to verify that the expectations were met. Behind the scenes, the viewMock will assert that each of the expected calls were received and issued with the right parameters. The following listing shows the code.

```
private IList getTestData()
{
    IList shoes=new ArrayList();
    shoes.Add(new Shoe("1001","Dancing
    Queen",Shoe.ShoeType.Dancing,199m,"Soft"));

    shoes.Add(new Shoe("1002",
    "Heavy Duty Master",Shoe.ShoeType.Safety,299m,"500 lbs"));

    shoes.Add(new Shoe("1003",
    "Tango Beginner",Shoe.ShoeType.Dancing,149m,"Medium"));

    return shoes;
}

[Test]
public void LoadView_test ()
{
    DynamicMock viewMock=new DynamicMock(typeof(ICatalogView));
    IList shoes=getTestData();
```

```
CatalogController ctrl = new CatalogController
    ((ICatalogView)viewMock.MockInstance, shoes);

// Set expectations on view mock
viewMock.Expect("ClearGrid");
viewMock.Expect("AddShoeToGrid",new object[]{shoes[0]});
viewMock.Expect("AddShoeToGrid",new object[]{shoes[1]});
viewMock.Expect("AddShoeToGrid",new object[]{shoes[2]});
viewMock.Expect("SetSelectedShoeInGrid"
    , new object[]{shoes[0]});

ctrl.LoadView();
viewMock.Verify();
}
```

With the tests all in place (although only one was shown in the previous listing), all that is left is to show the actual implementation of the CatalogController (see the following code listing).

```
public class CatalogController
{
    ICatalogView _view;
    IList _shoes;
    Shoe _selectedShoe;

    public CatalogController(ICatalogView view, IList shoes)
    {
        _view=view;
        _shoes=shoes;
        view.SetController(this);
    }

    public void LoadView()
    {
        _view.ClearGrid();
        foreach(Shoe s in _shoes)
            _view.AddShoeToGrid(s);

        _view.SetSelectedShoeInGrid((Shoe)_shoes[0]);
    }

}
```

Simplifying the View Interfaces Through Adapters

In Joe's Shoe Shop, the ICatalogView exposes a property for every possible detail that the Controller needs to access. It is perfectly OK to do so, but you might end up with very large interfaces if you have 10 input boxes and you need to be able to control the visibility, enabled, font, back color, fore color, border style, and so on of each of them. To prevent this problem you can create an Adapter/Wrapper [GoF Design Patterns] for each type of UI control you use. The Adapter for a TextBox could expose the mentioned properties, and the View interface would then only have to expose one property of the TextBoxAdapter data type for each textbox. Behind the scenes, the View would then provide references to the real UI controls to each Adapter during instantiation and the Adapter would simply delegate the call it receives to the actual implementation.

Decouple the Controller from the View

It can sometimes be advantageous to decouple the Controller from the View. This can be done in several ways. A simple solution is to create an interface for the Controller and have the View know about that only and not the actual implementation. A more complex way is to have Views raise events to anonymous subscribers (Observer pattern [GoF Design Patterns]). I'm not a big fan of this approach as I cannot imagine why one View would need to communicate user interactions to multiple subscribers—let alone subscribers of unknown types! If different Controllers or even other Views need to know about a change to a particular View, the Controller for that View should notify them. This can be done through events if needed—the point is that the Controller should have 100% control of who gets to know about it.

Regardless of the implementation details, the advantage of decoupling the Controller from the View is that we can vary the Controller behind the View. This can be very useful when a View can show up in a lot of different contexts, and it might not make sense to always have to enforce a particular Controller to go along with it. An example of this could be special logic that has to be applied to the View for particular customers. In this case, we could have a factory method that serves up the appropriate Controller depending on which customer the system is dealing with.

Combining Views/Controllers

More complex Views are often made up of multiple smaller Views. Examples are wizards where the user navigates through a bunch of Views through next and previous buttons or maybe even jump back and forth several steps at a time. Information might be saved along the way, but it does not really get committed until the user clicks Save on the final screen.

Another example is Master/Details Views where changes made to the details View might cause changes in the Master View as well.

Both examples can technically be coded with one huge Controller, but it will most likely be a messy experience minimizing the reuse possibilities. We may want to use some of the steps in the wizard elsewhere in the application, or we may want to show the Master View without the Detail View, for example. The solution here is obviously to separate the View and Controllers into smaller pieces. ("If you want to eat an elephant you have to do it in small pieces.") In the case of the wizard, we could have a `FlowController` that controls the basic flow back and forth through the wizard, and each step could have its own View and Controller.

In the Master/Detail, we might have the Controller for the Detail View raise an event on changes. Any other Controller could then subscribe to this event, including the Controller for the Master View.

Is It Worth It?

The key benefit of applying the MVC pattern is that it makes your UI code testable. Secondarily, it forces a very structured approach onto the coding/design process of the UI, which may in itself cause cleaner code in the end. You're forced to think a little more, so to speak.

On the flip-side it should be noted that just because we *can* test every line of code does not mean we *should*. With the MVC in place, it is possible to write an extensive test suite for every View, and it sure feels good the first couple of times getting a bunch of green bars for the UI logic. However, the value of tests that test something very simple that is unlikely to get broken with future changes because of low interdependence with other parts of the system may not be that huge. Especially if those UI test suites impose huge maintenance overhead on your codebase. Every time you change the UI slightly, you have to make a lot of changes to the corresponding UI tests.

◆

Thanks, Chris!

Whether we want to test the UI with rigorous unit tests or not, I think what Christoffer just showed us is a very valuable technique for making the view part of a Windows Forms application thinner, so it's just about painting the forms and for factoring out some of the presentation logic into a layer of its own.

That's pretty much the theme of the next section as well, but this time in the context of the Web. Ingemar Lundberg discusses how he applies the MVP pattern [Fowler PoEAA2] as the tool for testing a Web application.

The Model-View-Controller Pattern

Test-Driving a Web Form

By Ingemar Lundberg

How can you unit test—and thereby also use TDD for—your GUI?

In this short section I'll try to give you a general idea of how you can unit test your GUI. In the process, techniques such as self-shunting [Feathers Self-Shunt] and mocking will be shown. However, the TDD process in itself is not described. Self-shunting is (very briefly) a technique where you're letting the test class also act as a stub or mock.

Background

Typical GUI code consists of a bunch of callback methods that are called as a result of something the user does with the GUI, such as pressing a button. Typically, a callback method does something with a domain object (or possibly even executes some SQL). The problem is that the callback methods get called from an environment, such as WinForms or ASP.NET, that isn't easy to hook up in your NUnit tests. You simply can't do it.

The goal is to have as little untested code as possible. The first thing to do is to move as much code as possible out of the callback methods. If the code isn't tangled in the callback methods, you've created the possibility to unit test it.

But that isn't enough. What about the state of the GUI? You know, things like if the user has selected that row, this and that button should be disabled. This will not be covered simply by moving code out of the callback methods. Don't get me wrong—it is a good first step.

To take it further, we need to use the sharpest tool in our box: *abstraction*. We need a model of the interaction, and we need an abstraction of the form we're programming. At this point, I'll stop talking about the GUI in general terms and start talking about a form, or more specifically about an ASP.NET Web Form. However, this technique is also applicable to Windows Forms, and it is even platform neutral.

An Example

This is, in my opinion, by far the hardest part of writing about programming—finding a problem scenario that could be used to illustrate your point without sidetracking the reader. I need an example that makes my GUI change state; in other words, something needs to be disabled when the user does something special.

In Sweden we have the tradition of only letting our kids have candy on Saturdays. Let's say that I have one box of chocolate bars, one of lollipops, and one of portion-sized peanut bags. The kids can have three goodies of their choice, but no more than two of the same kind. A simplification of the model is that we never run out of candy.

This is without doubt another silly example, but hopefully it will do its job. In Figure 11-2 you can see the end result. I could have shown you my original pencil sketch of the GUI, but this will do too. In the left pane we have all the types of candy available. It is from this pane that the user (kids of all ages) picks candy for their Saturday candy stash, shown in the right pane. You can see how you're prevented from picking another chocolate bar while you might pick a lollipop or a bag of peanuts.

Chocolate	Chocolate
Lollipop >>	Chocolate
Peanuts >>	

Figure 11-2   Choices, limitations, and selections

The reader is kindly asked to disregard the lack of styling, which isn't covered here (and I should not express any opinions whatsoever on that subject).

Domain Model

To be able to move on with today's lesson, I need a domain model. It is shown in Figure 11-3.

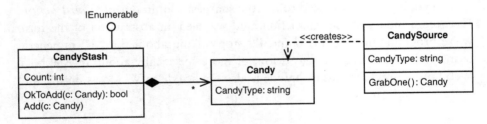

Figure 11-3   The Domain Model

I've tested this model separately. OkToAdd() checks the business rules I stated previously. It's OK to add three items, but only two of the same type (CandyType). This isn't rocket science.

Test-Driving a Web Form

TDD of GUI

Finally, we're coming to the point. Before we start, I'd like to remind everyone that even though we're introducing an abstraction of the form, we have a pretty concrete picture of how it is going to work, as shown in Figure 11-4.

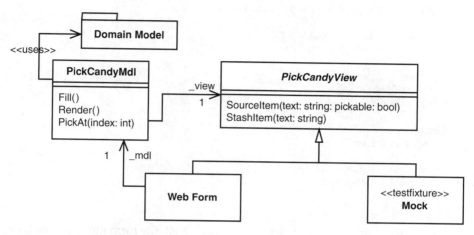

Figure 11-4 Model of the UI

Display Candy Types

When the form is first shown, we want to be able to fill the left pane with names of all the types of candy. It should be possible to pick from all of the sources. The test looks like this. (I'm going to take a fairly big step here based on my previous experience of this, dare I call it, pattern.)

```
[Test] public void FillSourcePanel()
{
    mdl.Fill();
    mdl.Render();
    // using A=NUnit.Framework.Assert
    A.AreEqual(SrcPanel, "a> b> c> ");
}
```

It doesn't even compile. I need to add Fill() and Render() to PickCandyMdl. That's easy; I just add two empty public methods, one named Fill() and one named Render(). But what is the test expressing? What am I asserting? The assertion is expressing what the "form" should look like now—in a very abstract way. The string SrcPanel is used instead of the HTML table (the left one in the form) that we're aiming for at the end.

Where does SrcPanel come from? Well, SrcPanel is a string in the test fixture (the class) that is manipulated by my self-shunted [Feathers Self-Shunt] implementation of the PickCandyView. This is the recurring pattern when I mock the view.

```
[TestFixture] public class PickCandyTests: PickCandyView
{
    void PickCandyView.SourceItem(string text, bool pickable)
    {
        SrcPanel += text + (pickable ? ">"
            : string.Empty) + " ";
    }

    PickCandyMdl mdl;
    string SrcPanel;

    [SetUp]
    protected void Setup()
    {
        mdl = new PickCandyMdl();
        SrcPanel = string.Empty;
    }
… snip …
```

It compiles, but it turns red. What's missing? Well, the form model, mdl of type PickCandyMdl, needs to know about its view. That's easy! I add a SetView() method to the model. (By the way, this is one of the few occasions where I use "interface implementation" the way I did with PickCandyView.SourceItem(), as in {interface name}.{member name}.)

Private or Public Implementation of Interface Methods?

Implementation of methods can only exist on classes. If a class, Foo, implements an interface, Bar, the interface's methods are a part of that class. I would in most cases implement Bar's members as public on Foo. Remember that the interface of the class itself is all its public members. Foo is a Bar, hence the members of Bar are a part of Foo. It just so happens that I implement an interface's members as private in other situations as a means to solve name collisions, as in the case of a self-shunting mock. Here I don't actually see the interfaces (PickCandyView and CandySourceRetriever) as a part of the test fixture's interface.

Test-Driving a Web Form

The form model needs to know how to obtain all Candy Sources. This could be easily fixed by just supplying the model with a list of Candy Sources. But instead I'm going to show you another little trick that improves testability in the general case. I'm letting the form model (or rather that package/assembly) own an interface representing the needed retrieve operation.

```
public interface CandySourceRetriever
{
    IList Retrieve();
}
```

Why Not the I-name Convention for Interfaces?

Let me ask you—what good would it do you? This convention came from an environment where the notion of an interface itself was a convention, a rule, and not a first-class language concept (that changed, more or less, with midl). When it comes to trying to instantiate an interface (with new) the C# compiler (at least my version) treats abstract classes and interfaces as one and the same.

```
public interface Bar {}
public class Foo { public static void Main() {new Bar();} }
ingo.cs(2,47): error CS0144: Cannot create an instance of the abstract class or interface 'Bar'
```

Why do we not have an A-name convention for abstract classes? Because when you refer to a type that has methods and properties, you don't care if it is an interface, abstract class, or concrete ditto. The I-name convention seems to have been adopted by the *Framework Class Library* (FCL) without further consideration.

Alternative Explanation/Rambling

The I-name convention made sense in COM. COM wasn't really object-oriented, was it? It was (well, *is*) component-oriented. Is there a reason to treat interfaces of components as something inherently different from the component itself? Maybe, but the question to ask is if interfaces in FCL are interfaces to components or if they are the answer/compromise to the difficult (compiler) problem of multiple inheritance. If so, an interface in CLR is very close to an abstract class. There's no A-name convention for abstract classes. Drop the I-name convention; it serves no purpose. When you refer/use a type that has methods and properties, you don't care if it is an interface, abstract class, or concrete ditto.

I'll also mock this interface as a self-shunt. Of course, the form model needs to know about its retriever. With all this in account, the test fixture starts as the following:

```
[TestFixture] public class PickCandyTests: PickCandyView, CandySourceRetriever
{
    void PickCandyView.SourceItem(string text, bool pickable)
    {
        SrcPanel += text + (pickable ? ">"
            : string.Empty) + " ";
    }

    IList CandySourceRetriever.Retrieve()
    {
        return sources;
    }

    PickCandyMdl mdl;
    ArrayList sources;
    string SrcPanel;

    [SetUp] protected void Setup()
    {
        mdl = new PickCandyMdl();
        mdl.SetView(this);
        mdl.SetRetriever(this);
        sources = new ArrayList();
        sources.Add(new CandySource("a")); // think chocolate
        sources.Add(new CandySource("b")); // ... lollipop
        sources.Add(new CandySource("c"));
        SrcPanel = string.Empty;
    }
… snip …
```

Of course, the test still comes out red because we haven't implemented anything in PickCandyMdl yet. Let's do it now.

```
[Serializable] public class PickCandyMdl
{
    public void Fill()
    {
        _retrieved = _retriever.Retrieve();
    }

    public void Render()
    {
        foreach(CandySource s in _retrieved)
            _view.SourceItem(s.CandyType, true);
    }
```

```
    public void SetView(PickCandyView v)
    {
        _view = v;
    }

    public void SetRetriever(CandySourceRetriever r)
    {
        _retriever = r;
    }

    [NonSerialized] PickCandyView _view;
    CandySourceRetriever _retriever;
    IList _retrieved;
}
```

As you can see, most of this is trivial. In Fill() we pick up the available candy sources and in Render() we iterate over them passing information to the view for it to display. Note that we've faked the implementation so far; the candy sources are not going to be "pickable" (the true constant) in all circumstances. SetView() and SetRetriever() are trivial. The [NonSerialized] attribute on _view is needed when you use out of process handling of the Session state in the ASP.NET application.

When we run the test now, it turns green. Hooray!

Picking Candy

We need to be able to pick candy from the source list. Let's express that as a test.

```
[Test] public void PickingCandy ()
{
    mdl.Fill();
    mdl.PickAt(0);
    mdl.Render();
    A.AreEqual(SrcPanel, "a> b> c> ");
    A.AreEqual(StashPanel, "a ");
}
```

StashPanel is of course the test fixture representation of the right-hand panel displaying what you (I mean your kids) have picked so far (a HTML table in the real form). A new method is needed, PickAt().We also need a new method on the view.

```
public interface PickCandyView
{
    void SourceItem(string text, bool pickable);
    void StashItem(string text);
}
```

PickAt() is an excellent incitement to introduce CandyStash to the form model, only hinted at as _stash in the following code:

```
public void PickAt(int index)
{
    Candy c = ((CandySource)_retrieved[index]).GrabOne();
    _stash.Add(c);
}
```

We also need to complement Render().

```
public void Render()
{
    foreach(CandySource s in _retrieved)
        _view.SourceItem(s.CandyType, true);
    foreach(Candy c in _stash)
        _view.StashItem(c.CandyType);
}
```

I'm sure you can implement the StashItem() method the same way I implemented SourceItem().

Running the test now takes us to green again. Before I move on, I complement my first test to assert that the StashPanel is empty (string.Empty).

Handling the Display Dynamics

When we picked two of the same candy type, that type is not supposed to be "pickable" anymore (have a look at the first figure of the application again). Let's express that as a test.

```
[Test] public void PickingTwoOfSameKind()
{
    mdl.Fill();
    mdl.PickAt(0); mdl.PickAt(0);
    mdl.Render();
    A.AreEqual(SrcPanel, "a b> c> ");
    A.AreEqual(StashPanel, "a a ");
}
```

The stash of candy now contains two "a"s. The missing greater than symbol (>) in SrcPanel after the "a" is the key thing here. This test doesn't introduce any new methods, but it comes out red due to the shortcut implementation of Render() we made earlier. Remember the true constant? Isn't the OkToAdd() method on CandyStash exactly what we're looking for here?

```
public void Render()
{
    foreach(CandySource s in _retrieved)
        _view.SourceItem(s.CandyType, _stash.OkToAdd(s.GrabOne()));
    foreach(Candy c in _stash)
        _view.StashItem(c.CandyType);
}
```

I grab one from the source (s.GrabOne()) and pass it to OkToAdd() to see if it is "pickable." The CandySource is an infinite source (it is actually an object factory). In real life you'd probably rather die than waste chocolate bars like this, but this isn't real life, this is software.

If we picked three of an allowed mix, we're not allowed to pick anything else, right? Let's express that as a test, too.

```
[Test] public void PickingThreeMix()
{
    mdl.Fill();
    mdl.PickAt(0); mdl.PickAt(0); mdl.PickAt(1);
    mdl.Render();
    A.AreEqual(SrcPanel, "a b c ");
    A.AreEqual(StashPanel, "a a b ");
}
```

This turns green right away. The OkToAdd() check for "pickable" was a stroke of genius, don't you think? We shouldn't be surprised, because it (OkToAdd()) captures the very essence of our business rule.

The Web Form Implementation

There are several ways to handle state in a Web application. In this scenario, I've disabled view state on the document form and am relying solely on the Session object on the server. I build the page upon hitting the Web form, and I rebuild it just before ending the processing (in the PreRender event) to reflect the model's current state. Remember that the model's state changes when we pick candy for our stash.

For this I've added a call to MyInit() first in the standard OnInit() method of the Web form created by Visual Studio .Net.

```
void MyInit()
{
    if (!IsPostBack)
    {
        _mdl = new PickCandyMdl();
        Session["PickCandyMdl"] = _mdl;
        _mdl.SetRetriever(CreateRetriever());
        _mdl.Fill();
    }
    else
    {
        _mdl = (PickCandyMdl)Session["PickCandyMdl"];
    }
    _mdl.SetView(this);
    MdlRender();
}
```

```
PickCandyMdl _mdl;
HtmlTable _srcTbl, _stashTbl;

void MdlRender()
{
    _srcTbl = new HtmlTable();
    srcpnl.Controls.Add(_srcTbl);
    _srcTbl.Width = "100%";

    _stashTbl = new HtmlTable();
    stashpnl.Controls.Add(_stashTbl);
    _stashTbl.Width = "100%";

    _mdl.Render();
}

private void WebForm1_PreRender(object sender, System.EventArgs e)
{
    srcpnl.Controls.Clear();
    stashpnl.Controls.Clear();
    MdlRender();
}
```

The srcpnl, the candy source panel, and stashpnl, the candy stash panel, are Panels (the control in the WebControls namespace) I've added with the form designer in Visual Studio.

Of course, the form implements PickCandyView. The code is fairly simple. Any decisions made (if statements) concern appearance only, not the state of the interaction. This is crucial. The model must be responsible for the latter.

```
void PickCandyView.SourceItem(string text, bool pickable)
{
    int index = _srcTbl.Rows.Count;
    HtmlTableRow tr = AddTR(_srcTbl);
    HtmlTableCell td = AddTD(tr);
    td.InnerText = text;

    td = AddTD(tr);
    if (pickable)
    {
        LinkButton lb = new LinkButton();
        td.Controls.Add(lb);
        lb.ID = "pick@" + index.ToString();
        lb.Text = ">>";
        lb.Click += new EventHandler(Pick_Click);
    }
}
```

Test-Driving
a Web Form

```
void PickCandyView.StashItem(string text)
{
    AddTD(AddTR(_stashTbl)).InnerText = text;
}
```

And finally, here's the pick callback method:

```
private void Pick_Click(object sender, EventArgs e)
{
    _mdl.PickAt(IndexFromID(sender));
}
```

Yes, I trust you to read between the lines. The only possibly non-trivial thing I left for you to figure out is the `CreateRetriever()` method. You've seen something similar to what's needed in the test fixture.

Figure 11-5 shows the app in sort of a comic strip. The kid picks two chocolate bars followed by a bag of peanuts.

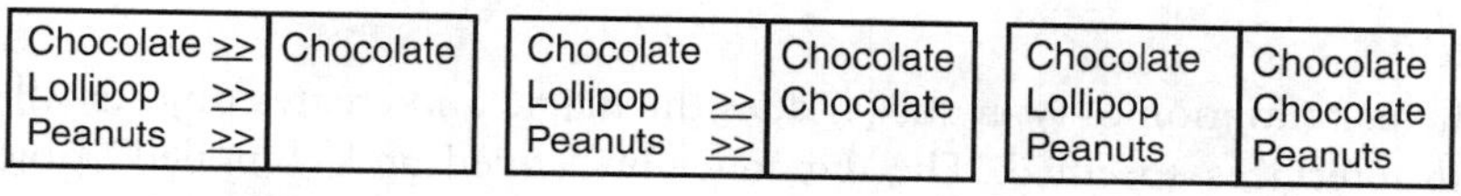

Chocolate >>	Chocolate	Chocolate	Chocolate	Chocolate	Chocolate
Lollipop >>		Lollipop >>	Chocolate	Lollipop	Chocolate
Peanuts >>		Peanuts >>		Peanuts	Peanuts

Figure 11-5 The candy-picking application

Summary

Most code for handling the GUI is in a model of the interaction. Only a small portion of trivial code is left untested. Graphical appearance is, however, not what's tested with this methodology but rather the dynamics of the GUI.

In this quite unfinished example I got away with very little handling in the form model. Wrapping the candy picked in, say, a `CandyItem` object is one possible development if we decided to add features for regretting a choice (return to the source).

Mocking with NMock

Let me, as a small addendum and appetizer, show you another way to mock during testing using NMock [NMock]. I'll be very brief, letting the test code speak for itself allowing you to compare it with the previous tests. Let's first have a look at the setup. Let me just point out that the test fixture class doesn't implement the interfaces `PickCandyView` and `CandySourceRetriever` as it did earlier in our self-shunting fixture.

```
PickCandyMdl mdl;
IMock data, view;
const bool Pickable=true, NotPickable=false;
```

```
[SetUp] protected void Setup()
{
    data = new DynamicMock(typeof(CandySourceRetriever));
    view = new DynamicMock(typeof(PickCandyView));

    mdl = new PickCandyMdl();
    mdl.SetView((PickCandyView)view.MockInstance);
    mdl.SetRetriever((CandySourceRetriever)data.MockInstance);
    ArrayList sources = new ArrayList();
    sources.Add(new CandySource("a")); // think chocolate
    sources.Add(new CandySource("b")); // ... lollipop
    sources.Add(new CandySource("c"));

    data.SetupResult("Retrieve", sources);
}
```

The instantiation of DynamicMock(s) does the magic and creates objects adhering to the interfaces specified. The dynamically "coded and compiled" object of a mock is found as IMock.MockInstance. With SetupResult(), we tell the data mock to return sources when it gets called with Retrieve().

Now let's have a look at the equivalence of the first test from earlier.

```
[Test] public void FillSourcePanel()
{
    // Expectations
    view.Expect("SourceItem", "a", Pickable);
    view.Expect("SourceItem", "b", Pickable);
    view.Expect("SourceItem", "c", Pickable);
    view.ExpectNoCall("StashItem", typeof(string));
    // Execution
    mdl.Fill();
    mdl.Render();
    // Verification
    view.Verify();
}
```

The comments in the code are there just to show you the general phases, besides setup, when testing with NMock. We declare that we're expecting SourceItem() of PickCandyView to be called three times and what values we expect. We also state that StashItem() is not to be called.

In the execution phase we, well, do the execution of the object we're testing by calling some methods on it. And finally, we ask the view mock to verify that our expectations were met during execution.

I think it is best to follow the red-green (-refactor) formula of TDD. In the previous test at least, if you forget to call Verify() you'll end up with a green test regardless of whether the expectations are met or not. If you first require a red run, you're sure that you're actually verifying (asserting) something.

Test-Driving a Web Form

◆

Thanks, Ingo!

Again, testing is an extremely important factor and something worth preparing and adjusting for. Now we have discussed two different variations regarding the UI, but with similarities on how that can be done.

Last but not least, we will discuss some aspects regarding the data for the UI in contrast to the data in the Domain Model.

Some might feel my approach is "I have a hammer; let's find nails" when talking about mapping for the presentation services just because mapping is a popular solution for the persistence services. But I think it's very much in the spirit of DDD to focus on the core, the Domain Model, as much as possible and then create simple, flexible solutions for dealing with the infrastructural problems "around" the Domain Model, such as transforming the Domain Model into another model for another tier. That's why I think object-to-object mapping and UI mapping have a lot of potential, especially for routine tasks that are just a waste of time to hand code.

In this section, Mats Helander discusses some aspects of UI Mapping, focusing on automatic mapping between a presentation friendly model (such as a Presentation Model [Fowler PoEAA2]) and the Domain Model. Over to Mats.

Mapping and Wrapping
By Mats Helander

With the aid of O/R Mapping, we are able to connect our Domain Model to the relational database. Together with the business methods that we add to the Domain Model classes and possibly to a Service Layer [Fowler PoEAA], we have a pretty solid architecture in place for the structural and functional foundation of the application.

That brings us to the last stretch—the *Presentation Layer* (PL). While you and I may consider the Domain Model to be the heart of the application, end users are likely to think of whatever they are presented with as the final basis for judgment.

This means that no matter how cool your Domain Model (and supporting Service Layer) is, no one will applaud your work (except a fellow developer) unless you provide access to your model via some whiz-bang UI.

The good news is that, if you're lucky, connecting a PL to your Domain Model can be a piece of cake. The bad news is that, whenever you're not that lucky, it can be quite a challenge.

In the simplest case, your Domain Model is already "presentable" and you could just data bind directly to the Domain Model objects. However, the interface of an application frequently demands that information is presented in a more "user friendly" form than it was in the Domain Model.

Mapping and Wrapping

Whenever the Domain Model objects fall short of being immediately presentable, you'll have to make a choice: Should you just *wrap* your DM objects or should you *map* a new set of objects to them?

For example, say that you have a DM class called Person, with FirstName and LastName properties. However, in the UI, you want to have a single text box for editing a person's full name.

One way of doing this, of course, is to have some code in your UI that simply reads from the DM Employee object's first and last names and writes to the textbox and that reads from the textbox and writes to the Employee object properties when the user hits Save.

A lot of the time, in the so called "real world," this is how UI requirements are solved—by what is essentially an accumulating heap of hacks.

In the end, this is not the path toward a maintainable application, and that is what motivates us to look for a design that will scale with increasing complexity and size of the application.

One recurring solution is to complement the Domain Model objects with a new set of objects, often referred to as the *Presentation Model* (PM).

The Presentation Model objects are a part of the PL and should have a structure and behavior matching the requirements of the PL (in effect, matching the needs of the UI). In our example, the PM Person class would have a FullName property rather than FirstName and LastName properties found in the Domain Model Person class.

Why not just put the GetFullName() method in the Domain Model Person class? We could, if it had a use in some business logic operation, but if the only use of the GetFullName() method is in the PL, the method should go in the PM and not in the Domain Model.

Keeping your Domain Model free of non-business aspects, such as presentation and persistence, is every bit as important as it was to keep the Business Logic Layer of yesteryear free of Presentation logic and Data Access logic, and for just the same reason: Keeping the Domain Model free from any non-business aspects is key to keeping the "heart" of your application understandable and maintainable.

So for this example, assume that GetFullName() is only used in presentation and is thus a good candidate for a method that should go on a PM rather than on the Domain Model.

The question becomes how we can connect the PM classes to the Domain Model classes, and thus we arrive at the choice: *Mapping* or *Wrapping*?

Wrapping the Domain Model with the Presentation Model

Wrapping is often the easier solution, requiring no additional framework for state management in the PM. The idea here is that you pass the DM Employee object to the constructor method of the PM Employee object. The PM Employee then keeps an internal reference to the DM object and delegates all calls to the DM properties. See the following code listing.

```
//Presentation Model wrapper object
namespace MyCompany.MyApplication.Presentation
{
    public class EmployeeWrapper
    {
        private Employee employee;

        public EmployeeWrapper (Employee employee)
        {
            this.employee = employee;
        }

        public int Id
        {
            get { return this.employee.Id; }
            set { this.employee.Id == value; }
        }

        public string FullName
        {
            get
            {
                return this.employee.FirstName + " " +
                this.employee.LastName;
            }
            set
            {
                //This should of course be complemented with
                //some more cunning logic, as well as some
                //verification, but this is just an example...
                string[] names = value.Split(" ".ToCharArray()
                    , 2);
                this.employee.FirstName = names[0];
                this.employee.LastName = names[1];
            }
        }
    }
}
```

Using the EmployeeWrapper class is a matter of bringing up an Employee object from the Domain Model and then passing it to the EmployeeWrapper constructor (see the following code listing).

```
//Using the Presentation Model wrapper object
Employee employee = employeeRepository.GetEmployeeById(42);
EmployeeWrapper employeeWrapper = new EmployeeWrapper(employee);

SomeControl.DataSource = employeeWrapper;
```

Big advantages with the wrapping approach include simplicity and flexibility. You can write pretty much any transformations you like in your wrapper objects, transformations far more complex than our relatively simple FullName transformation, if required.

A big drawback is that you will find yourself writing a lot of repetitive code in your wrapper classes for delegating to properties that don't need any transformation—like the Id property in the previous example.

This may make it tempting to just go ahead and let the Presentation Model objects *inherit* from the Domain Model objects instead, overriding whatever properties that need transformation, but leaving all others as they are. The problem with this is that then you are stuck with the public API of the Domain Model, because all public members of a superclass are inherited by the subclass.

In our example, we could have let the PM Employee inherit from the Domain Model Employee, and we could have added the FullName property to the PM Employee, but the PM Employee would *also* have exposed the FirstName and LastName properties from the Domain Model Employee, because these public properties would be inherited.

Wrapping your Domain Model objects rather than inheriting from them gives a higher level of encapsulation that is usually well worth the extra, admittedly tedious, work of delegating between PM and Domain Model properties.

Furthermore, the delegation code for properties that don't require any advanced transformations can be fruitfully attacked with code generation solutions or even just code snippet templates. If all else fails, let the intern write the boilerplate code!

Mapping the Presentation Model to Domain Model

The alternative to wrapping your DM objects with your PM objects is to actually copy the data back and forth between the DM objects and the PM objects. In this case, you'd be writing code like the following:

```
//Moving data manually between Presentation Model
//and Domain Model
```

```
Employee employee = employeeRepository.GetEmployeeById(42);
EmployeeView employeeView = new EmployeeView();

employeeView.Id = employee.Id;
employeeView.Salary = employee.Salary;
employeeView.FullName = employee.FirstName + " " +
employee.LastName;
```

As with the wrapping example, the code for copying the data could be placed in the constructor of the PM object, in which case the constructor would accept the DM object in a parameter. The previous example shows only the operative lines of code for clarity.

If you suffer from the same affliction as I, *abstractus manicus*, you will immediately recognize the potential for abstracting this work into a framework of some kind. In short, we should be able to specify (in, say, an XML file) what PM properties map to what DM properties and then let the framework use reflection to move the data.

Such a framework would have to map one set of objects to another set of objects, and so the logical term for this type of framework would be "Object/Object Mapper"—or O/O Mapper for short!

If you decide to write such a framework, you may realize that solving the non-transformational cases, such as mapping Id to Id and Salary to Salary in the previous case, should be a pretty straightforward task. Mapping FullName to First-Name and LastName, on the other hand, is trickier.

It is quite solvable, but the question becomes if it is the right approach to try to build advanced transformation services into the O/O Framework.

The alternative is to avoid charging the O/O Mapper with responsibility for actual structural transformations and let it concentrate on just moving data back and forth between objects that share the same or a very similar structure.

In our example, the solution becomes giving the PM Employee class a FirstName and a LastName property in addition to its FullName property, but also making the FirstName and LastName properties protected.

The O/O Mapper should have no problems accessing the protected PM properties using reflection, so it will be able to map to them from the Domain Model's FirstName and LastName properties, but only the FullName property will be exposed to the client by the PM object.

In fact, the O/O Mapper could even write directly to the private fields of the PM objects, so you wouldn't have to implement the protected properties at all—indeed, the mapper probably *should* access the private fields directly in order to avoid triggering side effects in the property getters and setters that should only be invoked when client code accesses the properties, not when the framework wants to move data.

However, some O/O Mappers may offer advanced features (such as Lazy Loading) that depend on properties being there so that access to them can be intercepted, and so you may want to keep the properties around for that reason. The following code listing shows a PM object that relies on O/O Mapping.

```
//Presentation Model object that relies on O/O Mapping
namespace MyCompany.MyProject.Presentation
{
    public class EmployeeView
    {
        private int id;
        private decimal salary;
        private string firstName;
        private string lastName;

        public EmployeeView() {}

        public int Id
        {
            get { return this.id; }
            set { this.id = value; }
        }

        public decimal Salary
        {
            get { return this.salary; }
            set { this.salary = value; }
        }

        protected string FirstName
        {
            get { return this.firstName; }
            set { this.firstName = value; }
        }

        protected string LastName
        {
            get { return this.lastName; }
            set { this.lastName = value; }
        }

        public string FullName
        {
            get
            {
                return this.firstName + " " +
                this.lastName;
            }
            set
            {
```

```
                string[] names = value.Split(" ".ToCharArray()
                    , 2);

                this.firstName = names[0];
                this.lastName = names[1];
            }
        }
    }
}
```

Of course, whatever you do in a framework, you could also do manually. If you were to copy the data manually from Domain Model to PM without the aid of an O/O Mapping framework, in order to write to the protected properties you could either use reflection or create shortcut methods for accessing your properties by name. Some code using the second approach might look like the following:

```
//Move data between Presentation and Domain Model without
//transformation
Employee employee = employeeRepository.GetEmployeeById(42);
EmployeeView employeeView = new EmployeeView();

employeeView.Id = employee.Id;
employeeView.Salary = employee.Salary;

//We have to use a method that lets us access protected
//properties by name to write to the protected methods.
//Alternatively, we could use reflection.
employeeView.SetPropertyValue("FirstName", employee.FirstName);
employeeView.SetPropertyValue("LastName", employee.LastName);
```

Using this approach, the task of moving the data between the PM and the Domain Model becomes straightforward—almost trivial, had it not been for the pesky reference properties.

Managing Relationships

When we take relationships between the objects into account, the task becomes more difficult again. Object graphs (a group of objects that are all interconnected via relationships) are potentially very large, and if asking the O/O Mapper to fill a PM Employee object from a DM Employee object also results in the filling up of a few hundred related objects, we may have effectively killed performance in our application.

Another issue is that you have to remember to return PM objects from PM reference properties. For example, when I read the AssignedToProject property of a PM `Employee` object, I want a PM `Project` object back, not a DM `Project` object. Consider a naïve implementation of a Wrapper object with a reference property as shown in the following:

```
//Naïve implementation of reference property in wrapper object
namespace MyCompany.MyApplication.Presentation
{
    public class EmployeeWrapper
    {
        private Employee employee;

        public EmployeeWrapper (Employee employee)
        {
            this.employee = employee;
        }

        public Project AssignedToProject
        {
            get { return this.employee.Project; }
            set { this.employee.Project = value; }
        }
    }
}
```

The problem here is that the `Project` property of the PM `EmployeeWrapper` object will return a DM `Project` object rather than a PM `ProjectWrapper` object. This is usually not at all what we want, and so we have to take care to write our PM reference properties in the fashion shown here:

```
//Slightly less naïve implementation of reference property
//in wrapper object
namespace MyCompany.MyApplication.Presentation
{
    public class EmployeeWrapper
    {
        private Employee employee;

        public EmployeeWrapper (Employee employee)
        {
            this.employee = employee;
        }

        public ProjectWrapper AssignedToProject
        {
            get
            {
                return new
                ProjectWrapper(this.employee.Project);
            }
            set
            {
```

Mapping
and
Wrapping

```
            this.employee.Project =
            value.GetDomainObject();
        }
    }

    public Employee GetDomainObject()
    {
        return employee;
    }
  }
}
```

Note the `GetDomainObject()` method on the `ProjectWrapper` class used in the `AssignedToProject()` setter method. When you write to the `AssignedToProject` property of the PM `EmployeeWrapper` object, you pass a `ProjectWrapper` object to the setter, but we have to pass a Domain Model `Project` object to the `Project` property of the wrapped `Employee` object. Thus we need a way to get to the required `Project` object from the passed in `ProjectWrapper` object, and the `GetDomainObject()` method fills this role.

So when we implement reference properties, we suddenly have to supply a method for getting at the Domain Model object referenced internally by a PM object—something that might not be needed otherwise.

For completeness, and in order to be able to implement a corresponding `AssignedEmployees` property in the `ProjectWrapper` class, we have also provided a `GetDomainObject()` method on the `EmployeeWrapper` class.

But even this isn't really enough. Looking critically at the code, we can't help but notice that each time we read from the `AssignedToProject` property, a new `ProjectWrapper` object is created. Assuming the Identity Mapping in our Domain Model layer is working, each new `ProjectWrapper` object created when reading the same property over and over will wrap the same DM `Project` object, and so we shouldn't run the risk of data inconsistency and corruption, but it is hardly ideal nonetheless.

In the end, we might want a full-blown solution that could handle Identity Mapping in the PM as well, making sure that there are never two different PM instances representing the very same Domain Model instance around in a session.

The code in the `AssignedToProject` property would then have to be rewritten so that instead of creating a new instance of the `ProjectWrapper` object itself, it would ask a PM Repository with an Identity Map for the `ProjectWrapper` object.

That means that the `EmployeeWrapper` object will need a reference to the `ProjectRepository` object. Say goodbye to the comforting simplicity that has hitherto graced the Presentation Model. The end result is that the whole slew of fascinating and entertaining horrors and hardships that we remember from managing reference properties in the Domain Layer will rear their ugly heads again.

Mapping
and
Wrapping

One way of "solving" these issues with reference properties is to simply avoid reference properties in your PM objects, using "flattened" objects instead that expose only primitive properties, quite possibly from referenced objects as well. See the following code listing.

```
//"Flattened" Presentation Model object, exposing only primitive
//properties
namespace MyCompany.MyApplication.Presentation
{
    public class EmployeeWrapper
    {
        private Employee employee;

        public EmployeeWrapper(Employee employee)
        {
            this.employee = employee;
        }

        public int Id
        {
            get { return this.employee.Id; }
            set { this.employee.Id == value; }
        }

        public string AssignedToProjectName
        {
            get { return this.employee.Project.Name; }
            set { this.employee.Project.Name = value; }
        }
    }
}
```

This approach is often very useful, especially because many UI controls are designed for showing tables of rows, and flattened objects adapt well to this paradigm. But whenever you are interested in representing navigable, deep structures rather than just grids of stuff, the flattened approach falls short. However, you may often find yourself complementing a fully partitioned PM with some flat objects specifically written for some grid in your application.

"Flattened" PM objects provide a good example of how the PM often looks very different from the Domain Model and, of course, the more different they are, the more motivated we are to have two separate models instead of just adding the features needed by the PL to the Domain Model.

Matters of State

Mapping
and
Wrapping

When making the choice between Mapping and Wrapping, special attention should be paid to the difference in how state is handled in the two approaches.

When wrapping your Domain Model objects, only one instance of the data is used by the application. If you have two views showing the same employee at the same time, and you update the employee's name in one view, the single instance of the data in the wrapped object is updated. If the second view is then refreshed, it should display the updated data, because it is also mapping directly to the same wrapped, updated object.

When mapping your PM objects to your Domain Model objects, however, you could potentially have several different sets of PM objects representing the same Domain Model object, but with different state in them.

Even if you have an Identity Map for your PM, you may have two different PM Employee classes that look slightly different for different presentation purposes, in which case the Identity Map is of no help at all.

This could lead to conflicts. On the other hand, it also opens up the possibility of more sophisticated, disconnected data management.

For example, a mapped set of PM objects may be worked with for a long time in isolation in some wizard. At the last step of the wizard, the user could decide to commit the work to the Domain Model (and then to commit the updated Domain Model to the database) or to discard the changes. Had the user been working with a set of PM objects that directly wrapped the Domain Model objects, this option of canceling the changes would not have been available because the Domain Model objects would have been continuously updated when the user worked in the wizard!

Certainly, the option of canceling so that the changes aren't forwarded to the database is there even without the PM, assuming your Domain Model supports disconnected operations (for example, by using a Unit of Work [Fowler PoEAA]). However, if you press cancel at the end of a wizard that works directly with the Domain Model, even if your database is spared from the changes, your Domain Model will still have been changed so that when you present it in the next screen of your application, the changes are visible.

If you are prepared to throw away your Domain Model if the user cancels, there is no problem. There is also no problem if the Unit of Work supports full rollback of the state in the Domain Model. But if you are writing a rich client where you intend to let the Domain Model live for the scope of the application (for example, you don't want to throw the DM away if the user cancels) and your Unit of Work does not support full rollbacks, you may well run into this issue.

In some situations, you'll find that wrapping best suits your needs, while mapping works better in other situations. Sometimes you'll use both in the same application, perhaps using wrapping as the default approach but using mapping just for wizards or other "batch jobs" that should be possible to discard without committing.

Mapping
and
Wrapping

Final Thoughts

Sometimes you're just plain lucky. Whenever you're able to present your Domain Model to the user right away (or with a minor amount of supportive hacks) you should thank your lucky stars, because there's no getting around the fact that connecting a PM to a Domain Model can be quite headache-inducing.

The headache is significantly reduced if you decide to go with "flattened" PM objects, because most of the more severe issues arise directly as a result of trying to manage reference properties.

The choice between wrapping and mapping is influenced by a number of factors, including how state is managed and the opportunities for reducing the amount of boilerplate code in your applications via code generation (wrapping) or via using an O/O Mapping framework (mapping).

By trying to keep structural transformations outside the scope of any frameworks or code generators you employ (instead placing all such advanced transformation logic in code within your PM classes and hiding non-transformed members in the PM by making them protected), you greatly reduce the complexity required by such frameworks/code generators and thereby improve your chances of writing something useful yourself or finding something available online.

If you doubt that all this extra architectural overhead in the form of PMs, O/O Mappers, and transformation logic methods is really necessary—fine, perhaps you're lucky enough to find yourself with a presentable Domain Model.

The bottom line, however, is that you should *really, really* try to avoid modifying the Domain Model in order to suit it to the needs of the PL—don't try to make your Domain Model work double as a PM unless you can get away with that without changing the Domain Model.

As soon as you recognize that there is a difference between the way you want to represent your Domain Model in the core of the application and the way you want to present it to the user, you recognize the need for a PM—at least as long as you want to follow the advice of *never burdening the Domain Model with PL aspects*.

I am slightly fanatic about keeping my Domain Model objects completely oblivious of PL aspects. This means that if my Domain Model could be data bound to directly and if only some attributes were added to the properties (like attributes for specifying category and default value for binding to the property grid), I'll refrain from adding those PL attributes to my Domain Model objects. Instead I'll opt for complementing my Domain Model with a PM even if it is in every detail exactly the same as the Domain Model, except for the attributes. If you can't identify yourself with the lunatic fringe demographic, though, perhaps you'll stop short of that.

But one reason I keep doing that is that as soon as the PM is there—as well as the supporting infrastructure for Wrapping or Mapping to the Domain Model—I usually find plenty of opportunity for refining the presentational aspects of the PM, and soon enough the two models will begin to become more and more different, making it easier and easier to motivate complementing the Domain Model with a PM.

◆

Thanks, Mats!

Summary

I think my friends just described how you can benefit from the Domain Model again through the discussions of presentation services.

Even though you focus on the core with the Domain Model, that's not the same as saying that the presentation service is less important. On the contrary! The importance of the presentation service is one of the reasons why you should work hard on the Domain Model. By moving out as many things as possible from the PL that are just distractions in that context, it is easier or more possible to create a first-class UI.

Epilogue

So we have been thinking about an application in something of a DDD-ish way. The book was pretty much structured the same way, by which I mean the following:

1. First we try to collect the requirements and understand the problem.

2. Next we think about which approach to use for structuring the main logic. According to Fowler, we can choose from Transaction Script, Table Module, and Domain Model [Fowler PoEAA]. If the requirements signal that this is a complex (regarding behavior and/or relationships) and long-lived project, we will probably choose Domain Model.

3. Then we need a certain style for the Domain Model, not only to avoid common traps, but also to create something really powerful. That's where DDD comes in. We try to settle the Ubiquitous Language [Evans DDD]. We work hard with the Domain Model, trying to make it knowledge rich.

Epilogue

4. After that it's time to think about the distractions: the required infrastructure. The most typical problem to consider is how to deal with persistence. If possible, object relational mapping is a popular choice for DDD projects. (Instead of the somewhat overloaded term "infrastructure," let's describe this as it's all about mapping the model to other tiers, such as presentation, persistence, and integration services.)

5. Finally, needless to say, there are lots of other things to consider, such as how to deal with presentation.

Not that I think it's a waterfall process, not at all, but a book is sequential by nature and consequently more often than not the description will be as well. It's important to remember and stress the iterative and incremental style of development that is required to mitigate risk and lead to a successful project.

OK, it's over. This book, that is. But as Dan said, it's just the beginning.

Just one more thing: I started this book talking about how I value "lagom" (something like not too much and not too little, but rather *balanced*). Has the book been "lagom"? Well, I think to some it has been extreme in some directions, and perhaps "lagom" in others.

What is balanced is all in the eye and in the context of the observer.

PART V

Appendices

There are two appendices providing further examples of Domain Model styles and a catalog with an overview of patterns.

The appendices are about other styles and collections.

PART IV

Appendices

Appendix A

Other Domain Model Styles

There are lots of variations on how the Domain Model pattern is used. I asked a couple of friends of mine to describe their favorite ways of applying Domain Models. As the input, they got the requirements listings from Chapter 4, "A New Default Architecture," and you will find their answers here in Appendix A.[1] I'll repeat those requirements here for you:

1. List customers by applying a flexible and complex filter.

   The customer support staff needs to be able to search for customers in a very flexible manner. They need to use wildcards on numerous fields, such as name, location, street address, reference person, and so on. They also need to be able to ask for customers with orders of a certain kind, orders of a certain size, orders for certain products, and so on. What we're talking about here is a full-fledged search utility. The result is a list of customers, each with a customer number, customer name, and location.

2. List the orders when looking at a specific customer.

   The total value for each order should be visible in the list, as should the status of the order, type of order, order date, and name of reference person.

3. An order can have many different lines.

   An order can have many order lines, where each line describes a product and the number of items of that product that has been ordered.

---

[1]Please note that when they received the input, the idea was to require an application server in the scenario, something I changed later on for Chapter 4.

447

4. Concurrency conflict detection is important.

    It's alright to use optimistic concurrency control. That is, it's accepted that when a user is notified after he or she has done some work and tries to save, there will be a conflict with a previous save. Only conflicts that will lead to real inconsistencies should be considered as conflicts. So the solution needs to decide on the versioning unit for customers and for orders. (This will slightly affect some of the other features.)

5. A customer may not owe us more than a certain amount of money.

    The limit is specific per customer. We define the limit when the customer is added initially, and we can change the amount later on. It's considered an inconsistency if we have unpaid orders of a total value of more than the limit, but we allow that inconsistency to happen in one situation and that is if a user decreases the limit. Then the user that decreases the limit is notified, but the save operation is allowed. However, it's not allowed to add an order or change an order so that the limit is exceeded.

6. An order may not have a total value of more than one million SEK.

    This limit (unlike the previous one) is a system-wide rule. (SEK is the Swedish currency, but that's not important.)

7. Each order and customer should have a unique and user-friendly number.

    Gaps in the series are acceptable.

8. Before a new customer is considered OK, his or her credit will be checked with a credit institute.

    That is, the limit discussed previously that is defined for a customer will be checked to see if it's reasonable.

9. An order must have a customer; an order line must have an order.

    There must not be any orders with an undefined customer. The same goes for order lines, they must belong to an order.

10. Saving an order and its lines should be atomic.

    To be honest, I'm not actually sure that this feature is necessary. It might be alright if the order is created first and the order lines are added later on, but I want the rule to be like this so that we have a feature request related to transactional protection.

OBJECT-ORIENTED DATA MODEL, SMART SERVICE LAYER, AND DOCUMENTS   449

Object-
Oriented
Data Model,
Smart
Service
Layer, and
Documents

11. Orders have an acceptance status that is changed by the user.

   This status can be changed by users between different values (such as to approved/disapproved). To other status values, the change is done implicitly by other methods in the Domain Model.

First up is Mats Helander with the variation he calls "Object-oriented data model, smart service layer, and documents." Here goes.

Object-Oriented Data Model, Smart Service Layer, and Documents

By Mats Helander

Sometimes, during dark winter nights, I recall faintly what life was like in the days before the Domain Model. It is at times like those that I pour a little cognac into my hot chocolate and throw an extra log on the fire.

The evolution of the architecture in my applications, finally leading up to the use of the Domain Model, followed a pattern some readers may feel familiar with. I'm going to outline this evolution quickly, as it helps put my current approach for using the Domain Model into context.

In the Beginning

I started out writing client-server applications where all the application code was stuffed into the client, which would talk directly to the database. When I started writing Web applications, they consisted of ASP pages with all the application code in them including the code for calling the database.

Because the result of this type of application architecture is, without exception, a horrific mess whenever the application grows beyond the complexity of a "Hello World" example, I soon learned to factor out most of the code from the presentation layer and to put it in a *Business Logic Layer* (BLL) instead.

Immediately, the applications became easier to develop, more maintainable, and as a bonus the BLL could be made reusable between different presentation layers. It should also be noted that in those days, it could make a big difference to the performance and scalability of a Web application to have the bulk of its code compiled in a component.

The next step was to lift out all the code responsible for communicating with the database from the BLL and put it in a layer of its own, the *Data Access*

Object-
Oriented
Data Model,
Smart
Service
Layer, and
Documents

Layer (DAL). I recall that I was slightly surprised to see that the DAL was often substantially larger than the BLL—meaning more of my application logic dealt with database communication than with actual business logic.

At this time, I was almost at the point where the Domain Model would enter into the equation. The PL would talk to the BLL that would talk to the DAL that would talk to the database. However, all data from the database was passed around the application in the form of Recordsets, the in-memory representation of rows in the database (see Figure A-1).

Presentation Layer(s)
Business Logic Layer
Data Access Layer
Relational Database(s)

Figure A-1　Classic, pre-Domain Model layered application architecture

Sometimes, working with the data in its relational form is just what you want, and in those cases the architecture described earlier still fits the bill nicely. But, as I was becoming aware of, relational data structures aren't always ideal for the business logic to work with.

Object-Orientation and Relational Data Structures

From some work I had done with an object-oriented database from Computer Associates called Jasmine, I had come to understand that an object-oriented data structure was quite often a lot easier to work with when developing the business logic than the corresponding relational structure.

Relationships between entities are simpler, for one thing. In the case of many-to-many relationships, this is especially so, because the relational data structure requires an additional table whereas no additional class is required in the object-oriented data structure.

Collection properties are another case where an additional table is used in the relational model but no extra class is required in the object-oriented data structure. Furthermore, object-oriented data structures are type safe and support inheritance.

The Domain Model and Object-Relational Mapping

The problem was that OO databases weren't that common. Most projects I encountered still revolved around the relational database. This is where Object-Relational Mapping entered the picture.

Object-
Oriented
Data Model,
Smart
Service
Layer, and
Documents

What Object-Relational Mapping does is to let you take an object-oriented data structure and map it to the tables in a relational database. The advantage is that you will be able to work with your object-oriented data structure as if working with an OO database like Jasmine, while in reality you're still using a relational database to store all your data.

Furthermore, you can add business logic to the classes of the object-oriented data structure in the form of business methods. As you may have guessed, the object-oriented data structure with business methods that I'm talking about is—that's right—the Domain Model.

By learning about Object-Relational Mapping I could finally take the step toward including the Domain Model in my application architecture. Inserted between the BLL and the DAL, the Domain Model Layer now allowed my business logic to work with an object-oriented data structure (see Figure A-2).

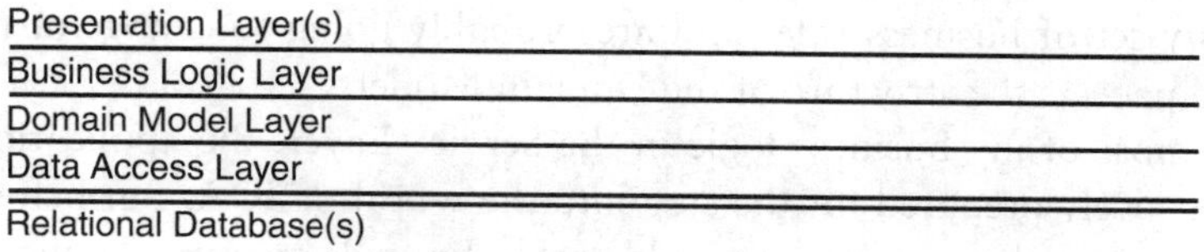

Presentation Layer(s)
Business Logic Layer
Domain Model Layer
Data Access Layer
Relational Database(s)

Figure A-2   Updated, layered application architecture including Domain Model

This meant that a BLL method that had previously been working with a Recordset containing a row from the Employees table would now instead work with an Employee Domain Model class. I gained type safety, and the code became shorter and easier to read—not to mention that I could navigate my data structure during development using Microsoft's IntelliSense feature!

Ever since, I've been a devoted user of the Domain Model and I haven't looked back—except during those cold, dark winter nights.

As I mentioned, another advantage with the Domain Model is that it lets you distribute your business logic over the Domain Model classes. I've experimented a lot with where to put my business logic. I've shifted between putting most of it in the Business Logic Layer to putting most of it in the Domain Model Layer and back again.

Service Layer

I've also come to prefer the term Service Layer [Fowler PoEAA] to Business Logic Layer, as it better covers what I'm doing at times when most of my business logic is in the Domain Model Layer. When most of my business logic is

Object-
Oriented
Data Model,
Smart
Service
Layer, and
Documents

in the Service Layer I see no reason to switch back to the term Business Logic Layer, though I sometimes refer to it as a "thick" Service Layer to distinguish it from a more conventionally thin Service Layer.

These days I almost always put most of the business logic in a "thick" Service Layer. While some OO purists might argue that structure and behavior should be combined, every so often I find it practical to keep the business logic-related behavior in the Service Layer.

The main reason for this is that in my experience, business rules governing the behavior of the Domain Model will usually change at a different pace, and at different times, from the rules governing the structure of the Domain Model. Another reason is that it easily lets you reuse the Domain Model under different sets of business rules.

Normally, the only business methods I would put on the Domain Model objects themselves are ones that I believe are fundamental enough to be valid under *any* set of business rules and are probably going to change at the same time and pace as the structure of the Domain Model.

With most of my business logic in the Service Layer, the application architecture is nicely prepared for the step into the world of SOA. But before we go there and take a look at how I would tackle Jimmy's example application, I'd just like to stress another particular benefit of this approach.

Combining Things

As I mentioned earlier, the object-oriented data structure offered by the Domain Model isn't the perfect fit for *every* operation you'll want to perform. There are reasons why relational databases are still so popular and why many people prefer to use Object-Relational Mapping before going with an actual OO database. For many tasks, the relational data structure and the set-based operations offered by SQL are the *perfect* fit.

In these cases, slapping methods onto the Domain Model objects that will actually be performing set-based operations directly on the relational data structures may not seem like a very natural way to go.

In contrast, letting Service Layer methods that access the database directly (or via the DAL) co-exist side by side with methods that operate on the Domain Model is no stretch at all. Converting a Service Layer method from using one approach to the other is also easily accomplished.

In short, I'm free to implement each Service Layer method as I see fit, bypassing the Domain Model Layer where it is not useful as well as taking full advantage of it where it *is* useful (which, in my experience, happens to be quite often).

Object-
Oriented
Data Model,
Smart
Service
Layer, and
Documents

Jimmy's Application and SOA

Having said that, let's return to Jimmy's application and the brave new world of SOA. So far I have only really described what my application architecture looks like on the server, which may be enough for a Web application, but now we're going to deal with a Rich Client, and I'd like to focus on application servers as a variation to the rest of the book.

In cases where a lot, if not all, of the business logic has been distributed over the Domain Model, a tempting approach is to try to export both data and behavior packaged together in this way to the Rich Client by giving it access to the Domain Model. With the architecture I'm using, where most of the behavior is found in the Service Layer, a more natural approach is to expose the behavior and the data separately.

Concretely, the Service Layer is complemented with a Web Service façade (a type of the Remote Façade pattern [Fowler PoEAA]), which is just a thin layer for exposing the business logic methods in the Service Layer as Web Services. The Rich Client communicates with the server by calling the Web Services, exchanging XML documents containing serialized Domain Model objects.

For our example application, this means that each time the Rich Client needs new information it will call a Web Service on the server that will return the information in the form of an XML document. To begin with, let's take the case of listing customers matching a filter.

I would begin by creating a GetCustomersByFilter() Service Layer method implementing the actual filtering. The Service Layer method would take the filter arguments and return the matching Domain Model objects. Then I'd add a GetCustomersByFilter() Web Service exposing the Service Layer method to the Rich Client.

The Web Service accepts the same filter arguments and passes them on in a call to the Service Layer method. The Domain Model objects returned by the Service Layer method would then be serialized to an XML document that would finally be returned by the Web Service. The Rich Client can then use the information in the XML document to display the list of customers to the user (see Figure A-3).

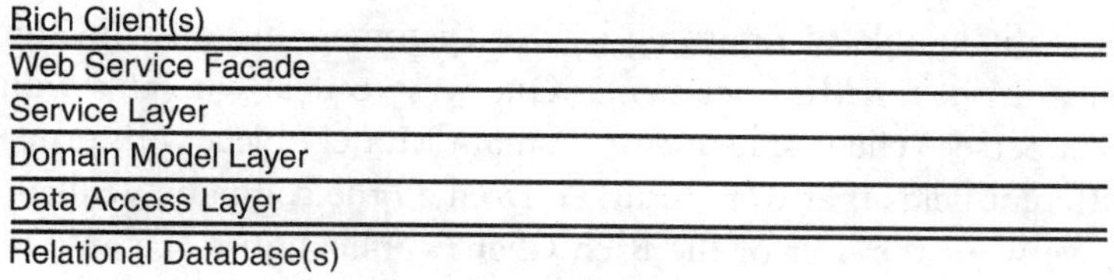

| Rich Client(s) |
| Web Service Facade |
| Service Layer |
| Domain Model Layer |
| Data Access Layer |
| Relational Database(s) |

Figure A-3 Rich Client Application Server layered application architecture including Domain Model

Object-
Oriented
Data Model,
Smart
Service
Layer, and
Documents

It is completely up to the Rich Client application developers if they want to create a client-side Domain Model that they can fill with the data from the XML document. They may also decide to store the information for offline use. One way is to just save the XML documents to disk. Another is to persist the client-side Domain Models to an offline database on the client machine.

Note that the eventual client-side Domain Model doesn't have to match the Domain Model on the server. Accordingly, if the client-side Domain Model is persisted to an offline database, the client-side database will presumably follow the design of the client-side Domain Model and thus doesn't have to look like the server-side database.

Note

One important difference regarding the schema of the server-side database and the client-side database is that if a server-side database table uses automatically increasing identity fields, the corresponding client-side database table normally shouldn't.

Say that a new employee is created on the server. As a new row is inserted in the Employees table it is automatically given a value in its auto-increasing ID column. The employee is then serialized and sent to the client, which fills a client-side Domain Model with the data and stores it in the client-side database for offline use.

The new row in the client-side Employees table should *not* be assigned with a new ID—the ID that was assigned to the employee in the server-side database should be used. This means that the properties for the ID columns may be different on the client and the server.

The point here is that the developers of the Rich Client application are free to decide whether or not they want to use a Domain Model at all, and if they want one they are free to design it as they see fit. The communication between client and server is 100% document-oriented, and no assumptions about the Domain Models on either side are made by the other.

For example, maybe the Rich Client calls Web Services of many different companies, all capable of returning lists of customers but all with slightly different fields in their XML documents. One way to deal with this would be to create a "superset" client-side Customer Domain Model object with properties for all the different fields that were returned from all the companies called.

Next, we want the user of the Rich Client application to be able to look at the orders belonging to a particular customer. The unique ID of each customer

OBJECT-ORIENTED DATA MODEL, SMART SERVICE LAYER, AND DOCUMENTS

455

Object-
Oriented
Data Model,
Smart
Service
Layer, and
Documents

was of course included in the XML document returned by the first Web Service, so we know the ID of the customer in which we're interested.

What I have to do is to implement a Web Service that takes the ID of a customer and returns the orders for that customer. Again, I begin by creating a GetOrdersByCustomerID() Service Layer method that accepts the ID of a customer and returns the Domain Model Order objects belonging to the customer.

I'll then proceed by adding a GetOrdersByCustomerID() Web Service that takes a customer ID, passes it along to the Service Layer method, and finally serializes the returned order objects into an XML document that can be returned by the Web Service.

However, in this case, some extra attention has to be paid to the XML serialization. We want the XML document to include the total value for each order, but the Order Domain Model object doesn't contain any TotalValue property because the total value of an order is not stored in any field in the database.

Rather, the total value is calculated whenever it is needed by adding the values of the order lines together. The value of each order line, in its turn, is calculated by multiplying the price that the purchased product had when it was bought by the number of items bought.

Because the order lines aren't included in the XML document sent to the client, the client application can't calculate the total values for the orders, which means that the calculation has to be done on the server and the result has to be included in the XML document.

The methods for calculating the value of an order line and the total value for an order are good examples of the type of method that many people would prefer to put on the OrderLine and Order Domain Model objects but that I prefer to put in the Service Layer.

Service Layer Design

This may be a good time to mention that I usually organize my Service Layer around the same entities that are used in the Domain Model, rather than by task, which is otherwise also popular. This means that if I have an Employee object in the Domain Model Layer, I'll have an EmployeeServices class in the Service Layer.

For services that don't need any transaction control, I also usually implement the Service Layer methods as static methods so that they can be called without instantiating any object from the Service Layer classes.

In the case at hand, I would thus place a static GetValue() method on the OrderLineServices Service Layer class and a static GetTotalValue() method on the OrderServices class. These methods will accept the objects they should work with as parameters. This means I won't be calling a method on the Order object itself in the following fashion:

```
myOrder.GetTotalValue();
```

Instead I'll be calling a Service Layer method, like this:

```
OrderServices.GetTotalValue(myOrder);
```

It is this kind of procedural syntax that has some OO purists jumping in their seats, hollering, and throwing rotten fruit, but I think that the benefits that follow from separating the behavior from the structure of the Domain Model are well worth the slightly uglier syntax.

Of course, the service methods don't have to be static, and sometimes they can't be—for example, if they should initiate a declarative transactions or if you want to configure your SL classes using Dependency Injection (see Chapter 10, "Design Techniques to Embrace").

But when static methods will do, I usually make them static simply because that means less code (no need to waste a line of code instantiating a SL object every time I want to call a service). Because it makes for less code, I'll continue using static service methods in my examples.

The point is that I don't really lose the opportunity for organizing my methods pretty much as nicely as if I had put them on the Domain Model classes. Because for every Domain Model class I have a corresponding Service Layer class, I'm able to partition my business logic in just the same way as if I had distributed it over the actual Domain Model.

The benefit comes when the rules for GetTotalValue() start changing even though the underlying data structure doesn't change—such as when suddenly a system-wide rule should be implemented stating that an order may not have a total value exceeding one million SEK. You can then just modify the relevant Service Layer methods without having to recompile or even touch your Domain Model Layer that can remain tested and trusted.

Returning to the GetOrdersByCustomerID() Web Service, I just add a call to the Service Layer OrderServices.GetTotalValue() method to which I pass each order during the serialization routine and add a field to the XML document for holding the result.

This provides us with a good example of how the Domain Model on the client, should the client application developer choose to implement one, can differ from the server-side Domain Model. The client-side Domain Model Order object might well include a property for the total value as presented in the XML document—a property that the server-side Domain Model Order object doesn't have.

OBJECT-ORIENTED DATA MODEL, SMART SERVICE LAYER, AND DOCUMENTS   457

Object-
Oriented
Data Model,
Smart
Service
Layer, and
Documents

Following this approach, we may decide to include even more fields in our XML document with values that have been calculated by Service Layer methods.

For instance, consider a system-wide rule specifying that a customer may not owe more than a certain amount of money. The precise amount is individual and calculated by some special Service Layer method. When designing the XML document to return from the GetCustomersByFilter() Web Service, you may want to include a field for the maximum amount each customer can owe, or at least a flag stating if the customer is over the limit.

This goes to demonstrate that the documents offered by the server don't have to match the Domain Model—communication between client and server is entirely document-oriented.

Looking at what we have at the moment, the user of the Rich Client application should be able to view filtered lists of customers and to view the list of orders belonging to each customer. Next, we want to let them check out the order lines belonging to a specific order.

There's no news in how this is implemented: The client calls a Web Service with the ID of the order, the Web Service forwards the call to a Service Layer method and serializes the results to XML. By now, we know the drill for letting the client fetch data. What about letting the client submit data?

Submitting Data

Let's say we want the user to be able to update the status of an order from "Not inspected" to "Approved" or "Disapproved." At first glance it may seem like a straightforward request, but we're really opening a Pandora's Box of concurrency problems here as we move from read-only to read-write access.

So let's begin by sticking with the first glance and not look any closer for a little while. How would we do it then?

The first thing to do is to create an UpdateOrderStatus() Service Layer method and a corresponding Web Service. The methods should accept the ID of the order and the new order status as parameters and return a bool value telling you if the operation completed successfully. (We won't go into any advanced cross-platform exception handling here—even though it's a whole bunch of fun!)

So far, so good; the Service Layer method is easy enough to implement, and the Web Service is just a wrapper, forwarding the call to the Service Layer method. Now let's look at the problems we're going to run into.

The problems arise if two users try to update the status of the same order at the same time. Say that user A fetches an order, notes that it is "Not inspected"

Object-
Oriented
Data Model,
Smart
Service
Layer, and
Documents

and goes on to inspect it. Just a little later, user B fetches the same order, notes the same thing, and also decides to inspect it. User A then notes a small problem with the order, causing her to mark the order as "Disapproved" in her following call to the UpdateOrderStatus() Web Service.

Just after user A has updated the status of the order, user B proceeds to call the same Web Service for updating the status of the same order. However, user B hasn't noticed the problem with the order and wants to mark the order as "Approved." Should user B be able to overwrite the status that A gave the order and that is now stored in the database?

A standard answer would be "No, because user B didn't *know* about the changes user A had made." If user B had known about the change that user A made and still decided to override it, the answer would be "Yes" because then B could be trusted not to overwrite A's data by mistake. So the challenge becomes this: How do we keep track of what B, or any other client, "knows"?

One approach is to keep track of the original values from the database for updates fields and then at the time when the modified data is saved to the database, check if the original values match those that are in the database now. If the values in the database have changed, the client didn't *know* about these changes and the client's data should be rejected.

This approach is called *optimistic concurrency*. Let's look at a very simple way that optimistic concurrency could be implemented for the case at hand.

To begin with, the client application has to be coded so that when the user changes the status of an order, the status that was originally returned from the database via the XML document is still kept around.

Then the UpdateOrderStatus() Web Service and the Service Layer method with the same name have to be modified to accept an additional parameter for the original order status value. Thus, when the client calls the Web Service, three parameters are passed: the ID for the order, the new order status, and the original order status.

Finally, the UpdateOrderStatus() Service Layer method should be updated to include a check if the current status for the order in the database matches that which was passed to the parameter for the original order status, executing the update only if the values match.

This version of optimistic concurrency, matching the original values of updated fields with those in the database, will give good performance and scalability, but it can be a bit cumbersome to implement, at least in a Rich Client scenario. An alternative way of using optimistic concurrency is to add a versioning field to the tables in your database.

Object-
Oriented
Data Model,
Smart
Service
Layer, and
Documents

Sometimes even strategies like optimistic concurrency won't work, so domain-specific solutions have to be applied in those cases. A normal theme is to use some sort of check-in/out system, where the user marks an object as "checked out" or "locked" when it is fetched for write access, preventing other users from updating it until she is done. Other, more sophisticated schemes include merging of concurrently updated data.

The only way to decide on what strategy is appropriate in the particular case is to ask the domain specialist—that is, the person understanding the business implications of these decisions—what behavior is desired. There's no general way to select a concurrency strategy.

Even so, I'm guessing that the appropriate way to go in this case would be to use optimistic concurrency, with or without a versioning field. The point is that it is still up to somebody who knows what the expected behavior is for their business to decide.

Perhaps the biggest problem with the approach we have used here is that we have asked the client to keep track of the original values for us. This is probably asking a bit too much of the client application developer, so a better alternative might be to store the original values on the server in a Session variable or a similar construct.

How Fine-Grained?

Another thing to consider is whether the service is too fine-grained. Rather than providing a separate Web Service for every field of an order that can be updated, could we, perhaps, implement a single UpdateOrder() Web Service instead?

In this case, rather than providing a parameter for each updateable field, the Web Service could accept an XML document representing the updated order. That is, instead of this:

```
[WebMethod]public bool UpdateOrder(int orderID, int orderStatus
, DateTime orderDate, int customerID)
```

you could use this:

```
[WebMethod]
public bool UpdateOrder(string xmlOrder)
```

In this way the client both receives and submits data in the form of XML documents. This strictly document-oriented approach helps in keeping the Web Services API coarse-grained and avoiding overly "chatty" conversations between the client and the server (see Figure A-4).

Object-
Oriented
Data Model,
Smart
Service
Layer, and
Documents

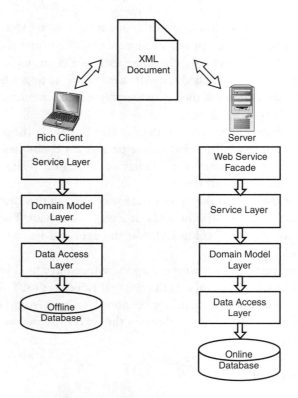

Figure A-4   Overview of full application architecture

A Few Words About Transactions

Finally, a note on transactions. As I mentioned earlier, I usually make my Service Layer methods static whenever I *don't* need transactions, but in the case of a business application managing orders, I'm inclined to believe transactions will be part of the solution.

This implies that, for example, the UpdateOrderStatus() method should be transactional. What this means is that instead of making this method static I turn it into an instance-level method and mark it with the [AutoComplete] .NET attribute. Because I'm also going to mark the whole class that the method belongs to with the [Transaction] attribute and let it inherit from ServicedComponent, I decide to lift this method out of the OrderServices class and into a new class called OrderServicesTx, where "Tx" stands for "transactional."

And that's it. All my UpdateOrderStatus() Web Service has to do now is to create an instance of the OrderServicesTx class and call the UpdateOrderStatus() on that object instead of calling the old static method on the OrderServices class. The execution

THE DATABASE MODEL IS THE DOMAIN MODEL 461

The
Database
Model Is
the Domain
Model

of the `OrderServicesTx.UpdateOrderStatus()` will use distributed transactions that will be automatically committed if the method finished without exceptions and rolled back otherwise.

The Service Layer is, in my opinion, the perfect place to enforce transaction control in your application. It is also a great place for putting your security checks, logging, and other similar aspects of your application.

Note that *all* the methods in the Service Layer don't have to be organized around the entities from the Domain Model layer. Just because I'll have `EmployeeServices`, `CustomerServices`, and so on, that doesn't mean I won't also have `LoggingServices` and `SecurityServices` classes in my Service Layer as well.

Summary

My preferred style is to put most of the business logic in the Service Layer and let it operate on the object-oriented data structure represented by the Domain Model. The communication between client and server is completely document-oriented, and no attempt to export the Domain Model to the client or even to let the client access the server-side Domain Model (for example, via Remoting) is made.

I hope I've been able to give some idea about how I use the Domain Layer—and why—as well as how I would go about designing Jimmy's application.

◆

The Database Model Is the Domain Model

By Frans Bouma

To work with data on a semantic basis, it's often useful to specify general definitions of the elements a given portion of logic will work with. For example, an order system works with, among other elements, *Order* elements. To be able to define how this logic works, a definition of the concept *Order* is practical: We will be able to describe the functionality of the system by specifying actions on `Order` elements and supply with that a definition of that element `Order`.

This `Order` element contains other elements (values like the `OrderID` and `ShippingDate`) and has a tight connection with another element, `OrderRow`, which in turn also contains other elements. You can even say that `Order` *contains* a set of `OrderRow` elements like it contains value elements. Is there a difference between the containment of the value `OrderID` and the containment of the set of `OrderRow` elements? The answer to this question is important for the way the concept of `Order` is implemented further when the order system is realized with program code.

The Entity's Habitat

Looking at the relational model developed by Dr. E.F. Codd [Codd Relational Model], they should be seen as two separated elements: Order and OrderRow, which have a *relationship*, and the elements itself form a *relation* based on the values they contain, like OrderID.

However, looking at the Domain Model, pioneered by Martin Fowler [Fowler PoEAA] and others, it doesn't have to be that way. You could see the OrderRow elements in a set as a value of Order and work with Order as a unit, including the OrderRow elements.

What's an Entity?

In 1970, Dr. Peter Chen defined the concept *entity* for his *Entity Relationship Model* [Chen ER], which builds on top of Codd's Relational Model. The concept of the entity is very useful in defining what Order and OrderRow look like in a relational model. Chen defined *Entity* as

> "**Entity** and **Entity set**. Let *e* denote an entity which exists in our minds. Entities are classified into different entity sets such as EMPLOYEE, PROJECT, and DEPARTMENT. There is a predicate associated with each entity set to test whether an entity belongs to it. For example, if we know an entity is in the entity set EMPLOYEE, then we know that it has the properties common to the other entities in the entity set EMPLOYEE. Among these properties is the afore-mentioned test predicate."

By using the Entity Relationship Model, we're able to define entities like Order and OrderRow and place them into a relational model, which defines our database. Using Eric Evans' definition of *Entity*, however, we are far away from the relational model, which I think comes down to the following definition: "*An object that is tracked through different states or even across different implementations.*" The important difference between Evans' definition and Chen's definition of an entity is that Chen's definition is that of an abstract element; it exists without having state or even a physical representation. With Evans, the entity physically exists; it's an object, with state and behavior. With the abstract entity definitions, we're not influenced by the context in which an entity's data is used, as the interpretation of the data of an entity is not done by the entity itself (as there is no behavior in the entity) but by external logic.

To avoid misinterpretations, we're going to use the definition of Dr. Peter Chen. The reason for this choice is because it defines the abstract term for things we run into every day, both physical items and virtual items, without looking at context or contained data as the *definition* is what's important. It is therefore an ideal candidate to describe elements in relational models like Customer or Order. A physical Customer is then called an entity *instance*.

Where Does an Entity Live?

Every application has to deal with a phenomenon called *state*. State is actually a term that is too generic. Most applications have several different kinds of state: *user state* and *application state* are the most important ones. User state can be seen as the state of all objects/data stores that hold data on a per-user basis (that is, have "user scope") at a given time T. An example of user state is the contents of the Session object of a given user in an ASP.NET application at a given moment. Application state is different from user state; it can be seen as the state of all objects/data stores that hold data on an application scope basis. An example can be the contents of a database shared among all users of a given Web application at a given moment. It is not wise to see the user state as a subset of the application state: When the user is in the middle of a 5-step wizard, the user state holds the data of step one and two; however, nothing in the application state has changed; that will be the case *after* the wizard is completed.

It is very important to define where an entity instance lives: in the application state or in the user state. If the entity instance lives in the user state, it's local to the user owning the user state, and other users can't see the entity and therefore can not use it. When an entity instance is *created*, like an order is physically created in the aforementioned order system, it is living inside the actual application; it is part of the application state. However, during the order creation process, when the user fills in the order form, for example, the order is not actually created; a temporary set of data is living inside the user's state, which will become the order after it is finalized. We say the entity instance gets *persisted* when it is actually created in the application state.

You can have different types of application state: a shared, in-memory system that holds entity instances, or you can have a database in which entity instances are stored. Most software applications dealing with entity instances use some kind of *persistent storage* to store their entity instance data to make it survive power outages and other things causing the computer to go down, losing its memory contents. If the application uses a persistent storage, it is likely to call the data in the persistent storage the actual application state: when the application is shut down, for example, for maintenance, the application doesn't lose any state: no order entity instance is lost, and it is still available when the application is brought back up. An entity instance in memory is therefore a *mirror* of the actual entity instance in the persistent storage, and application logic uses that mirror to alter the actual entity instance that lives in the persistent storage.

Mapping Classes onto Tables Versus Mapping Tables onto Classes

O/R Mapping deals with the transformation between the relational model and the object model: that is, transforming objects into entity instances in the persistent storage and back. Globally, it can be defined as the following:

A field in a class in the object model is related to an attribute of an entity in the relational model and vice versa.

A chicken-egg problem arises: what follows what? Do you first define the entity classes (classes *representing* entity definitions), like an Order class representing the Order entity) and create relational model entities with attributes using these classes, or do you define a relational model first and use that relational model when you define your entity classes?

As with almost everything, there is no clear "this is how you do it" answer to that question. "It depends" is probably the best answer that can be given. If you're following the Domain Model, it is likely you start with domains, which you use to define classes, some probably in an inheritance hierarchy. Using that class model, you simply need a relational model to store the data, which could even be one table with a primary key consisting of the object ID, a binary blob field for the object, and a couple of metadata elements describing the object. It will then be natural to map a class onto elements in the relational model after you've made sure the relational model is constructed in a way that it serves the object model best.

If you start with the relational model and you construct an E/R model, for example, it is likely you want to map an entity in your relational model onto a class. This is different from the approach of the Domain Model, for instance, because the relational model doesn't support inheritance hierarchies: you can't model a hierarchy like Person <- Employee <- Manager such that it also represents a hierarchy. It is, of course, possible to create a relational model that can be semantically interpreted as an inheritance hierarchy; however, it doesn't represent an inheritance hierarchy by definition.

This is the fundamental difference between the two approaches. Starting with classes and then working your way to the database uses the relational model and the database just as a place to store data, while starting with the relational model and working your way towards classes uses the classes as a way to work with the relational model in an OO fashion.

As we've chosen to use Chen's way of defining entities, we'll use the approach of defining the relational model first and working our way up to classes. Later on in the "The Ideal World" section we'll see how to bridge the two approaches.

Working with Data in an OO Fashion

Entity-representing classes are the developer's way to define entities in code, just as a physically implemented E/R model with tables defines the entities in the persistent storage. Using the O/R Mapping technique discussed in the previous section, the developer is able to manipulate entity instances in the persistent storage using in-memory mirrors placed in entity class instances. This is always a batch-style process, as the developer works disconnected from the persistent storage. The controlling environment is the O/R Mapper, which controls the link between entity instances in the persistent storage and the in-memory mirrors inside entity class instances.

A developer might ask the O/R Mapper to load a given set of Order instances into memory. This results in, for each Order instance in the persistent storage, a mirror inside an entity class instance. The developer is now able to manipulate each entity instance mirror through the entity class instance or to display the entity instance mirrors in a form or offer it as output of a service. Manipulated entity instance mirrors have to be persisted to make the changes persistent. From the developer's point of view, this looks like saving the manipulated entity instance data inside the objects to the persistent storage, like a user saves a piece of text written in a word processor to a file. The O/R Mapper is performing this save action for the developer. But because we're working with mirrors, the actual action the O/R Mapper is performing is *updating* the entity instance in the persistent storage with the changes stored in the mirror received from the developer's code.

The relationships between the entities in the relational model are represented in code by functionality provided by the O/R Mapper. This allows the developer to traverse relationships from one entity instance to another. For example, in the Order system, loading a Customer instance into memory allows the developer to traverse to the Customer's Order entity instances by using functionality provided by the O/R Mapper, be it a collection object inside the Customer object or a new request to the O/R Mapper for Order instances related to the given Customer instance.

This way of working with entities is rather static: constructing entities at runtime through a combination of attributes from several related entities does not result in entity-representing classes, as classes have to be present at compile time. This doesn't mean the entity instances constructed at runtime through combinations of attributes (for example, through a select with an outer join) can't be loaded into memory; however, they don't represent a persistable entity, but rather a virtual entity. This extra layer of abstraction is mostly used in a read-only scenario, such as in reporting applications and read-only lists, where a combination of attributes from related entities is often required. An example

**The
Database
Model Is
the Domain
Model**

of a definition for such a list is the combination of all attributes of the Order
entity and the "company name" attribute from the Customer entity.

To successfully work with data in an OO fashion, it is key that the functionality controlling the link between in-memory mirrors of entity instances and the
physical entity instances offers enough flexibility so that reporting functionality
and lists of combined set of attributes are definable and loadable into memory
without needing to use another application just for that more dynamic way of
using data in entity instances.

Functional Research as the Application Foundation

To efficiently set up the relational model, the mappings between entity definitions in the relational model and entity representing classes and these classes
itself, it is key to reuse the results from work done early in the software development project, the Functional Research Phase. This phase is typical for a
more classical approach to software development. In this phase, the functional
requirements and system functionality are determined, defined in an abstract
way and documented. Over the years, several techniques have been defined to
help in this phase; one of them is NIAM [Halpin/Nijssen Conceptual Schema],
which is further developed by T.A. Halpin [Halpin IMRD] to *Object Role
Modeling* (ORM). NIAM and ORM make it easy to communicate functional
research findings with the client in easy to understand sentences like "Customer
has Order" and "Order belongs to Customer." These sentences are then used to
define entities and relationships in an abstract NIAM/ORM model. Typically, a
visual tool is used for this, such as Microsoft Visio.

The Importance of Functional Research Results

The advantage of modeling the research findings with techniques like NIAM or
ORM is that the abstract model both documents the research findings during
the functional research phase and at the same time it is the source for the relational model the application is going to work with. Using tools like Microsoft
Visio, a relational model can be generated by generating an E/R model from
an NIAM/ORM model, which can be used to construct a physical relational
model in a database system. The metadata forming the definition of the relational model in the database system can then be used to generate classes and
construct mappings.

The advantage of this is that the class hierarchy the developers work with
has a theoretical basis in the research performed at the start of the project.
This means that when something in the design of the application changes, such

THE DATABASE MODEL IS THE DOMAIN MODEL

467

The
Database
Model Is
the Domain
Model

as a piece of functionality, the same path can be followed: the NIAM model changes, the relational model is adjusted with the new E/R model created with the updated NIAM model, and the classes are adjusted to comply to the new E/R model. The other way around is also true: to find a reason for code constructs the developer has to work with. For example, for code constructs to traverse relationships between entity instance objects, you only have to follow back the path from the class to the functional research results and the theoretical basis for the code constructs is revealed. This strong connection between a theoretical basis and actual code is key to a successful, maintainable software system.

Functional Processes as Data Consumers and Location of Business Logic

As the real entity definitions live in the relational model, inside the database, and in-memory instances of entities are just mirrors of real instances of entities in the database, there is no place for behavior, or Business Logic rules, in these entities. Of course, adding behavior to the entity classes is easy. The question is whether this is logical, when entity classes represent entity definitions in the relational model. The answer depends on the category of the Business Logic you want to add to the entity as behavior. There are roughly three categories:

- Attribute-oriented Business Logic

- Single-entity-oriented Business Logic

- Multi-entity-oriented Business Logic

Attribute-oriented Business Logic is the category that contains rules like OrderId > 0. These are very simple rules that act like constraints placed on a single entity field. Rules in this category can be enforced when an entity field is set to a value.

The category of single-entity-oriented Business Logic contains rules like ShippingDate >= OrderDate, and those also act like constraints. Rules in this category can be enforced when an entity is loaded into an entity object in memory, saved into the persistent storage, or to test if an entity is valid in a given context.

The multi-entity-oriented Business Logic category contains rules spanning more than one entity: for example, the rule to check if a Customer is a Gold Customer. To make that rule true, it has to consult Order entities related to that Customer and Order Detail entities related to these Order entities.

All three categories have dependencies on the *context* the entity is used in, although not all rules in a given category are context-dependent rules. Attribute-oriented Business Logic is the category with the most rules that are not bound to the context the entity is used in, and it is a good candidate to add to the entity class as behavior. Single-entity-oriented Business Logic) is often not a good candidate to add to the entity class as behavior, because much of the rules in that category, which are used to make an entity *valid* in a given *context*, can and will change when the entity is used in another context. Rules in the multi-entity-oriented Business Logic category span more than one entity and are therefore not placeable in a single entity, besides the fact they're too bound to the context in which they're used.

Pluggable Rules   To keep an entity usable as a concept that isn't bound to a given context, the problem with context-bound Business Logic rules in the category attribute-oriented Business Logic and the category single-entity-oriented Business Logic can be solved with *pluggable rules*. Pluggable rules are objects that contain Business Logic rules and that are plugged into an entity object at runtime. The advantage of this is that the entity classes are not tied to a context they are used in but can be used in any context the system design asks for: just create per-context a set of pluggable rules objects, or even more per-entity, and depending on the context state, rules can be applied to the entity by simply setting an object reference. The processes that decide which rules objects to plug into entities are the processes maintaining the context the entity is used in: the processes representing actual business processes that are called *functional processes*.

Functional Processes   In the previous section, The Importance of Functional Research Results," the functional research phase was described, and the point was made concerning how important it is to keep a strong link between researched functionality and actual implementation of that functionality. Often a system has to automate certain *business processes*, and the functional research will describe these processes in an abstract form. To keep the link between research and implementation as tight as possible, it's a common step to model the actual implementation after the abstract business process, resulting in classes that we'll call *functional processes* because they're more or less data-less classes with sole functionality.

The functionality processes are the ideal candidates in which to implement multi-entity-oriented Business Logic rules. In our example of the Gold Customer, a process to upgrade a Customer to a Gold Customer can be implemented as a functional process that consumes a Customer entity object and its Order entity objects, updates some fields of the Customer entity, and persists that Customer entity after the upgrade process is complete. Furthermore, because functional processes actually perform the steps of a business process, they are also the place where a context is present in which entities are consumed and the only correct place to decide which rules to plug into an entity object at a given time T for a given context state.

The Ideal World Using NIAM/ORM for Classes and Databases

For most people, reality is not always in sync with what we expect to be an ideal world, and everyday software development is no exception to that. In the functional research paragraph, physical relational model metadata were used to produce mappings and classes to get to the entity class definitions for the developer to work with. A more ideal approach would be if the NIAM/ORM model could also be used to generate entity classes directly, avoiding a transformation from metadata to class definition. It would make the ultimate goal, where the design of the application is as usable as the application itself, appear to be one step closer.

When that ideal world will be a reality, or even *if* it will be a reality, is hard to say as a lot of the factors that influence how a software project could be made a success can be found in areas outside the world of computer science. Nevertheless, it's interesting to see what can be accomplished today, with techniques developed today, like model-driven software development.

◆

Pragmatism and the Nontraditional Approach
By Ingemar Lundberg

When Jimmy first asked me if I was willing to write this "guest segment" I immediately said "Yes, of course." I must admit I was flattered. Not surprisingly, I became doubtful just a short while later. What do I have to say? Can I be precise enough to fit it in a very limited space? And above all, how can my .NET architecture fit into the Domain Model concept?

I will attempt to give you a general description of the architecture I've built for my former employer, which, without shame, I will call my architecture from now on. It is however not the architecture I'm using nowadays. I will also address some of the issues in Jimmy's exercise that I find interesting with regards to the strengths and weaknesses in my architecture. I can't possibly give you the whole picture in this limited space, but because the intention of this section is to show you that there is more than one way to skin a cat, I hope this brief description is sufficient enough to fulfill its purpose. When I talk about how things are done, please remember that the context is this particular architecture and not a general dogma.

Background and History

I need to bore you with some background and history in an attempt to explain why things in my architecture are the way they are. I want to point out two or three things that have been the main influence on the state of things. First, you need to know that before .NET I had designed a MTS/COM+ architecture. With the arrival of .NET, the (home-brewed) concepts from the old architecture weren't more than a few years old, and thus were barely "cemented" in people's (developers') minds and too expensive to lose.[2] The second thing you need to know is that my architecture isn't necessarily "the best" I could think of. I hope it is a good balance between state of the art design/development techniques, the skills of the personnel using it, and the quality/cost ratio requested.

Overview of the Architecture

What then are the concepts of my architecture? Those of you familiar with MTS/COM+ have been thoroughly taught the concepts of stateless OO programming (a contradiction in terms?). The process object [Ewald TxCOM+] is a stateless object representing a single, entire *Business Object* (BO) in one instance. It contains the full set of operations for one or a set of business objects of a particular business object type. The statelessness grants you this possibility.

The basis in the architecture is a framework of collaborating classes. It is usable by itself, but to be really effective it has a companion tool, BODef (for a snapshot of a part of it, look ahead to Figure A-11), where you define your business objects and generate boilerplate code. The code generator is more than a wizard because it lets you generate time after time without losing manual code additions. It uses the Generation Gap pattern [Vlissides Pattern Hatching] to accomplish this. In Figure A-5, you can see one (partial) definition of the BOs of the problem at hand.

The "standard" way of dividing application classes is shown in Figure A-6. All packages/assemblies, except those marked with <<framework>>, are application specific. The BoSupport assembly is supposed to be available not only in the middle tier but also in Remoting clients. The rich client required in Jimmy's problem challenge is going to communicate with the middle tier via Remoting.[3]

---

[2]If you work as a "technology leader" in an IT department, I'm sure you've noticed that when you are ready to move on to the next thing, people around you haven't really grasped what you've been talking about lately.

[3]Jimmy's note: As I mentioned in the introduction to this appendix, an application server was in the requirement from the beginning but was removed later on.

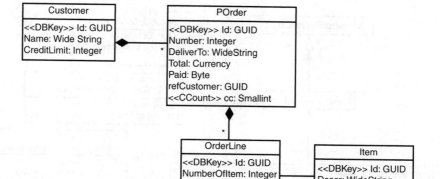

Figure A-5 BOs for the example

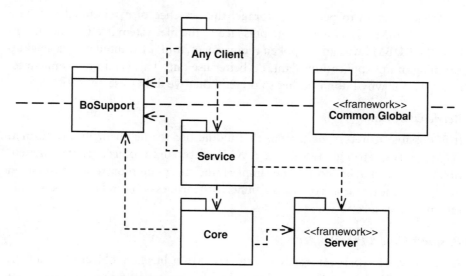

Figure A-6 Overall architecture

The Service assembly should contain at least one façade object that implements some basic interfaces to support basic CRUD, IBvDBOReq being the most important; see Figure A-7.

This façade isn't generated; instead, you inherit all base functionality (from FacadeBase), including the implementation of the mentioned interfaces.

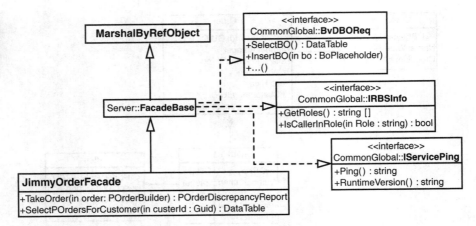

Figure A-7   Architecture for the facade

When it comes to persistent storage, the presence of a relational database system (RDBMS) is as sure as the presence of the file system itself at the site. In fact, the RDBMS was an unspoken requirement, and if I wanted proper backup handling of my applications data, I'd better use one. This is an important statement. This is why I don't bother to pretend that we didn't use an RDBMS.

Retrieval of Data

It is possible to return data from the middle tier to the client in any format: DataTable, DataSet, strongly typed DataSet, XML or serialized object graphs, to mention a few (or maybe most). The simplest and most common return format (in my case) is the DataTable. To return a bunch of "business object data," you simply return each as a row.

Business Object Placeholder

A row in the DataTable can easily be converted to a business object placeholder, BoPlaceholder. The BoPlaceholder class, located in the BoSupport assembly, is usable in its own right, but it's also the base class of specific business object placeholders.

The specific placeholders, one of them being POrderPh (purchase order) in Figure A-8, are generated by BODef. The Impl class is generated each time you choose generate. The leaf class is only generated once, which is pretty much the essence of the Generation Gap pattern.

You might think of these placeholder objects as information carriers or data transfer objects, but they might be used in more complex behavior scenarios.

And, yes, the BoPlaceholder derivates are in the BoSupport assembly, which is supposed to be present at both the middle tier and in the client tier (the rich/fat client).

You can return a DataTable from the middle tier to the client, leaving it to transform from DataRow instances to BoPlaceholder instances. You can also return a set (ArrayList, for instance) of BoPlaceholders to be used directly in the client. BoPlaceholder is serializable. However, remember that you can find loads of samples out there of how to databind a DataTable, but samples of data bound BoPlaceholders, although possible, are rare.

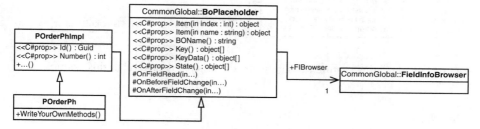

Figure A-8 Usage of BoPlaceholder

Process Objects

The final execution and enforcement of the business rules is a job for the core business objects, also known as the process objects. These objects are stateless and very short-lived. You can see the POrder process object in Figure A-9 and see that they follow the generation gap pattern. These objects are implemented in the Core assembly. Because I consider authorization to be a core part of business rules, it's no surprise that roles are specified on (public) methods of these objects.

Despite the fact that business rule enforcement is the responsibility of the core objects, one of them being POrder in Figure A-9, it is still very possible to implement the business rules in the BoSupport assembly and thus make them available in the rich client. However, when I do that I always make sure I double-check the rules in the process objects before persisting the changes. You see, it is very possible that a client has overridden a rule, say the upper order limit, perhaps via reflection, before submitting it to the façade object in the middle tier.

The process objects are often handed BoPlaceholders and are "hidden" behind a façade object. The process object and the placeholder, such as POrder and POrderPh, are conceptually parts of the same (logical) business object.

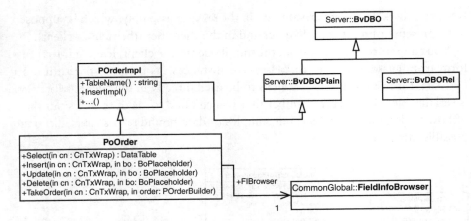

Figure A-9 Locating custom rules in `POrder`, the `TakeOrder()` method in this example

Metadata

As you might have noticed in some of the previous figures, there's plenty of metadata available in the framework classes. A more complete picture of the metadata, although not explained in depth, is found in Figure A-10. The metadata can give you some dynamics, both on data storage handling and UI handling.

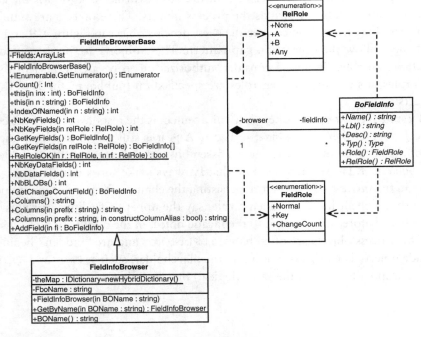

Figure A-10 A complete picture of the metadata

SQL statements in the middle tier are dynamically constructed from metadata, and you get a fairly good and very well-proven implementation. Should you discover bottlenecks, you have the freedom to implement the SQL handling your own way, such as by using stored procedures.

Jimmy's Order Application Exercise

Let's turn our interest to Jimmy's problem, the order-handling application. I imagine that the user of the order placement functionality (application) is someone speaking with (serving) a customer over the phone. Let's call this person an order taker. The fat client sort of implies this, if you see my point. One could easily imagine the desire for an e-commerce application, if not now then in the future. I don't think this has a big impact on the design should we go that way, but still, my interpretation of the scenario will affect, for instance, what roles we need in the system. I have the roles User and Admin. User can do most stuff and Admin can do just about anything. (With an e-commerce app you might need, say, a PublicUser role.)

I've cut out most real-world attributes to keep it compact. Most of that stuff, such as the customer's invoice address and order delivery address, isn't particularly difficult to handle. In the early phases of real application development, I often concentrate on the relationship between objects (and on their behavior and collaboration, of course) rather than on specific attributes anyway.

Simple Registry Handling

This problem demands the handling of customer data. This is what I would call a bread and butter registry handling functionality. I just have to show you my solution to this because it reveals some of my ideas and the potential for including metadata for the business objects.

Figure A-11 is a snapshot from my business object definition tool, BODef, showing you the Customer object. You can see that besides the field name and its type, there's more information attached to a field.

Figure A-11 The Customer class in BODef

In Figure A-12, which shows a form in the order application, the labels are taken from the metadata. With this grid you can add, edit and delete customers. The code to achieve this is rather compact (see the following code listing). The magic is all in the generic TableHandler, a class that takes advantage of the metadata of the Customer BO as well as of the generic façade interface, IBvDBOReq, and the BoPlaceholder and DataRow relationship of the architecture.

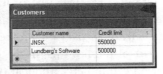

Figure A-12   A default implementation of the Customer

```
public CustomerFormList()
{
  InitializeComponent();

  _tabHndlr = new TableHandlerGuid(SvcFactory.Facade,
    CustomerPh.FieldInfoBrowser.BOName);
  _tabHndlr.TableChanged += new
    TableHandler.TableHandlerEventHandler
    (TableHandlerEventHandler);
  _tabHndlr.HookUpGrid(grd);
  _tabHndlr.FillGrid();
}
TableHandler _tabHndlr;

string[] confirmString = new string[] {
  "Do you want to add Customer?",
  "Do you want to save changes to Customer?",
  "Do you want to delete Customer?" };

void TableHandlerEventHandler(object sender,
  TableHandler.TableHandlerChangedEventArgs args)
{
  args.AcceptChanges = MessageBox.Show(
    confirmString[(int)args.TableHandlerChangeType],
    "Confirm", MessageBoxButtons.YesNo) == DialogResult.Yes;
}
```

There's no point in describing each little detail. You might want to take away ideas of what you can do with metadata. And not shown here, it's possible to have metadata describing the relationships between business objects, too. (Association objects are first-class citizens in my architecture.)

PRAGMATISM AND THE NONTRADITIONAL APPROACH

477

Pragmatism
and the
Nontraditional
Approach

Order Placement Business Rules

You can sort of read between the lines in Jimmy's problem description and see that this is where he wants us guest writers to dig in. Sure, I'm game.

Let me first tell you what I choose not to comment on in the problem description, which isn't the same as not having it implemented. The search problem is ignored. In my priority list, it was disqualified due to lack of space. The same goes for the per customer order listing. The creditability of a new customer went the same way. I have classified the unique number of the order as a minor challenge in my fake scenario. I simply assign it at the time when an order is submitted—the order taker gets it returned at that point and doesn't need it before then.

Good support for the order taking/fill-in process is a given. I pictured a "builder"[4] that's used to manipulate the order form (think piece of paper), the order form being the metaphor I'll reason around. I also imagined this builder as a serializable object that is, upon completion, submitted from the client to the middle tier.

The multi-user aspect adds a few tough issues to solve. For instance, when the order taker talks to the presumptive customer and the price of an item is changed, should he get to know that immediately? It doesn't help that the price is checked with the item repository because if you retrieve the price at 10:55 a.m. and list it on the screen, it might very well be changed at 10:56 a.m. The same problem exists for your stock; is the item available or do you need to order it from your supplier?

One way to solve this problem is to have the middle tier notify all clients (order takers) as soon as there is a price or stock change so that the client can take measures for this. However, this would complicate things considerably. The client is no longer only talking to the middle tier, the middle tier is also, on its own initiative so to speak, talking to all the (active) clients. And besides that, the timing problem isn't eliminated, only minimized.

I want to keep it simple but still support the needs. I need to look at the business process. The order taker talks with a customer on the phone. They discuss what the customer needs, and price and availability is communicated. Eventually the customer decides to buy, and the order taker submits the order to the middle tier. In response, the middle tier returns a report. The report states the final prices and availability. The latter will have an impact on delivery date. All discrepancies with the previously (orally) given facts are marked in the report (if any). The order taker discusses them with the customer and if he is unhappy

---

[4]You can, for instance, think of the StringBuilder class that is used to build a string.

with that, the order can be cancelled. Cancelling the order is a transaction of its own, an undo/delete transaction.

I understand that if you give a price to a customer you may have to stick to it—to some extent at least.[5] This can be corrected quite easily. One cheap way is to leave the price setting to a few people who only change prices after business hours. Another way is to have the system itself postpone effectuation of price changes to the next non-dealing moment. If the client caches price information, she must somehow have the knowledge to refresh (or drop) the cache on suitable/strategic occasions.

The problem with availability (stock) is, however, in contrast to prices, a dynamic one. Therefore, the need to have a report given as a response to an order submitted stands. It might as well report any price discrepancies found even if a policy to avoid that is implemented, just to be sure. The report will also have the final say on whether the order is within the global maximum limit or not and if the customer's credit is exceeded or not.

When an order is persisted, we stick to the price given. We don't want to tick our customer off with an invoice with higher prices than promised. This forces us to store the promised prices (OrderPrice in Figure A-5) with the order instead of just referring to the item (that has a price). An alternative is to have price history on the items, which is too much of a hassle. And, yes, we do not "reopen" submitted orders for complementing items in case of, say, the customer realizing he wants three instead of two of something shortly after talking to us. We might place an order with no cost for delivery and/or invoicing to take care of this situation.[6] Changing an order line to fewer items is another story that we can handle easily (it might affect high-volume discounts in the real world).

POrderBuilder   The support for taking and handling purchase orders is within the class POrderBuilder. It's a class meant to be used both in client and middle tier, and it's transported via serialization over the wire. POrderBuilder interacts with the warehouse on several occasions, such as when an order line is created when AddItemToOrder() is called. This interaction is captured in an abstraction called ItemStore consisting of one single method, GetItem().

The discrepancy report is created by POrderBuilder when calling the method CheckDiscrepancies(). The typical scenario is that the client uses a local version of ItemStore—see more in the section ItemStore—and different implementations in client, server and test, which gives prices and stock during the conversation with

---

[5]If you, an order taker, misread two zeros in the price, are you then liable?
[6]This is one of the many problems in a toy sample like this that are not stated well.

the customer. When the order is completed, the order taker submits it to the middle tier. At some point the middle tier calls CheckDiscrepancies() on the passed POrderBuilder to produce the report. At this point the ItemStore is an object living in the middle tier close to the database.

To have CheckDiscrepancies() as a method on POrderBuilder is appealing when it comes to unit testing. Take a look at the next code listing. A POrderBuilder, bldr, is created at [SetUp], where it is also populated with a few order lines. The itmStore is a stub ItemStore also created and associated with bldr during [SetUp]. The test simulates, in the first row, how the situation in the ItemStore has changed regarding stock when it is time to produce that discrepancy report. See the following code:

```
[Test]
public void Stock()
{
  itmStore.Items[0].Stock = 1;

  POrderDiscrepancyReport r = bldr.CheckDiscrepancies();
  Assert.AreEqual(0, r.PriceCount);
  Assert.AreEqual(1, r.StockCount);
  Assert.AreEqual(1, r.GetStockAt(0).NumberOfMissingItems);
}
```

Please picture how the discrepancy report is created early in the order submit handling before the order is committed. However, there is a problem concerning transaction handling here, a problem that is often overlooked or oversimplified. If you're not careful, the check can come out alright, in other words without any discrepancies, but when you commit the order, for instance the last item in stock has been "assigned" to another order and customer. I'm saying that the discrepancy check should happen in the same transaction as the order commit and with locks that prevent others from "stealing" items from the warehouse that you're about to sell.

ItemStore—Different Implementations in Client, Server, and Test It might be interesting to take a closer look at ItemStore. I talked about a local client version as well as a middle tier, transactional, version in the text earlier. What's that all about? Well, let me show you.

In Figure A-13 you can see how POrderBuilder holds a reference to an ItemStore. The reference is implemented as a public property that is assigned by the application code. In the client I use an implementation of ItemStore that is, and I'm sorry if I overstate this, very different from the transactional implementation that I use in the middle tier during order submit. ItemStore isn't much of an interface to implement when it comes to the number of methods; however, it is very central to the POrderBuilder. The ItemStore is, for instance, used by all methods showed in Figure A-13.

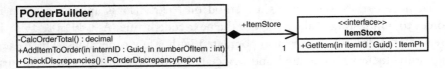

Figure A-13   The relationship between POrderBuilder and ItemStore

I've implemented the client version of ItemStore as a simple "read all items from store and cache." This strategy is fine as long as the number of items isn't too great. If it comes to that, it's no big deal to implement a version that queries the middle tier "smarter." In the client, when the order taker has the privilege to "work with an order," a POrderBuilder is instantiated and assigned an instance of the client side ItemStore implementation. At any time, a CheckDiscrepancies() against the client ItemStore is possible.

If the customer accepts, the next step is submission of the order to the middle tier. The POrderBuilder instance is serialized over the wire, but not the ItemStore instance. The reference to ItemStore is marked as [NonSerialized]. In the façade object, a connection/transaction is created and the job to take the order is handed over to the process object (the business object). This is shown in here:

```
public POrderDiscrepancyReport TakeOrder(POrderBuilder order)
{
  POrder bo = new POrder();
  CnTxWrap cn =
      CnTxWrap.BeginTransaction(bo.CreateConnectionForMe() );
  try
  {
    POrderDiscrepancyReport res = bo.TakeOrder(cn, order);
    cn.Commit();
    return res;
  }
  catch
  {
    cn.Rollback();
    throw;
  }
}
```

While we're at it, let's take a look at the process object's TakeOrder() method in the following listing:

```
[PrincipalPermission(SecurityAction.Demand, Role = Roles.User)]
[PrincipalPermission(SecurityAction.Demand, Role =
  @"InternalUnitTesting")]
public POrderDiscrepancyReport TakeOrder(CnTxWrap cn,
  POrderBuilder order)
{
  ItemStore itmStore = new TxItemStore(cn);
  order.ItemStore = itmStore;
  POrderDiscrepancyReport res = order.CheckDiscrepancies();

  POrderPh ordr =
    ((POrderBuilder.IOrderInternal)order.POrder).POrder;
  new POrder().InsertNoRBS(cn, ordr);

  OrderLine olproc = new OrderLine();
  for(int i=0; i<order.OrderLineCount; i++)
  {
    OrderLinePh ol =
      ((POrderBuilder.IOrderLineInternal)order[i]).OrderLine;
    olproc.InsertNoRBS(cn, ol);
  }

  return res;
}
```

You can see how ItemStore is actually an instance of TxItemStore that is passed the parameter cn containing/wrapping a database connection and an ongoing transaction. This implementation of ItemStore reads the store with an UPDLOCK hint (or whatever method you prefer), causing the store to be locked for update by others at this point. Granted, this is something of a bottleneck but correctness is high.

CheckDiscrepancies() will throw an exception in case there are severe business rule violations, such as if the global maximum limit is exceeded. If the only discrepancies are price differences or stock shortage, these will be noted in the report, but the order will be fully placed.

Do you remember what I said about double-checking business rules that "run" on both the client and the server? The essence is never to trust the client. Well, the checking is done in CheckDiscrepancies(). For instance, any tampering with the prices on the client side would come out as a discrepancy. In this particular situation, the client is running in your controlled environment, but you should nevertheless be cautious. Code executing on the server is much safer than code on the client. Remember that the server can't know (not generally) if the caller is your program sending information on the wire or if it's another program.

Summary

Some Final Points

Let's be honest. This isn't what most people would call pure OO. For instance, I'm not afraid of using somewhat "weaker" object references than the language itself provides. Have a look at my item reference in the form of a Guid in Figure A-13. But if you're a bit daring, ask yourself what's so obvious about using "pointer" references anyway. Compare it to proxy references, which give you an option of late/lazy instantiation.

What I want to say is don't get hung up on what's right and what's wrong. Generally, there is no such thing (I'm sure Jimmy agrees). Get the job done. Supply your business with the software it needs. Know what your design goals are (for instance, having the business rules in one place), and realize them.

◆

Summary

Now I'm back again; Jimmy, that is. It's time to summarize the style variations just described by Mats, Frans, and Ingo. Which one is best? It depends! Life is full of tradeoffs! Would you like to hear some more very good and useful nuggets? What is good and what is bad about the different styles? Here's another good nugget: Make your own decisions, for your own specific situations.

I'm sure you got my point here. As you understand, I didn't ask my friends to write some about their ideas on the subject to see which approach is best. I asked them write about this problem to get you some exposure to other points of view and some inspiration from other styles.

If I were to write micro-summaries of their styles, I would express it like this. In Mats' case, I believe the title is a great summary, namely "Object-Oriented Data Model, Smart Service Layer, and Documents." Mats is fond of locating the behavior in the Service Layer and seeing the Domain Model as an object-oriented representation of the data. "Documents" is about the exchange format between different tiers.

Frans stresses the importance of using the power of the database and that the representation in the database is the true one.

Ingo talks about the importance of finding the right abstractions and that you shouldn't expect to be able to use a single standard style for all situations. Add to that a big chunk of pragmatism.

Appendix B

Catalog of Discussed Patterns

This appendix is a catalog of the patterns that are discussed in the book. No new information is to be found here; instead, this is intended to be a service to the reader. You'll find here the source of the pattern where you can read more, a *very* condensed description, and most often a URL where you can instantly get more information.

Note

You find this appendix online as well if you would like it to be clickable: www.jnsk.se/adddp/patterns

---

When the description is written between quotation marks, that means that the description is taken directly from the provided URL (or from the mentioned book's inner cover in the case of some of the [GoF Design Patterns]).

Abstract Factory [GoF Design Patterns]

"Provides an interface for creating families of dependent objects without specifying their concrete classes."
http://patternshare.org/default.aspx/Home.GOF.AbstractFactory

Aggregate [Evans DDD]

Cluster Entities and Value Objects with a boundary. Let one of the Entities in the Aggregate be the access point (the Aggregate root).
http://patternshare.org/default.aspx/Home.DDD.Aggregates

Bounded Context [Evans DDD]

Define a boundary around a distinct model.
http://patternshare.org/default.aspx/Home.DDD.BoundedContext

Chain of Responsibility [GoF Design Patterns]

"Avoid coupling the sender of a request to its receiver by giving more than one object a chance to handle the request. Chain the receiving objects and pass the request along the chain until an object handles it."

Class Table Inheritance [Fowler PoEAA]

"Represents an inheritance hierarchy of classes with one table for each class."
http://www.martinfowler.com/eaaCatalog/classTableInheritance.html

Coarse-Grained Lock [Fowler PoEAA]

"Locks a set of related objects with a single lock."
http://www.martinfowler.com/eaaCatalog/coarseGrainedLock.html

Collecting Parameter Pattern [Beck SBPP]

An object to pass to methods for collecting information from the methods.

Concrete Table Inheritance [Fowler PoEAA]

"Represents an inheritance hierarchy of classes with one table per concrete class in the hierarchy."
http://www.martinfowler.com/eaaCatalog/concreteTableInheritance.html

Data Mapper [Fowler PoEAA]

"A layer of Mappers that moves data between objects and a database while keeping them independent of each other and the mapper itself."
http://www.martinfowler.com/eaaCatalog/dataMapper.html

Data Transfer Objects [Fowler PoEAA]

"An object that carries data between processes in order to reduce the number of method calls."
http://www.martinfowler.com/eaaCatalog/dataTransferObject.html

Decorator [GoF Design Patterns]

"Attaches additional responsibilities to an object dynamically. Decorators provide a flexible alternative to subclassing for extending functionality."
http://patternshare.org/default.aspx/Home.GOF.Decorator

Dependency Injection

Instead of letting the instance look up its own dependencies, inject the dependencies to the instance.

Domain Model [Fowler PoEAA]

"An object model of the domain that incorporates both behavior and data."
http://www.martinfowler.com/eaaCatalog/domainModel.html

Embedded Value [Fowler PoEAA]

"Maps an object into several fields of another object's table."
http://www.martinfowler.com/eaaCatalog/embeddedValue.html

Entity [Evans DDD]

"Many objects are not fundamentally defined by their attributes, but rather by a thread of continuity and identity."
http://patternshare.org/default.aspx/Home.DDD.Entities

Factory [Evans DDD]

"When creation of an object, or an entire aggregate, becomes complicated or reveals too much of the internal structure, factories provide encapsulation."
http://patternshare.org/default.aspx/Home.DDD.Factories

Factory Method [GoF Design Patterns]

"Define an interface for creating an object, but let subclasses decide which class to instantiate. Factory Method lets a class defer instantiation to subclasses."

Foreign Key Mapping [Fowler PoEAA]

"Maps an association between objects to a foreign key reference between tables."
http://www.martinfowler.com/eaaCatalog/foreignKeyMapping.html

Generation Gap [Vlissides Pattern Hatching]

"Modify or extend generated code just once no matter how many times it is regenerated."
http://www.research.ibm.com/designpatterns/pubs/gg.html

Identity Field [Fowler PoEAA]

"Saves a database ID field in an object to maintain identity between an in-memory object and a database row."
http://www.martinfowler.com/eaaCatalog/identityField.html

Identity Map [Fowler PoEAA]

"Ensures that each object gets loaded only once by keeping every loaded object in a map. Looks up objects using the map when referring to them."
http://www.martinfowler.com/eaaCatalog/identityMap.html

Implicit Lock [Fowler PoEAA]

"Allows framework or layer supertype code to acquire offline locks."
http://www.martinfowler.com/eaaCatalog/implicitLock.html

Layer Supertype [Fowler PoEAA]

"A type that acts as the supertype for all types in its layer."
http://www.martinfowler.com/eaaCatalog/layerSupertype.html

Layers [POSA]

(Also in [Fowler PoEAA].)
"Structures applications that can be decomposed into groups of subtasks in which each group of subtasks is at a particular level of abstraction."
http://patternshare.org/default.aspx/Home.POSA.Layers

Lazy Load [Fowler PoEAA]

"An object that doesn't contain all of the data you need but knows how to get it."
http://www.martinfowler.com/eaaCatalog/lazyLoad.html

Metadata Mapping [Fowler PoEAA]

"Holds details of object-relational mapping in metadata."
http://www.martinfowler.com/eaaCatalog/metadataMapping.html

Model View Controller [Fowler PoEAA]

"Splits user interface interaction into three distinct roles."
http://www.martinfowler.com/eaaCatalog/modelViewController.html

Model View Presenter [Fowler PoEAA2]

"Separates the behavior of a presentation from the view while allowing the view to receive user events."
http://www.martinfowler.com/eaaDev/ModelViewPresenter.html

Notification [Fowler PoEAA2]

"An object that collects together information about errors and other information in the domain layer and communicates it to the presentation."
http://www.martinfowler.com/eaaDev/Notification.html

Null Object [Woolf Null Object]

An object that provides default data and behavior when there would otherwise have been a null reference.

Optimistic Offline Lock [Fowler PoEAA]

"Prevents conflicts between concurrent business transactions by detecting a conflict and rolling back the transaction."
http://www.martinfowler.com/eaaCatalog/optimisticOfflineLock.html

Party Archetype [Arlow/Neustadt Archetype Patterns]

A way to represent information about people and organizations.

Pessimistic Offline Lock [Fowler PoEAA]

"Prevents conflicts between concurrent business transactions by allowing only one business transaction at a time to access data."
http://www.martinfowler.com/eaaCatalog/pessimisticOfflineLock.html

Pipes and Filters [POSA]

Channel the data through Pipes and process the stream in Filters.

Presentation Model [Fowler PoEAA2]

"Represent the state and behavior of the presentation independently of the GUI controls used in the interface."
http://www.martinfowler.com/eaaDev/PresentationModel.html

Proxy [GoF Design Patterns]

"Provides a surrogate or placeholder for another object to control access to it."
http://patternshare.org/default.aspx/Home.GOF.Proxy

Query Object [Fowler PoEAA]

"An object that represents a database query."
http://www.martinfowler.com/eaaCatalog/queryObject.html

Recordset [Fowler PoEAA]

"An in-memory representation of tabular data."
http://www.martinfowler.com/eaaCatalog/recordSet.html

Reflection [POSA]

Makes it possible via metadata to programmatically inspect the type of an instance and interact with the instance without knowing anything about the type beforehand.

Registry [Fowler PoEAA]

"A well-known object that other objects can use to find common objects and services."
http://www.martinfowler.com/eaaCatalog/registry.html

Remote Façade [Fowler PoEAA]

"Provides a coarse-grained façade on fine-grained objects to improve efficiency over a network."
http://www.martinfowler.com/eaaCatalog/remoteFacade.html

Repository [Evans DDD]

(Also in [Fowler PoEAA].)
An object for locating a certain Entity (or a set of Entities) that is in the middle of the life cycle.
http://patternshare.org/default.aspx/Home.DDD.Repositories

Separated Presentation [Fowler PoEAA2]

"Ensure that any code that manipulates presentation only manipulates presentation, pushing all domain and data source logic into clearly separated areas of the program."
http://www.martinfowler.com/eaaDev/SeparatedPresentation.html

Service Layer [Fowler PoEAA]

"Defines an application's boundary with a layer of services that establishes a set of available operations and coordinates the application's response in each operation."
http://www.martinfowler.com/eaaCatalog/serviceLayer.html

Service Locator [Alur/Crupi/Malks Core J2EE Patterns]

"Use a Service Locator to implement and encapsulate service and component lookup. A Service Locator hides the implementation details of the lookup mechanism and encapsulates related dependencies."
http://www.corej2eepatterns.com/Patterns2ndEd/ServiceLocator.htm

Services [Evans DDD]

Responsibilities that don't naturally fit into Entities or Value Objects can be factored out to Services.
http://patternshare.org/default.aspx/Home.DDD.Services

Single Table Inheritance [Fowler PoEAA]

"Represents an inheritance hierarchy of classes as a single table that has columns for all the fields of the various classes."
http://www.martinfowler.com/eaaCatalog/singleTableInheritance.html

Singleton [GoF Design Patterns]

"Singleton ensures a class only has one instance, and provides a global point of access to it."
http://patternshare.org/default.aspx/Home.GOF.Singleton

Specification [Evans DDD]

(Also in [Fowler Analysis Patterns].)
Captures and exposes predicates with concept describing names.

State [GoF Design Patterns]

"Allow an object to alter its behavior when its internal state changes. The object will appear to change its class."

Table Module [Fowler PoEAA]

"A single instance that handles the business logic for all rows in a database table or view."
http://www.martinfowler.com/eaaCatalog/tableModule.html

Template Method [GoF Design Patterns]

"Defines the skeleton of an algorithm in an operation, deferring some steps to subclasses. Template Method lets subclasses redefine certain steps of an algorithm without changing the algorithm's structure."
http://patternshare.org/default.aspx/Home.GOF.TemplateMethod

Transaction Script [Fowler PoEAA]

"Organizes business logic by procedures where each procedure handles a single request from the presentation."
http://www.martinfowler.com/eaaCatalog/transactionScript.html

Unit of Work [Fowler PoEAA]

"Maintains a list of objects affected by a business transaction and coordinates the writing out of changes and the resolution of concurrency problems."
http://www.martinfowler.com/eaaCatalog/unitOfWork.html

Value Object [Evans DDD]

(Also in [Fowler PoEAA].)
"Many objects have no conceptual identity. These objects describe some characteristic of a thing."
http://patternshare.org/default.aspx/Home.DDD.ValueObjects

References

[Alexander Pattern Language]
Alexander, Christopher, Sara Ishikawa, and Murray Silverstein with Max
Jacobson, Ingrid Fiksdahl-King, and Shlomo Angel. *A Pattern Language:
Towns, Buildings, Construction*. New York: Oxford University Press, 1977.

[Alur/Crupi/Malks Core J2EE Patterns]
Alur, Deepak, John Crupi, and Dan Malks. *Core J2EE Patterns, Second Edition: Best Practices and Design Strategies*. New Jersey: Prentice Hall, 2003.

[Arlow/Neustadt Archetype Patterns]
Arlow, Jim, and Ila Neustadt. *Enterprise Patterns and MDA: Building Better
Software with Archetype Patterns and UML*. Boston, MA: Addison-Wesley,
2004.

[AspectJ]
http://eclipse.org/aspectj/

[AspectSharp]
http://www.castleproject.org/index.php/AspectSharp

[Astels TDD]
Astels, David. *Test Driven Development. A Practical Guide*. New Jersey:
Prentice Hall, 2004.

[Bauer/King HiA]
Bauer, Christian, and Gavin King. *Hibernate in Action*. Greenwich, CT:
Manning, 2005.

[Beck SBPP]
Beck, Kent. *Smalltalk Best Practice Patterns*. New Jersey: Prentice Hall, 1997.

[Beck TDD]
Beck, Kent. *Test-Driven Development: By Example*. Boston, MA:
Addison-Wesley, 2003.

[Beck XP]
Beck, Kent. *Extreme Programming Explained: Embrace Change*. Boston, MA:
Addison-Wesley, 2000.

[Bloch Effective Java]
Bloch, Joshua. *Effective Java Programming Language Guide*. Boston, MA: Addison-Wesley, 2001.

[Booch OOAD]
Booch, Grady. *Object-Oriented Analysis and Design with Applications, Second Edition*. Reading, MA: Addison-Wesley, 1994.

[Bosch Product Line]
Bosch, Jan. *Design and Use of Software Architectures: Adopting and Evolving a Product-Line Approach*. Boston, MA: Addison-Wesley, 2000.

[POSA]
Buschmann, Frank, Regine Meunier, Hans Rohnert, and Peter Sommerlad, and Michael Stal. *Pattern-Oriented Software Architecture. A System of Patterns*. New York: Wiley, 1996.

[Castle]
http://www.castleproject.org/

[Cattell ODM]
Cattell, R.G.G. *Object Data Management: Object-Oriented and Extended Relational Database Systems*. Reading, MA: Addison-Wesley, 1994.

[CC.NET]
http://confluence.public.thoughtworks.org/display/CCNET

[Chen ER]
Chen, P. "The entity-relationship model—toward a unified view of data." *ACM Transactions on database systems*, vol.1 no.1, 1976.

[Cockburn Agile]
Cockburn, Alistair. *Agile Software Development*. Boston, MA: Addison-Wesley, 2002.

[Codd Relational Model]
Codd, E. F. "A Relational Model of Data for Large Shared Data Banks." *Communications of the ACM*, vol. 13 #6, 1970.

[Connolly/Begg DB Systems]
Connolly, Thomas M. and Carolyn E. Begg. *Database Systems, Fourth Edition: A Practical Approach to Design, Implementation, and Management*. Boston, MA: Addison-Wesley, 2004.

[Demeyer/Ducasse/Nierstrasz OORP]
Demeyer, Serge, Stéphane Ducasse, and Oscar Nierstrasz. *Object-Oriented Reengineering Patterns*. San Francisco: Morgan Kaufmann, 2002.

[Enterprise Library Logging]
http://msdn.microsoft.com/library/default.asp?url=/library/en-us/dnpag2/html/
entlib.asp

[Evans DDD]
Evans, Eric. *Domain-Driven Design: Tackling Complexity in the Heart of
Software.* Boston, MA: Addison-Wesley, 2004.

[Ewald TxCOM+]
Ewald, Tim. *Transactional COM+: Building Scalable Applications.* Boston,
MA: Addison-Wesley, 2001.

[Feathers Humble Dialog Box]
Feathers, Michael. "The Humble Dialog Box."
http://www.objectmentor.com/resources/articles/TheHumbleDialogBox.pdf

[Feathers Self-Shunt]
Feathers, Michael. "The 'Self'-Shunt Unit Testing Pattern."
http://www.objectmentor.com/resources/articles/SelfShunPtrn.pdf

[Fowler Analysis Patterns]
Fowler, Martin. *Analysis Patterns: Reusable Object Models.* Reading, MA:
Addison-Wesley, 1997.

[Fowler FixedLengthString]
Fowler, Martin. http://martinfowler.com/bliki/FixedLengthString.html

[Fowler FluentInterface]
http://martinfowler.com/bliki/FluentInterface.html

[Fowler HarvestedFramework]
Fowler, Martin.
http://www.martinfowler.com/bliki/HarvestedFramework.html

[Fowler InversionOfControl]
Fowler, Martin. http://www.martinfowler.com/bliki/InversionOfControl.html

[Fowler LW]
Fowler, Martin. "Language Workbenches: The Killer-App for Domain Specific
Languages?" http://www.martinfowler.com/articles/languageWorkbench.html

[Fowler Mocks Aren't Stubs]
Fowler, Martin. "Mocks Aren't Stubs."
http://martinfowler.com/articles/mocksArentStubs.html

[Fowler PoEAA]
Fowler, Martin. *Patterns of Enterprise Application Architecture.* Boston, MA:
Addison-Wesley, 2003.

[Fowler PoEAA2]
Fowler, Martin. http://martinfowler.com/eaaDev/

[Fowler R]
Fowler, Martin. *Refactoring: Improving the Design of Existing Code*. Reading, MA: Addison-Wesley, 1999.

[Fowler Snapshot]
http://www.martinfowler.com/ap2/snapshot.html

[Fowler UML Distilled]
Fowler, Martin. *UML Distilled, Third Edition: A Brief Guide to the Standard Object Modeling Language*. Boston, MA: Addison-Wesley, 2004.

[Fowler/Foemmel CI]
Fowler, Martin, and Foemmel, Matt.
http://www.martinfowler.com/articles/continuousIntegration.html

[GoF Design Patterns]
Gamma, Erich, Richard Helm, Ralph Johnson, and John M. Vlissides. *Design Patterns: Elements of Reusable Object-Oriented Software*. Reading, MA: Addison-Wesley, 1995.

[Greenfield/Short SF]
Greenfield, Jack, and Keith Short. *Software Factories: Assembling Applications with Patterns, Models, Frameworks, and Tools*. Indianapolis, IN: Wiley, 2004.

[Gregor Kiczales]
http://www.cs.ubc.ca/~gregor/

[Halpin IMRD]
Halpin, Terry. *Information Modeling and Relational Databases: From Conceptual Analysis to Logical Design*. San Francisco: Morgan Kaufmann, 2001.

[Halpin/Nijssen Conceptual Schema]
Halpin, T.A. and G.M. Nijssen. *Conceptual Schema and Relational Database Design: A Fact Oriented Approach*. New Jersey: Prentice Hall, 1989.

[Hay Data Model Patterns]
Hay, David. *Data Model Patterns: Conventions of thought*. New York: Dorset House, 1996.

[Hibernate]
http://hibernate.org

[Hohpe/Woolf EIP]
Hohpe, Gregor and Bobby Woolf. *Enterprise Integration Patterns. Designing, Building, and Deploying Messaging Solutions.* Boston, MA: Addison-Wesley, 2004.

[iBATIS]
http://ibatis.apache.org/

[Jacobson OOSE]
Jacobson, Ivar, Magnus Christerson, Patrik Jonsson, and Gunnar Overgaard. *Object-Oriented Software Engineering: A Use Case Driven Approach.* Reading, MA: Addison-Wesley, 1992.

[Johnson J2EE Development without EJB]
Johnson, Rod with Juergen Hoeller. *Expert one-on-one J2EE Development without EJB.* Indianapolis, IN: Wiley, 2004.

[Jordan/Russell JDO]
Jordan, David, and Craig Russel. *Java Data Objects.* Sebastopol, CA: O'Reilly, 2003.

[Kerievsky R2P]
Kerievsky, Joshua. *Refactoring to Patterns.* Boston, MA: Addison-Wesley, 2005.

[Lhotka BO]
Lhotka, Rocky. *Expert C# Business Objects.* Berkeley, CA: APress, 2004.

[Log4Net]
http://logging.apache.org/log4net/

[Loom.NET]
http://www.dcl.hpi.uni-potsdam.de/research/loom/

[Löwy Programming .NET Components]
Löwy, Juval. *Programming .NET Components.* Second Edition. Cambridge, MA: O'Reilly, 2005.

[Martin PPP]
Martin, Robert C. *Agile Software Development: Principles, Patterns, and Practices.* New Jersey: Prentice Hall, 2002.

[Meszaros XUnit]
Meszaros, Gerard. http://tap.testautomationpatterns.com:8080/index.html

[Meyer OOSC]
Meyer, Bertrand. *Object-Oriented Software Construction, Second Edition.*
New Jersey: Prentice Hall, 2000.

[MockObjects]
http://sourceforge.net/projects/dotnetmock

[MVC History]
http://c2.com/cgi/wiki?ModelViewControllerHistory

[NanoContainer]
http://www.nanocontainer.org/

[NHibernate]
http://nhibernate.sourceforge.net

[Nicola et al. SOM]
Nicola, Jill, Mark Mayfield, and Mike Abney. *Streamlined Object Modeling:
Patterns, Rules, and Implementation.* New Jersey: Prentice Hall, 2002.

[Nilsson COMB]
Nilsson, Jimmy. *The Cost of GUIDs as Primary Keys.*
http://www.informit.com/articles/article.asp?p=25862

[Nilsson NED]
Nilsson, Jimmy. *.NET Enterprise Design with Visual Basic .NET and SQL
Server 2000.* Indianapolis, IN: Sams Publishing, 2001.

[Nilsson NWorkspace]
Nilsson, Jimmy. http://www.jnsk.se/nworkspace

[NMock]
http://www.nmock.org

[NUnit]
http://www.nunit.org

[OMG MDA]
http://www.omg.org/mda/

[Pawson/Matthews Naked Objects]
Pawson, Richard, and Robert Matthews. *Naked Objects.* New York:
Wiley, 2003.

[Pfister Wolfpack]
Gregory F. Pfister. *In Search of Clusters.* Upper Saddle River, NJ: Prentice
Hall, 1998.

[PicoContainer]
http://www.picocontainer.org/

[POCMock]
http://www.prettyobjects.com/pocmock.aspx

[Prevayler]
http://www.prevayler.org/wiki.jsp

[Refactor!]
http://www.devexpress.com

[ReSharper]
http://www.jetbrains.com

[Richter .NET Framework]
Richter, Jeffrey. *Applied Microsoft .NET Framework Programming.*
Redmond, Wash: Microsoft Press, 2002.

[Ross BRB]
Ross, Ronald. *The Business Rules Book: Classifying, Defining and Modeling
Rules. Second edition.* Houston, TX: Business Rule Solutions, 1997.

[Rumbaugh OMT]
Rumbaugh, James R., Michael R. Blaha, William Lorensen, Frederick Eddy,
and William Premerlani. *Object-Oriented Modeling and Design.* New Jersey:
Prentice Hall, 1990.

[SnapDAL]
http://sourceforge.net/projects/snapdal

[Spolsky Leaky Abstractions]
Spolsky, Joel. *The Law of Leaky Abstractions.*
http://www.joelonsoftware.com/articles/LeakyAbstractions.html

[Spring]
http://www.springframework.org/

[Spring.NET]
http://www.springframework.net/

[Szyperski Component Software]
Szyperski, Clemens. *Component Software, Second Edition.* Boston, MA:
Addison-Wesley, 2003.

[Testdriven.net]
http://www.testdriven.net

[Valhalla]
http://www.jnsk.se/weblog/posts/part7.htm

[Vlissides Pattern Hatching]
Vlissides, John M. *Pattern Hatching: Design Patterns Applied*. Reading, MA: Addison-Wesley, 1998.

[von Halle BRA]
von Halle, Barbara. *Business Rules Applied: Building Better Systems Using the Business Rules Approach*. New York: Wiley, 2001.

[Windsor]
http://www.castleproject.org/index.php/Container

[Woolf Null Object]
Woolf, Bobby. "The Null Object Pattern," in *Pattern Languages of Program Design III*. By Robert C. Martin, Dirk Riehle, and Frank Buschmann (Eds.). Reading, MA: Addison-Wesley, 1998.

[XtUnit]
http://weblogs.asp.net/rosherove/archive/2004/10/05/238201.aspx

Index

T

THIS BOOK IS SAFARI ENABLED

INCLUDES FREE 45-DAY ACCESS TO THE ONLINE EDITION

The Safari® Enabled icon on the cover of your favorite technology book means the book is available through Safari Bookshelf. When you buy this book, you get free access to the online edition for 45 days.

Safari Bookshelf is an electronic reference library that lets you easily search thousands of technical books, find code samples, download chapters, and access technical information whenever and wherever you need it.

TO GAIN 45-DAY SAFARI ENABLED ACCESS TO THIS BOOK:

- Go to **http://www.awprofessional.com/safarienabled**
- Complete the brief registration form
- Enter the coupon code found in the front of this book on the "Copyright" page

Addison
Wesley

If you have difficulty registering on Safari Bookshelf or accessing the online edition, please e-mail customer-service@safaribooksonline.com.

Register
Your Book

at www.awprofessional.com/register

You may be eligible to receive:

- Advance notice of forthcoming editions of the book
- Related book recommendations
- Chapter excerpts and supplements of forthcoming titles
- Information about special contests and promotions throughout the year
- Notices and reminders about author appearances, tradeshows, and online chats with special guests

Contact us

If you are interested in writing a book or reviewing manuscripts prior to publication, please write to us at:

Editorial Department
Addison-Wesley Professional
75 Arlington Street, Suite 300
Boston, MA 02116 USA
Email: AWPro@aw.com

Visit us on the Web: http://www.awprofessional.com

AVAILABLE FROM MARTIN FOWLER, ERIC EVANS, AND ADDISON-WESLEY

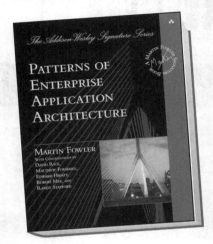

Patterns of Enterprise Application Architecture
MARTIN FOWLER

Patterns of Enterprise Application Architecture is written in direct response to the stiff challenges that face enterprise application developers. The author, noted object-oriented designer Martin Fowler, noticed that despite changes in technology—from Smalltalk to CORBA to Java to .NET—the same basic design ideas can be adapted and applied to solve common problems. With the help of an expert group of contributors, Martin distills over forty recurring solutions into patterns. The result is an indispensable handbook of solutions that are applicable to any enterprise application platform.

This book is actually two books in one. The first section is a short tutorial on developing enterprise applications, which you can read from start to finish to understand the scope of the book's lessons. The next section, the bulk of the book, is a detailed reference to the patterns themselves. Each pattern provides usage and implementation information, as well as detailed code examples in Java or C#. The entire book is also richly illustrated with UML diagrams to further explain the concepts.

Armed with this book, you will have the knowledge necessary to make important architectural decisions about building an enterprise application and the proven patterns for use when building them.

0-321-12742-0 • ©2003 • 560 pages

Domain-Driven Design
Tackling Complexity in the Heart of Software
ERIC EVANS

The software development community widely acknowledges that domain modeling is central to software design. Through domain models, software developers are able to express rich functionality and translate it into a software implementation that truly serves the needs of its users. But despite its obvious importance, there are few practical resources that explain how to incorporate effective domain modeling into the software development process.

Domain-Driven Design fills that need. This is not a book about specific technologies. It offers readers a systematic approach to domain-driven design, presenting an extensive set of design best practices, experience-based techniques, and fundamental principles that facilitate the development of software projects facing complex domains. Intertwining design and development practice, this book incorporates numerous examples based on actual projects to illustrate the application of domain-driven design to real-world software development.

0-321-12521-5 • ©2004 • 560 pages

Visit us online for more information about these books and to read sample chapters.
www.awprofessional.com

Addison
Wesley

informIT

www.informit.com

YOUR GUIDE TO IT REFERENCE

Articles

Keep your edge with thousands of free articles, in-depth features, interviews, and IT reference recommendations – all written by experts you know and trust.

Online Books

Answers in an instant from **InformIT Online Book's** 600+ fully searchable on line books. For a limited time, you can get your first 14 days **free**.

POWERED BY
Safari
TECH BOOKS ONLINE®

Catalog

Review online sample chapters, author biographies and customer rankings and choose exactly the right book from a selection of over 5,000 titles.